ADVANCE PRAISE FOR *FEEDING*



"Hooper meticulously reconstructs a convincing picture of how steady demands of European shipping and colonies for food supplies stimulated the emergence of state formation in western and eastern Madagascar."

—Edward A. Alpers, author of *The Indian Ocean in World History*

"Hooper has done a fine job by pushing the history of Madagascar's economic ties with the exterior into territory not adequately explored (or explored at all) by other historians."

—Pier M. Larson, author of *Ocean of Letters: Language and Creolization in an Indian Ocean Diaspora*

"This important book highlights Madagascar's key role in the Indian Ocean's maritime and commercial circuits as a provider of foodstuffs and provisions. These fueled the commodity and the slave exchanges, which in turn braided a variety of historical actors together within the ocean and beyond."

—Pedro Machado, author of *Ocean of Trade: South Asian Merchants, Africa and the Indian Ocean, c. 1750–1850*

"Jane Hooper sheds light on a crucial yet unexplored aspect of early modern globalization. *Feeding Globalization* chronicles the extent to which European shipping in the southwest Indian Ocean relied on provisions obtained in Madagascar to literally feed global trade across the Atlantic and Indian Oceans while fueling state formation and slaving on the island."

—Kerry Ward, author of *Networks of Empire: Forced Migration in the Dutch East India Company*

"Jane Hooper's groundbreaking study of Madagascar's provisioning trade offers a fascinating new perspective on Indian Ocean exchanges, European long-distance trade, Madagascan engagement with global markets, and the transformation of the island in the early modern era."

—Jeremy Prestholdt, author of *Domesticating the World: African Consumerism and the Genealogies of Globalization*

# FEEDING GLOBALIZATION

# Indian Ocean Studies Series

*Richard B. Allen, series editor*

Richard B. Allen, *European Slave Trading in the Indian Ocean, 1500–1850*

Erin E. Stiles and Katrina Daly Thompson, eds., *Gendered Lives in the Western Indian Ocean: Islam, Marriage, and Sexuality on the Swahili Coast*

Jane Hooper, *Feeding Globalization: Madagascar and the Provisioning Trade, 1600–1800*

# Feeding Globalization

*Madagascar and the Provisioning Trade, 1600–1800*

JANE HOOPER

OHIO UNIVERSITY PRESS
ATHENS, OHIO

Ohio University Press, Athens, Ohio 45701
ohioswallow.com


Printed in the United States of America
Ohio University Press books are printed on acid-free paper ∞ ™

27 26 25 24 23 22 21 20 19 18 17      5 4 3 2 1

**Library of Congress Cataloging-in-Publication Data**

Names: Hooper, Jane, 1981– author.
Title: Feeding globalization : Madagascar and the provisioning trade, 1600/1800 / Jane Hooper.
Other titles: Indian Ocean studies series.
Description: Athens : Ohio University Press, 2017. | Series: Indian Ocean studies series | Includes bibliographical references and index.
Identifiers: LCCN 2017008599| ISBN 9780821422533 (hc : alk. paper) | ISBN 9780821422540 (pb : alk. paper) | ISBN 9780821445945 (pdf)
Subjects: LCSH: Slave trade—Madagascar—History—17th century. | Slave trade—Madagascar—History—18th century. | Food industry and trade—Political aspects—Madagascar—History—17th century. | Food industry and trade—Political aspects—Madagascar—History—18th century. | Madagascar—Commerce. | Madagascar—Politics and government—17th century. | Madagascar—Politics and government—18th century.
Classification: LCC DT469.M31 H66 2017 | DDC 969.101—dc23
LC record available at https://lccn.loc.gov/2017008599

# Contents

# Illustrations

## FIGURES



## MAPS

# Acknowledgments

My interest in Madagascar began years ago, during the time I spent living on a small island off its east coast. My friends in Ambodifotatra on Île Sainte Marie welcomed me into their homes, patiently taught me Malagasy, and showed me how to properly cook rice. Their hospitality, present even when a cyclone was destroying the small island, will forever stick with me. It is to them that I dedicate this book.

The time I spent gazing across the waters of the Indian Ocean encouraged me to think about the ways in which the ocean has united, rather than divided, populations along its shores. Despite my continued interest in this topic, I have been fortunate to work alongside colleagues who study far different portions of the globe. My conversations with them over the years have profoundly shaped my thinking on the place of Madagascar in the world. First, I would like to thank the historians and art historians of George Mason University who helped support my efforts to bring this project to fruition. My colleagues at GMU have been unfailingly generous of time and knowledge. Benedict Carton and Rosemarie Zagarri, despite their own busy schedules, have been particularly helpful in offering comments on parts of this book. I'd also like to thank the members of the history department at Saint Joseph's University. My time as a David H. Burton fellow provided me with numerous opportunities to discuss my research and writing with the many accomplished historians there. Christopher Close deserves a special thank you for being willing to converse on so many occasions about the challenges involved in studying early modern history. I have benefited from the tireless support and encouragement of Clifton Crais. I am grateful for him and numerous other historians at Emory University, including David Eltis, Kristin Mann, and Roxani Margariti, for providing me with such very different perspectives on the study of history. My discussions with Kate

Armstrong, Dana Irwin, Amanda Madden, and Leah Weinryb Grohsgal have also shaped me as a scholar in more ways than I can count. Molly McCullers, a fellow Africanist, has been a particularly invaluable friend throughout this entire process.

If I had not met Richard Allen near the beaches of Zanzibar years ago, I can confidently say this book would not exist, at least not in its current form. I would like to thank him for sharing his enthusiasm, not to mention expertise, over the past several years. I have also benefited immensely from the work of talented and influential Indian Ocean historians such as Edward Alpers, James Armstrong, Gwyn Campbell, Pier Larson, Pedro Machado, and Kerry Ward. Not long ago, taking on a trans-regional research project such as mine seemed inconceivable, but fortunately that is no longer the case. Thanks to their efforts, it is exciting to contemplate the future of Indian Ocean studies as scholars continue to provide new perspectives on the history of the ocean. I would like to thank the director of Ohio University Press, Gillian Berchowitz, and two anonymous readers who have helped me transform my writing into a book. All remaining errors, however, are of course mine.

My family and friends have been a constant support, particularly during periods of travel and focused writing. I would like to thank my parents for their patience and feedback over the years. My husband Josh has given me the time to work while also encouraging me to take the breaks necessary to make it through such a lengthy endeavor. My children, Lizzie and Noah, have also enriched my life considerably by guaranteeing daily singing, dancing, and laughter to interrupt the sometimes weighty topics discussed in this book.

# Abbreviations

AN Archives nationales, Paris
  COL Colonial series, Archives nationales
  MAR 4/JJ Maritime records of ships, Archives nationales

ANOM Archives nationales d'outre-mer, Aix-en-Provence

BL British Library
  IOR East India Company Records, British Library
  Add MS Additional Manuscripts Collection

*COACM* Grandidier, Alfred, et al., eds. *Collection des ouvrages anciens concernant Madagascar.* 9 vols. Paris: Comité de Madagascar, 1903–20

NA Nationaal Archief, The Hague
  VOC 1.04.02 Records of the Dutch East India Company

NMM National Maritime Museum, Greenwich, London

WC Archives of the Western Cape, Cape Town, South Africa
  C Records of the Dutch East India Company

# ONE

## Feasts and Violence

MORE THAN EIGHT HUNDRED European and American ships arrived at the island of Madagascar during the seventeenth and eighteenth centuries. The men on board these vessels immediately sought fresh provisions from the coastal rulers who greeted them on the shores of the island. One such vessel was the Cape slaving ship, the *Brack*, which first arrived and anchored in St. Augustin Bay (alternatively, Saint Augustine's Bay) on July 26, 1741. O. L. Hemmy, the first *commies* (trade commissioner) on board, was responsible for securing slaves for the Dutch colony in southern Africa, but his first concern was finding food and water for the crew. Fortunately for Hemmy, although the shoreline appeared dry and barren, people approached the ship with oranges, chicken, and fish for sale. A leader identified as Prince William greeted the Dutch and agreed to supply them with cattle. Despite this warm welcome, Hemmy was told that he had to visit King Baba to the north if he wished to purchase more valuable commodities, namely rice and slaves.[1]

Hemmy and his companions were escorted by royal representatives to the nearby port of Toliara (Tulear, Tuléar). Hundreds of armed men surrounded the beach. King Baba was seated on a small bench, with an *asseegaye* (spear) to one side and a particularly handsome "English" gun on the other. The king was dressed in fine cloth and wearing an opulent necklace made of gold, silver, and glass beads. As Hemmy approached, the king immediately demanded to see a formal letter of introduction from the Cape Colony governor. One of the king's trusted advisers, Captain James, read and translated the letter for the king.[2] The king requested a bottle of arrack, a type of strong alcohol, which was quickly drained, as was a second bottle. Momentarily satisfied, King Baba invited the commies to dine and promised to kill a bull, as was his custom to celebrate the arrival of traders.[3]

Hemmy was led to the king's palace, where he sat beside low wooden planks and was invited to eat. The meal featured pieces of cooked meat with skin and hair still attached, complemented with dishes of cooked potatoes and rice stewed in milk.[4] As the king and commies began eating, the king also asked James and Jan, his other adviser, to join in the feasting. The king told the Dutchman that if the meat was not to his liking, he could have it prepared in the "English way." Hemmy replied that it was very good, as he was quite hungry, and he explained that he hoped they could "live as brothers."[5] During the meal, bottle after bottle of arrack was consumed by the participants after the king rejected a bottle of Cape red wine as "not healthy with such sweetness." In the king's estimation, arrack was the most suitable for a powerful ruler and Hemmy had no choice but to supply it in vast quantities. After the king had eaten his fill, the Dutch soldiers received the leftovers.[6]

As they were concluding their feast, King Baba announced to Hemmy that "I am a great king. I have people and livestock, greens, rice, and land in abundance. Come now with your ship and stay two or three months. I will give you slaves and all the things you may wish for."[7] The king's speech marked the end of formalities and the start of trading negotiations. His comments also served as a reminder that this scene of peaceful feasting took place during a period of intense violence, when many on the island were restricted from receiving even a bite of food from the feasts. Instead, these islanders were at risk of being enslaved and sold to foreign slavers. Between 1500 and 1800, an estimated 292,000 people from Madagascar were transported to slave markets on the Indian Ocean; a third of these were shipped to European forts and plantations that encircled the ocean's littoral. A further sixteen thousand traveled to the Americas where they would be sold, if they survived the extremely long journey, along with more than six million other Africans forcibly transported to the Americas.[8] The violence in and around Madagascar was on a scale typically associated with the transatlantic slave trade from western Africa. While persons taken from Madagascar formed a relatively small part of the magnitude crossing both the Atlantic and Indian Oceans, this traffic transformed Madagascar itself. Connecting populations on the island to the growing global demand for coerced labor, it introduced immense upheaval.[9]

Despite the central importance of the slave trade to the history of Madagascar, out of the more than eight hundred voyages to the island, only about a third of the English, French, and Dutch vessels that stopped there between 1600 and 1800 carried traders in search of slaves. The others loaded valuable supplies of food, wood, and water during their stays on the island.[10] The island's coastal ports and communities began to specialize in a bustling export trade in rice and cattle, with slaves sold to Europeans when food supplies were less abundant. The sale of captives became an alternative route for acquiring European imports. Following the intensification of food production on the island by the middle of the eighteenth century, slaves were relatively scarce and also expensive, being priced in silver coins that Europeans found challenging to procure.

Provisions, however, were still easy to obtain from coastal rulers. Without fresh supplies of food from Madagascar, European vessels would have struggled to carry silver to Asia and spices back to Europe. Colonists in the Mascarene Islands and in southern Africa relied upon frequent imports from the large island, as their colonies were located on lands of strategic importance but only marginal fertility. Rice from Madagascar filled the stomachs of the Europeans who supervised the labor of East African and Malagasy slaves working in plantations in Mauritius. English sailors eagerly consumed fresh beef from cattle originally purchased in Madagascar en route to India. Oranges and lemons from Madagascar revived soldiers suffering from scurvy following long months at sea. Pirates, including the famous Captain Kidd, spent time on the shores of Madagascar hoping to benefit from trading with prosperous island communities.

During the seventeenth and eighteenth centuries, these disparate groups arrived at the shores of Madagascar in search of fresh food and alliances. They "lived as brothers" with coastal rulers after sharing bowls overflowing with cooked beef and rice. That some of this food had been produced using slave labor or obtained through warfare scarcely concerned the Dutch or other visitors. The provisioning trade brought Madagascar to the center of global trading networks that intersected in the southwestern Indian Ocean. The resulting global connections enabled the islanders to sustain contacts with New York pirates and South African slavers, among others. Throughout, food served as a ritual marker of culture and status, imbued with social meaning going well beyond simple consumption. This was, after all, a world where only certain types of alcohol were deemed suitable for royalty. Only rulers and captains, those who participated in the ritual feasts, regularly consumed beef and white rice, while others were lucky if they received the leftovers.[11]

## FEEDING RULERS

For people in Madagascar, the seventeenth and eighteenth centuries ushered in dramatic political transformations, thanks in part to this provisioning trade. These two hundred years were a period of intense change for groups throughout Eurasia and along the Indian Ocean littoral.[12] The sudden appearance of Portuguese carracks in the bays of Madagascar during the sixteenth century likely did not initially shock the people of the island. Similar to coastal communities in Africa or Asia, many in northern Madagascar already participated in the long-distance trade networks that crossed the ocean.[13] A hundred years later, as more foreign sailors and soldiers had spilled onto their shores, the islanders found themselves fueling the oceanic explorations of not just Portuguese sailors, but also Dutch, French, and British. Their growing need for provisions spurred the expansion of food production within Madagascar and unleashed a ripple of changes on the island.

Madagascar has frequently fallen between the cracks in a historiography built upon an area studies framework, being neither a part per se of continental Africa nor completely within the Indian Ocean monsoonal wind patterns that had shaped premodern trade in the ocean.[14] The history of communities within Madagascar does not lend itself easily to comparisons with those along the shores of the Indian subcontinent, the Arabian Peninsula, or even nearby East Africa. In these locations, European influence was significantly blunted by a long history of oceanic trade connections. Much of Madagascar, by contrast, had been more removed from long-distance commerce and strong, externally focused political systems were only present in the north of the island before 1600. Yet, in spite of their distance from the African continent, the people of Madagascar have long lived at the crossroads of influences from both Asia and Africa. Movements of traders, slaves, and migrants ensured that the islanders were never completely isolated from other populations living along the shores of the Indian Ocean with whom they shared not only ancestry, but also vocabulary, farming techniques, and religious beliefs. These connections tended to be attenuated by the large distances between the island and major trading hubs throughout the ocean and were found most strongly in northern Madagascar.[15]

Between 1600 and 1800, rather than being a very minor player in the incipient world system, the island was a part of transoceanic trade networks that tied together various regions of the world. Throughout these centuries, the people of Madagascar enabled global commerce between the Atlantic and Indian Oceans and, as such, their story is as much a global one as one restricted to the Indian Ocean.[16] Yet Madagascar only remained a central provisioning location for a relatively brief period, with European visits in search of food peaking in the mid-eighteenth century. By the nineteenth century and with the advent of the steamship, fewer merchants tended to call at Madagascar for provisions as they crossed the oceans.[17]

Despite the short-lived role of the island as an important node in transoceanic trade, these years of exchanges would have far-reaching ramifications for both the islanders and Europeans who encountered one another across the feasting table. The sudden presence of kings wielding firearms in Madagascar's ports was the clearest innovation. As elsewhere in Africa, these individuals seemed to gain power as a consequence of the slave trade. Scholars from J. E. Inikori to Warren Whatley have repeatedly emphasized the negative impact of the transatlantic slave trade on African societies and noted an increase in political instability and economic impoverishment during the era of the slave trade. The transatlantic slave trade produced "a series of unfortunate transformations" in Africa, in the words of Patrick Manning.[18]

More recently, some historians have presented a more nuanced version of this history. By identifying the traffic in slaves as part of broader economic transformations within the continent, they suggest that while the slave trade was disruptive, it did not completely sever trading connections between African communities, nor did the trade completely destroy opportunities for economic advancement for some Africans. Some of this literature focuses on understanding the transition to "legitimate" (non-slave) commerce, frequently in agriculture, following abolition, but a number of historical studies have been published recently that examine the florescence of other production, also agricultural, in the midst of the transatlantic slave trade. Despite these efforts to consider the slave trade in a broader context, most historians would still agree that it is impossible to write about African communities on the shores of the Atlantic without examining the role the transatlantic slave trade played in their histories.[19]

The history of Madagascar reveals even more powerfully that the traffic in slaves was not the only factor contributing to violent political transformations within Africa. Guns were purchased not only with slaves but also with bags of rice on the shores of Madagascar. In 1600, individuals sold cattle for iron wire or colored beads in St. Augustin Bay. Scarcely a century later in the same location, a ruler known as Prince Will dictated the exact weight of gunpowder he would accept for a strong bull. State rulers also engaged in frequent battles with their neighbors, which contributed to a brief period of large-scale slaving from the island and the intensified use of unfree labor within the island itself. Leaders in Madagascar sought to defend and expand their political authority; as in Dahomey, this was a "period marked by war, political instability, and economic turbulence."[20] However, unlike West Africans, the islanders engaged in warfare to obtain and protect food supplies, as well as to acquire captives.

Until the early seventeenth century, much of the island's trade was overseen by merchants in the north of Madagascar who wore robes of imported cloth and spoke some Kiswahili. In their harbors, East India ships anchored beside East African vessels, as the captains of both sought to purchase captives from coastal rulers. The merchants of Madagascar, emboldened by this competition for their exports, demanded fine Asian cloth and silver from passing European merchants but did not rely on this trade as a base for their continued political power.[21] This picture would change dramatically by the close of the century. Although the political changes that came to the island following the arrival of Europeans were felt first and most strongly in the south, not the north, even this part of the island was eventually enveloped by waves of warfare emanating from elsewhere on the island.

The history of provisioning from Madagascar thus brings together two seemingly disparate pasts and processes, of African societies negatively impacted by the slave trade and communities along the Indian Ocean engaging with European merchants from a position of strength. Direct engagement with global commercial networks contributed to turmoil throughout Madagascar by providing new opportunities for some, but not all, on the island.[22] The provisioning trade from Madagascar predated, complemented, and contributed to the large-scale export of slaves, yet the rise of this trade was in some senses a historical accident. That the island became a center of provisioning was due as much to the island's geographical advantages and the unique demands of European maritime trade as to the availability of food on the island's shores.

## PROVISIONING INDIAN OCEAN COMMERCE

This perspective on trade from Madagascar is at odds with that presented in some publications examining early modern global commerce. The maps and accompanying narratives in these publications suggest that trade from Africa was primarily in captives (from West Africa to the Americas) and, from Asia, in pepper and silk intended for elite European consumption.[23] In both cases, the distraction posed by the horrific sale of humans on one hand, and that of luxury goods on the other, has led us away from studying the more routine and short-distance exchanges that supported global commerce. By focusing on higher-value goods, entire parts of the world, including Madagascar, disappear from maps of commerce that also ignore the complex trade routes that existed within regions and between the land and sea.[24] In fact, frequent short-haul trips by vessels carrying woods, foodstuffs, and simple cloth underpinned exchanges in the Indian Ocean for centuries prior to the arrival of European ships. These premodern exchanges, according to Michael N. Pearson, had a much longer history and proved more stable over the *longue durée* than more expensive exports of luxury items. The circulation of necessities by land and sea also shaped trade routes within the ocean well before the arrival of Europeans in 1498, although such trades have proved difficult to trace and have attracted only limited attention from scholars.[25]

The continued emphasis on luxury goods is apparent in publications on European oceanic explorations after the fifteenth and sixteenth centuries.[26] In his *Histoire de l'océan Indien*, Auguste Toussaint describes how spices fueled European competition, but gives no consideration to how men on board the vessels transporting these commodities were fed.[27] In his lengthy histories of the Indian Ocean, K. N. Chaudhuri likewise restricts food to discussions about regional patterns of consumption among coastal populations.[28] In spite of these omissions, alongside the trade in silks and spices were indispensable exports of food that forced regular contact between Europeans and a diverse number of communities around the world. Spices, after all, were nutritionally "superfluous," according to one popular history.[29]

The focus on spices and silks can lead historians to exclude the participation of groups such as the people of Madagascar who engaged frequently in trade, but rarely provided Europeans with expensive exports.[30] In recent years, scholars such as Judith Carney have focused on the role that African agricultural labor played in the expanding global economy.[31] The food production and exports from Indian Ocean societies likewise reveal the contributions of a more diverse group of people in fueling resource-intensive global commerce during the early modern period. It is unsurprising that the few scholars of Indian Ocean history who do mention provisioning primarily focus on coastal East African communities.[32]

Access to food supplies motivated Europeans to explore the Atlantic and determined the conduct of their trade in the ports of West Africa and the Indian Ocean.[33] Trade between Europe and Asia was even more resource intensive than that within the Atlantic, particularly in terms of the materials required to build, maintain, fuel, and sustain the crews of merchant fleets on extremely long voyages. Building upon experiences trading in northwestern Africa and the Mediterranean, European merchants at first tried to carry necessities from Europe, and only occasionally purchase additional supplies during their time in the Indian Ocean.[34] This strategy quickly proved unfeasible. Europeans realized that they needed to find reliable sources for obtaining additional provisions before arriving at their destinations in India and the Middle East, especially as the risk of sudden, unforeseen challenges ran high on lengthy voyages. Storms could place stores of food in danger and delay voyages, with deadly consequences. Leaky barrels ruined meat and bread; spoiled food led to the under-nourishment of crew members, which further imperiled the success of a voyage. With the existence of such serious dangers, finding and maintaining access to reliable sources of food became paramount.

In a competitive environment where the speed with which merchants delivered nutmeg and silks to Europe determined the profit from their trading missions, securing rapid local access to the right types of food was crucial. Unlike Indian Ocean merchants, European traders did not arrive during one season and wait for a change in the monsoon winds to depart again. European arrivals in the ocean were less predictable and required much larger supplies of provisions than vessels working within the Indian Ocean. European traders also focused on acquiring certain food items to supplement stores of hard biscuit and dried meat, either because they kept well on long transoceanic voyages or due to beliefs about their medicinal powers. Ships required rice, legumes, tubers (including manioc, widely used to feed slaves by the late eighteenth century), fruit to prevent and treat scurvy, and, above all else, fresh or salted beef, believed at the time to be capable of curing numerous diseases and conditions.[35] Rice was particularly valued for its portability and was perceived in multiple cultural contexts as suitable for elite consumption.[36] Europeans shipped rice from India, Indonesia, and Madagascar to their settlements throughout the entire Indian Ocean.[37] Scholars have tended to understand the transformation of certain food items into commodities, goods with identifiable values and produced for export, as a development of the nineteenth and twentieth centuries.[38] Yet certain desirable food staples such as rice reached this status much earlier in provisioning locations such as Madagascar. In this case, the markets were not in distant Europe but instead within European ships themselves.

Europeans, unlike other traders circulating through the Indian Ocean, needed to acquire these items quickly, and in extremely large quantities, to avoid long waits and an increase in the mortality rate on board their vessels while at anchor. Given these constraints, Europeans learned to frequent certain ports and develop preferential trading relationships with the communities, including those within Madagascar, that had adjusted to their demands. Not all parts of the ocean's shores were as welcoming to European traders. Many port cities in the Indian Ocean lay beside regions poor in natural resources where food needed to be transported from far in the interior to the coast or imported from overseas.[39] John Richards and Edmund Burke III have noted that increased food production during the early modern period had a negative impact on the environment. This was likely the case for many locations along the ocean's littoral where food had to be brought from increasingly distant hinterlands, making supplies of food more limited and expensive for Europeans.[40]

Even within Madagascar, food had to be transported from the interior of the island to the coasts. Tracing the movement of food highlights lines of connection, as well as differentiation, between hinterland and littoral societies. The transportation of goods to the coast relied upon either coordinated independent traders or state-controlled commerce. As rice was harvested in the interiors of Africa and Asia and shipped to shores, it changed hands dozens of times and moved through diverse landscapes of power. Without examining the exports of mundane provisions alongside those of luxuries and slaves, it would be impossible to trace the deep roots of globalizing trade in the lands surrounding the Indian Ocean. By looking at the movement of food within Madagascar in particular, it becomes clear that almost the entire island, including its highly productive interior, was responsible for provisioning European voyages.

European trading companies also developed settler colonies that would serve as centers for growing or accumulating the necessary provisions, an action that further increased the impact of human populations in previously unpopulated areas or regions of low population density. Many of these colonies, whether in Southeast Asia, Africa, or on offshore African islands, required vast supplies of food and labor to be regularly imported from neighboring Indian Ocean communities.[41] Europeans in these locations encountered similar challenges as other groups living along the ocean's littoral and struggled to grow sufficient supplies of food in only marginally fertile soil.[42] Their unremitting efforts to spur on agriculture in spite of these challenges reveal the heightened value of food during an era of globalizing commerce and the need for stable locations for refueling vessels throughout the ocean.

## FEEDING COMPETITION

An examination of the provisioning trade from Madagascar provides new insights into the history of European trade in the Indian Ocean by calling attention to how these practical concerns shaped European activities. Historians have been aware of the rivalries, divisions, and competition between European trading groups in the Indian Ocean starting with publications by scholars including C. R. Boxer and Holden Furber.[43] Yet Portuguese, Dutch, English, and French merchants shared one characteristic that few historians note: frequent purchases of food from Madagascar to support their commerce in the ocean. Even if they did not stop at Madagascar, many European sailors consumed food produced in Madagascar at some point during their voyages within the Indian Ocean.[44] For this reason, access to provisions from Madagascar helped determine the success of various merchant groups within the Indian Ocean; as such, European groups as well as African and Asian ones competed for access to the trade of the island.

Beginning in the sixteenth century, the Portuguese Estado da Índia made many attempts, but few inroads, at creating a trading monopoly in the Indian Ocean. In Madagascar as well, despite early efforts to set up commercial and missionary outposts on the island, the Portuguese were unsuccessful at securing a foothold. Representatives of the Portuguese crown, Portuguese traders, and Mozambican colonists all briefly tried to obtain spices and slaves from Madagascar during the sixteenth century but were eventually drawn to more profitable parts of the ocean in pursuit of commodities. Portuguese attempts at converting the islanders were likewise abandoned by the early seventeenth century. Following these failures, the Portuguese settled on Mozambique continued to engage in trade with groups living within the southwestern Indian Ocean region, including with those in Madagascar who had large supplies of rice and cattle for sale. Portuguese (or Portuguese-sponsored) vessels continued to arrive in Madagascar's ports in search of provisions well into the nineteenth century.[45]

A major shift occurred during the first half of the seventeenth century, on the shores of Madagascar as well as throughout the Indian Ocean, as other European trading groups arrived to compete with the Portuguese. Between roughly 1590 and 1650, European rivalries for access to the spice trade meant groups such as the Dutch and English fixated on spices and little else. Their efforts led to the creation of monopoly trading companies such as the English East India Company (EIC) in 1601 and the Dutch East India Company (Vereenigde Oost-Indische Compagnie, or VOC) in 1602. The French followed shortly thereafter with their own series of trading companies in the ocean, most noteworthy being the Compagnie des indes orientales, which went through several iterations throughout the seventeenth and eighteenth centuries.[46]

Initially lacking strong provisioning centers in the southwestern Indian Ocean, all three European groups were drawn to Madagascar.

The Dutch were interested in using food and slaves from Madagascar to support their ventures in Indonesia and along the Red Sea. Dutch visits to the island predated the founding of the VOC, with the first ships sailing from the Netherlands to Madagascar in 1695. Once VOC voyages into the Indian Ocean began, their settler colonies in Batavia (Jakarta), Mauritius, and the Cape all imported rice and enslaved laborers from Madagascar. EIC captains were first drawn to the southwestern coast of Madagascar, distant from parts of the island visited by the Portuguese and Dutch. For two centuries, several EIC ships visited the west coast of the island annually on their way to EIC posts in India and Indonesia. Searching for a strong base to support their commerce in Asia and the Middle East, the French settled on the nearby Mascarene Islands by the late seventeenth century, abandoning attempts to live on Madagascar itself. Even once they set up homes and ports in the islands of Mauritius (Île de France) and Réunion (Île Bourbon), the French imported hundreds of slaves, cattle, and bags of rice annually from the larger island to their west.

Between 1600 and 1800, the English, Dutch, and French all tried to create colonies and permanent trading posts on Madagascar but made few intentional and successful incursions inland, as the islanders fought firmly against European settlement. The French alone sponsored at least four failed settlements on the island during the eighteenth century. French persistence reveals the central importance of Madagascar to European plans for expansion in the ocean, but also the severe shortcomings in their perceptions of the reality of life on Madagascar's shores. Even as these colonies failed, European captains repeatedly turned their ships to the island when they needed laborers or food.

In Madagascar, as elsewhere in the Indian Ocean, local and intra-ocean trade remained vibrant throughout this entire precolonial period, in spite of the sudden rise of military states on the island's shores.[47] European merchants discovered that they faced strong competition not only from other Europeans and Americans on the shores of Madagascar but also from non-European groups operating throughout the ocean. European, African, and Asian merchants interacted, cooperated, and clashed, as Europeans attempted to insert themselves into centuries-old patterns of exchange. Operating from a position of strength, islanders, usually under strong oversight by their rulers, could afford to strike tough bargains. In

Madagascar, Europeans consistently dealt with trading partners who were aware of the Europeans' need for food and took advantage of their desperation whenever possible.[48] In light of this competition, European weakness in terms of dominating commerce in the ocean, as highlighted by Sanjay Subrahmanyam and Sugata Bose, was apparent on the shores of Madagascar.[49] Even on this relatively distant island of seemingly limited value, Europeans struggled to maintain their access to trade, a reminder that European economic and political expansion was checked by other thriving exchange networks within and around the ocean's littoral.

As the end of the eighteenth century approached, a period that many historians of the Indian Ocean identify as ushering in a major shift of power in favor of European (especially British) imperialism, European trading companies came increasingly into conflict with non-European states and empires. Most of the historical scholarship dealing with this shift focuses on the Indian subcontinent, but even from the perspective of Madagascar, a shift in engagement was clearly occurring.[50] Although formal European annexation was still more than a century in the future for the islanders, new colonial ventures by Europeans in Asia had a lasting impact on the provisioning trade from Madagascar. Battles between the British and French in the northern Indian Ocean attracted European vessels into the ocean in larger numbers. These fleets of warships relied upon Madagascar for food to feed their sailors and soldiers with increasing frequency. During a single visit, the British might buy hundreds of bags of rice from the northwest coast of the island, while the French shipped hundreds, or even thousands, of live cattle from the opposite coast of Madagascar to the Mascarene Islands. By the close of the eighteenth century, after years of repeated and growing demands for food, the imports provided by the provisioning trade had led to not just an expansion of military state control on Madagascar, but greater economic connections within the island and perhaps the increased use of enslaved laborers to produce food for consumption and export to meeting this rising demand for provisions.

## EUROPEAN SHIP RECORDS AS SOURCES

This book uses the vantage point of the shores of Madagascar to examine the impact of global trade on Indian Ocean communities during the seventeenth and eighteenth centuries. This history is revealed through a careful reading of records left by the European and American traders, missionaries, and colonists who visited the shores of Madagascar. *Feeding Globalization* relies heavily on almost three hundred ship records similar to the journal left by the commies of the *Brack*.[51] European ship logs from such vessels provide detailed daily commentary, as seen in the many recent publications that focus on single slaving voyages in the Atlantic or Indian Oceans.[52] The records kept on board vessels in the Atlantic such as the *Diligent* reveal the experience of slave loading, the brutality of the Middle Passage, and the cruel calculations involved in the sale of Africans in the Americas. Such revelations reach beyond the experience of a single slaving voyage and speak to the uneven connections forged between Europeans, Africans, and Americans during this globalizing era.[53] The complex calculus involved in the slave trade, as Stephanie Smallwood points out in her study of the trade from the Gold Coast, enables historians to uncover both how Europeans attempted to create commodities from human bodies and the ways in which Africans resisted this development.[54]

Ship records do not simply illuminate the inner workings of the slave trade, but also provide context for understanding the evolution of trade within Africa, as is clear in the records of both slaving and merchant vessels. In these sources, European observations include, out of necessity, reference to major political, economic, and social changes in the ports they visited, whether they halted in search of slaves or provisions. The observations were preserved by trading companies and colonial governments seeking to amass knowledge about far-flung locations.[55] These ship records are even more valuable for understanding historical developments within Madagascar than elsewhere in Africa, as we have fewer details about political and economic shifts on the island prior to the nineteenth century. The close relationship forged between merchant and creole populations, enabled by the presence of resident Europeans on the Atlantic coast of many West African regions, was entirely absent from most of Madagascar until the late eighteenth century.[56] Instead, the brief interactions described in ship logs provide some of the most in-depth written sources available for the seventeenth and eighteenth centuries, especially given the almost complete lack of Malagasy written sources and recorded traditions for this period.

Many historical studies of pre-nineteenth-century Madagascar rely on an influential compilation of sources entitled *Collection des ouvrages anciens concernant Madagascar* (*COACM*).[57] The editors of this collection translated a variety of documents, including some ship journals and logs, from Portuguese, English, and Dutch into French during the early twentieth century. The sources fill nine volumes and most are now available for free online. The collection, as some historians have suggested, is far from comprehensive and not always accurate, and every attempt has been made to consult the original sources for this book.[58] EIC records, for instance, are almost entirely absent from *COACM*, as are many VOC sources. When they are present, the editors provide highly abridged versions and historians have challenged the translations provided in the volumes. The very detailed logs and journals kept by VOC merchants have garnered attention in recent years, thanks to the efforts of James Armstrong and R. J. Barendse. Their publications further reveal the shortcomings of the *COACM* collection.[59] French documents are also poorly represented in *COACM*, particularly colonial records from the Mascarenes.

In order to understand the role that the people of Madagascar played in feeding globalization, this book draws upon these colonial sources, in addition to English, French, and Dutch ship logs.[60] Regrettably, Portuguese archival holdings have not been consulted for this book, although publications by Edward Alpers and Thomas Vernet reveal that there is much to be done in those archives.[61] The records kept by the European trading companies that were consulted provide detailed descriptions of the men, women, and children who approached the newcomers on the shores of Madagascar. When looked at individually, the records of a ship's brief visit to a port or ports in Madagascar make few apparent contributions to our understanding of the history of the island. Usually only a few pages long, such accounts might note the purchase of a certain number of cattle and barrels of rice, in return for guns or coins. After a stay lasting a few weeks, a European ship would continue to sail toward harbors in the northern Indian Ocean, where the captain could engage in trade for more valuable items. European would-be merchants would not only examine the details of a single earlier voyage, but make their navigational decisions based on a history of regular successful visits to the island. An examination of multiple ship records, for instance, reveals how the negotiations that occurred on the coast of Madagascar between rulers and captains became more reliable and regimented by the middle of the eighteenth century, thanks to this accumulated knowledge of places and people. Ship logs regularly demonstrate that assumptions were made about the goods available in a particular region and the control certain island merchants and leaders exercised over the export trade. Such beliefs became self-fulfilling prophecies, as officers sought out certain titled rulers, identified on the basis of earlier trade, to fulfill their provisioning and slaving needs.

These sources also demonstrate the challenges that European captains and officers faced over this entire period, not just in acquiring goods, but also in maintaining order on board their vessels. Life at sea enabled captains and officers to dominate the movements of their subordinates, but, once ashore, sailors were "notoriously free," in the words of Michael Fisher, and were able to evade control to a much greater extent.[62] Incidents of sailor disobedience, desertion, and disputes on the shore punctuated otherwise peaceful voyages and occurred on almost half of the recorded eighteenth-century EIC visits to Madagascar. The frequency of this resistance suggests that European leaders struggled to control their subordinates. Access to fresh food on the island could mean life or death for both sailors and slaves. Indeed, many acts of resistance were rooted, at least in part, in struggles for adequate food supplies.[63] The words of the merchants that visited the island thus illustrate the fears of Europeans as much as they provide insights into developments within Madagascar. This anxiety over provisioning only disappeared during the nineteenth century, after European states had developed firmer colonial holdings throughout the Indian Ocean and Europeans traveled in faster seagoing vessels.

Despite opportunities for scholars to trace the shifting relationships between European traders and coastal rulers through these documents, the use of such sources can encourage us to overstate the impact of Europeans upon the island's history, society, and culture. The provisioning trade presented new opportunities for many in Madagascar, allowing for the creation of new coastal trading enclaves as well as providing new idioms of power and leadership to the islanders. In spite of this fact, the most important (in terms of both quantity and frequency) and longest-running exports from the island were probably via the northwest ports of the island to the Comoros, East Africa, and the northern Indian Ocean. Europeans knew little of these exchanges or how the networks had become intertwined in complex ways with their own by the nineteenth century.

The information found in ship logs is also limited by the nature of European visits to Madagascar. Europeans rarely had time to learn much of island cultural practices or their language during their stays. Most strikingly, European references to locations visited on the shores of the island were frequently confused and it is sometimes hard even to discern which parts of Madagascar they visited and with whom they traded.[64] The other major shortcoming of these sources is clear from the outset: the writers had only limited knowledge of the goings-on in the interior of the island. With their stays almost entirely limited to the beaches and direct shoreline, captains and trading officials knew little about (and demonstrated an overall lack of interest in) events occurring in the interior. This coastal focus limits our understanding of the sources of slaves for sale, the origins of rice sold in ports, and the expansion of highland states far into the interior during the eighteenth century. Europeans provide relatively reliable information about prices and items purchased, but their grasp of political dynamics on the island was limited and tinged by their own understandings of states and leadership.

It is also worth noting that the unevenness of the sources, with some of the writers limiting their discussion of trade to a few sentences or pages, prevents reliable numerical analysis, such as about the exact amounts of food available for purchase in any given year or even the precise price given for each slave purchased. Moreover, records are not available for all voyages; the figures displayed in this book are based on the records I was able to consult or uncover, but there were certainly many more stops at Madagascar by ships in search of slaves and food. Not all voyages left a record of their travels. For instance, ship journals are unavailable for almost a hundred of the 211 EIC voyages that are listed as halting in Madagascar in the online catalog of the British Library.[65] While we know the itineraries for many of these voyages, most of the daily details have been lost.

Despite the challenges presented by the use of European ship records, these sources provide valuable, if limited, glimpses into the opportunities presented by this rapidly globalizing world to coastal leaders and rulers. When examined in combination with the findings of archeologists and later recorded Malagasy traditions, these sources allow us to reach the conclusion that the provisioning export trade shaped political and economic developments on the island for more than two centuries. The sources also provide a potent reminder that European merchants relied on the assistance of local communities within Madagascar to complete transoceanic voyages that contributed to significant transformations back in Europe.

## CHAPTERS

*Feeding Globalization* recounts the history of this global feasting table by starting with the first European arrivals on the island. The second chapter uses European letters, ship logs, and published accounts to uncover the optimism that visitors felt upon first encountering Madagascar. Perceptions of a verdant and relatively unpopulated island encouraged the Portuguese, Dutch, French, and English to repeatedly send merchant vessels. Their experiences also led to efforts to colonize Madagascar, but European desires for unfettered access to the resources of the island were never fulfilled. Local leaders quickly forestalled all attempts to take control by refusing to provide European colonizers with adequate food and support. European optimism during this early period, however, did contribute to the island becoming a provisioning stop for merchant fleets entering the Indian Ocean.

European sources only hint at the massive political transformations occurring on the island throughout the seventeenth and eighteenth centuries. Two expansive military states formed during this period and began to take control of the export trade. Relying upon a variety of sources, including oral traditions, the next two chapters chart the rise of the Sakalava on the west coast and the Betsimisaraka to the east. The leaders of these states used violence to wrest control of coastal exchanges from other groups and to develop supply routes that stretched across the entire island. The less coordinated Betsimisaraka state had a harder time securing supplies of food and slaves for export than the Sakalava leaders who dominated the export trade from the entire west coast of Madagascar throughout the eighteenth century.

Following the rise of these two states, visits by European vessels to Madagascar became more regular and reliable, as described in chapter 5. This increased regularity was facilitated by the development of secure relationships between rulers and the Europeans who frequented the island. These alliances were cemented through elaborate rituals that included feasts and gift exchanges, with these rituals effectively eliminating other coastal people from participating in exchanges. In the explosion of documentation that accompanied their visits, European officers revealed that they were in fear during their stays on the island due to a lack of control over sailors on shore and on ship. Their fears manifested themselves in both a desire for the quick loading of provisions as well as a growing dependence on rulers to help them maintain control over subordinates on the beaches of Madagascar.

Chapter 6 describes how European struggles for dominance within the Indian Ocean during the mid-eighteenth century culminated in the battles of the Seven Years' War. The outbreak of war led to the French and British forging closer relationships with coastal rulers as their ships halted frequently in the ports of Madagascar for provisions. The French in particular invested a great deal of energy and resources in attempting to colonize the island repeatedly during the second half of the eighteenth century. As a result, by the start of the nineteenth century both the French and British were interested in a more permanent trading presence in Madagascar.

Competition for food and labor increased sharply within the region by the late eighteenth century, as described in chapter 7, and resulted in several important shifts in the use and sale of slave labor from the island. The rising demand from Europeans, particularly the French, for slaves from Madagascar coincided with a marked decline in the availability of enslaved laborers from the shores of the island. Slaves became scarcer and more expensive. The transformation of the slave trade, in terms of prices and availability, only makes sense in the context of the expanding provisioning trade, as coastal rulers were retaining slaves to work in a productive capacity on the island, and selling them, along with food, in return for silver coins. By the close of the century, communities within Madagascar even began to import enslaved laborers from East Africa to augment this work force.

Chapter 8 reveals how coastal populations responded to the heightened demand for laborers by turning beyond the island's shores to acquire slaves. Between roughly 1790 and 1820, hundreds of islanders left the eastern and western coasts of Madagascar annually in fleets of canoes, paddling toward the nearby Comoro Islands and East Africa. These armed men launched attacks on coastal populations, kidnapping large portions of the Comoro Islands population and forcing East Africans to flee into the interior of the continent. According to Comorians remembering the chaos decades later, all those who could fight were killed and those who could not fight were captured and enslaved by the soldiers. These exceptionally large and coordinated attacks, which unsettled communities throughout the region, can only be understood in the context of the competition introduced by the provisioning trade to Madagascar as well as the Comoros.

The slaving raids on the Comoro Islands and in coastal East Africa at the turn of the nineteenth century were the culmination of pressures introduced by global trade. The pressures that accompanied the arrival of global commerce by the nineteenth century, while distinct from those placed by the demand for slaves or luxury exports from Atlantic Africa or Southeast Asia, were very real. European merchants originally entered the Indian Ocean in search of lucrative trading opportunities. The pepper and cloves they returned with fetched astronomical prices back in Europe, at least initially. To make these multiyear journeys, Dutch merchants found themselves bartering with merchants in Madagascar for a few bags of rice. The English used glass beads to buy live cattle on the island to sustain their voyages to the Arabian Peninsula. The French staved off famine with food staples from Madagascar. The provisioning of European vessels did not just shape island societies but also European successes and failures.

Throughout this period of violence and negotiation, the feasting table provided a moment of repose for European and coastal elites. The feast also serves as a metaphor for understanding the important, if tenuous, relationship formed between those who came to the beaches of Madagascar in search of trading partners. Access to the table was a mark of status and power for Europeans and islanders alike. The coercion involved in the growing and sale of the food was beneath the notice of those who ate plentiful amounts of beef stew and rice at the feast, but it provided a constant threat to the continued success of this celebratory moment.

# TWO

## "The Richest and Most Fruitful Island in the World"

AN ENGLISH VISITOR TO Madagascar published a pamphlet with this title in 1643, following the publication of his other tract (*A Paradox: Prooving, That the Inhabitants of the Isle called Madagascar . . . Are the Happiest People in the World*) just three years prior.[1] Expressing such a positive view of Madagascar was not unusual in the seventeenth century. In fact, notions of Madagascar as a fertile land for both settlement and agricultural production date back a century earlier, when the first European ships arrived at its shores. In their sixteenth-century reports back to Europe, the Portuguese emphasized the plentiful supplies of food and slaves they had found. By 1609, people all over Europe had heard of the "extremely rich, powerful, and famous island of Madagascar . . . which in our days is considered as the largest in all the world."[2] The island was rumored to be home to exotic wildlife such as giraffes and elephants, as well as gold and silver mines.[3] Such legends encouraged a widespread fascination with the exotic flora and fauna on Madagascar, while making little mention of the people already inhabiting this apparent paradise.

European writers celebrated the natural fertility of an island perceived as an untouched and sparsely populated Eden.[4] An English poem was even written celebrating this point and imagining the glory of conquering such an island, "scenting of rich gummes."[5] Throughout Madagascar, according to one visitor, "Glens and slopes, hills, mountains, and valleys are enhanced by beautiful glimpses of dense woods, flourishing acres, and verdant fields. The fruitful earth only has to thank mother nature, that it, through her more than any effort of a zealous farmer, yields more fruits than there are hands to pick."[6] This and other such descriptions imply that the land was so naturally productive that Europeans with their agricultural skills could quickly transform the land into a granary to support their operations throughout the ocean.

Not only was the island described as richly fertile, but it was also known to be a huge landmass, almost continental in size. In one report defending the French decision to place a colony on the island, the writer noted that Madagascar was the fourth largest island in the world, larger even than England.[7] The idea that a small French settlement could eventually control the entire island attracted interest back in Europe. In fact, virtually every seventeenth-century description of Madagascar began with an estimate of the size of the island and noted that it was far larger than necessary to support its small (according to Europeans) human population. Indeed, the island was so expansive that it would be several centuries before a European successfully crossed it and described the interior accurately. Before they did so, fantastic descriptions of the island's animals featured prominently in early modern European publications.[8]

Practical concerns were initially responsible for attracting Europeans to the shores of the island, located roughly at the halfway point for voyages from Europe to Asia. Europeans learned that provisions were not as readily available in all islands and ports throughout the Indian Ocean. Unlike other coastal trading centers and settlements in the western Indian Ocean, such as Mozambique Island or Aden, the entrepôts of Madagascar drew upon a relatively rich foreland and hinterland, both capable of producing a wide variety of items for export.[9] Early traders reported acquiring cattle, poultry, rice, legumes, tubers, and plenty of fruits during their visits. The seventeenth-century French colonial governor Étienne Flacourt described Madagascar as home to a wide variety of ecosystems: mountains with gold mines, dense forests, pastureland capable of supporting large herds of cattle and sheep, rich soil for grain production, and rivers full of fish. The diversity provided abundance in every imaginable food item.[10]

For all these reasons, Madagascar was viewed as a favorable base for trading operations, but, as an island, it was viewed as especially ripe for colonization. When Europeans began to explore the great oceans, many of their first settlements were on islands. Since the Phoenicians, maritime merchants and empires had used islands as stopover locations for ships seeking to rapidly refuel.[11] By the seventeenth century, European plantations already existed on islands in the Mediterranean, in the Canaries, and along the Atlantic coastline of Africa. As T. Bentley Duncan argues, during early phases of European global travel islands became important "out of all relation to their size and resources," enabling merchants to set up limited colonies and conduct trade with land-based states and empires.[12] Islands also provided safety from hostile indigenous groups on the mainland of Africa.[13] This preference for occupying islands did not cease after Europeans sailed around the Cape of Good Hope. Shortly after their arrival in the Indian Ocean, Portuguese colonists were drawn to the islands of East Africa, including Mozambique and Kilwa, as well as those found elsewhere in the ocean. About a hundred years later, the Dutch focused their efforts on securing a foothold in the islands of Southeast Asia and the French in the Mascarenes. Many of the islands that attracted transoceanic merchants, such as St. Helena in the Atlantic and those in the Indian Ocean such as Mauritius, were completely uninhabited and first colonized by Europeans leaving animals to provide provisions for passing vessels. Convenient oases in the middle of transoceanic routes, such colonies on uninhabited islands were without threat from indigenous human populations, but they lacked laboring populations. As Europeans sought to settle and develop these islands, workers had to be imported along with supplies of food.

There would be no such labor problem on Madagascar itself, given that the island was believed to be incredibly fertile and home to a small population that could be made to work for European colonists. The island was also unclaimed by any powerful state or empire during the early seventeenth century, unlike the more hotly contested islands elsewhere in the Indian Ocean that became the battlegrounds for Portuguese, Dutch, English, French, and Ottoman competitors. Madagascar, the French argued in 1664, was more fertile, more friendly, and more welcoming to the spread of Christianity than the island of Java, then dominated by the Dutch.[14] Around the same period, one Englishman described how a successful English colony would turn Madagascar into a "Second Ormuz" (Hormuz) and make the English "Emperor of all of India."[15] Another Englishman, Robert Hunt, advocated a settlement on the northwest coast of the island in 1650. Once developed, he argued, the settlement would eventually rival Barbados in terms of sugar cane production, but agriculture would be "far cheaper," as laborers could be procured within Madagascar or brought from nearby East Africa. The settlement would also facilitate trade with India. Hunt, along with many other colonial planners, primarily focused on how this settlement could exploit the land and labor of Madagascar, in addition to taking advantage of the proximity of the island to other trading centers in the Indian Ocean.[16]

European desires and imaginings of Madagascar did not conform with reality and, despite lofty aspirations, attempts to possess the island failed repeatedly. After all, many of those advocating colonization had never seen Madagascar. English poet William Davenant had only visited Madagascar in a dream, yet penned a lengthy poem about the landmass.[17] In her book on English piracy, Margarette Lincoln notes that this "distant island" served as a sort of blank slate in the English imagination for "a range of topical debates."[18] But Madagascar was not really a blank slate, as it was home to a large indigenous population. Island rulers encouraged early European perceptions of the island's bays as safe shelters for their ships. Given the long history of maritime trade there, Europeans found valuable goods already for sale on Madagascar's shores when they arrived. From the beginning, however, colonists faced opposition from coastal leaders who were favorable to trade but would not allow Europeans to control their land or labor, particularly in areas of relative food scarcity such as the southern portion of the island. English and French settlers in these areas struggled to survive. European settlements also failed to thrive elsewhere on the island. The plans of Hunt were shattered after his proposed "plantation" and its settlers disappeared entirely from northwestern Madagascar.

Despite the shortcomings of their accounts, descriptions from early visitors provide us with some of the first glimpses of populations on the island. Portuguese, Dutch, French, and English traders, priests, and settlers wrote reports and letters about their successes and, especially, failures in dealing with island communities. For example, between 1648 and 1655 the French colonial governor Flacourt recorded lengthy observations about the islanders he encountered, including outlines of social customs, religious beliefs, and political structures, many of them hostile to French rule in the region. French officials were still referring to Flacourt's influential writings more than a century later.[19]

Through their attempted settlements, European trading companies gained extensive knowledge of the island, and such information encouraged them to continue visiting Madagascar in search of provisions. Competition between the Portuguese, Dutch, French, and English for continued access to food and slaves lay just beneath the surface in European interactions with the islanders. These rivalries rarely developed into overt conflict, but instead encouraged Europeans to carve out separate spheres of influence and frequent a wide variety of regions. This story of failed colonial attempts and continued optimism explains how the island became a center for provisioning during the late seventeenth century and remained so throughout the following century.[20]

## THE PORTUGUESE IN EAST AFRICA

Within a few years of sailing into the Indian Ocean in 1498, Portuguese sailors stumbled upon the island of Madagascar. In 1500, a ship commanded by Diego Diaz sailed off course to the west coast of Madagascar on the day of Saint Lawrence. While ashore, Diaz discovered he could obtain supplies of water and fish, as well as other provisions, from the islanders in return for knives, iron, cloth, and mirrors.[21] Subsequent voyages of the Portuguese to the island of "São Lourenço" were similarly unintentional, as their ships landed on the island following harsh storms in the Mozambique Channel. Later voyages were sometimes intended to discover any survivors from shipwrecks.[22] For the first decades of Portuguese exploration and trade in the Indian Ocean, Madagascar remained firmly outside of European commercial and military interests.

Portuguese vessels tried to fight against the powerful Agulhas currents that pushed southward around both sides of Madagascar. The debris left by the Portuguese ships on the southern shores of the island, an area that lacks natural harbors, was a testament to the power and danger of these currents.[23] As European vessels entered the Indian Ocean, they were forced to choose between the inner or outer passage around Madagascar on their way to the northern Indian Ocean; both choices offered challenging sailing conditions.[24] The Portuguese frequently opted for the inner passage, despite it being fraught with unpredictable

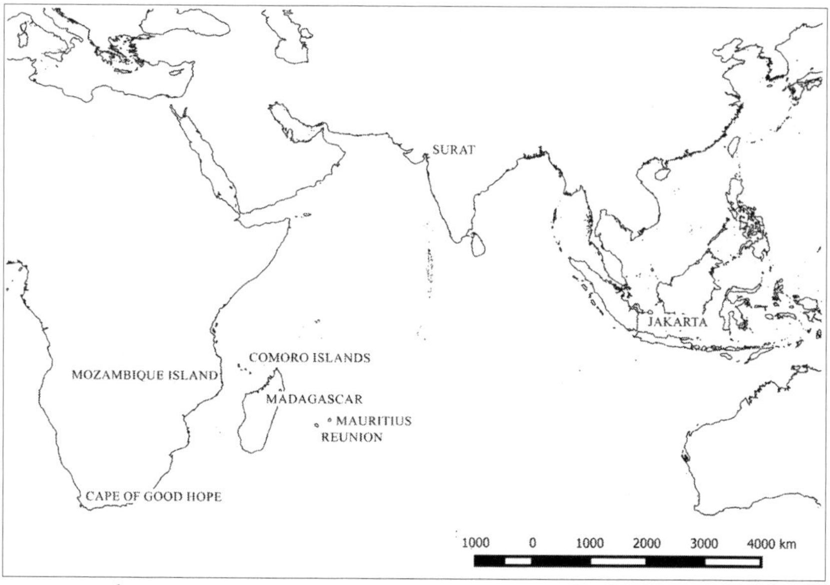


MAP 2.1. Indian Ocean

winds and currents. By contrast, taking the outer passage around Madagascar meant fewer chances of running aground or losing time on their way to Asia, but the route presented dangers to the passengers on board, who usually required additional food and water by this point in the journey. To take the outer passage meant "the almost certain death of many," according to one sixteenth-century Portuguese observer.[25] Many Portuguese captains preferred to brave the channel and stop on the East African coast before continuing their voyages.[26] Even after ships arrived safely at Mozambique Island (Ilha de Moçambique), their route to India was not assured. From November to January, monsoon winds blow from the northern Indian Ocean toward eastern Africa and then reverse between April and August.[27] The Portuguese quickly discovered that to be caught in the southwestern Indian Ocean at the wrong time of year could mean slowed travel or deadly encounters with cyclones.[28]

Ships from the Portuguese Estado da Índia rarely visited Madagascar at first, but after the gradual accumulation of information about the large island, so close to their settlements on the East African coast, Portuguese explorers and traders expressed interest in visiting it more frequently.[29] They hoped to find untapped supplies of spices and precious metals on the "very large island" so close to their East African trading posts.[30] In 1507, Afonso de Albuquerque, the second viceroy of Portuguese India, wrote a letter celebrating the ready availability of cloth, gold, silver, and rice on the island.[31] One man they encountered even suggested that clove trees grew along the northwest coast of Madagascar.[32] In an effort to gain support from the Portuguese crown for further expeditions, Albuquerque asserted that the ginger in Madagascar was superior to that of India.[33] Another Portuguese official later reinforced Albuquerque's contentions, promising "that, if a caravel is brought to these parts [Madagascar and the Comoros] in the monsoon, great service will be done to Your Highness and that much gain will come to you."[34] In Madagascar, officials believed, the Portuguese could purchase "things which made them imagine they had reached India." Once there, they would find that the "good people" on the island sold a type of pepper, as well as scented wood and wild cinnamon, in return for iron goods and cloth.[35]

For Europeans residing in East Africa, there were far more practical (and realistic) reasons to visit the island. Provisions had to be acquired continually for the many soldiers and merchants who lived in Portuguese forts and trading posts. The Portuguese could purchase rice, millet, sugar, and cattle from key trading centers in East Africa near Sofala and Kilwa Island, but these exchanges were prone to disruption thanks to frequent (often Portuguese-instigated) conflict in the region. Over the long term, these supplies were insufficient for the Portuguese military as well as their small, but growing, settler population.[36] As early as 1506, Portuguese officials in charge at Kilwa Island complained they were unable to feed not only the men at the fortress, but also sailors left ashore by shipwrecked vessels, and African leaders were refusing to provide them with food.[37] The Portuguese colony at Mozambique Island, a dry and largely barren island, faced similar challenges as it grew, especially after the building of a hospital for sick sailors by the middle of the sixteenth century.[38]

The Portuguese believed that large quantities of food could be obtained from northwest Madagascar, especially rice and livestock.[39] This belief was reinforced when they became aware of frequent commercial traffic across the Mozambique Channel. Since the tenth century, ports in the north of Madagascar, home to an Islamized population, had attracted merchants and migrants from East Africa, the Middle East, and even the Far East.[40] At least a dozen ports were identified in northern

Madagascar by the late fifteenth century by the Arab geographer Ibn Mājid.[41] The most prominent, at least according to sixteenth-century Europeans, was Massaliege (also referred to as Mazalagem, Mathaledge, etc.). The port was home to six or seven thousand people, many of them Muslim with ties to East African populations.[42] Ports throughout northwest Madagascar functioned as entrepôts for the fertile interior of the island, as the bays on this coastline, such as Boina, were connected to long rivers.[43] These rivers provided access to rich agricultural land and enabled the easy transportation of provisions as well as other trading commodities to the island's shores. The Portuguese learned that the "fair Island of St Laurence" was home to "sheep and much rice and maize, also many oranges and lemons." Fish were plentiful along the coast and in rivers. The availability of goats, cows, corn, fruits, cloth, and timber also enticed Portuguese captains.[44] Rice particularly interested the Portuguese, who became aware of a brisk export in the grain to the Middle East via Kilwa.[45] During their early explorations, they noted that rice supplies in the northwest of Madagascar were so plentiful that twenty ships could not exhaust supplies of the grain.[46]

Food exports were complemented by a traffic in captive laborers. According to one visitor, the large ports along the northwestern coast were surrounded by farmland and large herds of cattle, with much of the work completed through slave labor.[47] While this Portuguese assessment was made on the basis of only tenuous evidence, it was clear from other sources that thousands of people were sold on the shores of the island throughout the sixteenth and seventeenth centuries. As early as 1506, Portuguese passing by the northwest coast of Madagascar observed a bustling slave trade conducted by "Moors."[48] Other sixteenth-century visitors to the island described a traffic with "Arab" traders whose ships carried as many as five thousand slaves from the northwestern ports of Madagascar annually.[49] The exact magnitude is difficult to judge, in part because the enslaved individuals were shipped to a wide variety of destinations, including Malindi, Mombasa, Mogadishu, Muscat, and Aden.[50]

Many slaves came from the interior of the island, along with quantities of foodstuffs. In 1640, the captain of the English vessel *Frances* described his visit to "Mattaledge" (likely Massaliege), where he observed the trade between the people near "Mackamby island" (Nosy Komba?) and those on Madagascar. In March and April of each year, he reported, people from the interior (the "Hoves") moved in a *caffalo* (caravan) with ten thousand head of cattle and two to three thousand slaves, both to sell on the coast. Other exports included rice, hides, goats, hens, and various exotic woods.[51] The trade the Portuguese first observed may have been conducted in a similar manner, with slaves being sold for luxury goods such as fine cloth and precious metals.[52] By the mid-seventeenth century, Portuguese traders had established a regular slave trade on the northwest coast, judging by Dutch mentions of a Portuguese trading agreement with the "strongest king" on the island, perhaps residing in Massaliege.[53] Slaves that originated in Madagascar may have been purchased by Portuguese merchants visiting the Comoro Islands or on the East African coast.[54] The Portuguese preferred other sources for slave labor, although the trade from East Africa was not particularly large before the late eighteenth century.[55]

Even with the establishment of this food and slave trade with the islanders, misunderstandings were rife. Following their visits to the ports of Madagascar, Portuguese noted the lack of strong centralized authority, with the rule of coastal leaders rarely appearing to stretch far beyond their port cities. Portuguese visitors viewed political, religious, and linguistic divisions among the islanders as a positive feature, making the island more easily conquered.[56] This was not the reality. Northern coastal communities participated in trading networks that were openly hostile to the Portuguese, particularly in light of their frequent battles for control with Muslims. In 1506, shortly after their discovery of Madagascar, Portuguese sailors and soldiers raided the port cities of "Sada" and "Langane" in northwestern Madagascar. They burnt homes and seized supplies as coastal inhabitants fled.[57] The Portuguese attackers pursued them into the interior, where they captured the frightened islanders, while other Portuguese watched from the shore as "the sea [became] strewn with drowned men, women, and children." In a letter to the king, Albuquerque estimated that over a thousand people had died in the two raids. Those who survived were taken captive and given to the Portuguese soldiers, with each "to take as many as he liked." As their final act of treachery, the Portuguese commander oversaw the theft of goods from the ports, including fine cloth from India, some silver and gold, as well as a large quantity of rice. It took the Portuguese forces three days to complete their plundering.[58]

Further aggravating tensions, Portuguese missionaries endeavored to convert coastal peoples in Madagascar, including Muslim populations.[59]

The inhabitants of northwestern Madagascar were willing to trade with visiting European merchants in times of peace, but showed increased concern when the Portuguese threatened to become a more permanent presence on their shores, such as when they established a settlement for trade and Catholic missions at Massaliege in 1585.[60] The growing antagonism between the missionaries and the coastal people resulted in the murder of a Portuguese priest. Portuguese officials also accused the "Muslims of Madagascar" of harboring their enemies following attacks in East Africa and used this "alliance," along with the death of the priest, to justify a Portuguese attack on Massaliege in 1587.[61] By the early seventeenth century, some Portuguese blamed an implacable hatred of Christians and the strength of the "commercial sphere of the Arabs" for discouraging the Muslims of the northwest ports of Madagascar from trading with them, although Portuguese violence was a more likely cause of this hostility.[62]

Even outside of the north of Madagascar, further from the influence of East Africa, the Portuguese were unable to develop a stable trading presence. Portuguese missionaries focused some of their earliest conversion efforts in Antanosy (near Taolagnaro), a region in the southeastern portion of Madagascar where Portuguese settlers were lured by promises of abundant silver and gold.[63] Portuguese missionaries, traders, and soldiers formed a small trading post there in 1510. Their attempts to convert rulers were unsuccessful. The search for gold and silver mines was also abandoned. The Portuguese once again blamed their failures on religious differences, although the influence of Islam in this area was far more diffuse than in the north.[64]

By the seventeenth century, many Portuguese still struggled to maintain peaceful relationships with island leaders. An English visitor reported the following story in 1640 and some portions of his narrative can be confirmed by referring to a letter written by a Portuguese priest around the same period.[65] King Tinguimaro (Itongomaro), the ruler of "Mangakelly" (Mangakely) on the island of "Assada" (likely Nosy Be) had been trading with the "Moors" and Portuguese for decades.[66] These interactions were described as generally peaceful, until two of the king's wives (or concubines) were found missing after the departure of some Portuguese merchants. The English narrator tells us that "it was knowne" to the islanders that the merchants had taken the women back to Mozambique. The king sent a message to Massaliege informing the

Portuguese that they should not return to his island until they returned the women. He explained that he had already converted to Christianity and expected a certain level of respect from the Portuguese.[67] Portuguese merchants returned the women to Nosy Be two years later and the king assured the kidnappers that he was not angry. Instead he told them that "they were wellcome and made them a great feast."[68] Yet after one of the women appeared with a light-skinned child of European parentage, the king was offended and killed one of the Portuguese men. Both women were also put to death. The king died soon after, his heirs suspecting poisoning by the Portuguese and vowing revenge, although there is no evidence they were ever able to achieve this aim.[69] The English, trading rivals of the Portuguese by 1640, may have been told an exaggerated version of the story, but this incident suggests violence continued to mar relationships between Portuguese and island officials.

Another encounter, described by one of the first Dutch to visit the region, provides further evidence of Portuguese influence. When the ruler of the Comorian island of Mwali (Mohéli), dressed like a "Turque," boarded a visiting Dutch ship in 1601, he instantly began questioning the Dutch captain, Admiral G. Spilberg, about navigation and European maps.[70] By the time other European groups arrived in northwestern Madagascar, many of the leaders and traders could speak passable Portuguese and this ruler was no exception.[71] The king on this small island, to the surprise of the captain, not only proved knowledgeable in the art of navigation, but also had recently traversed the Red Sea during a trip to Mecca. His ease in trade with the European merchants also reflected a century of engagement with Portuguese traders. As if to confirm this fact, a few days later Spilberg spotted a ship sailing between East Africa and Madagascar, carrying Indian cottons and slaves. Even more remarkably to Spilberg, "mulattoes" manned the ship. These "half-Portuguese" spoke Portuguese, were dressed in Portuguese clothing, and carried Portuguese firearms.[72]

Such trade was the norm between the ports of northern Madagascar and Portuguese settlements on the East African coast by the seventeenth century.[73] By the early seventeenth century, a ship was reportedly dispatched annually from the Portuguese base at Querimba for cows, goats, ambergris, slaves, and cloth woven of "rushes" from northern Madagascar.[74] Many of the ships that crossed the channel were African-owned, African-operated vessels, spurred on by Portuguese demand, and this trade remained free of Portuguese monopoly controls. The Portuguese used Indian cloth and firearms to buy food and slaves from the African merchants who frequented visited Madagascar.[75] In spite of this regular commerce, the trade of the Estado da Índia remained far more focused on commodities found in the northern Indian Ocean and the East African interior.[76] Without further research into Portuguese archives, the extent of the trans–Mozambique Channel traffic remains unknown, but Mozambique Island's proximity to East Africa suggests that exports from Madagascar were less essential to the Portuguese colonists than those from the continent.[77]

Perceptions of Madagascar as an island both "beautiful and fertile" still persisted among the Portuguese.[78] In 1667, the Jesuit Manoel Barretto argued that "if any European nation should take possession of St. Lourenço [Madagascar] Portugal may well give up all desire of the whole conquest from the Cape of Good Hope to the entrance of the straits, of which they will be masters who are masters of St. Lourenço."[79] Many seventeenth-century Portuguese may have agreed with him. Portuguese officials in East Africa looked on with dismay as the Dutch, English, and French all attempted to establish themselves on the large island to their east. In fact, when other Europeans expressed interest in settling Madagascar, the Portuguese reacted by attempting to prop up their own claims in East Africa. Newitt suggests that Portuguese dependence on the food of Madagascar and, by extension, the Comoro Islands, may also explain why the Portuguese never attempted to conquer the Comoros, as they feared disrupting regional commerce.[80] Exports from Madagascar, even absent the fine cloth and desirable spices found elsewhere along the ocean's littoral, still wielded a noticeable influence over Portuguese officials.

## THE DUTCH AT MAURITIUS AND THE CAPE

By the middle of the seventeenth century, the Portuguese were no longer dominant in the trade of Madagascar. Their Dutch, English, and French rivals were newly influential on the island, as they were throughout the entire ocean.[81] The Dutch began regularly visiting Madagascar after 1595 and the French and English followed less than a decade later.[82] As Michael N. Pearson argues, the Dutch and English trading companies, unlike the Portuguese, "adroitly mixed skilful trade with the selective

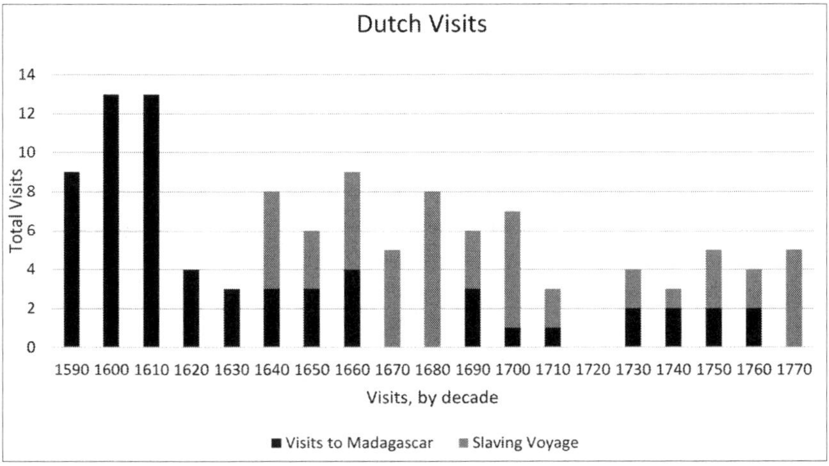


FIGURE 2.1. Dutch VOC ships visiting Madagascar, by decade, 1590–1780. *Sources: See appendix for full documentation.*

use of military force."[83] The careful focus on economic advantage that the Dutch brought to their plans for control in the ocean led them to only engage with Madagascar to support their trade elsewhere within the Indian Ocean. They had fewer colonial and religious aspirations on the large island than the Portuguese a century earlier and yet the Dutch had a greater impact on political and economic life on the island.

The rivalry between the Dutch and Portuguese formally began in 1602, with the formation of the Dutch Vereenigde Oost-Indische Compagnie (VOC). The VOC intended to forcibly and violently dominate European trade in the ocean. In addition to competing in Southeast Asia, VOC merchants targeted Portuguese holdings in East Africa, already weakened by Arab and African hostility, and mounted an unsuccessful attack on Mozambique Island in 1607.[84] Madagascar rarely enters into this history of conflict. The Dutch themselves knew little about Madagascar initially, as the sixteenth-century reports of Jan Huygen van Linschoten make clear.[85] The Dutch were so focused on securing spices, as highlighted in historical studies of the VOC, that their engagements with Madagascar seemed to be an afterthought. Stories of negotiations for rice pale in comparison to those detailing bloody conflicts over nutmeg and cloves in Southeast Asia.[86]

It is true that most early Dutch fleets only landed on Madagascar by accident or out of great necessity. Yet, given the length of their voyages and the challenges involved in crossing the Indian Ocean, these stops were more frequent (and influential) than one might suspect. When the first Dutch ships, a fleet of four vessels, arrived in the ocean in 1595, they spent several months replenishing their stores in southwestern Madagascar and along the east coast of the island. After loading fresh food and water, the ships sailed to Java and Sumatra.[87] This southern route would eventually enable the Dutch to traverse the ocean more quickly than the Portuguese, particularly after they developed other provisioning stops on the way to Southeast Asia.[88]

Only about ten percent of Dutch trading ships sailing into the Indian Ocean between 1595 and 1630 stopped at the shores of Madagascar, but this small percentage is misleading. Such was the level of Dutch involvement in commerce in the ocean overall that at least thirty-nine ships sponsored by Dutch trading companies stopped at Madagascar during these years. The ships came to anchor in Antongil Bay, St. Luce Bay (Bay of Saint-Lucia), and St. Augustin Bay.[89] None of the islanders living in these locations were accustomed to frequent trade with European merchants, so their stays proceeded with predictable consequences—food supplies were in short supply and recognizable trading partners were not always available. For example, the merchants in the 1595 fleet stopped in "St Augustijn" and visited the arid, sparsely populated land beside the bay, home to pastoralists who herded humped zebu cattle along with sheep and goats. The rivers near the bay, the Onilahy and the Fiheraña, would later provide easy transportation for foodstuffs, but Dutch sources provide no indication that there were direct trading connections with the interior during the late sixteenth century.[90] The Dutch visitors bartered with the *Andriana* (nobles, lords) for fish, cattle, fowl, sheep, and fruit. Despite the availability of food, when the Dutch departed after less than a week only 127 out of the 249 men who had boarded in Europe were still alive. The fleet then sailed around to the east coast of Madagascar, where the crews spent one month at Nosy Boraha (Île Sainte Marie) and Antongil Bay.[91] Subsequent trading voyages to Madagascar continued to visit these same locations. In 1598, a fleet spent almost a month in St. Augustin Bay, then several more weeks in the Comoros, visiting both Mayotte and Ndzuwani (Nzwani, Anjouan, Johanna).[92] The Dutch were pleased to report that only two men died during the 1598 visit to the island.[93]

Despite occasional visits to St. Augustin Bay, twenty-six of these early voyages halted on the east coast, in St. Luce Bay or Antongil Bay.[94]

FIGURE 2.2. A Dutch visit to southeastern Madagascar, c. 1618. *Source:* Willem Ysbrandsz Bontekoe, *Ovrnael ofte gedenckwaerdige beschrijvinghe vande Oost-Indische reyse* . . . (Hoorn: Ghedruckt by I. Willemsz, 1646), opposite page 10 (image from Library of Congress Prints and Photographs Division).

The Dutch later observed that "there was not a single Portuguese on this entire outer coast so that no difficulty need be feared from them."[95] During the early seventeenth century, rice seemed plentiful in eastern Madagascar. The Dutch described vast amounts of rice which the islanders would sell in return for small trinkets and cloth.[96] In spite of these positive descriptions, the results from provisioning in eastern Madagascar were mixed. One Dutch commander complained in 1598 that the people around Antongil were at war and there was a lack of food for purchase at the nearby island of Nosy Boraha.[97] On this small island, only about sixty kilometers long and ten kilometers wide, the inhabitants were fishermen, skilled in the capture of whales. They exported ambergris (a whale secretion used in perfume production) to the northern port cities of Madagascar, from where it would be sold to African and Arab merchants.[98] Apparently the production of foodstuffs for sale was less common on Nosy Boraha.

The challenges the Dutch had faced in eastern Madagascar encouraged them to send ships to St. Augustin Bay the next year, but the islanders now fled from the Dutch merchants and provisions were scarce. This failure forced the Dutch to visit the island of "Anschuan" (Ndzuwani) to the north instead.[99] Despite these challenges, Dutch ships continued to visit both coasts of the island and it seems that provisions were usually available, if in somewhat limited quantities.[100] For instance, in 1601, the crew of the *Zwarte Leeuw* was sailing from Antongil Bay, where they had stayed for a few days and sought fresh supplies, when they went aground near Nosy Boraha. They were forced to spend considerable time on the island repairing the vessel, buying food from the island's residents.[101]

In spite of the frequency of these early visits, fewer VOC vessels bought food from people in Madagascar after 1620 and interest in the island only revived following the founding of a Dutch settlement on nearby Mauritius. While sailing together in the southwestern Indian Ocean in 1598, a Dutch fleet became separated in a storm near Madagascar. In attempting to return to Madagascar, the vice admiral Wybrand van Warwijck arrived at an uninhabited island that he named Mauritius. Following years of visits to Mauritius for food and water, the VOC finally dispatched a governor and colonists to create an outpost on the island in 1638. During their first occupation, between 1638 and 1658, only a few settlers lived on the island. The Dutch hoped to create a strategic base, not a large populated colony, and made little effort to invest in growing food. At least two ships stopped annually during this phase of colonization to load ebony wood, along with some water, exhausting the limited food supplies on the island.[102] The focus on acquiring easy exports of ebony and consuming tortoises, birds, and wild fruits prevented focused agricultural production on Mauritius. Settlers on the mountainous island also complained about unreliable rains, strong winds, and frequent cyclones.[103] According to Megan Vaughan, the perennial lack of food on Mauritius was produced as much from mismanagement and the "unruliness" of the Dutch settlers, who eventually included a large contingent of convicts from Jakarta, as from the shortcomings of the natural environment.[104]

Madagascar was only a short sail from Mauritius so colonial officials tried to establish regular trade between the two islands. The Dutch seem to have viewed Madagascar as a reservoir for both food and laborers; the latter they hoped to purchase to replace the convicts who were currently employed by the company.[105] In 1639, Adriaan van der Stel, the commander on Mauritius, was instructed by VOC officials to sail to the east coast of Madagascar and sign treaties with leaders for slaves. The Dutch also signed a treaty with the Portuguese in 1641 in which the Portuguese agreed to recognize the east coast of Madagascar as within the Dutch sphere of influence and promised to restrict their visits to the west coast.[106] Van der Stel made a total of three voyages to the east coast of Madagascar in search of rice and slaves.[107] In 1641, the commandant sailed to St. Luce Bay where he was apparently successful at obtaining rice, but not slaves. He continued on to Antongil Bay, where he purchased 105 slaves with Spanish reales (silver coins), as well as combs, mirrors, linen cloth, and iron pans.[108] In 1642, he signed a treaty with the king "Filo Bucon" that placed the leader and his allies under the protection of the VOC and the United Provinces. In return, the king agreed he would not trade with the French, English, or Danish.[109] Shortly after van der Stel returned to Mauritius, half of the slaves he had purchased marooned and disappeared into the forests of the largely empty island, following a pattern that would become common in future years.[110] The slaves who did remain under Dutch supervision were kept busy harvesting and moving ebony to the coast.[111]

When van der Stel finally returned to Antongil Bay several years later in 1644, the king told him that the two Dutchmen left behind had died more than a year earlier (murdered by the islanders, according to French contemporaries, although it seems just as likely that they had died from tropical diseases).[112] In addition, the ruler had not adhered to his side of the treaty. Three times the king had assembled slaves for the Dutch. After van der Stel failed to arrive, the king sent the slaves across the island to the northwest ports of Madagascar.[113] The islanders also reported that a French ship had recently visited. In an effort to fight this competition, the Dutch continued to pursue a trading partnership with the king.[114] Another treaty was signed in 1645 in which the king agreed not to supply slaves to the French or Portuguese, only the Dutch. During a short stay in 1645, van der Stel purchased a hundred more slaves. When van der Stel set sail for Mauritius, he again left on shore a head merchant and five sailors, along with goods for trading.

The new commander of Mauritius, Jacob van der Meersch, continued the efforts of van der Stel and undertook two additional voyages to Madagascar. In October 1645, he procured 108 slaves from Antongil Bay and, the following year, sent traders to build a fort on the shores of the bay. The traders also visited Taolagnaro in 1646 and bought slaves from the French living there. Despite these efforts, the VOC was reluctant to continue its investment in the slave trade from Madagascar. VOC vessels had been taking slaves from Madagascar to Jakarta, but with the first arrival of slaves came fears that the importation of a large number of enslaved individuals speaking the same language would encourage them to rebel or flee in groups, as they had on Mauritius.[115] Likewise, the long distance to sail between Mauritius and Jakarta meant a relatively large number of the slaves died en route, far more than perished on much shorter voyages between Jakarta and slaving locations in Southeast Asia. In 1646, the governors at Jakarta announced that they no longer desired slaves from Madagascar.[116]

VOC support for the colony on Mauritius also faltered and they abandoned the island briefly in 1658. Settlers returned only a few years later, amid fears over English and French competition in the region. During their second occupation of Mauritius, between 1664 and 1710, VOC ships seldom stopped at the island. The Dutch outpost on Mauritius remained small, its inhabitants numbering fewer than two hundred people, and even this group was ungovernable. The Dutch finally decided to abandon their settlement on Mauritius in 1710, thanks to difficulties produced by locusts and rats, as well as the dangers posed by the runaway slave population, marauding pirates using the island as a base for operations, and the frequent violent storms that buffeted the ports and fields of Mauritius. Even after the administration officially left the island, many unwilling subjects, both free and unfree, had to be rounded up and forcibly shipped to Jakarta.[117]

By this period, the VOC had refocused their energies on developing a colony in southern Africa at the Cape of Good Hope, first founded in 1652.[118] In contrast to Mauritius, the Cape eventually became a successful center for supporting VOC fleets crossing into the Indian Ocean. For crews of ships seeking to refuel, the new colony was perfectly located, even if the land was not a fertile breadbasket. The colonists struggled to grow food and also faced challenges in procuring supplies from their hostile African neighbors.[119] Even though VOC ships were instructed to call at the Cape, not Madagascar and Mauritius (these islands became known as a "troublesome way to the Indonesian archipelago," according to historian Jaap Bruijn), the Dutch colonists at the Cape had to turn to Madagascar to fulfill their need for laborers and food.[120] Such was the interest in this trade that the Cape governor Jan van Riebeeck sent a message to Mauritius in 1655 asking for all of van der Stel's papers describing eastern Madagascar.[121] After reading several optimistic accounts and hearing from French traders about the plentiful food and "large numbers of slaves" available, van Riebeeck decided to send several ships to Madagascar.[122]

As a result, a total of fourteen VOC ships visited Madagascar during the1650s and 1660s.[123] The first two voyages from the Cape were to Antongil Bay, but the traders failed to load more than a few slaves, despite signing an agreement with a local king.[124] Undeterred, the VOC sent another ship to eastern Madagascar, but the vessel went ashore near Antongil Bay.[125] In his journal entries from 1656, van Riebeeck describes a well-timed encounter with an Englishman who had visited Mozambique and brought promising news to the hungry colonists at the Cape. The English visitor reported that the Portuguese obtained "all their supplies of rice, beans, peas, wax, honey &c" from the northwest coast of Madagascar, where they sent several small vessels annually. These ships were commanded by one or two native Portuguese, the rest being "8 or 10 half castes with better courage."[126]

By 1662, van Riebeeck had decided that western Madagascar could provide the food needed at the Cape "in the least expensive manner possible." Other sources for food, such as Jakarta, were far too distant to be reliable. Van Riebeeck also confessed a desire to diminish the power of the Portuguese by directing some of this valuable trade away from Mozambique Island, crippling the ability of the Portuguese to provision their merchant fleets. He made plans to have a company ship set aside for a regular provisioning trade with Madagascar (as the French would later do in the Mascarene Islands).[127] Van Riebeeck identified St. Augustin Bay as a place with "an abundance of cattle . . . whilst always no rice, or at least, very little." Gaining access to these cattle stores was important, as their African neighbors seemed resistant to providing the Dutch with this valuable resource. Furthermore, St. Augustin Bay would be "distant enough from the French, who profess to have the right of possession mostly everywhere on the Eastern side."[128]

Despite van Riebeeck's resolution, it took several more years for the VOC to send its ships to western Madagascar, the Dutch preferring to visit the more familiar east coast. In 1663, for instance, the ship the *Waterhoen* sailed to eastern Madagascar but only managed to obtain seven slaves and five "lasts" of "rice, cadjangh [peanuts], beans and peas." The day before they left the bay, five people from the vessel deserted, "evidently hoping to reach the French in the neighbourhood," and took guns with them on their escape. Once the ship returned to the Cape, the scale of the *Waterhoen* failure became evident. The slaves, whose number included two little boys and a girl, were all suffering from scurvy. The rice was crushed like meal and barely edible. Despite this failure, the *Waterhoen* again visited Antongil Bay the following year but could not obtain any slaves. According to Dutch records, the king "Fillo Horiva" told them he was unable to sell any slaves but could provide them with plentiful rice.[129] It was during this period, in 1663, that a Dutch ship, *Wapen van Amsterdam*, carried 354 slaves (of whom only 265 survived) to New York.[130] While the ship was able to obtain a large number of slaves, perhaps from the northwest coast of Madagascar, the high mortality rate foreshadowed the challenges European slavers would face later.

The Cape colonists only began to pursue trade on the west coast after 1672, when the Dutch captured an English slaving vessel which had 184 slaves on board, all procured from the ports of northwestern Madagascar.[131] Inspired by this success, a Cape slave ship, the *Voorhout*, sailed in 1676, the slavers on board purchasing 276 captives in "Mazalagem" and "Maningaar."[132] Following this success, the VOC sent the ship again to the same ports, but found slave prices higher amid competition from three Arab vessels. The health of the slaves was poor.[133] Likewise, in 1678, the VOC ship the *Elisabeth* bought 114 slaves from "Magalage" for Jakarta, but 51 died on the voyage across the ocean.[134]

Undeterred, the Cape government continued to send ships to the west coast of Madagascar for rice and slaves.[135] Trade became relatively predictable and Madagascar was seen as a reliable supplier for the Cape when the colonists faced dangers of food shortages and also for slave ships visiting East Africa.[136] Ships would leave southern Africa in May, sail for a month to Madagascar, and then spend three or four months visiting several ports along the west coast of the island. Even on such short voyages time was of the essence, as the return could take as long as six months and the risk of revolt on board or while near the shore was always high.[137] Historian Richard Allen estimates that 1,069 slaves were brought from Madagascar to the Cape on VOC-sponsored voyages between 1652 and 1699, with a further 1,756 slaves carried from Madagascar during the eighteenth century.[138]

While Madagascar remained important to the Dutch both as a victualing source as well as supplier of slaves for Mauritius and the

Cape Colony, the impact of Dutch trade on the people of Madagascar was mixed. The Dutch never managed to attempt anything larger than a small trading post on the island. Nevertheless, the Dutch were the first to try to conclude written trading agreements in eastern Madagascar, an area previously distant from frequent oceanic commerce. Even though trade was relatively small and infrequent compared to what was being carried out on the opposite coast, material traces of seventeenth-century Dutch trade have been found in the interior of Madagascar. The experience of van der Stel, describing the continued pull of trade toward the west coast of the island, suggests that this period was one still dominated by interisland commerce. There is also archeological evidence of the continued importation of goods into northeastern Madagascar throughout this entire precolonial period from as far away as China, even as more Europeans arrived on the island's shores.[139] In light of these trading opportunities, the decision of the king of Antongil to send his captives to northwest Madagascar, rather than reserving them for the Dutch, made perfect sense.

## THE FRENCH AT FORT DAUPHIN

In 1529, two French vessels visited Madagascar before continuing to Sumatra. They were followed by several other French attempts to intervene in the commerce of the ocean. Reports of ample food being bought with "things of little value" in Madagascar may have helped place the island at the center of French commercial schemes.[140] In 1642, Cardinal Richelieu founded the Compagnie française d'Orient, intended to be an imitation of the Dutch VOC.[141] The following year, the first French settlers landed near St. Luce Bay. Early Dutch sailors had recently visited this region and bought a great deal of fruit, rice, and boiled milk from a king who was conversant in "Spanish" (likely Portuguese).[142] The French hoped that this location might be ideal for a commercial base. Control of the establishment was given to a company agent named Jacques Pronis. His initial plans were ambitious, as he sought to control the entire east coast of the island, but they were rapidly halted by tropical diseases. After the first two months, only fourteen of the original forty settlers remained alive. Pronis decided to move his people to the south, where he oversaw the building of Fort Dauphin. This part of the south was cooler and Pronis hoped it would be healthier. The nearby bay was

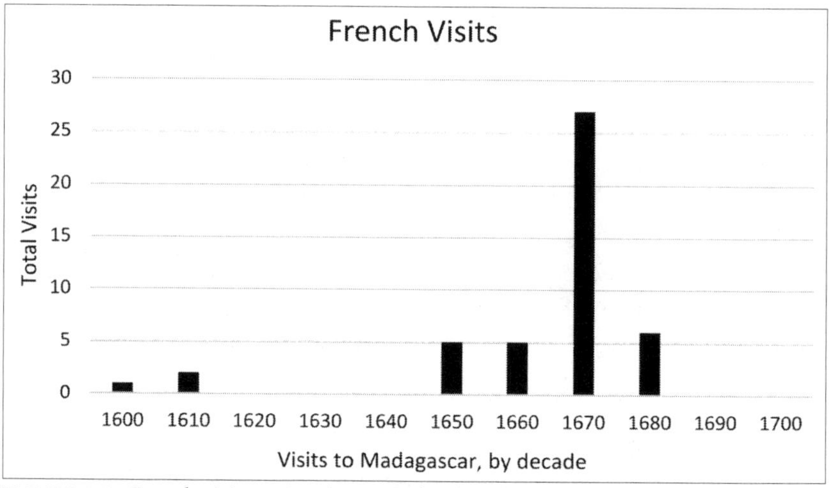


FIGURE 2.3. French visits to Madagascar, by decade, 1600–1700. *Sources: See appendix for full documentation.*

seen as a favorable location for ships to stop and load livestock. Shortly after his arrival, multiple ships sailed from France to Madagascar carrying colonists and trading goods to replenish the colony.[143]

Even after their move to Taolagnaro, the French settlers struggled. According to seventeenth-century accounts, Pronis was responsible for many of the difficulties these colonists would face. He married an island woman and tried to ally with leaders known as the *Raoandriana*. French sources list dozens of kings living near Anosy, each of them carried around in litters by their subjects. The kings traced their ancestry to the Middle East through oral traditions and written sources known as the *sorabe*, recorded using an Arabic script.[144] The Raoandriana secured their power through relationships with religious specialists known as *ombiasy*.[145] The French noted that the kings were less concerned with selling provisions to the French than with benefiting militarily from alliances with foreigners.[146] People lived in villages surrounded with strong palisades to protect their populations and cattle herds from theft. One of the leaders reportedly had 14,000 men under his control, presumably recruited to protect villages and their herds. Pronis contributed to this regional conflict when he decided to sell islanders as slaves to visiting Dutch slavers.[147] By the time Pronis's replacement, Étienne Flacourt, arrived in 1648, there were only twenty-eight Frenchmen living on the coast, the rest residing in the interior.[148] Flacourt despaired over the lack of religion apparent among these Frenchmen, who were more at home with their island wives than in Fort Dauphin. Food was in short supply at the fort, suggesting that the decision to ally and live with local families was a practical choice for many. Flacourt noted that the "*grands*" of the country had asked Pronis what riches he possessed, as he lacked both rice and meat. Pronis replied that while he lacked food, at least he had slaves. His response effectively demonstrates why the colony, intended to be a provisioning base for French merchants, was failing miserably.[149]

Flacourt had brought with him eighty additional colonists, including priests, and high hopes for reinvigorating the French settlement. The priests were meant to convert the islanders, but they also spent considerable time trying to restore the French to the faith and foster obedience to their new commander. Several more ships were sent between 1654 and 1660 with yet more settlers and priests to expand the Madagascar settlement.[150] In spite of his goals, Flacourt faced repeated difficulties. His reports describe a province at war, disrupted by the presence of French soldiers and firearms. Flacourt decided to return to Paris to ask for additional aid, but drowned in 1660 before returning to Madagascar. The account Flacourt left of his time on the island, providing lengthy descriptions of the religious and political practices of the Raoandriana, would be more influential on French commercial plans in the ocean than his time on the island itself.[151]

The French did not abandon hopes of settling Madagascar. By the 1660s, the mercantilist policies of Jean-Baptist Colbert had contributed to a French interest in undermining Dutch domination in the Indian Ocean. In 1664, Louis XIV granted the "island of Madagascar and its dependencies" to the Compagnie française des Indes orientales (the third French company to be awarded an exclusive monopoly on trade in the Indian Ocean). Unlike earlier attempts, this colony was to be under the close oversight of the French government and operated under a royal charter that gave the colonists a monopoly on trade from Madagascar.[152] Madagascar was once again chosen, according to Ames, "out of both historic and strategic necessity."[153] It seems that the French were still unable to envision a plan for the Indian Ocean that did not involve the island. They persisted in believing that southeast Madagascar had "the most gentle climate in all the Indies," and they hoped to begin to produce their own food on the island. In 1670, French admiral Jacob de la Haye described the land as "fertile" and naturally favorable to a number of crops.[154] Any food shortages, he argued, were produced by the failure of the islanders to cultivate the land correctly. Several times a year locusts ate all the plants to the roots, but he suggested that, with French oversight, this scourge could be easily wiped out. Hardworking French farmers could make the region far more productive.[155] These settlers believed, as a Frenchman expressed over a century later, that "the fortunate inhabitants of Madagascar never moisten the earth with their sweat; they turn it up slightly with a pick-axe; and this labour alone is sufficient" to produce rice and potatoes.[156] A seventeenth-century French observer likewise noted that "the common Food of the Inhabitants of this Island . . . is Rice boil'd with Salt and Water, which serves them instead of Bread; not but that the Ground will bring forth good Wheat, but the laziness of those, who should cultivate it, deprives them of the advantage of this so useful Commodity."[157] It was obvious to the French that, in spite of the islanders' shortcomings as farmers, supplies were readily available. If the islanders were able to acquire ample food from the island, imagine what industrious French farmers would be able to achieve?

Ships dispatched to Taolagnaro in 1664 contained almost three hundred passengers, including colonists and soldiers as well as carpenters, masons, and gardeners.[158] Their numbers included thirty-two women and some children. In spite of hopes for growing their own food, the climate of southeastern Madagascar was not amenable to French settlement and the new settlers faced the same challenges as others had under Pronis and Flacourt. The crops planted by the French failed. Wheat did not flourish in the hot, dry climate. Disease kept the mortality rate of colonists shockingly high, a number increased by the continued lack of nourishment. Even if they could purchase food, there was little, beyond cattle, that the people of Anosy had in large quantities. Water was in short supply, as were items for trade. The French realized that most of the people were materially poor, living in small, impermanent huts, storing their things in baskets, and only attired in bark cloth. During times of scarcity, people consumed "roots" and the locusts that plagued the area, practices that the French found appalling.[159] The picture of an endlessly fertile land proved to be a mirage.

As they lacked food in the south of Madagascar, the French in 1664 established trading posts in the rice-exporting regions of "Ghalemboule" (likely Fénérive), Antongil Bay, and Nosy Boraha.[160] French hopes were rather inflated. They believed, for instance, that Ghalemboule could provide ten or twelve vessels annually with rice, along with large amounts of honey and poultry.[161] One of the Frenchmen posted to the east coast, François Martin, left a detailed account of his time as an under-merchant between 1665 and 1668.[162] Martin lived near Ghalemboule with several other merchants in a small enclosed palisade with several huts, intended to store trading goods for purchasing rice. He explored the interior of the island in search of food, frequently in vain, as he encountered communities destroyed by cyclones, locusts, and warfare. People suffered in the lean months and, when the rice harvests did come in, they rarely sold their food, preferring to keep any surplus in reserve. Hunger was so widespread that people had to consume roots, locusts, and "monkeys" (lemurs). Far in the interior, people lived in more affluent circumstances. They sold large quantities of rice, along with slaves, to the ports of the northwest in return for firearms and silver "pieces of eight." The French made little effort to tap into this trade, due to the distances and terrain involved, and preferred instead to negotiate with east-coast leaders. Even this strategy was a failure. It was clear that the French merchants were wearing out their welcome within a few years. By the time Martin left Madagascar, he noted that the leaders tried to prevent their subjects from trading with the French. When the latter attempted to force them to sell food, people fled to the interior.[163]

Meanwhile, the French in the south of the island were living in increasingly perilous conditions.[164] Local kings became known as the "enemies of our religion" by French priests.[165] According to one eighteenth-century French traveler, "Dian Manangue," the sovereign of "Mandrarey" and a "faithful ally" of the French, attracted the attention of Father Stephen, the superior of the mission of Madagascar. The king made a speech to his people in which he rejected Christianity's strictures around polygamy and asked the priest why his "countrymen at the fort" did not follow the laws of his religion themselves.[166] The missionary confronted Dian Manangue and "snatched from him his *oli* [talisman] and his amulets, threw them into the fire, and declared open war against him."[167] The missionary was "instantly butchered" and the king declared he would "extirpate the French from the island." He sent his (baptized) son to gather support.[168] In the ensuing clashes, dozens of French were killed and the Frenchmen, in return, slaughtered men, women, and children and set fire to many villages. Thousands of people fought on both sides as communities throughout the region starved.[169]

Seventeenth-century French reports suggest that such conflict was frequent and more rooted in competition between the French and islanders for cattle and slaves than in religion.[170] The French at the fort continued to associate themselves with island women, despite official censuring of such relationships, with disastrous results.[171] More than a century later, a Frenchman named Alexis-Marie de Rochon described the exploits of a Frenchman he identifies as La Case, a man also mentioned in Arabico-Malagasy documents.[172] La Case reportedly married "Dian-Nong," the daughter of a sovereign who became a ruler after the death of her father. La Case and Dian-Nong raided the countryside, pillaging and attacking their enemies, and selling the proceeds (chiefly rice, cattle, and slaves) to the French at Fort Dauphin. Despite the violence described in his account, Rochon looked with favor on the exploits of La Case as he managed to successfully ally with many leaders. He even blamed the eventual collapse of the French colony on La Case's death.[173] While La Case was a particularly notorious example, French marriage with island women was common along the entire east coast. Martin tells a story of one French merchant, Sieur de Belleville, who decided to remain at Antongil with his wife for five or six years.[174] Once the French decided to close their posts on the east coast in 1671, some of the Frenchmen also chose to stay with their wives after one of the captains would not take the women on board.[175]

By 1672, only 250 French remained in the southeast of the island, most of these having set up household with women and refusing to leave.[176] The French settlers were "an impoverished, ill, and nearly naked lot," according to historian Pier Larson.[177] The French had arrived full of hope but found that Anosy was in fact "the most wicked land in the world."[178] They had discovered little worthy of exporting from the island, other than very limited supplies of food, and violent conflict between rulers continued to threaten trade.[179] French men and their families, including wives, their children, and household slaves originally from Madagascar, were finally moved to Réunion and Surat.[180] Attempting to colonize Madagascar had almost ruined the French trading company financially and had diverted their commercial energies from other ventures in the ocean. Only one or two French ships a year entered the Indian Ocean during the next few decades until another French

Compagnie des Indes was founded in 1719.[181] After this date, the French sent far more vessels into the ocean, as they refocused their attention on acquiring cloth in Surat and settling the Mascarenes.[182] After the collapse of Fort Dauphin, French ships took both the inner and outer routes around Madagascar on their way to Asian ports.[183] In the Mascarenes, Madagascar still was viewed as an ideal location for a colony, as eighteenth-century French observers attributed the collapse of the seventeenth-century settlement to the incompetence of colonial officials, not the local environment or the hostility of local communities.[184]

The seventeenth-century French settlements left their mark on the communities of southeastern Madagascar. Malagasy sorabe documents describe the events of the seventeenth century, including memories of the warfare instigated and perpetuated by French settlers. During one battle c. 1659, large portions of the southwest were described as "ravaged." The narrator observes that ten thousand cattle were taken from the inhabitants. When some villages did not give "whites" their cattle, gold, silver, and cloth, there was extensive bloodshed.[185] The murderous exploits of La Case, so lauded by Rochon, were remembered in particular detail. On one occasion, "Lakasy" (La Case) led an alliance of rulers who burned entire villages and stole three thousand cattle. Following several such raids, La Case returned to Fort Dauphin with ten thousand cattle and ten thousand captives.[186] One of the leaders at war with the French declared, "I must flee, as [my] people have died from hunger."[187] The violence that accompanied these French attempts at settlement had become intimately linked to starvation, not only for the settlers but also the islanders.

## ENGLISH PLANTATIONS

The English East India Company (EIC) sent its first ships into the ocean in 1601. The first fleet sailed into the Mozambique Channel and stopped at St. Augustin Bay as they entered the ocean. English reliance on provisioning in the Mozambique Channel would set the stage for, and determine the locations of, English settlements on Madagascar several decades later. Despite increasing interest by historians such as Alison Games and Emily Erikson in seventeenth-century English plans for Madagascar, there have been few attempts to link the success of early provisioning visits to later English desires for colonies on the island.[188]

It was only following frequent, peaceful refueling in western Madagascar that some in England decided to include the large island in their "struggle for power and wealth through overseas expansion," to borrow Games's phrasing.[189]

When the English arrived in southwestern Madagascar in the first decades of the seventeenth century, they discovered that local communities were initially unaccustomed to supplying visiting vessels with plentiful provisions. For example, four EIC trading vessels came to anchor in St. Augustin Bay in 1614.[190] When they arrived, the English discovered the shoreline was sparsely populated. No kings, queens, or courtiers approached the visitors or offered to board their ship. No coastal inhabitants arrived in their own dugout canoes or clamored to sell the sailors produce of the island. At the time of the Englishmen's arrival in August, rain would have been almost completely absent from the region.[191] When the English boarded canoes and came ashore, they discovered a collection of huts made of "bark" (woven palm leaves) near the shoreline. Herds of cattle may have been wandering nearby, but no people. The lack of people made the English at first assume that the islanders hid in fear, and perhaps they did, given European descriptions of recent encounters near the bay.[192] After all, seventeenth-century Portuguese had boasted that there were so many cattle in Madagascar that sailors could come ashore and easily "kill the cattle as unowned or disregarded property, simply for the sake of the tallow, leaving the flesh for the vultures."[193]

Fortunately for these English merchants, men and women eventually approached the merchants and agreed to provide them with much-needed supplies. The coastal people sold the English several head of cattle and provided them with other invaluable sources of nutrition. They also helped the sailors in securing such fresh water and wood as was available in this arid region. Among the most important English purchases were baskets of lemons and oranges to help them combat scurvy. The English made these food purchases with various small items, including silver chains they assumed would be used "to hang about [the traders'] necks."[194] Indeed, silver and beads were the only items that could be used to purchase cattle from the inhabitants living near the bay and EIC merchants quickly learned to carry such trading goods with them on their voyages into the Indian Ocean.[195] Knowing that the season was growing short, the EIC captains only stayed in St. Augustin Bay for about two weeks.[196] The four ships left Madagascar, their supplies refreshed and their captains full of memories of a friendly people and a fertile island. The English captains were eager to arrive at the richer shores of India before their ships fell into further disrepair. To stay longer would also increase the number of their sailors catching malaria and other tropical illnesses, provide them with more opportunities to run away, and even risk large-scale revolts by disgruntled crew members. These EIC ships visited the island of "Comara" before continuing to Socotra and Surat. The precarious survival of crew members in this crossing is clear in the experience of one of the vessels, the *Hector*, which had undertaken four journeys into the Indian Ocean previously. It had to be abandoned in the northern Indian Ocean for being "rotten" in 1616, within a few months of their departure from Madagascar. The crew members and all the cargo on board had narrowly escaped disaster.[197]

Following their arrival in Asia, the EIC officers issued reports back to company officials in Europe. Their positive experiences in Madagascar, when combined with earlier EIC reports, recommended the island to future expeditions. One English merchant, John Sandcrofte, wrote approvingly of the bay, describing the "excellent good" cattle. In the same year, the merchant Robert Preston reported that "the people [showed] themselves both civil and loving, being the properest men that I have seen." He found the islanders to be "reasonable" and amenable to trade, despite their lack of experience in dealing with European merchants.[198] The bay was easy for sailors to find after crossing under the Cape of Good Hope and the people here provided cheap and plentiful food to visiting fleets. These positive descriptions of southwestern Madagascar began circulating among EIC captains and, within a few years, the bay in Madagascar was recommended as a good meeting place and the "fittest place of refreshing" for EIC fleets on long voyages into the Indian Ocean.[199] From 1607 to 1700, at least fifty-two EIC ships stopped in St. Augustin Bay before sailing onward.[200]

Despite the recent introduction of oceanic trade to southwestern Madagascar and occasional clashes, coastal communities welcomed the opportunities presented by the arrival of European ships, not just those of the English, but Dutch and French as well. Visitors to the bay described the arrival of people in canoes full of food to sell to the sailors. When news of a ship's arrival spread, inhabitants along the rivers would approach the bay with their herds or in canoes to bring goods for trade. "Chiefs" (the Andriana) sold the English small supplies of rice, cattle,

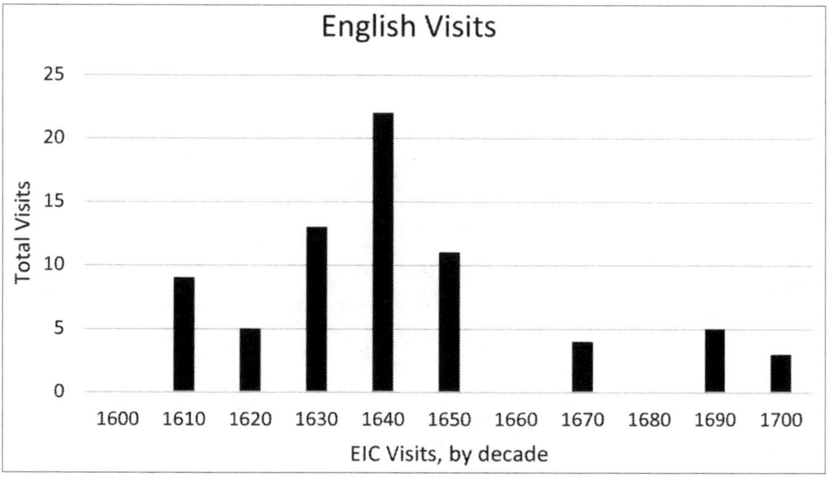


FIGURE 2.4. English East India Company visits to Madagascar, by decade, 1600–1700. *Sources: See appendix for full documentation.*

"callavances" (also written calavances, likely the hyacinth bean, *Lablab purpureus*), and lemons in return for metal and red carnelian beads that the Europeans had brought from India or the Persian Gulf region.[201] The Andriana also requested military support and firearms from the English. In return, these leaders promised to provide visiting Englishmen with cattle or slaves obtained in raids on groups in the interior of the island.[202] Such was the extent of English success that the French at Fort Dauphin made repeated requests to move their settlement to the opposite side of the island.[203]

The islanders were so obliging that one English trading group, the Courteen Association, decided to finance two colonies on the island in 1645, one based at St. Augustin Bay and a second on the northwest coast at "Assada," near or on Nosy Be.[204] With these colonies, the English hoped to create export centers for moving slaves from Madagascar to EIC establishments in the Atlantic and Indian Oceans, as well as securing provisions within Madagascar.[205] After their arrival in 1645, the 140 settlers built a fortified camp along the southern side of St. Augustin Bay.[206] The colonists, expecting a fertile (if sparsely inhabited) paradise, complained to a passing English merchant about the "extreme barrenness of the soil" and the difficulty in keeping their cattle safe from thieving people.[207] They may have exaggerated these difficulties, since coastal communities had long managed to survive in the region, but the English were not prepared for the environment, which was not suitable for growing wheat and the other English crops that they had hoped to plant in the colony. They had to rely upon the islanders to herd their purchased cattle. After only a few short weeks the settlers were close to starvation and the neighboring communities refused to sell them food. At the peak of tensions, some of the settlers complained that once the islanders had sold cattle, they stole them back after only a short period.[208] English soldiers were dispatched to recover cattle but some of their island neighbors killed the men and then set fire to the colony's forge and bellows.[209] When ships sent elsewhere in the ocean failed to return with food and trading goods for the colonists, the few remaining English settlers decided to abandon the hostile shores of Madagascar. Of the 140 colonists, men, women, and children, who had arrived at the island in March 1645, only twelve sailed from Madagascar in May 1646.[210]

Intended to rival the sugar plantations of Barbados, the settlement at Assada founded in 1650 met with an even more disastrous fate, despite being located in what would seem a more favorable location for coordinating trade and developing agriculture. When an English captain, James Berblocks, visited Assada a few months after the colonists were to have arrived, he discovered that all signs of the settlement had disappeared entirely, along with all of the "planters" (settlers).[211] He suspected the worst after eventually finding the remains of what he described as an "English fort."[212] After facing down an attack on the shores of the island and fearing an ambush if he lingered any longer, the captain ordered his ship to sail to nearby Ndzuwani. The captain spoke with the king of "Demonio" (Domani) in Ndzuwani while purchasing provisions on that island and learned that the kings of Madagascar "would not admit any of our people to inhabit his land or islands."[213]

After deciding to return to Madagascar and visit the port of "Martaledge" (Massaliege), the captain urged his crew to make no mention of the Assada colony. Instead he instructed them to tell the people that they were sailing to India and only in search of water and provisions. While at anchor near Massaliege, the English encountered a Portuguese ship off the coast with several slaves hidden aboard. The English captain learned that these slaves had to be held below deck, as the slaves had been reserved for "Arabians" who exported them to Ndzuwani and the islanders feared reprisals if they were found selling slaves to Europeans. Berblocks negotiated with traders in Massaliege and managed to purchase twenty-four slaves in poor condition. He also bought plenty of cattle and sheep from the traders for excellent prices before sailing to Bantam.[214]

Berblock's account reveals a great deal about the relationship formed between Europeans and islanders by the 1650s. The disappearance of the Assada colonists was attributed to the hostility of the coastal communities, but the failure of both English settlements on Madagascar suggests a deeper-running challenge to European colonization on Madagascar. As the English and French experiences repeatedly proved, the islanders were willing to provide merchants with provisions and even slaves, but Europeans faced considerable animosity when they attempted to seize supplies of rice, cattle, and laborers.

As a result of these failures, never again did the English attempt to create a permanent trading post on the island, but EIC vessels continued to visit ports in western Madagascar to provision their ships before sailing to India. By the mid-seventeenth century, the EIC expressed a particular interest in purchasing slaves from the island, particularly on the west coast, where, according to one English guide, "you need not doubt of meeting of slaves enough at some of these places."[215] One of the first English purchases of slaves in the southwestern Indian Ocean region was in 1639, when an EIC trader bought a shipment of slaves with cloth in the Comoro Islands.[216] These slaves may have originated in northwestern Madagascar, a region the English frequently visited and described as connected with slaving in the Comoros. In 1644, for instance, an EIC captain observed "a junk" carrying five hundred slaves from Massaliege and sailing toward the Comoros.[217] This and other similar observations of a preexisting traffic in captives on the west coast of Madagascar, as well as some luck in obtaining small cargoes of slaves, contributed to the English proposing that ships sent to Surat should stop and "buy up what slaves they can procure at St Laurence [Madagascar], Mozambique, Johanna [Ndzuwani] and the [Comoro] Islands."[218] The EIC issued orders in 1663 for several ships to visit the island of Madagascar, "either to the Eastward or westward of the island as . . . most advantageous and soonest gained . . . [and if to the west], sail for Masiladge [Massaliege], or any other place within judgment" to purchase thirty or forty slaves, aged from fifteen to twenty-one, for EIC settlements.[219] The promise of the slave trade, as well as the continued pursuit of provisions, encouraged EIC visits to western Madagascar for slaves and provisions into the eighteenth century.[220]

The periodic arrival of Europeans in the ports of Madagascar during the sixteenth and seventeenth centuries has usually been dismissed as peripheral to European interests elsewhere in the ocean. The Portuguese cared more for gold in East Africa than rice from Madagascar, and paid the price.[221] The Dutch wanted spices from Asia, cloth from India, and ebony from Mauritius, and much more, but only slaves from Madagascar.[222] In a recent history of Madagascar, Stephen Ellis and Sofolo Randrianja argue that the island offered few exports that Europeans were interested in carrying long distances, other than slaves.[223] But a focus on luxury goods and slaves ignores the need of fresh food and water that spurred European merchant fleets to spend weeks at a time on the shores of Madagascar in the middle of their transoceanic voyages, to say nothing of the multiple attempts to settle and convert the islanders by the mid-seventeenth century.

In the midst of the fantastic and speculative claims made by Europeans about Madagascar there are also the detailed descriptions of the islanders they encountered. Through European eyes, we primarily receive information about the commodities for sale on the shores of Madagascar. In the southern half of the island, cattle and citrus fruits were abundant, while the people of the north and east of Madagascar had rice for sale, but fewer cattle. The north was also home to a bustling slave trade. Food supplies were frequently limited and subject to disruption. Absent are the descriptions of royal ceremonial feasts that would be a hallmark of eighteenth-century trading rites. Our knowledge of seventeenth-century Madagascar is not only limited by the information that Europeans chose to record but also where they decided to visit. Merchants only halted at locations that offered secure harbors for sheltering their ships. These harbors usually were deep bays and river basins. Few vessels came to land directly to the north and south of St. Augustin Bay, for instance, so descriptions of these regions largely come from shipwrecked sailors.

It is clear that European trade networks, as shown in the experiences of Berblock or van der Spil, were secondary to those already operating within and around Madagascar throughout the seventeenth century. Slaves were reserved for East African and Arabian traders, not Europeans. Sixteenth- and early seventeenth-century European trading records reveal that a ready market for Asian cloth already existed, as well as knowledge of its relative value, particularly in the north of the island. To the south, beads, firearms, and miscellaneous manufactured goods were more frequently used to purchase foodstuffs. The nuanced demand for certain colors and types of beads changed over time, from the red "rangoe" beads of the seventeenth century to the yellow glass beads requested during the eighteenth. The portability and durability of these forms of currency gave them higher demand in the south of the island and they may have been transported across trade routes stretching deep into the interior of the island before the seventeenth century.[224]

Work completed by prominent archeologists, including Robert Dewar, Chantal Radimilahy, and Henry Wright, confirms that communities throughout Madagascar had been connected through frequent migration and commerce for centuries prior to the arrival of Europeans on the island's shores.[225] Judging by the distribution of imported goods, merchants on the northwest coast traded (directly and indirectly) with a variety of groups throughout Madagascar by the thirteenth century. On an island of fluctuating rainfall and crop productivity, the ability to access and control food supplies may have contributed to political centralization by the sixteenth century. As agricultural communities in Madagascar's interior produced more commodities for export, such as ironware, cloth, and other manufactured goods, they also supported leaders who could oversee these and other exchanges.[226] Such economic and political changes have been noted throughout much of the island, even among the less populated pastoral communities in the south.[227] There may have also been a population boom in the interior of the island as the first European ships began visiting Madagascar, although details are elusive.[228]

Thus island communities may have been in the midst of a major phase of reorganization just as the first Portuguese were arriving on their shores.[229] Given these conditions, was the arrival of European merchants at the shores of Madagascar immediately transformational? Scholars have debated the importance of European intervention on communities along the shores of the Indian Ocean, but, by and large, most would agree with Abdul Sheriff who, along with others, concludes that the initial arrival of Europeans was less of a shock to the littoral societies of the Indian Ocean than it was to the economies of Europe.[230] After all, Europeans not only competed with each other in these early years, but also faced challenges from other maritime and land-based powers.[231] In Madagascar, Europeans needed to adapt to the economic conditions they encountered. Trade with Europeans in the northwest of the island was perhaps initially an outlet for surplus agricultural production that was already being accumulated for sale to African and Arab merchants. In the south of the island, by contrast, it would take an economic and political revolution for the people to secure dozens of bags of rice annually to sell to European merchants. Following this revolution, leaders could dictate the prices of the commodities they knew Europeans most needed. While European merchant groups introduced additional competition into trade in Madagascar, the real threat to coastal leaders did not come from these European visitors and colonists, but from populations elsewhere on the island.

# THREE

## The Sakalava

### *From Warriors to Merchants*

THE ENGLISH VESSEL THE *Sussex* was returning from a visit to China in 1738 when strong winds suddenly tore apart the ship's sails and damaged the mast. The crew panicked. Their commanding officers decided to board another English ship sailing in company with the *Sussex*, but sixteen men chose to stay on the damaged vessel.[1] Four days after the departure of their officers, the remaining sailors sighted St. Augustin Bay. Upon entering the bay, the men signaled to the people on the shore to approach by hoisting a flag and firing several guns toward the beach. Two men, including a "linguester" (linguist) who could speak English, approached the vessel in a canoe. These newcomers brought with them a jar of honey, a present from the "King of Barbar." The king's representatives asked the captain to go ashore and visit with the king at his residence to the north, in the port of "Toliar." They were informed that the king had just returned from war and had plentiful slaves and provisions for the Englishmen.

Despite this demonstration of trade and hospitality, the two islanders were suspicious of the English. They asked why so few men were on board such a large vessel and did not believe the evasive lies they were told, that most of the men were doing work in the hold of the ship. The "King of Barbar" was even more knowledgeable about the typical conduct of EIC traders. When the sailors tried to use "China ware" to purchase provisions, the king informed them that he knew that these goods were "private trade" and not typically used for such purchases. Feeling vulnerable to attack, the crew left the bay, traveling as fast as they were able in their rapidly disintegrating vessel.[2]

As the *Sussex* sailed along the west coast of Madagascar, it literally fell to pieces. Only a handful of sailors, including one named John Dean, made it to the shore alive. Once they arrived, the four men sought assistance from a variety of individuals: a Frenchman (perhaps a former pirate) who had lived in Madagascar and spoke the language of the islanders, a number of "headmen" who were constantly going off to war, the wives of the headmen who sheltered and fed the castaways, and the king, "Renauf," who lived in "Moharbo" (Mahabo).[3] According to Dean, the European arrivals were largely treated with indifference, as the king and other leaders were more interested in pursuing war with neighboring communities than helping them return home, although the visitors were generally able to obtain food and shelter from the islanders. Dean, the sole surviving crew member, was finally rescued by an English vessel visiting the king's port of "Youngoult" (Young Owl, Iongoeloe, near Morondava) about a year later.[4]

Upon his return to England, Dean wrote a brief account of his time in Madagascar. His writing touches on dress and culinary practices, as well as the political organization of the state. The king in Mahabo ruled the west-central portion of Madagascar through violence but also exercised ritual authority over his subjects. One of the king's chief friends and a "man of power," Rabbalow, was frequently "out on the scout, with about fifty armed men."[5] Dean's comments suggest that these military excursions were aimed at acquiring both slaves and cattle. Dean also described pausing at the town of "Munghavo" where "most of the deceased kings are laid in small houses." Each time the king's entourage passed through, "they killed an ox, beat drums, blowed their conches, and fired guns over the houses of the deceased kings."[6]

Dean's sketch of leadership in western Madagascar can be compared with the better-known account provided by Robert Drury.[7] Drury, another shipwrecked sailor, spent about fifteen years living in southern and west-central Madagascar several decades before Dean set foot on the island. According to his published account, Drury encountered numerous monarchs during his stay on the island during the first years of the eighteenth century. At the time of his visit, the Sakalava king of "Moherbo" (Mahabo), "Rer Trimmonongarevo," ruled over the port of Morondava, home to individuals who supplied milk and other provisions to European vessels.[8] Drury outlined how the king's brothers had formed predatory states directly to the north and south of Morondava and described personally observing their battles for control over land near St. Augustin Bay.[9] Less than four decades after Drury's stay on the island, the kings Dean encountered had consolidated their control over trade from the entire west coast of the island, which they used as a base for military operations against their enemies.

The kings depicted by both Dean and Drury demonstrated their power through the use of violence and demanded ritualized obedience from their inferiors, but the accounts left by the two sailors tell us little else about the beginnings of these states in western Madagascar.[10] When Europeans halted at the coast of Madagascar during the seventeenth century, most were unaware of transformations occurring within the island. European knowledge was limited to the "continual quarrels" and "bloody wars" between "petty princes" that they observed during their brief visits.[11] By the eighteenth century, however, European reports from their time on Madagascar supported the experiences of Drury and Dean. Although European sources are limited both in scope and content, they do suggest that Sakalava kings and queens preyed upon weaker communities that provided food to the leaders at gunpoint (or spearpoint) or as tributaries. In the southwest, the English and Dutch negotiated for rice and slaves with a King Baba who resided in the port of Toliara, just to the north of St. Augustin Bay. Morondava, a new port located in the west-central Menabe region, was controlled by a powerful king who provided Europeans and Americans with plentiful slaves and provisions. The northwest was no longer dominated by Muslim merchants and leaders, as Sakalava kings and queens began overseeing exchanges with Europeans in this region as well.

Sakalava rulers have been described by historians as "slave-trader kings," and indeed their power to dominate the export trade from the island was central to their control over western Madagascar, although they chose to monopolize not only the sale of slaves, but also of rice and cattle.[12] The value accorded to these desired provisioning items, priced

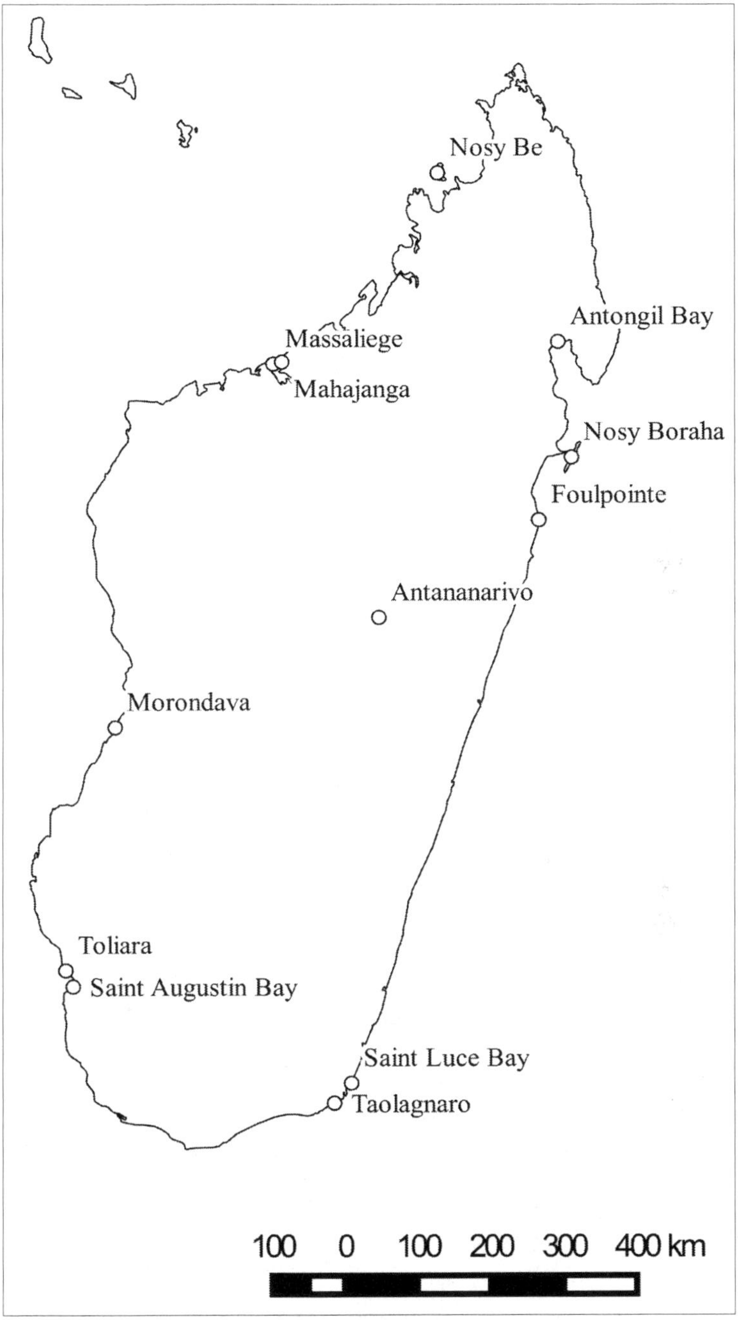


MAP 3.1. Madagascar, c. 1600–1800

in firearms and silver coins, approached that which Europeans had paid for slaves. By manipulating European demands for laborers and provisions as well as expanding their control over the island, Sakalava rulers maintained a tight grip on the exchanges on the west coast of Madagascar. The term merchant kings would be a more apt description for these monarchs.

## IDENTIFYING THE SAKALAVA

Sixteenth-century Portuguese visiting northwestern Madagascar either described the islanders they encountered as "Moors" (African Muslims) or referred to them as "Boucki" (also written as "Bouckes," "Buki," or "Buqua") if they were not Muslim.[13] Visitors to Madagascar suggest that these identities were not only rooted in religious differences, but were linguistic ones as well, as the Boucki spoke a language distinct from the Moors, who sounded more similar to the "Kaffirs" from East Africa[14] During the seventeenth century, an Englishman identified a third group on the island, the "Hoves" (Hova), who "agree[d] in their speech" with the Boucki and lived in the interior of Madagascar.[15]

By the early eighteenth century, Drury noted very few differences, aside from minor variations in vocabulary and pronunciation, between the languages spoken in southern and western Madagascar. Instead he identified people by the regions in which they lived (the countries of "Saccalauvor," "Merfaughla" (Mahafaly), "Anterndroea" (Antandroy), etc.), each distinguished by slightly different patterns of governance, land use, and social customs.[16] He mentioned that Sakalava also functioned as a family name, noting that Sakalava rulers were related by blood and joined together in an "amicable alliance."[17] Yet many other eighteenth-century visitors in western Madagascar, including Dean, do not use the term Sakalava to describe the kings and queens of this region, even if the names of the leaders they encountered appear in Sakalava royal genealogies. Throughout the eighteenth century, the term Sakalava was used more frequently to describe major ports on the west coast of the island.[18] In light of such inconsistencies, it is difficult to uncover how the term Sakalava was understood in western Madagascar.

By the mid-nineteenth century, the term Sakalava was being used to describe not only kings and queens, but also their subjects in the western portion of the island.[19] The history of the Sakalava monarchs was recorded in a series of publications penned by foreign missionaries, government officials, and, most influentially, a French naval captain, Charles Guillain, who composed one of the earliest collections of Sakalava royal traditions, *Documents sur l'histoire, la géographie et le commerce de la partie occidentale de Madagascar.*[20] The compilation of these traditions and, relatedly, the use of the label Sakalava, served to confirm the legitimacy of the coastal rulers who inherited power from their Sakalava ancestors.[21] The writers, including Guillain, were concerned with identifying rulers with whom the French could form alliances and their writings reflected Western perceptions of statehood, leadership, and empire.[22] Nineteenth-century Europeans frequently sought to fix firm boundaries around the territory controlled by the Sakalava rulers, despite the fact that the area dominated by these monarchs had been ruled through a variety of familial ties, alliances, and tributary states.[23] In spite of their efforts, conceptions of nation and state rarely overlapped in any meaningful way, at least in western terms. In fact, it was likely impossible to say with certainty where the borders between one state and another lay at any given time, nor the significance of the label Sakalava for most people in western Madagascar during the nineteenth century. The term Sakalava almost certainly did not have the same connotations it would acquire by the mid-twentieth century, when it would become the label for a sizable ethnic group in Madagascar.[24]

The use of the identifier Sakalava in the eighteenth century, while distinct from that of later periods, nonetheless colored the political landscape and was used to express political alliances to visitors on the island. European sources, including those left by Drury and other visitors to western Madagascar, reveal that there were indeed leaders who self-identified as Sakalava and exercised sovereignty over the western portion of the island. In perhaps the most powerful connection between past and present, eighteenth-century Sakalava rulers used ceremonies and physical monuments to express the power of their ancestors.[25] As Dean's account reveals, royal tombs had been sacred places for worship, as they are today, although the shape of these ceremonies has changed dramatically. In recent years, the commemoration of Sakalava and other prominent ancestors in Madagascar has found expression, for instance, in the practice of *tromba* (trance) ceremonies and in *fitampoha*, the ceremonial washing of royal relics.[26] These frequent reminders of the past reflect an abiding interest in royal genealogy. In northwest Madagascar during the 1980s, the sovereign clan could still trace their ancestors back twenty-seven generations. Nobles could name between nine and fifteen generations, commoners, about three or five, and slaves had no kin, "by definition."[27] Such differences might have existed in earlier centuries. The coastal Vezo fishermen have reported that the Sakalava used genealogy as a manner of control and domination during the years when they attempted to assert sovereignty over Vezo communities.[28]

The challenge for historians is to note these potent memories of genealogy and royal ancestry while not projecting a contemporary Sakalava identity onto our study of the past. Although leaders along Madagascar's west coast represented themselves, and the trading ports that they projected power onto, as Sakalava to European traders during the eighteenth century, it does not mean that others who lived there saw themselves as part of a distinct and united Sakalava ethnic group. Indeed, the comments of the Vezo suggest that they did not.

## THE RISE OF THE SAKALAVA

The few Europeans who visited the west-central coast of Madagascar prior to the eighteenth century only hinted at the political, economic, and military revolutions that were occurring within this part of the island.[29] In 1616, a Portuguese priest described bloody battles between people living in the west-coast village of Sahadia and their enemies, the "Suculambes," but we know little else about this particular set of struggles.[30] By the close of the seventeenth and into the eighteenth century, observers noted that a powerful group was attacking communities along the entire west coast of the island, although it was rarely identified by name.[31] Sakalava royal traditions, by contrast, provide detailed descriptions of the divine rulers who founded the Sakalava kingdoms.[32] According to these, Sakalava ancestors were originally from the southeast of the island, their traditions suggesting Raoandriana origins and many of their religious practices echoing those found in the Anosy region of the island.[33] After leaving the southeast, these ancestors moved to the north and west, halting when they reached the Morondava River, where access to fresh water and fertile soil helped convince them to stay near its shores.[34] To the north was the wide Tsiribihina River, a stark break in the dry landscape, according to one nineteenth-century European traveler who described the "rich alluvial soil" between these two rivers as "remarkably fertile."[35] Archeological studies reinforce some of these Sakalava traditions by revealing that small polities lived along the rivers in the region and were probably ruled by interrelated dynasties prior to the seventeenth century. These studies also suggest that much of the export trade in the west-central portion of the island was directed toward entrepôts in northwestern Madagascar.[36]

Sakalava rulers may have settled along the shores of the Morondava and founded the Maroseraña kingdom in the early years of the seventeenth century.[37] Traditional histories assert that the Sakalava established this kingdom not only due to their superior organization and military power, but also thanks to divine intervention, apparent in the names they provided for their kingdom and the region they ruled.[38] According to one interpretation, the word *serana* in Maroseraña refers to the close relationship rulers forged with priests and their amulets.[39] Over time, this privileged access to spirits may have contributed to a belief in divine kingship, along with the practices of ancestor worship and divination. The Sakalava renamed this region Menabe, or "very red," the red symbolizing power and strength, as well as describing the color of the rich soil in the region.[40] Motifs of strength and fertility are interwoven in other traditions on the founding of the kingdom. In one of these, the ancestors placed the bodies of "a man, a woman, a magnificent red steer, and a goat" into a deep pit. Then they poured the blood of the steer over the others.[41] Another tradition described how divine intervention, in the form of an enormous red bull descending from the sky, led a Sakalava king to victory over his opponents.[42]

From its base in Menabe, the kingdom gradually expanded to dominate the west-central region within a few decades, according to traditions, and Sakalava rulers tried to maintain good relations with the groups they encountered and eventually conquered.[43] Neighboring states became tributaries to Sakalava royalty, either willingly or after defeat by Sakalava forces. Sakalava rulers integrated prominent families into their own through a process of intermarriage and blood-brotherhood ceremonies (*fati-dra*). The fati-dra ceremonies, described at length by European visitors to the island in later years, served to create quasi-familial alliances between the royal family and local leaders.[44] Sakalava rulers also married into these families and, from them, may have adopted many local religious practices, including ancestor worship. Thanks to these ceremonies and marriages, the descendants of rulers from incorporated communities were now celebrated as part of the Sakalava ruling family and dynasty. Sakalava rulers also allowed the groups they conquered to remain on their land, thus benefiting from the commerce and labor of their newly acquired tributaries.[45] By the early eighteenth century, Europeans observed that tributary groups sent the Sakalava royalty annual gifts in the form of silk, rice, sheep, vegetables, and slaves, in return for peace.[46] Tributary leaders appear to have retained, at least ostensibly, some of their independence and freedom, as long as they continued to send regular supplies of food and slaves. In remembering the process of incorporation into the Sakalava state, the Vezo fishermen of the west coast stated that, despite being tributaries to the Sakalava for the past few centuries, they were never fully subservient.[47]

Sakalava traditions insist that the expansion of the state was due to the military power of their rulers. European observations suggest two other reasons why neighboring groups joined the Sakalava state: for protection against a growing slave trade and to safeguard food supplies. Other communities in the region may have agreed to be incorporated into the expanding Sakalava state as they sought protection from slave raiders, who seem to have been expanding their activities throughout Madagascar in response to demands from both European and non-European slavers.[48] Although large numbers of slaves were not exported directly from the west-central coast until later in the seventeenth century, the slave trade from the northwest coast may have been carrying away men, women, and children from the interior of the island decades earlier. For instance, in 1665, a Frenchman living on the east coast of Madagascar described the devastation wrought by predatory slave raiders operating throughout the island.[49] These attackers likely targeted the west-central region of the island as well, given the trading links that existed between port cities to the north and the Menabe region. According to seventeenth-century Portuguese visitors, the Sakalava king Andriamandazoala had at least five hundred armed men at his side in 1613.[50] People living on the west coast of Madagascar may have desired the stability and protection of these men. By the early eighteenth century, men living in western Madagascar told Drury that they came willingly to the Sakalava king's side, knowing that they "fight for their own security and ease, and when they get any plunder from their enemies, they think themselves sufficiently rewarded."[51] Drury also argues that Sakalava rule had enabled the country to grow "not only vastly populous, but rich, and the people live in plenty as well as peace."[52]

In addition to protecting their subjects against enslavement, the Sakalava rulers also secured and redistributed food supplies within a relatively arid region. Exports of foods such as rice, beans, and tubers from St. Augustin Bay and Massaliege may have been stressing local communities by the mid-seventeenth century. It is telling that food, along with slaves, was included in tributary payments to Sakalava rulers. Supplies of cattle and rice were seen also as rewards for serving the king.[53] Furthermore, around 1527, a Portuguese visitor to western Madagascar described finding little food for purchase, and there are no records of the Portuguese attempting to purchase provisions from the west-central region during the sixteenth century.[54] It seems unlikely that large supplies of cattle and rice were for sale on the west-central coast, as rice was primarily grown further in the north and interior of the island and cattle were highly valued and seldom eaten, except on ceremonial occasions. This situation changed within the next century, at least in the west-central portion of the island. Portuguese sources describe how the king Andriamandazoala provided visiting priests with plentiful food in 1613, suggesting either increased agricultural production or the ability of the Sakalava to tap into additional supplies of food for export, through trade or frequent raiding.[55] While the Portuguese did not list the food they obtained during this visit, we do know that people in the ports directly to the north at this time possessed rice, millet, "mungo," beans, peas, nuts, bananas, ginger, sugarcane, and limes.[56] Likewise, by the time Drury visited the island, coastal communities had devised means for supplying vessels with ample food and water during their stays in west-central Madagascar.[57] During the early eighteenth century, the Sakalava king himself owned thousands of cattle, many of them acquired through warfare.[58]

According to seventeenth-century Portuguese reports, Andriamandazoala possessed a supply of unfree laborers obtained from throughout the island. One slave woman told the Portuguese that she had been marched across three countries ("*pays*") before arriving at the ruler's capital.[59] Sakalava rulers probably used a variety of strategies to acquire these laborers, with some purchased from other groups and others captured through warfare or given in tribute. Drury mentions that many of the captives seized in warfare, especially women and children, were only kept as ransom and were returned to their families once the latter agreed to ally with the Sakalava.[60] Those who remained enslaved may have been used for cattle herding, in addition to some agricultural and household labor. Royal ownership of slaves may have served to bolster Sakalava power, as it did in later periods.[61]

It appears, as historian Stephen Ellis has argued, that the Sakalava wars of the mid-seventeenth century predated the rise of a large slave trade with Europeans from the region.[62] Despite the lack of slave exports to Europeans, there was evidence that Sakalava rulers were becoming more interested in engaging in trade with passing ships. According to traditions, the Sakalava ruler Andriandahifotsy (also referred to as Lightfoot, c. 1614–1683) established a permanent seat of power at his palace in Mahabo, a town along the shores of the Morondava River.[63] Mahabo was a convenient base for controlling long-distance trade in the region, as the Sakalava ruler could easily reach interior portions of the island along the river as well as have access to the coastal port of Morondava. By the 1730s, Andriandahifotsy was particularly revered for the role he had played in consolidating Sakalava control over commerce from the region.[64]

European sources confirm that Andriandahifotsy began to take tentative steps toward forming a relationship with European merchants visiting western Madagascar, although this period was marked by considerable misunderstandings, as the following story makes clear. According to French merchant François Martin, a group of forty-five Frenchmen sailed to the west-central coast of Madagascar in the mid-seventeenth century.[65] The French commander found a welcoming river inlet and went ashore to negotiate with a local ruler, named "Lahe Foutchy" (likely Andriandahifotsy). The French narrator described Lahe Foutchy as not only one of the richest lords of this region, but one of the greediest. After the king refused to sell the Frenchmen provisions for cheap prices, the French commander led his troops inland into a region rich in cattle and, the French hoped, gold. On their march into the interior, the French forces encountered an army numbering twelve to fifteen thousand men, all armed with spears. The men, led by Lahe Foutchy, massacred all of the soldiers save one, a Portuguese man who later escaped to the French trading post at Fort Dauphin.[66]

A few years later, the French sent another ship to explore the western coastline.[67] In passing the region controlled by Andriandahifotsy, the French captain sent representatives to the shore, where the sailors met with some islanders. They appeared peaceful, so the French ship came to anchor along the coast. Around four or five hundred people approached the shoreline with refreshments and several of them asked for permission to see the ship. About fifty came aboard, including, Martin remarked, the wife of one of the local leaders. The captain remained onshore with some of his soldiers to sign a trading agreement with an unnamed local monarch, perhaps Andriandahifotsy.[68] The people visiting the French ship suddenly seized the French pilot and fired the cannon on board the ship. At that sound, locals on the shore fell upon the French, who had not brought their weapons ashore, and massacred all of the unarmed men. On board, the visitors killed two French sailors and injured three or four others. As the sailors reached for their weapons, the islanders jumped into the ocean and swam ashore. The woman remained on board, but they quickly discovered she was a "slave," wearing noble clothing as a disguise. How they determined this deception is unclear. The pilot quickly set sail from the coast with only six healthy sailors aboard. He returned to Fort Dauphin with news of the deaths and the French mourned the loss of their compatriots, especially the captain and *commis* (trade commissioner).[69]

The French narrator, Martin, retold these two events to provide an example of the problems Europeans encountered in negotiating with groups on the west-central coast of Madagascar and to serve as a warning to merchants. He probably had heard these stories secondhand, but they still served as cautionary tales to the French. In both episodes, the Sakalava ruler demonstrated his mistrust of Europeans, maybe arising from his knowledge of European conduct elsewhere on the island, as the French and English were both attempting colonies in Madagascar during these years. The story of the girl, if we accept Martin's argument that she really was a slave dressing as a noblewoman, suggests recognition of shared European and Sakalava ideas of hierarchy.

Martin's account concludes on a more peaceful note. Shortly after the second massacre, a Sakalava king sent a troop of soldiers and representatives overland to Fort Dauphin, where they had an audience with French colonial officials. Following negotiations, the ruler apparently made peace with the French and agreed to welcome them as traders into his territory.[70] Indeed, by the end of his reign, the king known as "Lightfoot" supplied hundreds of captives to at least five European slave ships.[71]

At the close of the seventeenth century, a newly enthroned Sakalava king, Andriamanetriarivo ("Rer Timmononngarevo," "Timovareva," ruling from roughly 1685 to 1712), decided to use military force to expel both of his brothers from the Menabe region.[72] Rather than continue fighting for control of the kingdom, one of the brothers led a group of armed supporters south to St. Augustin Bay. Battles between the Sakalava and people who lived near the bay had begun decades earlier, during earlier periods of Sakalava expansion, but this new incursion brought fresh waves of violence to the region.[73] Known as the "northern enemy," the Sakalava continued to attack communities near St. Augustin Bay into the early eighteenth century, when Drury himself observed the clashes.[74] The repeated efforts by Sakalava rulers to conquer the south, rather than venturing into the more fertile interior of the island, may have been prompted both by opportunity (perhaps there were stronger opponents to be found in the more populated interior) as well as a desire to benefit from the export trade from St. Augustin Bay.[75]

Following the conquest of southwestern Madagascar, European visitors to the region in 1698 noted a dramatic change.[76] When they arrived at St. Augustin Bay, the merchants were directed to trade at Toliara to the north for the first time.[77] In the bay and at Toliara, Europeans now dealt with two rulers, holding the ceremonial titles of "King Baba" (also written as "Kinne Baba," "Barbar," "Baubau," or "Bawbaw") and "Prince William" ("Will" or "Ouil"). From his home in Toliara along the Fiherenana River, King Baba had access to stores of rice and slaves. The ruler in St. Augustin Bay, Prince William, was subservient to King Baba. As one observer noted later, Prince William "appears to me to be appointed by and to derive his authority from the king of Baba."[78] In spite of this dependent relationship, Prince William was still a powerful merchant in his own right. He was responsible for supplying Europeans with water, cattle, and miscellaneous other food items such as fish, poultry, and fruit, although he rarely had quantities of rice or slaves for sale. For those, Europeans learned that they had to negotiate with King Baba in Toliara.

The titles of Prince William and King Baba appear to have been hereditary and adopted to reflect European (particularly English) terms of nobility.[79] The titles of prince and king were conscious choices, as the words are not related to Malagasy or East African words for king or ruler. It is hard to be sure of the exact origin of these titles, as we have little evidence beyond European observations.[80] Given the long history of Euro-American visits to this part of the island and the presence of English speakers among the islanders, it would be hard to believe that the use of the titles was accidental. It seems far more likely that their use was a conscious effort at "similitude," to use Jeremy Prestholdt's terminology. Prestholdt deploys the term to describe how people in the Comoros strategically adopted cross-cultural practices, for instance in echoing the European political formations that they wanted their visitors to acknowledge.[81] In southwestern Madagascar, the titles of Prince William and King Baba were readily adopted by European visitors, who would request to see these rulers upon their arrival at the island.

Judging by the frequency and size of food exports from Toliara, as well as comments made by the king himself, King Baba had access to the production of large tracts of land in the interior worked by laborers, including slaves, who grew food and oversaw the herding of cattle.[82] The growth of the provisioning commerce following Sakalava conquest suggests that the king also drew upon trade routes and tributaries in the interior of the island to provide him with reliable supplies of desirable exports. The firearms, gunpowder, and bullets King Baba and Prince William acquired from the Europeans spread far into the southern interior of the island throughout the eighteenth century, further confirming that trade routes stretched across portions of southern Madagascar.[83] Without these routes, the coastal rulers would have been unable to sell rice or other foodstuffs to European merchants, but we know little about the apparatus for this trade.[84] It does seem that the export of food and slaves typically went hand-in-hand in this part of Madagascar, as slaves would carry food to the coasts and then would be sold to visiting slavers, although fewer slaves were exported from this (less populated) part of the island than elsewhere in Madagascar.[85]

European observers also described frequent wars between King Baba and neighboring groups.[86] The close proximity of antagonistic neighbors to the south and east, along with the need to secure trade routes in the region, meant that King Baba and Prince William had to be able to raise a strong army of supporters and build fortifications.[87] Prince William tried to prevent Europeans from trading with the Mahafaly "Prince Grimm" who lived to the south of the Onilahy River.[88] Even when Europeans were able to strike up a trading agreement with the

Mahafaly leader, they discovered that he lacked the supplies of provisions and slaves commanded by Prince Will and King Baba.[89] Archeological findings confirm that warfare was frequent in southwestern Madagascar and some communities moved to more defensive locations in the drier interior of the island, fearing attacks by coastal groups. Evidence provided by European observations, paired with the construction of larger earthwork forts throughout southern Madagascar by the eighteenth century, suggests that coastal leaders were trying to protect themselves against rivals who may have wished to control exchanges with European visitors themselves.[90]

It does not seem, however, that King Baba went to war frequently with the Sakalava of Menabe. During the eighteenth century, most Europeans did not recognize any connections between the rulers of the Menabe region and those to the south, although Toliara was described as the most southern limit of the Sakalava Empire in European sources by the nineteenth century.[91] Sakalava traditions recorded during the nineteenth century assert that the rulers in these regions were blood relatives and thus allied.[92] Earlier European sources appear to confirm the existence of an alliance between the rulers of these two regions, although we know little about the networks of trade and migration that crossed western Madagascar.[93]

Far more is known about the connections between Sakalava rulers in west-central and northwestern Madagascar. While one brother ruled over Menabe and the other brother went south to St. Augustin Bay, Andriamandisoarivo (Tsimanato, Tsimenata) journeyed north. He may have even received support from his brother's rivals in Menabe.[94] According to traditional histories, his men fought for control of the northwestern coast of Madagascar through a series of clashes, including with Muslims long resident in the region. Throughout his march, Andriamandisoarivo relied upon an ombiasy to advise him (as the Raoandriana had in Anosy) and Sakalava traditions would later credit divine support as well as the power of an enchanted *vy lava*, a long iron knife, for his victories.[95] By the early eighteenth century, Andriamandisoarivo, with the support of his eight-hundred-man army, founded a new Sakalava dynasty in the north which he named Volamena, meaning red money or gold. His descendants were known as the Zafibolamena, children of the Volamena.[96] He died in the northern city of Bezavo around 1710, having cemented his name in traditions as the founder of a powerful new kingdom.[97] His kingdom contained the port of Mazalagem Nova, or Massaliege, already a prosperous center for trade, as well as the new ports of Boina and Mahajanga (Majunga).[98] Within decades, the rulers of the northern Sakalava branch had surpassed the Maroseraña dynasty of Menabe to the south in both military and economic power, as the Zafibolamena benefited from bustling trade networks already operating in the northwestern region.[99] Traditions describe the respect the Sakalava held for the communities they defeated in the north, likely tied to their desire to maintain access to commerce with the Comoros and East Africa. During their march northward, Sakalava followers reportedly respected local grave sites and the sacred trees that surrounded them. They granted religious freedom and allowed Arab and Muslim traders to continue their trade with visiting merchants.[100]

These histories may have overemphasized the respect that Sakalava rulers paid to the people of the northwest, as the slave trade underwent a sudden burst of activity directly following Sakalava conquest.[101] In 1695, Dutch slavers described their slaving negotiations with "Andiaximanatte" (Andriamandisoarivo?), the present king of Magelage (Massaliege) and "Maringande" (Manigare, a northwestern port). This king had used firearms, supposedly acquired through trade with the English, to overpower "unarmed tribes" in his battles for control. In a dramatic reversal of earlier slave-trading practices, the king told the Dutch that he would only accept guns, no cloth or other merchandise, in return for his slaves.[102] American slave traders visiting the island during this period also reported that the king told them he had six thousand slaves for sale, obtained in his wars of expansion.[103] Two years later, when Dutch merchants returned to the northwestern ports, they discovered that slaves were suddenly more expensive, costing two guns instead of one, although, thanks to the continuation of these "internecine wars" in western Madagascar, captives remained plentiful. The king told them that he still required "good muskets with which to destroy his enemies." Even though the Dutch were able to acquire slaves with guns during this second voyage, most of the 119 slaves died shortly after their arrival at the Cape Colony. Their poor health was due to being "prisoners of war," or so the Dutch speculated.[104]

Despite this period of intense violence, it does seem, judging by later observations, that relations between the Muslim merchant elites in the northwest of the island and the new Sakalava rulers were quickly eased, as reported in the traditions. Portuguese visiting "Maselagache" in 1726 described dealing with the "principal Moors" and, a few years later, meeting a king who spoke Arabic fluently.[105] Sakalava involvement in the export trade was also clear in other European observations. One English captain described the northwestern town of Mahajanga as a bustling, cosmopolitan port in 1764. He wrote that the town, built "after the Indian fashion," contained many stone buildings and mosques. Inhabited by "native" Muslims and others from "Surate, Johana, Mosembeck, and the Commoro islands," Mahajanga was clearly a prosperous and cosmopolitan port. Within the city, the Sakalava rulers allowed Muslims to practice their religion freely. In return, the Sakalava instituted a series of trading controls. The king appointed a "purser authorized to carry trade on in the king's name, in conjunction with another purser that comes down from the king."[106] Sakalava kings and queens even allowed visiting European merchants to trade with local "Arab" merchants as well as with Sakalava representatives and appeared to be increasingly tapped into these networks crossing the southwestern Indian Ocean region.[107] A Sakalava queen married an East African (or Comorian) man around the middle of the eighteenth century, according to English and Dutch reports.[108] Sakalava kings and queens also incorporated Islamic beliefs and rituals into their practice of divine kingship and some converted to Islam by the early nineteenth century.[109]

Instead of destroying trade networks along the northwestern coast, Sakalava rulers reestablished them, under their control, and continued to expand the export trade by extending their power, directly and indirectly, even further into the island. From the northwest coast, the Sakalava rulers gained significant influence over the north of the island during the eighteenth century, but we have few details about how this occurred, as Europeans largely avoided the rocky northern coast of Madagascar prior to the mid-eighteenth century. For example, a 1665 Dutch map displays, with some accuracy, ports around the coast of Madagascar, except in the north. The mapmaker labeled this region "*pays incogneu*," an unknown land.[110] By the end of the eighteenth century, following several European visits, it became clear that the Sakalava rulers indirectly controlled much of this region as well.[111] As the French observed in 1742, several coastal rulers throughout the northern region had familial ties to the Sakalava king at Boina to whom they owed tribute.[112]

As other Europeans began to frequent major ports dotting the northern coastline, including Nosy Be, Diego Suarez (Antsiranana), and Vohémar, they also noticed that the rulers in these locations all claimed to be blood relatives of the Sakalava ruler of Boina.[113] In the 1770s, the French sent several expeditions to explore the north of the island. One representative, Nicolas Mayeur, discovered that a Sakalava leader ruled over a northern province stretching from the west coast to Vohémar in the east. The king, named Lamboine (L'Amboine, Lamboeny), lived in the extreme north of the island in Ankara and oversaw some twenty local leaders controlling smaller provinces. These monarchs ruled over smaller villages located along rivers, which both enabled the easy transportation of trade items to the coast and provided water for growing crops.[114] Local leaders sent Lamboine annual tributary payments in rice, cattle, and slaves, which were later sent to Boina. A benevolent ruler, Lamboine exempted the communities from the tributary payments during times of war and privation.[115]

This picture of tolerance was not without violence. In 1774, the French observed that Lamboine sent five hundred armed men to attack various villages throughout the north. His army raided and stole cattle from villages not already under his control. As a result of their growing military and commercial power, the influence of the Sakalava was expanding all the way to northeastern Madagascar. By 1780, the French discovered that the Sakalava king also had an alliance with a king named "Raminti" ruling over the port of Vohémar on the northeast coast.[116] When the French tried to negotiate for cheaper cattle prices from the people of the north and bypass the Sakalava monopoly at Boina, they discovered the extent of Sakalava control over the commerce of northern Madagascar. The Sakalava kings and queens forbade the people in the north to sell cattle directly to French merchants.[117]

## THE LIMITS OF SAKALAVA POWER

By the close of the eighteenth century, the Sakalava king in Boina was known to be a "despotic" king who treated "all of his subjects" as slaves, just as his ancestors had "since time immemorial."[118] Despite this description, it is far from clear that Sakalava queens and kings exercised any sort of absolute domination over communities in western Madagascar. Indeed, the continued reliance on various other elites, translators, and merchants to complete trading agreements with Europeans suggests otherwise. Rather than exercising direct rule, the Sakalava leaders appear to have controlled portions of Madagascar by forming tributary relationships with other communities and marrying into the families of their neighbors. Powerful military, religious, and political leaders thus became kin and part of the Sakalava family.

Karen Middleton has described a similar pattern of political rule among the Karembola in south-central Madagascar. She has argued that "power is concentrated at the center; at the outer margins the ruler's power fades imperceptibly away. Beyond a core zone the boundaries of a kingdom are unstable and ill defined."[119] Her description has been echoed by Maurice Bloch, who explained that political control in Madagascar came from "force and cattle" as well as "ritual and *hasina* [the power of the sacred]."[120] Such pictures of political power suggest that the incentives for communities to supply Sakalava merchant kings with cattle, rice, and slaves may have been produced both by the monarchs' purchasing power as well as their ability to coerce, frequently with violence, the exports of these commodities.[121] Along with these more material means to power, Sakalava rulers emphasized their links to a divine past, demonstrated through royal worship and commemoration and remembered through oral traditions. This ritual power was clearly expressed to European visitors such as Dean and Drury, who observed powerful men communicating their obedience to the king and worshiping at the burial grounds of prominent ancestors.

The limits of this model of political leadership, based as it was around violence, ritual, and access to cattle, may explain the frequent conflicts that Europeans encountered during the eighteenth century. Many of these conflicts were struggles over royal succession, never simple in a world of complex familial ties and blood-brotherhood.[122] Although the tributary model suggests more diffuse power relations than suspected by European visitors to the island who saw the Sakalava king as an absolutist despot, European records confirm that obvious hierarchical relations existed, not only between the rulers and the ruled, but also between various leaders. The adoption of the title "prince" by a leader who could sell cattle to the Europeans and that of "king" by his superior, who could supply not only cattle but also rice and slaves, does not appear accidental. Instead, it suggests that the islanders were attempting to make their political standing clear to visitors by using foreign terms of leadership to label those who could sell provisions and slaves. These terms, however, were adopted following the expansion of the Sakalava to control coastal trading enclaves, revealing that global trade had shaped, but did not trigger, political centralization in western Madagascar.

Did Sakalava rulers thus create an empire? It was not an empire in the European model, or even as successful as the nineteenth-century Merina kingdom of Madagascar, in terms of exacting labor and resources from its subjects.[123] It may make more sense to think of the Sakalava as related rulers who controlled the western ports of the island through a network of alliances and had to maintain their power by controlling the circulation of key imports, at first firearms but eventually silver coins as well.[124] Stephen Ellis has suggested that the Sakalava kings of Boina were political innovators on the island, developing "a new form of sovereign power by their recruitment of European military advisers and their domination of the slave trade."[125] Yet the domination of the provisioning trade was also key to Sakalava maintenance of other sources of power, including supplies of slaves. After all, Drury noted that Menabe was one of the richest provinces on the island, not due to the slave trade, but thanks to plentiful supplies of foodstuffs. Drury describes how, during a feast following a series of successful battles, military leaders (all of whom ritually communicated their submission to the Sakalava king by licking his feet) consumed four calabashes of "toak" (*toaka*, alcohol), along with honey, sugar cane, rice, and a large amount of beef. It was the best meal Drury had consumed during his many years on the island.[126] This food, acquired through a complex alliance of tributaries as much as through warfare, attested to the ability of Sakalava rulers to access labor and resources on Madagascar.

# FOUR

## The Betsimisaraka, Pirate Kings

BETWEEN THE 1680S AND 1720s, dozens of Anglo-American pirates spent months living on the shores of Madagascar.[1] These privateers and pirates of the Caribbean were seeking richer shores for plunder, and the lands of the Indian Ocean were more distant from increasingly critical politicians in Europe and the Americas.[2] Piracy in the Indian Ocean, as in the Atlantic, offered opportunities for those seeking an alternative social order, as well as material advancement otherwise barred by current legal frameworks.[3] Yet the distinction between merchant and pirate was fuzzy, in part due to the long-running history of maritime violence within the Indian Ocean.[4] Piracy was present well before 1498 and, after this date, the labeling of individuals or groups as pirates became a means for advancing the economic and political goals of European merchants operating in the ocean.[5] As soon as the Portuguese arrived in the Indian Ocean, they attempted to label their competitors as pirates but would turn the other way when their allies attacked merchant vessels. As other European groups arrived in the ocean, many Portuguese themselves were labeled as pirates, and traders of any nation who flouted monopoly laws became known as interlopers.[6] Madagascar became a space where these contests over legitimacy and sovereignty would play out.

By the late seventeenth century, many Anglo-American pirates had chosen Madagascar as their destination. The choice to visit and stay there was not haphazard but instead predicated on the geographical opportunities afforded by the island as a base of operation, as well as the supplies of food and slaves already known to be available on its shores. The absence of European company control over Madagascar was an additional attraction. In short, the pirates came to Madagascar for the same reasons the Portuguese, Dutch, French, and English had been arriving for decades: the island offered convenience, security, and economic opportunities.

The pirates were some of the most memorable of visitors to the island during the seventeenth and eighteenth centuries. The exploits of swashbucklers filled numerous broadsheets and novels back in Europe and contributed to a major shift in attitudes toward Madagascar.[7] The history of pirates on the island has, in turn, received considerable attention from scholars.[8] In fact, Madagascar is only mentioned in some histories of the Indian Ocean when they discuss this "Golden Age" of piracy, despite the limited political and economic influence the pirates exercised on the island.[9] Public interest in the activities of pirates far predated the twenty-first century and the sensationalist and popular literature spawned by the pirates has resulted in substantial liberties being taken with the history of the island. For instance, a popular but largely fictionalized account of the pirates on the island, perhaps penned by Daniel Defoe, presents Madagascar as a pirate paradise, welcoming to all seeking liberty.[10]

These sensationalist stories of Madagascar as a pirate safe haven are at odds with the more reliable sources that reveal the quotidian nature of interactions between pirates and islanders. The pirates who came to Madagascar could be placed into one of two categories: they were either maritime raiders who preyed upon shipping in the ocean or resident merchants who sought to evade monopoly controls. The most important foreigners, those who spent significant time on the island, were more akin to the latter, acting as independent merchants and rarely taking part in the clashes at sea popularized in pirate literature. The pirate communities that inhabited Madagascar maintained frequent commercial and legal contact with North America, as historian Kevin McDonald has recently revealed.[11] Once the pirates arrived on the island, many of them followed the model set by French colonists decades earlier and incorporated themselves into local families. Many of these pirates were slave traders. Trading in southeast Africa was illegal under the charter of most of the East India Companies, but it was much easier to escape the attention of authorities on the east coast of Africa, where the volume of trade and shipping was far below that of West Africa.[12] In one famous case, Frederick Philipse of New York switched his focus from slave trading in the Congo region in the 1680s and dispatched traders to arrange the purchase of slaves from Madagascar. These traders would be described as pirates by the English.[13] The pirates were able to oversee the transportation of thousands of people from Madagascar in one of the longest (and most deadly) Middle Passages in world history.[14] These pirates primarily served as cross-cultural brokers, in parallel roles to the Indian Ocean merchants who operated outside of state control. They learned the languages of the ports in which they resided and visited and acquired homes and families in far-flung ports around the ocean's littoral, including in northern Madagascar.[15]

While the slave trade between Madagascar and North America was encouraged by the pirates' presence in Madagascar, the deeper roots of transoceanic commerce from Madagascar cannot be neglected. Anglo-American pirates were just another group of newcomers who had been stopping at the island for decades (or even centuries), although maybe the first to be so singularly focused on slaving. These pirates were not the first Westerners to marry with island women and father children, nor were they the first to enslave and deliver their captives to waiting vessels. They were not even the first to bring firearms to the island. Their presence did not eliminate other trade from the island. In spite of new fears provoked by the pirates inhabiting the shores of Madagascar, Europeans continued to acquire fresh water and food from the island. Ships stopped at the shores of Madagascar annually and some even visited known pirate haunts, even though Madagascar had become "a byword for mutiny and desertion," according to McDonald.[16] The alternatives, of sailors dying from dehydration and scurvy, were comparably more dangerous.[17]

After the decline of piracy on the island's shores, European ships came in increasing numbers, as the French sought support for their Indian Ocean establishments. This commerce—the arrival of ship after ship from the Mascarenes in search of slaves and food—would leave more of a mark on the lives of most islanders in eastern Madagascar than the comparatively brief pirate-led slave trade. The records created by this growing trade, unconnected to the history of piracy in eastern Madagascar, reveal the limited impact of the Euro-American interlopers on the island. Suddenly, by 1730, trade with the French for the Mascarenes was conducted through a new port, Foulpointe. As on the west coast, the king of Foulpointe sought to monopolize the import of firearms and silver coins into the east coast of the island, although with more limited success than his Sakalava counterparts. By the close of the eighteenth century, this king identified himself to French merchants as Betsimisaraka.[18] In these political innovations, the islanders were more influenced by new political patterns within Madagascar than the presence of pirates on their shores.

## THE PIRATE ISLAND

The first Anglo-American pirates who sailed into the Indian Ocean during the 1680s visited Madagascar for provisions. Shortly after this first visit, other pirates decided to settle on Nosy Boraha, an island off the east coast of Madagascar.[19] When these foreigners began arriving at Nosy Boraha, they confronted communities in the midst of upheaval, perhaps provoked by the presence of Dutch and French merchants in the region. Communities on the east coast of Madagascar were struggling to control and benefit from commerce with Europeans, but they likely found this task impossible without dominating the trade routes that stretched far into the interior. By 1655, the French found that frequent warfare between populations on Nosy Boraha and Antongil Bay was contributing to a strong demand for guns by populations living near the bay.[20] A decade later, the people near the bay were still fighting with those to the interior.[21] Constant conflict took a toll on local communities in eastern Madagascar. This region, known for its rice production in 1671, was lacking in both cattle and rice only a few decades later following periods of frequent warfare, or so French observations suggest.[22]

It was into this unsettled world that the pirates arrived and began to cultivate alliances with local leaders who sought to gain access to these new trading opportunities. From their base in eastern Madagascar, the pirates raided both European and Muslim shipping throughout the northern Indian Ocean before returning to the island to regroup.[23] By 1697, forty-five of these pirates may have lived on Nosy Boraha, although the EIC could not confirm the exact number.[24] Despite linguistic and cultural ties to the European North Atlantic, these itinerants had diverse origins, including England, France, Jamaica, and North America. Many of them were later described as "negro'" or "*nègre*" by Europeans. The pirate community on Madagascar eventually included retired pirates, ambitious traders, and runaway sailors, all male.[25]

While on Madagascar, the pirates did not only purchase goods but also established "a residence and fortification" to coordinate illegal trading with the Americas.[26] Around 1691, the slave merchant Philipse sponsored a trading post on Nosy Boraha.[27] He sent a small ship with trading goods and experienced sailors (mostly former pirates) to the small island. Following the quick death of most of the would-be colonists, a man named Adam Baldridge took control. Benefiting from his experiences in the Caribbean and assisted by a black servant he had brought on his journey, Baldridge asserted himself as the leader of the colony and began to establish relationships with his neighbors on Nosy Boraha.[28] A king sent over his daughter to form a marriage alliance with Baldridge, despite his reputation as a murderer and fierce leader. In eastern Madagascar, such marriages between local elite daughters and European pirates became common, as they had been just a few decades earlier.[29] Baldridge reportedly assisted people who arrived from the larger island searching for their family members who had been enslaved and brought to Nosy Boraha. In so doing, he gained their support.[30] Echoing the actions of the French just decades earlier, Baldridge constructed a fort or palisade on Nosy Boraha, fortified with guns and manned with a collection of armed local soldiers. Baldridge began stockpiling goods in his fort. He sent letters to prospective European traders and traded with the pirates who were raiding ships around the Red Sea, Persian Gulf, Madagascar, and the Comoros.[31]

Baldridge and the other pirates imported American and East Indian goods, including stolen India cloth, gems, and gold, to buy slaves from islanders. We know little about the conduct of this commerce. They may have attacked communities but it seems more likely that they tapped into existing slaving networks within the island. Perhaps for this reason, these pirates were far from successful in establishing themselves as permanent commercial leaders. For example, Baldridge was blamed by his sponsor, Philipse, for loading a ship in 1691 with only 34 slaves, 15 of them children and "3 years suckling."[32] To gain sufficient quantities of slaves, on several occasions capturing and enslaving neighbors appeared one of the only options to fill cargo holds. The sale of their erstwhile allies would have grave repercussions for the survival of the pirates on the island, as it had for Pronis decades earlier.[33] On the slave ships that sailed to the Americas, the mortality rate was extremely high, to be expected given the long distances involved. The health conditions of the slaves who were still alive were shockingly poor.[34]

These challenges were compounded by a growing determination on the part of European monopoly companies to halt the activities of pirates in the northern Indian Ocean.[35] When the English arrived in eastern Madagascar at the close of the seventeenth century to combat piracy, several pirates boarded the English ships voluntarily, a testament to the difficulties they had faced in Madagascar. Even after the English ships departed, a few more pirates returned to America following the issuance of an English pardon. Some of the accused made their escape at the Cape of Good Hope, and the VOC, probably wishing to defy the English, refused to extradite them.[36] Others decided to relocate to the Mascarene Islands, where they periodically antagonized Dutch and French settlements for several decades.[37]

A few decided to remain in Madagascar and there was a resurgence of piracy on the east coast of Madagascar as the eighteenth century began. Out of fear of more pirate attacks, the English banned legal shipping to Madagascar for a time and this ban appeared warranted.[38] Baldridge's replacement, Edward Welch, was dispatched from the Americas toward the end of the seventeenth century. He may have lived on the east coast of Madagascar until his health deteriorated under the strains of the tropical climate and he died in 1708.[39] During the late seventeenth century, an unknown number of pirates lived and operated on the west coast of Madagascar. Many pirates, such as William Kidd, frequented the Comoro Islands, from where they attacked ships periodically.[40] The narrow entrance of the Mozambique Channel enabled easier seizures of ships and their victims included one English vessel, the *Prosperous*, which was taken near southwestern Madagascar in 1702.[41] In 1720, an EIC ship was seized off the west coast of Madagascar near Ndzuwani as the ship was sailing to India.[42] Two Ostend East-India Company ships were also taken during this period near Madagascar.[43] As late as 1727, Portuguese visitors to Nosy Boraha found a few pirates still residing on the island.[44]

Some pirates sheltered under the protection of the Sakalava rulers on the west coast after the arrival of the English fleet. The Sakalava reportedly welcomed them as traders and translators.[45] When Drury visited western Madagascar, white men were a fixture in Sakalava courts and resident along the coastline.[46] Other observers noted during this period that there were "nine or ten white men who were under the king of Boarare [Baba?]."[47] Some of the former pirates also reportedly stayed in the northwestern port of Boina in "a very handsome manner" and owned houses with pewter dishes as well as "many cattle and slaves."[48] These pirates may have provided a linguistic education and taught the islanders how to use firearms with great skill. The people of St. Augustin Bay knew how to curse in English thanks to the tutelage of the foreigners, making frequent statements such as "G–d D—n ye, John, me love you."[49] For European sailors, the pirate lifestyle was so appealing that many passing European captains complained of "fractious fellows" trying to flee inland at St. Augustin Bay and other ports, in hopes of a better life under the protection of Sakalava leaders.[50]

In spite of the continued threat posed by pirates, English merchant fleets resumed provisioning visits to St. Augustin, Morondava, and Massaliege by the early eighteenth century. The English even attempted to expand their trade with Madagascar, undoubtedly influenced by the rumored successes of the pirates and new hopes of recovering pirate booty from the island.[51] The pirates had proved that a slave trade from the island could be lucrative and there was an assumption, although wholly unfounded, that they were the first to introduce this "horrid traffic" to Madagascar.[52] After 1711 and the creation of the South Sea Company, more English merchants tried to purchase slaves from the island for the Americas.[53] The South Sea Company would oversee the importation of thousands of slaves from (mainly western) Madagascar into the Americas for several decades before abandoning the effort after 1730.[54]

The threat of piracy remained on the east coast during the first decades of the eighteenth century, although we have fewer details about these pirates. By contrast, the western ports of Madagascar were seen as fairly peaceful.[55] Until the 1720s, French colonial officers in the nearby Mascarenes continued to complain that pirates threatened their trade in eastern Madagascar and they again sent several warships to capture the interlopers, apparently successfully on at least one occasion.[56] One infamous pirate, Olivier La Buze (Buse), was seized and hung in Réunion by the French after being captured in Taolagnaro in 1730.[57] After this date, both the English and French were more concerned with the increase in piracy along India's coast than the presence of any pirates in Madagascar.[58]

## THE BETSIMISARAKA

In the years following the departure of the pirates from the shores of Madagascar, French traders began to note references to the former pirate-trader Baldridge, even though it was several decades after he had left the island. In 1733, French traders visiting Antongil Bay were approached by a local king named "Baldrich mulâtre" or "Roy [king] Baldrige." The king was dressed in rich "French" clothing, including a jacket decorated with gold buttons.[59] This French-speaking king was accompanied by five hundred armed men, as well as two women, probably his wives, and their "mulatto" sons.[60] A few years later, King Baldridge's "uncle," a king living near Antongil Bay, traded with the French. He was dressed similarly and had three light-skinned wives who were wearing fine clothes.[61] French sources fail to connect the name of Baldridge to the pirate who previously inhabited these shores. Instead, it appears that people in Madagascar adopted these titles for themselves and may have been his descendants or assumed his name, thanks to the blood-sharing ceremonies that had made them kin.

These elites became known later to visitors to the island as the *zanamalata*, people of mixed Euro-American and island ancestry.[62] Other mixed-descent kings began to assert their control over trade in eastern Madagascar. On Nosy Boraha in 1733, a light-skinned king instituted a trading ritual that he stated had been learned from the pirates, sharing a drink of seawater and gunpowder with visiting captains.[63] Then the king and the captain concluded their alliance by becoming blood-brothers through a modified fati-dra ceremony. This ceremony joined the local practices of fati-dra, used extensively on the west coast of the island, with rituals perhaps gained from contact with Euro-American pirates. The ceremony of blood-sharing had evidently extended to include gunpowder as an additional ingredient in establishing trading alliances.[64]

As on the west coast, political changes in the east were accompanied by an attempt to attract European merchants to new ports on the island. During the 1730s, Europeans who used to frequent Antongil Bay began to visit a port known to the French as Foulpointe and became acquainted with a powerful ruler there.[65] A "mulâtre" of a pirate reportedly named Tom Tew and the daughter of a local leader, Ratsimilaho (Ratsimilahoe, "Tamsimalo," or "Tom Similo") had established his capital at Foulpointe.[66] As with the Sakalava, much of what we know about this legendary king is derived from later histories repeated by his descendants. They continued to venerate his remains for decades after his death, even moving them to Nosy Boraha.[67] According to a French history recorded at the close of the eighteenth century, Ratsimilaho united leaders on the east coast at the start of the century in what the French would later call the Betsimisaraka Confederation. Ratsimilaho used a series of ceremonial meetings, with speeches (*kabary*) and blood-sharing ceremonies, to bring together neighboring kings into a broad-based alliance that would rule over the region around Foulpointe and Antongil Bay. The goal of these meetings during the first half of the eighteenth century was to establish them as the unquestioned leaders of the east coast of Madagascar. Once united, the rulers would take the place of the previously scattered kingdoms of the east coast.[68] Island legends recorded by the French in the 1760s described how Ratsimilaho had voyaged to Bombay and Malabar in his youth.[69] He also may have spent extensive time on the west coast of the island in the Sakalava court at Boina, suggesting that he was influenced as much by the models of leadership he found among the Sakalava and the English as he was by the pirates.[70]

Observations by French traders in eastern Madagascar during the 1730s seem to confirm parts of this history, although they also highlight that the confederation may have begun for defensive reasons, as east coast leaders sought protection against attacks elsewhere on the island. Several sources suggest that their main foes were the Betanimena who were their immediate neighbors, but there are also hints that the Sakalava may have been responsible for fomenting unrest as well.[71] After the Sakalava seized control of the northwestern ports, they may have looked eastward to expand their influence over trading networks in the interior of Madagascar where commercial networks linked the ports on both sides of the island prior to the eighteenth century.[72] The French, frequent visitors to the east coast, were the first to make note of political transformations occurring in this region. Before the French attempted to form a colony in Antongil Bay in 1732, they first sailed to the northwest coast of the island and asked the Sakalava king at "Massaly" (near Boina) for permission to settle in the bay. With little explanation, it appears that French officials believed it was necessary to ask the west coast king before attempting to establish a permanent presence on the east coast of Madagascar, suggesting that the Sakalava ruler exercised an informal influence in the region.[73]

Furthermore, as French merchants and colonists visited the east coast more frequently during the eighteenth century, they began to report repeated incidents of aggression on the coast from either their neighbors or from the Sakalava. Following several brutal raids by the "king of Massaily" on villages around Antongil Bay around 1734, several east coast communities were left close to starvation and begging for the French to sell them firearms, presumably to be used in protection against further attacks.[74] The islanders readily offered slaves to the French but the merchants complained that they lacked the food to feed them and refused to buy many of the captives. After the raids from the interior had ceased, different coastal rulers joined in a defensive federation led by the king Ratsimilaho. Even though his port of Foulpointe was not under attack, Ratsimilaho sent thirty canoes with armed soldiers to assist his allies in Antongil Bay, the Baldriches, against their enemies.[75] Following the dispersal of these enemy forces, the goals of these coastal rulers turned from defensive to offensive.[76] Beginning in 1738, the "white" kings of Antongil (Roi Baldriche and his uncle) joined forces with Ratsimilaho to attack their neighbors throughout the east coast and seize rice and slaves to sell to French merchants. To become more powerful, Ratsimilaho reportedly concluded a commercial treaty with the Sakalava, in which he made the leaders of the Betsimisaraka allies of (and perhaps tributaries to) the Sakalava kings.[77] Ratsimilaho himself became part of the Sakalava dynasty following fati-dra ceremonies which created familial bonds between him and Sakalava rulers. He even convinced the Sakalava king to send his daughter to him in marriage.[78]

The rise of Ratsimilaho appears to have had a lasting impact on the trade of the east coast of Madagascar by the middle of the eighteenth century. Under Ratsimilaho's rule, the Betsimisaraka-allied kings reportedly conquered a stretch of almost seven hundred kilometers along the east coast throughout the 1740s. While few contemporary European sources describe this expansion, archeological examinations of the region suggest that during this period there were dramatic shifts for the communities inhabiting eastern Madagascar. Previously the east coast had been home to small villages stretching along the coast, with larger villages located along major river estuaries. By the middle of the eighteenth century, however, many communities had shifted inland and were often fortified. Populations may have been moving to the interior to escape from the attacks of the Betsimisaraka and the growing tension created by the export of slaves to the French. Archeological studies also reveal that the largest villages of this period were the two capitals of Ratsimilaho, suggesting a consolidation of power by the ruler and his descendants.[79] French observations appear to confirm these developments. In 1769, a French scientist visiting eastern Madagascar noted that, despite good soil and plentiful rice, recent wars had devastated the country and there were no longer any sizable villages along the coast south of Foulpointe. Those that remained appeared depopulated.[80]

Along with these developments, the port of Foulpointe attracted far more ships from the Mascarenes after the 1730s. Even though French vessels continued to frequent Antongil Bay, Nosy Boraha, and Taolagnaro in search of provisions, they began to go to Foulpointe when they wanted to purchase not just rice and cattle, but slaves as well. By 1800, at least 140 European ships had visited the port, versus 87 that travelled to Taolagnaro. Almost half of the ships to Foulpointe were in search of slaves, and this trade resulted in a large influx of firearms into the region.[81] Meanwhile, coastal populations benefited from the increasing dependence of the French on the region for food and slaves for the Mascarene Islands, which transformed Foulpointe into an entrepôt for mediating trade with the interior of the island.[82] As trade with Foulpointe grew, the French sometimes left a number of traders on the island to help coordinate trade, and this additional tenure resulted in greater information about the political workings of eastern Madagascar.[83] Although slaves were never available in the quantities that the French might have desired, the French were more frequently able to purchase rice and cattle than a century earlier.[84] French merchants celebrated the great abundance of provisions available for purchase in Foulpointe, including fowl, fresh and saltwater fish, cattle, goats, and sheep.[85] Increasingly connected to rice-producing regions several days' march to the interior, the port of Foulpointe remained influential in east coast trade for the next several decades.[86]

During the 1760s, one Frenchman noted that the "Betsemirac" were still so closely allied at Foulpointe that they were obligated to be buried in their own country.[87] Despite this rhetoric of support, the confederation appears to have been only weakly united after Ratsimilaho's passing, around 1750. When the founder of the confederation died, his daughter, Béti ("Betty"), assumed the throne briefly. She signed a treaty giving the French control over Nosy Boraha, where they built a small colony.[88] Following a major revolt against the French and the colony's subsequent collapse, she was blamed for the unrest and sent to Mauritius to stand trial. After her name was cleared, she became the first free person of color to receive a land grant in Mauritius.[89] A French document also suggests that she imported eight of her own personal slaves from Nosy Boraha to Mauritius.[90]

After her departure, Béti's brother Andrianjanahary (Zanhare, Zanahary, "Jean Hare," or "Jean Hard") assumed the throne at Foulpointe and ruled for over a decade.[91] Andrianjanahary, reportedly the offspring of a Sakalava princess and Ratsimilaho, was only sixteen years old at the time of his father's death and would struggle throughout his reign to maintain control over the east coast port.[92] A French scientist, Guillaume de la Galaisière, was in Foulpointe in 1762 when several kings threatened to attack Andrianjanahary. Galaisière observed a battle that involved an estimated six hundred men and a flotilla of forty canoes. The use of canoes appears to suggest attacks from the coast, not the interior, although the Frenchman's discussion of battle techniques is far from conclusive. This and other battles were seen as particularly disastrous to trade with the French, as local soldiers frequently destroyed crops and set fire to their enemies' fields.[93]

By the 1770s and 1780s, however, trade from eastern Madagascar appeared relatively more stable to the visiting French, despite frequent shortages in supplies of slaves for export and high prices demanded for them. This stability may have been due to continued commercial support from the Sakalava rulers. Throughout the 1770s, the Betsimisaraka king of Foulpointe, Yavi (Hiavi), sent a "levy" of slaves to Boina each year in return for two hundred cattle from the west coast.[94] Clearly, Yavi benefited from his alliance with the Sakalava and used this trade to export cattle to the French during the second half of the eighteenth century.[95] Such was the sway of the Sakalava in the region that the French accused the Sakalava of trying to incite the people of Antongil Bay against the

French during the late eighteenth century.[96] The French, however, were crucial allies to Betsimisaraka leaders, who had more difficulty than the Sakalava in maintaining their access to supplies of slaves and food in the interior of the island.[97]

## THE PROVISIONING TRADE AND STATE DEVELOPMENT

Anthropologist Henry Wright has written about the Sakalava and Betsimisaraka states as "failures" in terms of developing and sustaining state apparatus, as well as in contrast to the more successful highland states that originated in the interior of Madagascar during the eighteenth century and would eventually form the Merina state. Both the Sakalava and Betsimisaraka kingdoms experienced difficulties in establishing peaceful royal successions. Wright argues that the northern Sakalava state was unstable after the death of Andriandisoarivo in 1710. All that was left was "a network of small polities of varying sizes throughout the west coast."[98] The Sakalava were capable of mobilizing soldiers and demanding ritual tribute payments, he explains, but they were unable to form an administration powerful enough to monopolize trade networks in the rural interior of the island. Likewise, the death of Ratsimilaho, the father of the Betsimisaraka state, led to the collapse of the confederation and no other powerful leader managed to dominate the east coast during the eighteenth century. Betsimisaraka power was limited to the domination of a single port, Foulpointe, and even that rule was frequently contested. The leaders of Sakalava and Betsimisaraka coastal states were also unable to assert themselves with European traders who sought permanent treaties, unlike the Merina who were able to negotiate an alliance with the British during the early nineteenth century.[99]

Despite "failing" to found stable states, however, the rulers of Toliara, Morondava, Boina, and Foulpointe all managed to coordinate a sizable export trade from the island throughout the eighteenth century. Although there was a similar pattern of rule on both coasts, with a focus on dominating foreign imports, these kings and queens exercised different tactics for accessing commercial networks on the island. There is little indication of divine royalty on the east coast of Madagascar, for instance. Descriptions of funerals and the worship of ancestors reveal that, although the "great families" had finer tombs, there is little indication that annual worship ceremonies approached the same scale or pomp as found among the

Sakalava.[100] Likewise, trance ceremonies do not appear to have been as definitively linked to royalty as they were on the west coast.[101]

The presence of states on the west and east coasts of the island, moreover, can be contrasted with the disordered trade the French continued to find in the southeast of the island, likely produced by environmental constraints and a lack of access to trading networks in the interior of Madagascar. When visiting Taolagnaro throughout the eighteenth century, the French noted that multiple leaders and dynasties vied for dominance in the region.[102] These kings regularly led men, armed with both guns and sagayes, to war with neighboring groups for cattle (and small numbers of slaves) to sell to Europeans.[103] One trader in 1736 described at least twenty-five kings in the region around Taolagnaro, each ruling over a few thousand people. At times, these kings appeared to work together and presented themselves as siblings, but, at other times, they were engaged in constant conflict.[104] As a king informed a French visitor in the 1760s, one explanation lay in the religious beliefs of the southeast region: the divine talismans owned by each king allowed them all to be viewed as equally powerful and this fact prevented any single leader from gaining the upper hand. While revealing in some ways, this observation is still rather unhelpful in understanding the political situation in and around Anosy.[105] After all, the Sakalava rulers traced their religious heritage to the southeast but their use of such talismans supported, rather than placed limits on, political centralization. It is noteworthy that, even after residing for over a year in Taolagnaro, the French colonial leader Comte Dolisie de Maudave (Modave) frankly admitted to his French patrons in 1768 that he was at a loss to figure out the local political situation and identify a reliable trading partner for the French.[106]

The kingdom of the Antemoro to the north likewise never managed to attract and maintain a sizable export trade, despite being located closer to zones of rice production. Stephen Ellis has suggested this was due to a lack of openness to European influence such as was found among the Sakalava and Betsimisaraka rulers.[107] In addition, the rulers in southeastern Madagascar also had fewer opportunities for trade. Although earlier Dutch and French ships had visited St. Luce Bay and Matitanana with some regularity, this part of the island was far less frequented throughout the eighteenth century, the ports here being seen as more dangerous to ships.

By contrast, while leaders on both coasts of Madagascar had established rather diffuse power structures, they benefited from European recognition of their sovereignty and preference for their ports. In return, Sakalava and Betsimisaraka kings and queens provided their subjects with some measure of economic and political stability. During periods of expanding slave trade, diminishing natural resources, and increasing pressure from rival trading groups, individuals sought out leaders who could protect their interests. The ritual and military power of certain leaders enabled them to offer their subjects this protection. These relationships became more unequal and hierarchical throughout the eighteenth century, thanks, in part, to the ability of coastal rulers to monopolize access to European trade networks through their use of trading rituals.

# FIVE

## Rituals of Consumption, Rituals of Domination

FOLLOWING THESE DRAMATIC POLITICAL developments, European traders could almost immediately determine whether their visit to Madagascar would be a successful stop by the greeting they received from the islanders. From the start, contact was mediated by a series of elites accustomed to dealing with the needs of Europeans. During successful voyages, when a ship first became visible on the coast, a welcoming party would approach the vessel in a canoe. Once on board, the islanders would tell the captain where to anchor and addressed his immediate concerns (locating a supply of fresh water usually being among the most pressing). In the southwest of the island, this welcoming party was dispatched by Prince Will from St. Augustin Bay. The group usually included a skilled navigator, a translator, and a messenger from the Sakalava monarch in Toliara, King Baba.[1] These representatives, particularly in western Madagascar, were identified by the Europeans as minor leaders, traders, or royal relatives. A similar greeting party reached European ships in most ports of the island and Europeans came to depend on them. By the mid-eighteenth century, captains expressed their surprise if such a group did not approach the ship as it first arrived off the coast of Madagascar. While approaching Taolagnaro, for instance, the French would fire cannons to induce islanders to approach the ship in their canoes before anchoring off Madagascar.[2]

Europeans had long relied on the assistance of local navigators to bring their ships safely to anchor. Just as Vasco da Gama had engaged a pilot on the East African coast for assistance in sailing to India centuries earlier, European captains used local help to approach Indian Ocean harbors throughout the eighteenth century.[3] Captains complained that they needed to find a secure place to keep their ships at anchor in the bays and rivers around the coast of Madagascar, as it was surrounded in many locations by shallow reefs and dangerous surfs.[4] Island navigators could read European maps and use their instruments. They were also knowledgeable about monsoonal wind schedules.[5] Such was the confidence in their maritime skills that, if the hired navigator failed to lead the ship to anchor successfully, frustrated European captains punished them for sabotaging the ship. In one case, a French captain threatened to cut off the head of a navigator who led him astray, "whether by mistake or design was not known."[6] Relying upon the help of these sailors, European monopoly companies failed to improve their own geographical knowledge of Madagascar's coastline until the nineteenth century. Before 1800, European sea charts remained rudimentary and captains relied heavily upon local assistance to navigate the treacherous waters around Madagascar.[7]

The second member of the welcoming party to arrive on board in most ports was a translator. This individual developed a long-lasting relationship with the crew, as the interpreter remained on board throughout the entire stay of a ship on the coast and assisted in communication between Europeans and islanders. These linguists appear to have been the same from year to year, or at least assumed similar titles. Interpreters sent to ships in St. Augustin Bay and Morondava introduced themselves to Europeans with names such as "Captain William Bush," "Tom Bush," or "Captain Martin."[8] We know little about these interpreters, their role in coastal communities, how they had managed to gained such fluency (whether it was from contact with European pirates, as many contemporaries argued, or not), and if Europeans had given them these names or if they were adopted by the Sakalava rulers and elites themselves.[9] It is only clear that the translators worked for the local rulers and they demonstrated their loyalty to them.

The languages spoken with fluency in different ports reveal the frequency with which different European nationalities visited the island. The translators in Sakalava-controlled ports by the 1730s usually spoke English, even with French and Dutch merchants.[10] In Taolagnaro, the French would be approached by canoes carrying translators who spoke both French and English.[11] In the northwestern coast of Madagascar, there were translators who spoke Portuguese as well as English.[12] In Ndzuwani, many people spoke either English or Portuguese, and some ships carried an Arabic or Swahili speaker on board to assist with translation when visiting the Comoro Islands or the northwest coast of Madagascar.[13] Instead of relying upon the islanders to provide a translator, the Dutch and the French typically brought a slave from the Cape or the Mascarenes to act as translator in Madagascar.[14]

Some knowledge of English and French had also become widespread among elites on both coasts. During the 1730s, Betsimisaraka rulers in eastern Madagascar spoke some French and Prince Will of St. Augustin Bay knew "broken English," although these rulers still depended on skilled interpreters to assist in concluding trading agreements.[15] Many other coastal elites also demonstrated a knowledge of European languages, such as the navigators who helped the ships come to anchor.[16] In contrast, few Europeans before the late eighteenth century learned the Malagasy language with sufficient competency to not rely upon the help of interpreters. Whether secured on the coastline or brought from European settlements, translators served a rather dangerous function as interpreters and informers during slave-trading voyages. In fact, the first victims of slave-ship uprisings were frequently the interpreters, just as they were in the Atlantic.[17]

Other individuals approached European captains shortly after their arrival in Madagascar. These men (and sometimes women) were described as "ambassadors" but we could more correctly identify them as local elites, given their close relationship with the kings and queens of the coasts.[18] They offered to assist Europeans in getting in touch with rulers and concluding trading agreements, all in return for a "present." These islanders frequently spoke English or French, as in the example of "James Martin," who met the crew of the *Onslow* in St. Augustin Bay in 1741.[19] The ambassadors appeared to be subordinate to local rulers, as they assisted the visiting merchants but seemed to be unable to trade directly with them. James Martin, for instance, advised the captain of the *Onslow* that the real ruler of southwestern Madagascar resided in Toliara and offered to help him in his voyage to that port.[20] The ambassadors also helped European officers in transporting presents to the king or queen.[21] The dispatch of the present to a ruler, "according to custom," was the first step in opening trading negotiations. In Taolagnaro, the initial "present" demanded by rulers was usually a bottle of *eau de vie*, which they reportedly drank like water.[22] In western Madagascar, it was more customary to send a fine gun to the local king, along with some alcohol. The ruler would then send a gift of his own in response, typically a slave or bullock. In Toliara, in fact, many captains expected that, after royal representatives delivered presents to the king, they would receive in return "a fat ox or some other valuable thing."[23]

The islanders who greeted the Europeans made clear that only certain rulers in each region of Madagascar were able to sell the most valuable trading commodities, chiefly rice, slaves, and cattle, to visiting Europeans. These leaders tended to live in the interior of the island and, in the case of Sakalava monarchs, along the rivers stretching far inland.[24] Coastal people would inform captains how long they would be waiting for the ruler to arrive at the coast and also transmit considerable information about trading prospects for these desired items. They could tell the ship's captain where to accomplish certain tasks while waiting for the arrival of the king or queen. These crucial tasks included obtaining fresh water, constructing their trading factory, and fetching wood for the ship.[25] They would also inform them of dynastic changes in the region.[26] Some of the people living on the shoreline even knew intimate details about commerce, politics, and the needs of European traders. These elites were a critical source of information on events in the Indian Ocean, as European captains could go months without any updates and, during times of war, such information was invaluable for the safety of ships.[27] Captains routinely asked messengers if any English, French, or other European ships had stopped in the port recently.[28] Knowing that trade was continuing without disruption encouraged visiting captains to remain in port and open trading channels with local rulers. Likewise, the absence of these assurances prompted some captains to travel elsewhere in Madagascar in search of food supplies.[29]

Messengers also knew enough of European politics to manipulate rivalries to their advantage, especially those between the English and French. Royal representatives in Sakalava ports usually expressed a great friendship with the English when they spoke with English traders and the opposite when they met with Frenchmen.[30] In 1714, a messenger reassured a French captain that, after some English ships stole three hundred cattle without paying in St. Augustin Bay, the people there would no longer trade with the English and that they preferred the French.[31] Despite this statement, English merchants continued to trade peacefully in the bay for the next several decades, suggesting the English affront was quickly forgotten, if not completely fabricated (by either the messenger or the Frenchman). Further north, at Massaliege, a local vessel with a French flag approached an English ship, the *Diligent*, in 1761. After a confrontation with the English captain, the people on board the boat quickly explained that some nearby merchants owned this flag. The boat carried rice for local trade and "it was customary to hoist French colours when they had trade." This response apparently reassured the English that the people living in the region still desired to trade with them, not their enemies.[32] By contrast, the traders of eastern Madagascar described their close relationship with the French and expressed surprise when English ships arrived in their ports.[33] The Dutch were at a disadvantage on both coasts, where islanders would tell the Dutch that both the English and French, more frequent visitors, paid higher prices for food and slaves.[34] By playing off perennial European competition, the rulers and their representatives ensured they received favorable trading deals with passing traders.

After receiving the initial welcoming party on board, Europeans lowered smaller boats, known as *chaloupes,* longboats, or "pinnaces," overboard to reach the shore. If the captain was only in need of supplies of water and wood, he could hire local help to load the necessary items and leave without dealing with a local monarch. Of course these individuals expected payment from merchants in return for their assistance, usually in alcohol and firearms.[35] Most Europeans, however, waited for several days (or weeks, on rare occasions) at anchor off the coast of Madagascar for rulers to arrive and agree on prices for cattle, rice, and slaves. While they waited, Europeans could purchase various food items from the local men and women who typically brought foodstuffs to the ships in their canoes. These foods included oranges, lemons, and honey, all items locally obtainable.[36] The rapid appearance of these entrepreneurial traders amazed less experienced sailors, as few houses and buildings were visible on the "grand and beautiful" shorelines.[37] It seems likely that the islanders anticipated the annual arrival of ships and were prepared to sell produce to the Europeans. Following good harvests, coastal communities throughout Madagascar sold surplus food items to sailors for alcohol, Indian cloth, and beads, although access to firearms and coins was more restricted. European observers described how crew members interacted with the "very civil" locals with "joy." Hungry sailors peddled their personal belongings, including clothing and bedclothes, for food, while officers also used some of the ships' money to buy some small provisions to feed their crew.[38] As one sailor explained, "The commodities they dealt in, though of a different specie from ours, were, like them, calculated for that prime object, the belly."[39]

## FEASTS WITH KINGS AND QUEENS

After several days of waiting, the captain would be alerted that the king had arrived at the shoreline. The meeting between the monarch and the ship's captain would be undertaken with "ordinary ceremony" shortly thereafter.[40] A meeting with the local monarch was a significant event because, as all passing captains knew, the disposition of the king or queen determined the success of a provisioning stop.[41] The establishment of trust between rulers and captains was accomplished in different ways around the coast and these steps were crucial to establishing a strong trading relationship, as it was in the Atlantic. In the Bight of Biafra, as Paul Lovejoy and David Richardson have demonstrated, the slave trade was also dominated by a set of merchants who communicated their relationship to visiting merchants through the adoption of Western trading patterns and practices.[42]

The first issue that preoccupied Europeans was identifying a ruler who could sell a large amount of desirable food items. Given the time and effort involved with establishing relationships with rulers, Europeans usually preferred to deal with the single most powerful monarch in a region. On the Sakalava-controlled west coast of the island, this individual was fairly easy to identify. Upon their arrival, Europeans were directed by the people they spoke with to the ruling king or queen of the port. Although Sakalava leaders were frequently at war and there were occasional disputes following the death of a monarch, it was rare that Europeans could not quickly ascertain the whereabouts of the local leader or find a royal representative, if the ruler was away, who could provide them with rice and cattle.[43] In southeastern Madagascar, finding trading partners was more fraught with tension. Having multiple rulers to discuss prices and amounts of gunpowder with appears to have slowed trade in Taolagnaro, as each wanted to discuss prices, drink alcohol, and exchange presents.[44] Throughout the eighteenth century, Betsimisaraka rulers on the east coast also fought for dominance in coastal exchanges. At the start of the century, French merchants would trade with any kings or leaders who approached their ship while they were anchored in Antongil Bay.[45] By the 1730s, the French preferred to trade in Foulpointe with Ratsimilaho and his descendants until about 1768, when other rulers more successfully vied for access to exchanges.[46] French merchants continued to seek out other trading partners along the coast and the French expressed uncertainty over who to trade with, given frequent disputes over legitimacy.[47] Due to this uncertainty, French voyages to east-central Madagascar for provisions became longer and less successful, particularly as wars along the east coast decreased the amount of food available for sale.[48] As a result, the French colonists in the Mascarenes eventually sent their own representatives to reside on the east coast by the 1770s. During the late eighteenth century, French traders were greeted by these men on the shore. In these cases, the local French representative arranged housing for the officers and would attempt to quickly load the vessels.[49]

In general, before the 1770s, once merchants identified who they perceived to be the legitimate and most powerful ruler in the port they were visiting, the Europeans would invite the king (or, occasionally, the queen) on board their vessel. Prior to boarding, the captain would order his crew to fire cannon salutes to greet the ruler and his entourage. The king also frequently ordered the European longboat to come to the shore and carry him on board. The boat would transport a large number of elites to the ship, these men being described by one English visitor as the king's "black princes" in 1759.[50] Some of the merchants were already acquainted with these elites from their earlier encounters on the shores of the island and greeted them like friends. Another Englishman observed that when King Baba arrived, he was "attended by full fifty of his nobles and a vast retinue of commoners." The "nobles" in St. Augustin Bay had titles such as Prince George, John, Dick, Frederick, and "Robin Hood."[51] The rulers and nobles were all dressed in "oriental panoply," presenting a spectacle for the visiting Europeans and effectively distinguishing them from the other islanders.[52] In almost all cases, kings would also be accompanied by a large number of armed soldiers carrying guns and spears, as well as wives, children, and slaves.

On board, on the shoreline, or far in the interior, near the ruler's palace, the formal ceremonial meeting of the Europeans and rulers typically consisted of two parts: the consumption of an elaborate meal and the exchange of more presents. The ruler and his or her favorites sat down for the feast with the Europeans, although the majority of the retinue did not partake. In addition to consuming vast quantities of food, kings and other guests drank copiously, as the alcohol made the feast a real celebration as well as a diplomatic occasion.[53] The ceremonies echoed those in West Africa in which rulers redistributed food amongst their subjects. J. Cameron Monroe and Anneke Janzen describe how feasting in Dahomey was a means for both stitching together society and asserting political dominance by elites.[54] Within many parts of Madagascar, as well, feasting occasions, including elaborate funerals, were a means for both sharing and demonstrating wealth.[55] By inviting Europeans to feasts that included valuable foods such as freshly slaughtered cattle and white rice, the leaders were consciously asserting their domination and access to supplies of food while also acting as gracious hosts to their guests.

Europeans, in turn, tried to contribute to the feasting. A common gift to the king at this meal was several bottles of brandy, arrack, or eau de vie.[56] Alcohol consumption acted as a cross-cultural social activity that both groups enjoyed and bottle after bottle had to be provided if Europeans hoped to establish a positive trading relationship with the coastal communities, as the rulers appeared to view alcohol as central in setting up trading relationships with European merchants.[57] Alcohol was also one of the few items that Europeans could contribute to the feasting occasion and they frequently used it as a bargaining chip for lubricating trade on the island. In eastern Madagascar, kings and traders sometimes engaged in a *serment de fidélité* which involved imbibing a drink of gunpowder and alcohol.[58] The captain of the *Diligent* found he received only a "cool reception" from King Baba until he was given a bottle of brandy as a present.[59] After supplying large quantities of alcohol, many Europeans professed to be shocked by how much liquor the islanders could consume. On one occasion on ship, the rulers and their representatives "behaved very ridiculous, [and] being much in liquor professed a great deal of friendship and made large promises" to the crew.[60] Consumption by women seems to have provoked consternation among many English observers. When the Sakalava king's sisters and eldest daughter came on board in 1753, they were "not easy [until] they got more" brandy to drink, the captain of the *Dragon* noted, much to his dissatisfaction.[61] Even the "Moors" on the northwest coast consumed alcohol in great quantities, much to the surprise of Europeans.[62] In truth, it appears that both rulers and Europeans drank large quantities of liquor and many Europeans boasted about their high tolerance to the local alcohol, *toaka,* while coastal officials would be falling down after drinking the same amount.[63] This ability seems hardly worth bragging about, as it attests to the frequency with which crew members drank to excess and captains sometimes even encouraged such drinking to placate disgruntled sailors. At least one English sailor died of alcohol asphyxiation on the shores of the island.[64]

After the meal, the king and captain formally exchanged additional gifts.[65] Rulers frequently brought the commodities most desired by Europeans: food items. In southern Madagascar, the gift was usually a cow or bull. On the northwest coast, this present might include a quantity of rice as well as live pigs and fresh potatoes (or some other type of tuber).[66] Even if the visiting Europeans were not slave traders, rulers still offered slaves as gifts. The captain and their officers sometimes received young female slaves for their "use" during the duration of their visit.[67] The exchange of these presents functioned as a sort of port duty for establishing trade on the coast of Madagascar, but the captains had to appear appreciative of the presents they received as well. When, in 1742, King Baba brought an English captain five bulls, one from himself and one from each of his four wives, the king was "affronted" when the cattle were not killed immediately. The captain, not wanting to seem ungrateful, felt obliged to kill two and have them salted.[68]

Rulers of western Madagascar highly valued presents of foreign clothing, as well as beads and jewelry.[69] These gifts were used to make visible the connection between foreign traders and island kings, queens, and elites, but they also became more expected and formalized as the decades continued, just as they did in Atlantic Africa. John Thornton notes, for instance, that ceremonies of gift giving by the Portuguese on the Gold Coast transformed into carefully controlled forms of taxation, although always in "the guise of a gift."[70] The same could be said for present giving in Madagascar. The presentation of these gifts was hardly free, according to one captain visiting western Madagascar. He explained that "the present is more properly selling them," as a king expected a present in return, frequently alcohol, supplemented with various beads, mirrors, cloths, and pieces of jewelry.[71] One European captain presented a Sakalava king with a "second-hand imperial blue silk coat" from India, along with some other worn European clothing. The pleased king danced a "jig" with his attendants before leaving, without "showing the least token of gratitude," likely implying he did not provide a gift of his own in return.[72] The demand for foreign cloth and clothing explained why some of the goods (other than firearms) most frequently stolen from Europeans were the ship's canvas and dirty laundry.[73] European gifts also included finely decorated guns and their accoutrements; at times, the king refused to accept any other "gifts."[74] For example, in 1749 a captain gave the king of Massaliege a "buccaneer" gun, a "half buccaneer" gun, and a small keg of powder, as well as a case of cordials, a looking glass, and some pewter and clothing.[75]

Other elites would receive similar, if smaller, presents from the Europeans, particularly if they were unusually helpful as private merchants or translators. Some of the monarchs had several wives, as many as twelve in the case of the king of Morondava in 1759.[76] All of these wives required presents from European traders, a practice that became "customary" during the eighteenth century. For instance, when a royal representative took presents from an English ship in 1761 to King Baba in Toliara, gifts to his wives were included as well.[77] Despite some women possessing significant political power in Madagascar, evidenced by the Betsimisaraka queen Béti or the Sakalava queen Ravahiny, European captains rarely gave women guns as presents. It is perhaps revealing of the gendered nature of (European) trade in the region that men received guns, while women received beads, mirrors, scissors, and cloth from Europeans, even in the cases where queens were the dominant political rulers.[78]

As the king, queens, and their entourage returned ashore and then back into the interior with their presents, a final gun salute usually had to occur upon their departure for the shore. European ships commonly saluted one another as they arrived in the ports of Madagascar, just as they would have in European-controlled areas.[79] Coastal trading representatives learned to request this gesture from visiting ships and it became essential both in greeting the ruler upon arrival and for starting trade on the coast. In Morondava, "Capt. John the linguist" informed the captain that he had to fire the guns twice to show they were there for trade (in addition to sending a gift of brandy to the king).[80] Sometimes "natives of distinction" were also saluted by gunshots, including John Nick and Prince Gregory by the EIC ship *Beckenham* in St. Augustin Bay in 1764.[81] Once, when a captain failed to salute the monarch upon coming on board, the king ordered the captain to do so immediately, although he seemed a bit startled by the result.[82]

After the king or queen visited the ship, their royal trading representatives began the work of concluding prices for rice, cattle, and slaves.[83] The royal purser usually remained on the coast to settle any trading disagreements that might arise after the ruler returned to his or her residence.[84] Prices for food were generally described as reasonable and comparable to those elsewhere in Africa but were still heavily debated, in any port along the coast, at any point in time, by English, French, and Dutch captains alike.[85] Between disputes over the size of cattle, the age of the slaves, and the size of a measure of gunpowder, the captain and his representatives were kept busy negotiating with the purser during their stays, as prices could vary over time.[86] As one captain observed, prices were never hard and fast: "The agreeing on the price of cattle is merely a matter of form for they deceive you in the size and age of the cattle as much and whenever they can."[87] The purchase of rice had to be carefully done to avoid deception from the islanders, who would sometimes add sand or rocks to rice baskets to increase their weight, or so Europeans claimed.[88] At the start of the eighteenth century, Europeans purchased cattle with gunpowder, but less expensive food, such as "yams, potatoes, fowls, goats, plantains, bananas, milk, honey, tamarinds, or wax," could be obtained with diverse trading goods, such as flints, bullets, knives, and glass beads.[89] Guns were required for the purchase of slaves and gunpowder for cattle in places such as St. Augustin Bay and Taolagnaro through the 1750s.[90] By the end of the century, however, most rulers priced rice, cattle, and slaves in silver coins.[91]

On the west coast of the island, the price for items was directly decided by kings and queens, even when provisions and slaves were occasionally obtained from local merchants.[92] It seems likely, although difficult to prove, that the situation was similar to that found in Atlantic Africa, where, according to Thornton, even "private" trade was carefully controlled by the rulers.[93] As the eighteenth century continued, Europeans visiting Madagascar dealt more with a variety of local merchants, described as "chiefs," "assistants," "ministers," or relatives who coordinated the trade in slaves and provisions from the coast, particularly while the ruler was away at war.[94] This situation was obviously the case on the northwest coast, where many of the traders appeared to be Muslim and specialized in supplying African and Arab vessels as well.[95] In 1764, for instance, the English set up trading with "the Chief man residing here . . . a Purser authorized to carry trade on in the king's name."[96] On the northwest coast, a Dutch trader also described trading with an "Arabisch koopman [trader]" in 1775, but only with the Sakalava king's permission.[97] Wealthy traders who were originally from the Comoros were also allowed to offer goods for sale in Morondava by the middle of the century.[98] Perhaps the Sakalava monarchs were too busy leading war campaigns at their borders to spend significant time negotiating with European captains on the coast.

## CONTROLLING SAILORS

As trading in provisions and slaves began, the captain negotiated with local elites to provide him with men to "build a storehouse" on the shore, as it was rare that there was already a European resident in the port who could arrange for one. Unlike the stone trading centers Europeans constructed and inhabited in West Africa or Asia, the "factories" or storehouses constructed in Madagascar were little more than huts, impermanent and to be taken down by the islanders after the ship left.[99] European traders hired people to assist in this necessary "drudgery" and ease the work of sailors. These workers built factories with local materials and the buildings sometimes lacked even a roof if the ship visited during the dry season. Europeans also hired coastal workers to help with filling water barrels and transporting food to their ships. At the start of the century, captains paid the workers "some powder, beads, looking glasses, etc." for their assistance in construction. Referred to as *marmittes* by the French, these hired laborers began to demand firearms and coins for their labor by the close of the century.[100]

After the storehouse was built, one trading manual advised captains to divide it "into two parts, one end for trading in and the other for salting and packing your meat [beef]."[101] A factory also contained trading goods, under strict guard by the crew members. Keeping guns and gunpowder dry was their primary concern, although this was next to impossible during the rainy season. Wise captains did not send large amounts of supplies to the shore at a time, in order to reduce theft and damage. Despite this precaution, thievery was common. The islanders frequently took clothing from drying lines, which was likely easy to accomplish when local women were hired to do the wash. Even after losing items, captains had little recourse, as they relied upon the local communities to provide them with the necessary food and water (and labor) to continue their voyages.[102] Ideally, the factory and tents were located as close to the shore and rivers as possible, to facilitate the transportation of goods from the interior of the island. Captains still complained of the difficulties involved in loading cattle and slaves onto longboats and bringing them to the ship, particularly in bad weather. Once again, they relied upon the assistance of the islanders in accomplishing these tasks.[103]

Most of the sailors and soldiers would live in simple tents on the shoreline.[104] After European sailors, also with the help of paid laborers, erected the factory and tents on shore, soldiers and sailors disembarked with their trade goods of mostly guns and gunpowder, and waited for the arrival of the slaves and food. Slave traders, in particular, spent significant time in the factories on the shores of Madagascar because it sometimes took several months for slaves to arrive on the shoreline.[105] Even when they simply wanted food, Europeans could sometimes wait up to a month to purchase the desired numbers of cattle and bags of rice. There was little evidence of stockpiling of rice ashore in preparation of the arrival of Europeans, unlike supplies of cheaper foodstuffs; instead it seems that rice and cattle were kept in villages a distance in the interior and had to be brought to the coast. In many cases, slaves themselves would transport food, such as bags of rice, to the shoreline, where both the slaves and provisions would subsequently be sold.[106]

Captains ordered tents to be erected for the quartering of soldiers and sailors onshore as well, as they were responsible for guarding the firearms in the factory and assisting in the transportation of slaves on board ships. Europeans also used tents for the rehabilitation of sick sailors, who were sometimes quite ill with scurvy.[107] Once again, coastal rulers determined the location of these shelters.[108] The soldiers living on the shore, however, had increased contact with the diseases of

Madagascar and the inhabitants of the island. Sick men sent ashore to recover frequently got sicker and sicker, particularly if a ship arrived during periods of hot weather. During this time of year, European sailors were more vulnerable to catching illnesses, such as the experience of those on board the *Delaware*, which visited Madagascar in December and January. The crew suffered greatly from worms as well as dysentery, "the bloody flux."[109] Rumors of the threat that Madagascar posed to their health circulated among the sailors. Dutch sailors were described as afraid of the diseases of Madagascar and many argued that the diseases seemed to be more prevalent on the island than elsewhere in the tropics.[110] The French also complained that sailors who slept ashore in the Comoros could catch the "fever of Anjouan."[111] Already weak with scurvy, the sailors' sickly condition could be exacerbated by heat, exposure to tropical diseases, and unclean drinking water, especially if they stayed on shore for longer than a few months. The crew of the *Beckenham* was unlucky and spent all of November and December, months of intense heat, ashore in St. Augustin Bay. The captain complained that the "number of our sick [was] still increasing" throughout their entire stay.[112] In general, as another Englishman stated, "Natives here seem to wonder much at the White men's dying."[113] As Stephen Behrendt suggests for the Atlantic world, the mortality rate for the crew members on slave trading vessels visiting Madagascar was quite high, as the sailors dealt with some of the same diseases and food shortages that contributed to slave deaths.[114]

Another danger of lingering on the shore came from the islanders themselves who, on more than one occasion, attacked the crew members who were sleeping on their beaches. The causes of these attacks are not usually identified in European log books, but we can assume that sailors living on shore had more opportunities for angering coastal communities, either in their attempts to set up liaisons with local women or steal from the local people. The results of these conflicts, however, are described in great detail in the sources. In 1761, for instance, the chief mate of an EIC ship went ashore with some armed men at St. Augustin Bay. A great number of islanders, "armed with muskets and lances," approached the beach and tried to get into the English canoes. The chief mate called upon "Captain Frazier," a local elite, to ask why his people had attacked his crew. Captain Frazier replied that, contrary to English promises, his subjects had been treated "very ill" by the sailors and some of the English sailors had attacked and killed one. The chief mate appealed to King Baba, who appointed a royal guard to be left at the English tent to prevent future disagreements.[115] While the use of pawns to safeguard the safety of crew members and the continued conduct of trade was not as frequent as it was in some parts of West Africa, occasionally elites or royal family members were also detained on board European vessels for the duration of their stay off the coast of Madagascar to ensure peaceful trading.[116] Unlike in Atlantic Africa, the use of presents and feasting appeared to be central to the formulation of this relationship, with pawnship rarely relied upon other than as a last resort in Madagascar.

The people of Madagascar also knew about the discontented mood of many of the sailors and took advantage of it. Silas James, an English sailor, was stationed on shore to guard the tents at St. Augustin Bay in 1783. He complained of frequent hunger, as the crew was not fed a wholesome diet even while anchored off Madagascar. When he observed some local fishermen bringing fish to the beach, James offered his assistance with bringing in the nets, in return for some of the catch. The men, observing James's poor state, invited him to their fire and gave him some sweet potatoes and fish, which made "a most exquisite supper." James fell asleep and woke to discover that, while he was sleeping, the fishermen had "cut away almost the whole tent," taken the iron hoops off the water casks, and rolled the casks into the sea. The captain soundly beat James for neglecting his duty.[117]

On another occasion, in 1752, an English captain blamed two of his sailors for mistreating the islanders in St. Augustin Bay. The captain decided that, due to the actions of these two, some of the coastal people had become inclined to "do us some injury" and took some of King Baba's representatives hostage on board his ship until the peaceful conclusion of trade.[118] While the ship's journal gives us little hint of the relationship struck up between these sailors and the islanders, impoverished sailors clearly had many incentives either to ally with or take advantage of the people they encountered in Madagascar. By trading items from the ship illegally, including clothing, mattresses, and sails, sailors could purchase supplementary food. Unsurprisingly, stories of such trades appear frequently in the archives.[119] One particularly humorous encounter involved three sailors stealing gunpowder to sell to the locals in St. Augustin Bay in 1783. The sailors stole gunpowder from the large cannons mounted on the ship in order to escape detection. They reportedly sold the powder in return for some pots of honey from islanders. The following day, King Baba came aboard and the officers ordered an eight-gun salute. "To the astonishment of everyone on board . . . only one cannon made a report, the other seven had no more powder in them than what was contained in the tube, and these went off with a fizz!" Fearing the wrath of their captain, the three sailors fled into the interior of Madagascar.[120]

The work demanded of sailors tempted many of them to rebel or flee, as the three described above did.[121] Maybe some of them, like one sailor on board a nineteenth-century whaler, got "heartily tired of the monotony and dirt" of their lifestyle. They also carefully weighed their chances for success against the opportunities for finding employment in different ports in the ocean.[122] In making this decision, Madagascar's infamous history as a pirate haven may have encouraged desertion.[123] By the 1730s, European pirates had vacated Madagascar, but captains still worried about maintaining ship discipline and reacted harshly to any hint of insubordination. Some of the crew of the *Dragon* simply called the captain an "old dog" and the captain placed them in irons.[124] On the *Delaware,* a sailor named James Morrice refused to bring a shipment of rice on the pinnace. Morrice "damned the officer of the factor[y] and said he would not bring the rice forever, a son of the bitch you all." Morrice and the officer began to strike each other. When the captain arrived to stop the fight, Morrice informed him that he thought there were "too many officers on board and denied what he had said on shore." As punishment, Morrice was to receive two or three lashes. He retorted that he would swim ashore to escape, but the captain placed him in irons as an example to other crew members.[125]

In defense of the captain who punished Morrice, one sailor could influence others and convince them to escape ashore.[126] Sailors tended to escape in groups and steal items from the ship, including the longboat and "the ship's canvas," items invaluable for the ship's functioning.[127] Many of the escaping sailors were repeat offenders.[128] The most frequent runaways from EIC vessels were lascars, seamen acquired in the Indies and the Arabian Peninsula for working on ships, perhaps suggesting that British control over this particular labor force was even more elusive.[129] On the *Houghton,* in addition to five other sailors attempting to run, three "black lascars" were successful: "Hattular, Shaw

Mahomett, Shecoseen."[130] Two sailors from the *Talbot* escaped at St. Augustin Bay with "Cock eye," a lascar from Bengal, as well.[131] One Englishman even offered a cautionary tale to sailors thinking they could have a better future under local rulers. He told of three runaways who became "wretched objects of [King Baba's] capricious cruelty." To ingratiate himself with the king, one of the sailors constructed the king a palace "in the English taste." Even this carpenter became a victim of the king's ill will and was eventually forced to board a Portuguese ship going to China to escape the island.[132]

This warning did little to decrease the incidence of desertion on the shores of Madagascar. When sailors ran away, European captains had to enlist the help of local rulers and elites to find them, given how little they knew of the interior of the island and how to traverse its terrain. For instance, when the captain of the *Delaware* found a longboat stolen by several runaways, he had to ask King Baba to help him recover his sailors.[133] When a seaman of the *Oxford* ran away, the captain offered a reward of "six quarts of gun powder to any of the natives who shall apprehend him." The captain thought this reward would be "cunning enough to entice" them to help the English. Despite the captain's confidence, the runaway sailor was not found before the ship departed for England. Whether the reward was not sufficient to gain the assistance of the coastal peoples or the sailor had simply managed to flee into the interior is unknown.[134]

Captains frequently described the men they picked up in Madagascar ports as sailors "left" by earlier vessels. More likely, these sailors had been runaways from previous voyages or even former pirates, but the desperation of European captains meant that they cared little about the origins of willing laborers. These men sometimes worked as intermediaries for Europeans, as some had learned rudimentary Malagasy and had knowledge of trading negotiations. Sakalava kings were reportedly extremely welcoming to foreign sailors and, unlike in the south of the island, they were rarely enslaved.[135] When the captain of the *Chesterfield* took on a Frenchman at St. Augustin Bay, he sent the man to Morondava to lead negotiations with the king because he spoke Malagasy.[136] Another English ship, the *Devonshire,* recovered two lascars who, supposedly, had been taken in a "Moor's ship" belonging to Bombay and carried to the Red Sea two years earlier, before gaining passage on a French ship to Taolagnaro, via Mauritius, and traveling across the island to St. Augustin Bay.[137] The vast majority of runaways, however, seem to have remained on shore and either became part of coastal society or, more likely, perished.

The increasing frequency of acts of resistance committed by sailors, whether minor (illicit trading) or major (running away), represented a shift in how Europeans and others encountered the island. Work by historians such as Peter Linebaugh and Marcus Rediker suggests that resistance from sailors in the Atlantic world became more frequent by the middle of the eighteenth century. In the midst of the "revolutionary Atlantic" period, collective action by sailors threatened the success of many voyages.[138] It is clear that European sailors and soldiers also had greater opportunities to rebel on the shores of Madagascar by the mid-eighteenth century. Thanks to the spread of warfare from the Americas and into the Indian Ocean basin, larger numbers of European vessels visited the island than ever before. No longer was Madagascar an unknown space to be claimed by European trading companies, but rather an integral part of the exchange networks that connected and crossed the two oceans.

In spite of the frequency of European visits, the island's ports remained distant from European colonial centers. The absence of European power on Madagascar's shores gave discontented sailors and soldiers opportunities to escape. By staying behind in Madagascar, Europeans and lascars alike could seek employment elsewhere in the ocean, on the vessels that passed by the island, or seek their fortunes within the island itself, as the French colonists and pirates had in previous years. These deserters appeared confident in their abilities to survive and prosper in these cosmopolitan ports, frequently visited by ships of various nations. The threats posed by a lack of access to food and the possibility of enslavement, both very real threats as demonstrated by the experiences of those who shipwrecked on the shores of Madagascar, were perceived as less serious than the discipline they experienced on board European merchant and naval vessels.[139]

## THE ROLE OF TRADING RITUALS

Between 1700 and 1800, more than five hundred Dutch, English, and French traders spent at least a week off the coast of Madagascar purchasing food. This number includes merchant ships sailing to the northern and eastern Indian Ocean, numerous ships on short-haul voyages from European settlements in the Mascarenes and Cape, and fleets of French and British warships.[140] Only about 168 of these were in search of slaves along with provisions. Dutch ships sailed from the Cape of Good Hope to Madagascar, their captains lingering for months in the ports of the west coast, purchasing both food and slaves for the Dutch colony.[141] Almost a hundred English ships stopped along western Madagascar for provisions, with the vast majority of them halting for only a couple of weeks at St. Augustin Bay before continuing to India or Indonesia. Others visited the Comoro Islands where local merchants engaged in a brisk trade with the ports of western Madagascar. Dutch and English ships typically restricted their visits to the west coast of the island. When they were in search of slaves, they directed their ships to visit multiple ports in this region, including St. Augustin Bay, Toliara, Morondava, Massaliege, and Mahajanga.[142] There were hundreds of French visits to Madagascar during the eighteenth century. Some French ships passed by the western coast for quick refreshing on their way to Asia or for cargoes of slaves, but, far more frequently, their destinations were the east coast of Madagascar where they hoped to find both laborers and food for the Mascarene Islands.[143]

Throughout the eighteenth century, island leaders, particularly the Sakalava and, to a lesser extent, the Betsimisaraka, were able to guarantee plentiful food for sale to these Europeans, even when slaves were in short supply. In order to establish a trusting environment conducive to this cross-cultural trading, Europeans engaged in complex rituals to cement alliances with kings, queens, and royal representatives. These rituals were so important that European records of voyages to Madagascar appear almost formulaic in their descriptions of trade, as discussed above, with very little variation between about 1700 and 1780. This regularity enables us to reproduce the visits with much detail. Almost every ship log from this period describes the initial meeting between the captain, local rulers, and prominent merchants, the exchanging of extravagant presents, and subsequent negotiations over prices. If the trading rituals were carefully followed, Europeans were able to purchase enough food to feed their sailors and slaves, and there is considerable evidence that the negotiations themselves were typically quite successful for Europeans. The regularity of these visits was in part a consequence of the political innovations that had occurred within Madagascar in earlier years.

These consistent trading rituals are important for understanding the history of Madagascar for two reasons. Most clearly, these encounters demonstrated the extent to which the islanders reproduced European ideals of leadership through similitude.[144] Europeans sought to identify recognizable forms of governance in various parts of the island. Their ship logs described the rulers and elites mentioned above as kings, princes, pursers, governors, and royal soldiers, and the writers of these sources clearly attempted to cast these islanders in roles similar to individuals found in Europe. The use of English titles in southwestern Madagascar by many elites, for instance, amused European visitors but also served to create easily identifiable trading partners. In the ports of the east coast and southeast, by contrast, trading was less guaranteed, but also less ritualized.

Beyond reassuring European traders and attracting them to the region, trading rituals also firmly established the control of certain coastal leaders over the sale of high-value goods and the importation of firearms and coins into Madagascar. As in trading ports along the Atlantic coast of West Africa, the preference for "trusted" merchants allowed certain African commercial and political elites to be the chief mediators for commerce on the African shoreline.[145] Unlike in many parts of West Africa, Europeans visiting Madagascar lacked resident traders to assist in their negotiations, making them more dependent on coastal leaders. Most debates over pricing and supplies had to occur after the merchants had already arrived at Madagascar, when the visitors would be completely at the mercy of islanders for their sustenance. Disagreements over pricing produced heated disagreements on the shores of the island, casting doubt and uncertainty over the interactions of merchants and rulers. Despite these disputes, most Europeans and island rulers developed a common ground in which to conduct their exchanges for most of the eighteenth century. These relationships would become even more important for ensuring rapid trade and stable interactions, between rulers and captains as well as captains and their crew members, by the middle of the eighteenth century, when maritime warfare within the Indian Ocean reached a new peak and Europeans relied upon food from Madagascar like never before. The feasting and gift exchanges served to ease the minds of uneasy captains visiting Madagascar, but, in an era of rising Western military strength, these Europeans still had to beg for the assistance of coastal rulers to fetch their runaway sailors.

# SIX

## European Warfare and Imperialism

IN 1760, THE GOVERNOR-GENERAL of Mauritius wrote a letter complaining of food shortages on the island.[1] "It is cruel," Antoine Desforges-Boucher wrote, "to struggle each instant against famine."[2] He explained that he had sent ship after ship to Madagascar to purchase rice to feed the island's colonists, soldiers, and slaves. The captains of these vessels reported back that wars along the east coast between the ruler of Foulpointe and his neighbors prevented the French from buying food. In fact, for several years, conflicts had greatly diminished supplies of provisions and created shortages along Madagascar's coastline. A devastating cyclone and the spread of epidemic disease in past years had reduced further the rice stores of communities in eastern Madagascar.[3] Without fresh supplies from Madagascar, settlers in the Mascarenes were precariously close to starvation. Many slaves on Mauritius had already died, even as the governor sent more and more ships to Madagascar in search of food as well as slaves to replace those who had perished.[4]

Throughout the eighteenth century, French traders repeatedly purchased cattle, rice, and slaves in Madagascar to supply the islands with food and labor, as agricultural production on the two main Mascarene Islands was barely sufficient to support their populations.[5] When the food shortage of 1760 struck, however, it was during the Seven Years' War, also referred to as the Third Carnatic War in the northern Indian Ocean. British, French, and Indian forces were battling for control over southern India's coastline, the Carnatic. The majority of clashes occurred on the land and sea immediately surrounding India. These battles culminated in the British gaining a foothold on the coast of the Indian subcontinent in 1757 and defeating the French in 1761, effectively turning the tide in favor of British domination in the Indian Ocean.[6] Even after their defeat, the French continued to supply the Maratha Empire in India with firearms and military training to fight against the British.[7]

Throughout the entire eighteenth century, different European powers had sought to monopolize access to lucrative textile exchanges on the Indian subcontinent. As a result, even before the battles of the mid-eighteenth century, European involvement in the Indian Ocean appeared to be shifting decisively away from coastal trade and toward more direct control over land and production around the ocean. Despite the transformation in European goals and strategies, this shift was not felt uniformly throughout the ocean. The rise of British imperialism may have represented a decisive change in the history of the northern Indian Ocean region, but the nature of this impact has yet to be fully explored for the southwestern Indian Ocean region. In this periphery (Madagascar) of a periphery (East Africa), the most obvious way in which these struggles played out was in the increased presence of British and French vessels within the ocean.[8] Even after some marked improvements in shipping, European fleets still relied upon coastal communities in the southwestern Indian Ocean region for supplies. The ports of Madagascar in particular would continue to provide convenient reprovisioning stations for wartime vessels over a period of nearly twenty years, as the French and British governments sent squadrons of five or more naval ships into the ocean annually to support their struggles.

Prior to 1757, British and French involvement within Madagascar had followed different paths and, once war broke out, the British again relied on western Madagascar. They were able to obtain sufficient quantities of food, wood, and water to restock quickly and easily in Sakalava-dominated ports. The French, by contrast, faced considerable challenges in making such purchases on the less stable east coast of the island. The perilous situation of 1760 described above highlights the degree to which the French had come to rely upon exports from

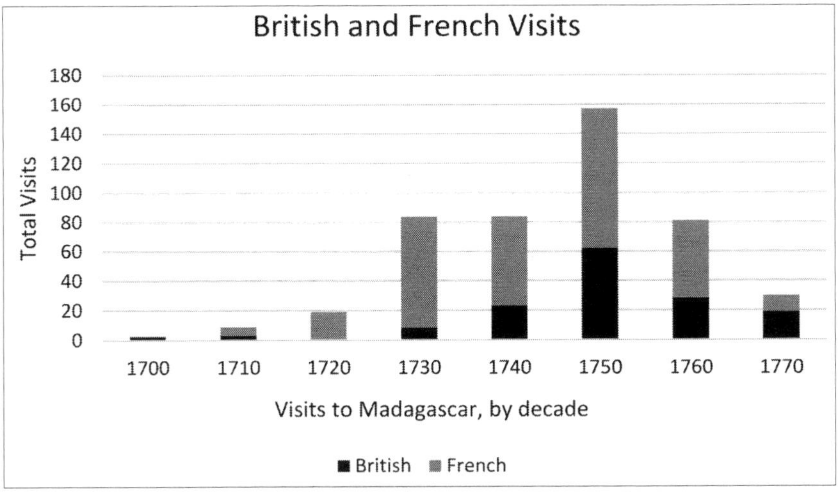


FIGURE 6.1. British and French visits to Madagascar, by decade, 1700–1780. *Note:* The voyages include British merchant and admiralty vessels, and French merchant and naval vessels, but exclude pirate or interloper ships, as well as ships sailing to the Americas. *Sources: See appendix for full documentation.*

Madagascar for their survival during this era of frequent conflict. Access to supplies in Madagascar thus contributed to British successes and French failures elsewhere in the ocean.

## PATTERNS OF PROVISIONING

Repeated struggles in the Atlantic between British, Dutch, Portuguese, and French forces frequently (but not always) spilled into the Indian Ocean throughout the early modern period. Years of European competition had resulted in different groups carving out separate spheres of influence not only in Madagascar, but throughout the Indian Ocean. During the seventeenth century, EIC merchants focused on establishing trading forts at valuable commercial centers along the shores of the Indian subcontinent, including Madras (Chennai), Surat, and Bombay (Mumbai).[9] As the EIC expanded its trading and colonial operations, more and more ships were dispatched into the ocean and toward the bustling ports of the northern Indian Ocean. The EIC competed first with the Portuguese and then the Dutch for trade in this region. The eighteenth century ushered in a period of accelerating demand, particularly for the goods of Asia, back in Europe.[10] By the 1720s, the main competition for the British came from the reinstated French Compagnie des Indes, which had redoubled its commercial efforts in both Asia and the Mascarene Islands.[11] Between that time and the close of the eighteenth century, the British and French battled with each other and also participated in dynastic struggles on the Indian subcontinent, all with the hopes of expanding their commercial presence in the northern Indian Ocean region.[12]

The Dutch VOC influence over trade in Madagascar, always minimal in comparison to the British, French, or Portuguese, was significantly diminished by the mid-eighteenth century, as it was elsewhere in the Indian Ocean. As Chris Nierstrasz has remarked, VOC commercial endeavors throughout the Indian Ocean were in decline for much of the century, while the English and French companies were on the ascendant.[13] By the early eighteenth century, the VOC had invested in a provisioning settlement in southern Africa and maintained a foothold in Indonesia. The company demonstrated little desire to expand its control beyond these enclaves.[14] Most Dutch merchant ships to India continued to avoid the Mozambique Channel and instead skirted eastern Madagascar on the way to India, only visiting Madagascar or Ndzuwani when sailing to the Arabian Peninsula.[15] Dutch attempts to safeguard their outposts and trading ventures in the ocean against European rivals, especially the British, led to larger numbers of VOC vessels and their personnel sailing into the Indian Ocean by the middle of the eighteenth century, but their provisioning demands were mostly filled at the Cape of Good Hope.[16] Given this increased pressure on food supplies at the Cape, the VOC sent thirty-one ships on short-haul voyages to Madagascar for food and slaves throughout the eighteenth century, but these voyages steadily decreased in frequency by the close of the century, when Cape slaving ventures were aimed more at East Africa than Madagascar.[17]

Likewise, the Portuguese demonstrated little interest in directly controlling trade from Madagascar as they turned their attention to ivory and then slaves from East Africa, although short-haul voyages between Madagascar and Mozambique continued throughout the eighteenth century and into the nineteenth.[18] Frequent importations of livestock and rice fed settlers in Mozambique Island, according to historian Eugénia Rodrigues, and were transported via East African merchants. In Mozambique, fresh beef was particularly in demand and became, as it was on Madagascar, "a strong indicator of belonging to the island elite."[19] Yet it was consumed rarely by the average Portuguese soldier or colonist due to the need to import the cattle from Madagascar or the Comoros. Both Dutch and Portuguese traders likely knew that food was relatively plentiful on the west coast of Madagascar, as the continued dispatch of vessels to this portion of the island suggests, although neither the Dutch nor the Portuguese depended solely on the island for provisioning, nor did they attempt to develop formal settlements on Madagascar during the eighteenth century.

When hostilities between the British and French broke out in the northern Indian Ocean in 1746, the EIC was already accustomed to directing their vessels to stop in western Madagascar. These provisioning stops remained crucial in maintaining the health of crews on naval vessels and were carefully planned for success. British naval officers knew to visit Madagascar primarily between May and September, as these were the cooler months.[20] The EIC had learned that a visit during this period would allow ships enough time to provision and reach the lower extent of the monsoonal trade winds around the Comoro Islands before September or October. In 1748, for instance, the captain of the East India merchant ship, the *Houghton,* was forced to sail into St. Augustin Bay when he had "26 men down with the scurvy etc, uncapable [*sic*] of duty and others falling down daily."[21] After sending the sick to the shore to recover, the captain filled his ship with fresh water, wood, and provisions. The *Houghton* set sail three and a half months later for English holdings in "Bencoolen" (Benkulen, in Sumatra), Chennai, and Surat. Most of the crew had recovered during their stay in Madagascar, probably in part thanks to the arrival of the ship during August.[22] To speed the recovery of his crew, the captain likely bought oranges, lemons, fish, and milk, in addition to the usual purchases of rice and cattle in St. Augustin Bay.[23]

After years of visits, the British knew of the customs necessary for successfully trading at Toliara, Morondava, and Boina. On the east coast of the island, however, British captains had trouble purchasing provisions.[24] British did not know how to negotiate in Foulpointe or Taolagnaro, where silver coins, not guns, were the typical currency by the middle of the eighteenth century. The British also complained that food supplies were far more limited on the east coast than on the west and they worried about sailing so close to the French-controlled Mascarene Islands.[25] In fact, so rare were British visits to the east coast that the people in southeast Madagascar expressed surprise in 1736 when the

EIC ship, the *Harrington,* arrived in the region to buy slaves and food. The islanders had heard the British were afraid of the French and so did not frequent that part of the island. The British were quick, of course, to dismiss this idea. In spite of their bravado, after "some trouble with the natives" and their "deceitful" promises to bring slaves, the captain directed his ship to leave the east coast.[26] In fact, few EIC vessels passed this way in the future. Trade on the west coast remained sufficiently reliable that they did not need to look elsewhere for provisions.

By contrast, the French faced repeated challenges with acquiring food. From the beginning, it appeared that colonists would benefit from the relatively short distance between their settlements on the Mascarenes and the larger island to the west. It only took two weeks (or less) to sail to the east coast of Madagascar from the Mascarene Islands in good weather, although return voyages could take considerably longer.[27] Throughout the early eighteenth century, the company sent several ships annually to eastern Madagascar in search of food and slaves, as they attempted to transform their two islands, especially Mauritius, into provisioning centers for French merchant fleets.[28] French ships began to avoid the more treacherous interior route through the Mozambique Channel and instead visited the Mascarenes to provision before continuing to India. After loading goods in Asia, the ships would return to the islands, where they would sometimes wait for months before continuing their voyages back to Europe.[29] Such navigational patterns placed high demands upon the production of food at Mauritius and Réunion to support not only the slaves and settlers who lived on the islands but also visiting merchants, sailors, and soldiers.

As early as 1698, French colonists on Réunion required frequent imports of slaves from Madagascar to help with clearing land and establishing agriculture and the settlers on Mauritius followed a similar pattern after the French assumed control of the island in 1721.[30] The islands' governors, however, were not satisfied with growing wheat and herding cattle to supply passing ships. They wanted to develop plantations that would grow valuable exports. The governors envisioned the islands becoming even more profitable than Saint-Domingue, France's lucrative colony in the Caribbean. Company governors dictated export quotas to the settlers and began encouraging coffee cultivation by 1735.[31] The list of desired exports eventually included not only coffee but also sugar cane, indigo, and cotton.[32] The demand for slaves to work these crops remained high throughout the eighteenth century, with the number of slaving voyages to the islands peaking in the last decades of the century and continuing well into the nineteenth.[33]

Production on Mauritius and Réunion never lived up to French expectations and would never rival that of Saint-Domingue, in part due to the constant need to import supplies from eastern Madagascar and elsewhere in the Indian Ocean. Throughout the entire century, ships were dispatched almost annually from the Mascarenes and would return from Madagascar with a small number of *captifs* along with the rest of their cargo, primarily rice and cattle.[34] The French sailing from Mauritius and Réunion tried to avoid sailing between November and March, when there was a great chance of encountering cyclones, and attempted to visit the island primarily during the "healthy" time of year, before the heat and rains set in.[35] Voyages between Port Louis, the main port on Mauritius, and Foulpointe, Toamasina, and Antongil Bay typically lasted between three and four months.[36] Given the frequent demand for food on the islands, however, French ships sometimes undertook multiple trips to Madagascar in rapid succession and ships set aside specifically for this commerce were sent to the island five times in the space of twelve months, forcing them to travel in periods of bad weather and heavy storms.[37] It became common practice for colonial authorities to send these *particulier* ships (short-haul ships owned by the colonial governments) to multiple ports during their trips. The French also sent ships occasionally to western Madagascar when they were desperate for slaves, but these voyages were more lengthy and, even prior to the outbreak of the Seven Years' War, seen as more dangerous.[38]

Even with frequent inputs of new slaves, the plans of the company's directors to promote exports from the islands unraveled. In good years, the French-owned islands could produce enough food for the colonists as well as supply some of the visiting ships, but environmental problems consistently reduced the productivity of agriculture in the Mascarenes. Crops on the islands failed repeatedly following a series of natural disasters, in 1725, 1728, 1730, and 1737, and again at a similar (or even increased) pace during subsequent decades. The colonists and their slaves struggled to grow wheat, maize, and rice, as well as successfully raise cattle on the islands. Growing coffee proved even more difficult in the sometimes marginally fertile soil, and it was backbreaking work for the laborers. Locusts and rats consumed crops, especially the prized wheat. Droughts dried up grain fields and diseases struck down valuable cattle and slaves. Cyclones wiped out crops and destroyed recently constructed ports. In some years, the mortality rate among the company's slaves was well above ten percent.[39] On top of these problems, the danger of bringing large numbers of slaves speaking a common language (Malagasy) to a sparsely inhabited island became clear thanks to the growing incidence of desertion, as slaves followed a pattern that had begun during the years of Dutch rule. Some of the colonists came to believe that "Madagascar slaves are always much more inclined to desert their master" and flee into the mountains. The maroons robbed French colonial farms and encouraged rebellion among slaves. Some even stole canoes in seemingly suicidal efforts to return to Madagascar. The governors constantly debated what to do about the maroon communities and the threats they posed.[40]

To address some of the problems that faced the colonies, French leaders made several pragmatic decisions. One of the most important was the introduction of manioc as a food for slaves. By the middle of the eighteenth century, manioc had been adopted in the Mascarenes, as it grew in poor soil and would store for months.[41] Despite this innovation, French colonists still preferred to eat wheat themselves and, when that crop failed, rice, which had to be imported from Madagascar or Asia. This continued demand encouraged traders to regularly visit eastern Madagascar to purchase extremely large quantities of rice in the ports of Foulpointe, Nosy Boraha, and Antongil Bay. For instance, in 1725, a small ship belonging to the colonial government, the *Ruby,* returned from the east coast of Madagascar with several thousand tons of rice, along with thirty-two male and four female slaves. This supply of rice appeared to the grateful colonists as "manna fallen from the sky," to be used in protecting them against the next famine. The food was retained for distribution among the troops on the island and the company's various workers, until the next harvest.[42] During the 1720s, the French also began a concerted effort to purchase hundreds of live cattle at a time from Taolagnaro, with one ship ordered to carry hundreds back to the islands, although relatively few cattle survived the journey.[43]

The events of the 1730s also ushered in a new era in terms of heightened French involvement in Madagascar. In 1730, following a particularly violent cyclone, many homes and buildings were destroyed on the French islands. In 1733, again, the survival of the colonists was threatened when mice and rats consumed much of the harvest.[44] These years were ones of recurrent food crises in South India as well, suggesting that supplies for purchase were limited in Asian ports.[45] With little food available in the Mascarenes, the governors sent more ships than usual to eastern Madagascar.[46] These voyages sparked a desire among the French governors to form a trading settlement on Madagascar that would allow ships to more easily and cheaply obtain food for export to the Mascarenes. In 1733, the governors decided to found a small colony on the small island of Île Marotte (likely Nosy Mangabe) in Antongil Bay, an island that was previously uninhabited but located very closely to the coastal settlements that ringed the bay. Almost immediately after their arrival, however, the settlers had trouble securing provisions and many of the soldiers sent to live on the island died quickly after disembarking. The colony was abandoned only months after its founding.[47]

## BRITISH AND FRENCH CONFLICT

This failed endeavor was just one of many during a period in which the French repeatedly exhausted the resources of the colonial governments in the Mascarenes trying to found settlements on the east coast of Madagascar. The failure of the French colony in 1733, however, coincided not just with increasing French dependence on the produce and labor of Madagascar but also with the rise of Betsimisaraka leadership in eastern Madagascar. As a result, for the next several decades, French merchants complained that the islanders were frequently at war. The French explicitly connected island conflicts with disrupted trade, while also hoping that these battles would result in large numbers of enslaved individuals for sale.[48] By examining political developments in early modern Europe, however, the people of Madagascar could have made similar observations about the warlike nature of Europeans, especially as British and French competition reached new heights around the mid-eighteenth century and extended into the lands surrounding the Indian Ocean basin. A heightened demand for provisioning accompanied this new involvement in the ocean, with periodic food shortages and even famines occurring on the Indian subcontinent, in part produced by periodic failures of monsoon rains but possibly exacerbated by the increased presence of soldiers and slave laborers in the region.[49]

A rising demand for food was clearly present in 1744, when ten British warships joined the usual EIC "India ships" and stopped briefly at St. Augustin Bay in what would become a common pattern.[50] When another fleet arrived at the bay two years later, one British officer lamented the "melancholy condition of the ship's company," with 110 men sick, "most of which were dangerously ill."[51] The men went ashore where they recovered by sleeping in tents and eating every "sort of food or fruits that could be proper for their different disorders."[52] The British commanders found plentiful beef and water in the bay, after sending the usual presents to King Baba in Toliara.[53] On this occasion, the ships set sail with little salted meat, rice, and callavances (Hyacinth beans) on board because, according to the commander, they did not wait long enough for the traders to bring more food to the shores of St. Augustin Bay. He also mentioned that, if they had had more salt, he would have purchased many more cattle from King Baba to dry extra beef for their voyage.[54] Such reports were recorded in letters dispatched back to the British admiralty and encouraged continued visits by British fleets. As before, the large bay in southwestern Madagascar became a meeting spot for ships that may have separated during the voyage into the Indian Ocean. In return for provisions, the British provided the Sakalava Empire with a constant infusion of firearms and other foreign imports, in amounts that may have far exceeded previous imports into the island.

The French also turned to Madagascar for supplies of food and labor during the wars, but were not as fortunate as the British. The arrival of warships in the harbors of the Mascarenes had increased pressure on the colonies' already precarious food stores. To try to circumvent the need for the fleets to visit Madagascar, French officials at Mauritius and Réunion sent their own ships more frequently to eastern Madagascar in search of cattle and other livestock to supply the warships.[55] Fresh beef was deemed absolutely necessary for nourishing soldiers and supporting French naval actions. For this reason, the French government in the Mascarenes bought hundreds of live cattle, including 470 cattle from Foulpointe in 1747 alone, to fill this new demand.[56] Two years later, a single French ship bought 400 cattle at Taolagnaro, but lost all but 180 of them on the return voyage.[57] The French administrators argued that these constant importations of food, especially cattle, were necessary to restore the supplies of the islands after the annual visits of the French fleets and their "*grande consommation*."[58]

Even though citrus fruits and vinegar were the preferred cure, a few French officials argued repeatedly for the need for beef to treat scurvy.[59] The need to purchase and transport cattle, however, was taking a toll on the treasuries of the islands, so the French sought alternatives. Out of desperation, the French turned to tortoise meat to feed soldiers and sailors. They sent ships to the nearby island of Diego Rodrigues (present-day Rodrigues), where sailors captured hundreds of tortoises and likely pushed several species into extinction. This choice was only made when absolutely necessary. Some people appeared to believe that turtle meat, unlike beef, was less effective at curing diseases and ailments.[60] In spite of this belief, throughout the eighteenth century the French relied upon the small island as a fishery and colonial outpost.[61]

The emphasis on beef and rice consumption, even in the midst of dire food shortages, pushed the French to trade even more frequently with Madagascar. The French colonial government had profited from exports of coffee and other commodities from the Mascarenes, at least for a brief period, and hoped to purchase food in Madagascar with the proceeds in order to feed the visiting fleets.[62] These plans might have succeeded, except that supplies of provisions from Madagascar were not forthcoming on most mid-eighteenth-century voyages, thanks to frequent disorder within eastern Madagascar. The French professed to be constantly worried about the threat of British attacks on their vessels or even the eventual invasion of the islands. For these reasons, the French did not frequently visit the west coast. French worries were not unwarranted, however, as the British did contemplate invading Mauritius and repeatedly conducted surveillance of the French forces on the islands during the second half of the century.[63]

The growing dependence of the French on trade in eastern Madagascar can be noted in the dispatch of a large fleet of French warships to India in 1746. Bertrand-François Mahé de la Bourdonnais (Bourdonnaie), the governor-general of the Mascarenes, formed an expedition to sail to the northern Indian Ocean and fight the British.[64] His fleet of ten ships left the Mascarene Islands in March and headed to Madagascar for provisions, as the ships had obtained only enough food from the Mascarenes to last a few months.[65] Once the fleet arrived at the east coast of Madagascar, a strong cyclone struck and damaged many of the ships, forcing them to sail into Antongil Bay. The French landed the ships' crews near the bay and set up a hospital to help the sick recover.

Bourdonnais led an expedition into the interior of the island for wood to rebuild their masts and sent other ships along the coast for additional food.[66] It took several months to complete these tasks, as supplies in Madagascar were not plentiful, perhaps due to the cyclone. When the fleet finally left the bay months after its arrival, it consisted of nine ships, the French having lost one, but fortunately 3,042 men were still on board the vessels, 720 of them described as "blacks." Bourdonnais was worried about losing the "blacks" (slaves brought from the Mascarenes, it seems) to desertion while in Madagascar. The French did lose 30 of these men but used gunpowder to bribe "the chief of Manahar" to return most of the deserters. In spite of their lengthy and expensive detour to Madagascar, the ships continued on to the coast of India and forced the British to capitulate in Chennai on 21 September 1746.[67]

The experiences of Bourdonnais and his fleet had once again convinced the French of the utility of a settlement on the east coast of Madagascar, despite their failure in Antongil Bay only a decade earlier. The French decided in 1750 to sponsor a small trading and military colony on Nosy Boraha, the former haunt of Anglo-American pirates.[68] In this year, French officials signed a treaty with the east coast ruler of Foulpointe, Queen Béti.[69] Béti and twenty-nine other leaders agreed to give the French possession of the small island of Nosy Boraha in "perpetuity."[70] Despite this lofty language, the French colony on the island was extremely short-lived. After the signing of the treaty, a small contingent of soldiers arrived to take control of the island, but, within a few months of their landing and following several threats from the island's inhabitants, the French soldiers were forced to relocate their settlement to Île aux Cayes, located off the main island and surrounded by a deep harbor. In this more protected location, the soldiers continued to struggle to obtain sufficient provisions until the colony was disbanded by 1754, following a violent attack on the settlement. The people of Nosy Boraha had massacred a French officer, Gosse, and other French soldiers in that year for reportedly abusing communities in Madagascar.[71] Many of the perpetrators fled from the small island to the mainland of Madagascar in fear of French reprisals.[72] During the 1760s, Nosy Boraha remained relatively depopulated, according to visitors' reports, and the French continued to seek vengeance for the destruction of their colony.[73]

It quickly became clear that while the French had failed to build a lasting trading settlement on Nosy Boraha, they may have also contributed to unrest in the region. For the first time, French traders arrived to find communities along the east coast entirely without rice or cattle for sale. Not only was food scarce but entire communities had completely disappeared from the east coast. Many coastal inhabitants appear to have migrated into the interior or elsewhere in Madagascar in the aftermath of conflict.[74] French merchants also blamed droughts and the spread of a virulent epidemic during the 1750s and 1760s for further reducing supplies on the east coast.[75] Despite the presence of a French-appointed *chef de traite* residing in Foulpointe, with secondary French trading posts installed along the east coast of the island, food was at times difficult to obtain.[76] The smallpox epidemic in Mauritius in 1756 that killed half of the slaves on the island further challenged the French.[77]

Even when they were able to purchase food, French merchants discovered that prices for provisions, not just slaves, had increased dramatically as island traders demanded the French make payment in silver coins.[78] In seeking to buy food on credit, French warships contracted debts at Foulpointe that the company could not pay, effectively halting trade there even further.[79] Without a ready supply of coins, the French negotiators could neither pay off their debts to the island leaders nor procure new supplies.[80] In the words of French merchants, the trade of eastern Madagascar was "ruined."[81] By the outbreak of the Third Carnatic War in 1756, the French worried seriously about food shortages affecting their populations. Despite their fears of the British warships, the French had already been sending traders to western Madagascar and even East Africa in search of supplies.[82] The governors also dispatched vessels to the Cape of Good Hope to buy food from the Dutch.[83] The French begged their merchant ships to bring rice to the islands from Indonesia.[84] Even these attempts did little to bolster food supplies and the governors began urging colonists to focus on growing food, not coffee and other export crops. Historian Huguette Ly-Tio-Fane Pineo refers to this agricultural shift as only a "half-hearted endeavour," and it seems to have had little impact on the food shortage.[85]

In the midst of these French failures, British ships continued to visit St. Augustin Bay on their way to India throughout the 1750s and 1760s. The British successfully purchased large supplies of provisions during each visit before continuing on to the northern Indian Ocean.[86] In contrast, the lack of sea support for French troops in India clearly damaged French military operations in the northern Indian Ocean. In 1758, the

French navy, under the command of the French admiral Anne Antoine, Comte d'Aché, sailed from the Indian coast to provision their ships at the Mascarenes. Upon arriving at Mauritius, the admiral discovered that the islands were lacking food supplies.[87] He sent most of his fleet to the Cape for food and sailed to India with a smaller contingent of sailors and soldiers. The admiral had left French land forces in India unprotected and, in the absence of naval support, they were forced to retreat.[88] A year later, d'Aché returned to the Mascarenes for food and water but, in January 1760, a cyclone hit the islands and crippled his fleet at anchor. Given this setback, d'Aché decided it was wiser to remain in the Mascarenes to protect the islands against the threat of British invasion, rather than risk the long voyage back to India in damaged and under-provisioned ships. Without the benefit of naval protection, the French forces in India lost a major battle in 1760 and surrendered their control of major ports in India by the following year.[89]

## RENEWED OPTIMISM

Even after this setback, some French officials still thought that control of Madagascar would make them "the masters of commerce in the Indies."[90] At least one believed, despite experiences to the contrary, that there were "few countries in the world where navigators can find, in greater abundance, and at less expense, refreshments of every kind."[91] Yet another permanent trading settlement on the island would hopefully solve French problems. The French sent a merchant, a M. de Laval, to reside in the region near Antongil Bay and coordinate trade from his palisade near the coast during the 1760s.[92] Laval and other visitors reported that the land near the coast was extremely fertile, home to small rice farms and fields suitable for feeding large herds of cattle.[93] In short, the location had "*ressources infinies*" for a colony.[94] Such suggestions were all the French governors needed to renew their search for a colony on the island.

In 1768, the French set up a colony in Taolagnaro, near the location of the seventeenth-century French colony, Fort Dauphin. The French desperation for supplies appears to have repressed memories of their numerous failures in this arid region. After some debate, the company officials decided that a colonial administrator who had considerable experience in India, Comte de Modave, would lead a small settlement aimed at increasing trade, particularly in cattle and rice.[95] Despite residing in Taolagnaro for about two years, however, the administrator failed to create a prosperous settlement in the region. Modave and his troops were constantly embroiled in local political disputes and had trouble gaining food supplies, not just for export, but also to support his own colonists.[96] Modave pleaded for greater investment from the French, for more soldiers as well as trading goods, but eventually was forced to return to Europe, from where he continued his plans to reestablish the colony.[97] His greatest contribution to the history of Madagascar was likely his part in introducing the prickly pear cactus to southern Madagascar, an action that would have far-reaching consequences for the livelihood of many communities in the region.[98]

By 1767, the company was experiencing severe financial difficulties that hampered the continuation of their commerce with Madagascar as well as support for the island colony.[99] These financial problems eventually resulted in the French government assuming formal control of the Mascarene Islands. Trading restrictions were eased, with all French citizens allowed to participate in trade with Madagascar and the islands, leading to a rapid increase in commerce, particularly in slaves, with Madagascar.[100] In yet another attempt to slow the flow of silver out of their colonies, the French government outlawed the slave trade from eastern Madagascar for a few years during the 1770s.[101] Instead, more ships went to East Africa and the west coast of Madagascar for slaves. The slaves they returned with were particularly in demand after an outbreak of the "*petite verolle*" (*vérole* or smallpox) in 1771 damaged slave populations on the islands.[102] Food supplies were scarce in eastern Madagascar during this period as well and too expensive to buy at the Cape.[103]

The difficulties the French had faced in the past did not deter plans for a fourth attempt at creating a permanent French colony on the island of Madagascar. This settlement was perhaps the most spectacular failure yet, and while several sources documented Modave's attempt to settle the south of Madagascar, the new venture is preserved in multiple volumes of the Madagascar colonial series held in the French archives. The documents reveal that the French government, finally heeding the words of Laval in support of a colony near Antongil Bay, invested considerable energy and resources into this new French settlement beginning in 1774, as this settlement appeared "absolutely necessary to procure for

Île de France the help which it needs."[104] The unlikely leader of this colony was a Hungarian nobleman named Maurice Auguste Benyowsky (Benyovszky) who first arrived at Mauritius in 1772.[105]

From the start, despite gaining support from the French metropolitan government, the governors on Mauritius and Réunion had their doubts about Benyowsky.[106] Benyowsky was ordered to engage in defensive warfare only, yet he arrived at the Mascarenes with architectural plans already drawn up for an elaborate military fortress on the island to be named "Louisbourg."[107] Shortly after his arrival on Madagascar, if his memoir is to be believed, Benyowsky quickly gained the confidence of local rulers through a mixture of benevolent governance and military force.[108] Benyowsky leaned heavily on French translators who had years of experience on the coast of Madagascar. Many of these men had married island women and had strong networks of contacts throughout the island.[109] Benyowsky formed lengthy descriptions of his plans for dominating the commercial networks that crossed the island.[110]

Despite such lofty claims, French sources suggest that his colony disrupted commerce and antagonized neighboring communities from the beginning.[111] The death toll among his soldiers was immense.[112] Reportedly, by 1776, out of an original contingent of 400 men, more than 260 had died from disease and lack of food. The remaining men were sickly.[113] In addition, Benyowsky lacked the food supplies to provision a visiting French vessel in 1775, and all of the local leaders referred to him as "*le Mauvais Blanc*" (the Bad White). Given these evident antagonisms, Benyowsky requested military assistance against local communities. Several hundred French soldiers stormed one of the villages on the east coast that was threatening the French settlement. The French soldiers set fire to all of the homes and fields of the hostile islanders.[114]

After this attack, rulers in the region signed a treaty with Benyowsky recognizing him as "ampanscabe" (*mpanjaka-be,* literally, big king or ruler) in 1776.[115] He told the French that leaders throughout the east and north of the island recognized him as "their glorious monarch" and frequently thanked him for his rule.[116] Benyowsky's military efforts on the east coast, unsurprisingly, attracted the hostility of Sakalava rulers who were influential in the region.[117] In addition, far from abolishing slavery, Benyowsky tried to set up an export business to sell slaves at the Cape of Good Hope for his own personal profit. He ran into trouble with the Mascarene governors when they discovered his plans.[118] Benyowsky was recalled back to France in October of 1776.[119] As Benyowsky sailed back to Europe, his ship stopped at the Cape to sell slaves from Madagascar.[120] Benyowsky briefly returned to Madagascar with American soldiers hired in Baltimore in 1784, but the French dispatched a troop of sixty soldiers to the island. He was attacked and killed near Antongil Bay, either by the French or by his own men.[121]

Benyowsky's history foreshadows impending conflicts in "unclaimed" locations such as Madagascar, where European attitudes regarding commerce and political power would increasingly challenge local leadership. He was able to influence European leaders who knew little of the conditions on the ground in places as remote as Madagascar. He deployed details such as his adoption of the title "*mpanjaka-be*" as evidence of his authenticity as an island leader (echoing the use of the English title "king" by the people of Madagascar themselves). Meanwhile, the leaders on the island, despite "signing" a treaty with him, took little notice of this authority. Europeans, by contrast, appear to have believed him capable of such achievements. British and French visitors to the island for the half century following Benyowsky's death blamed any chaos they encountered within Madagascar on his marauding policies. While there is little evidence to suggest that he and his several hundred soldiers were that influential on the internal workings of the island, it was a period of increasingly violent competition over the control of resources, including food and slave labor. His actions also reveal the growing ambivalence of Europeans toward slavery and the slave trade, an ambivalence that would have important ramifications by the start of the nineteenth century. The fact that his manic plans were supported at all suggests a desperation on the part of Europeans to dominate production on the fertile island within the southwestern Indian Ocean.

## FRENCH FAILURES?

Megan Vaughan has argued that the frequent conflicts of the eighteenth century played a considerable role in shaping the Mascarene Islands and perhaps were also important in Madagascar, as the islanders dealt with the rising demands presented by large fleets of European ships off their shores.[122] After the war in the northern Indian Ocean ended with a British victory, both British and French governments demonstrated interest in maintaining access to trade in the southwestern Indian Ocean region, including Madagascar, as it had proved so valuable during wartime. They both maintained large contingents of soldiers and sailors in the ocean after the war ended.[123] The British fought with the Marathas for the next few decades and these battles required the continuous dispatch of British ships into the ocean. These ships still frequented western Madagascar.[124] More ships sailed from the Mascarenes to Madagascar in search of slaves by the close of the century.[125]

Much of the scholarship on the seventeenth- and eighteenth-century French East India companies fixates on the failures of the French traders and administrators in comparison to their Portuguese, Dutch, and English counterparts. The French did not send enough ships, make cogent plans, or invest adequate financial resources in these endeavors. Many historians focus on the economic imperatives that determined the formation of the French trading companies and contrast these with English and Dutch monopoly companies. Philippe Haudrère, for instance, describes the various financial challenges the company faced as hampering their attempts to profitably organize trade within the Indian Ocean.[126] Some scholars blame constant funding struggles for preventing French access to prime markets in the Indian Ocean.[127]

As a result, there is a tendency to isolate the decisions of the companies' directors in France from events within the Indian Ocean. Few scholars have examined the role of communities in Madagascar (or even those in the Mascarenes) in shaping French commerce in the Indian Ocean.[128] In spite of this absence, it seems clear that French plans centered on the island of Madagascar and French officials became obsessed with painting a "rosy picture" of Madagascar.[129] The numerous failed colonies of the eighteenth century suggest how reliant the French had become upon Madagascar. The French were thus hampered when the agricultural production of the communities in eastern Madagascar proved to be unreliable. Likewise, the possession of Mauritius has been seen as a crucial link in developing French commerce, as it provided the French with safe ports near the center of the ocean.[130] The utility of the island's ports, however, was less than expected, in light of frequent cyclones and food shortages.[131] The battle for the control of the Carnatic coast further exacerbated challenges for French colonists. Thus, French colonial failures should be equally attributed to the negative influence of diseases, such as dysentery, malaria, or various *flux* described by Europeans, and natural disasters, such as *sauterelle* (locust) infestations, rather than blamed entirely upon poor management or a lack of funding.[132] Environmental conditions on the two Indian Ocean islands, as well as on Madagascar, helped produce precarious survival conditions for the French colonists and negatively affected the commercial plans of the company.

Further complicating the picture is what (little) we know of provisioning in the Indian Ocean. The rice-producing portions of the Indian Ocean were linked through complex weather patterns, and when crops failed in India, they may have failed in other regions visited by Europeans. Scientists have found evidence of a widespread "megadrought" throughout Southeast Asia between 1756 and 1768, in the midst of British and French battles for control in the ocean.[133] Furthermore, according to one estimate, "more than a third of the entire population of Bengal died between 1769 and 1770, while the loss in cultivation was estimated as closer to one-half."[134] Sunil Amrith argues that this drought encouraged British imperial policies that were aimed at more directly controlling agricultural production in the Bay of Bengal region.[135] It is conceivable that this eighteenth-century drought influenced British and French military conflict on land and at sea. A lack of food would most certainly have forced the British and French to identify alternate provisioning centers in Asia and perhaps drove their ships to visit Madagascar with more frequency.

In his book *Late Victorian Holocausts,* historian Mike Davis links the devastating famines (and resulting deaths and political instability) that occurred in Asia and Africa in 1876–79 and 1896–1902 to particularly intense El Niño events.[136] Similar correlations between weather disruptions, food shortages, and political upheaval likely existed in earlier years. One El Niño event between 1789 and 1793, for instance, may have contributed to famine, riots, and epidemics in Europe, Asia, and the Caribbean.[137] While we know relatively little about food shortages within the southwestern Indian Ocean during the eighteenth century, as most research has focused on "Monsoon Asia," the region was connected with the northern Indian Ocean not only through weather but also through trade.[138] Although there is no evidence of concurrent crop failures in the Bay of Bengal and the southwestern Indian Ocean, crises occurring in Asia would have influenced the ability of Europeans to obtain food in Asian ports, perhaps driving them to secure alternate sources for provisions. Regular food shortages in East Africa and Asia may have also resulted in hundreds or even thousands finding themselves enslaved and sold to Europeans, while also increasing the demand for food and laborers in European colonial settlements throughout India, Indonesia, southern Africa, and the Mascarene Islands.[139]

# SEVEN

## Slaving Failures

THE PRESENCE OF A visibly bustling slave traffic in northwestern Madagascar had drawn European and American merchants to the island in search of laborers throughout the seventeenth century.[1] As R. J. Barendse, Gwyn Campbell, and others have argued, the island would become a "central link" in the global slave trade by the nineteenth century.[2] For much of the eighteenth century, however, relatively fewer slaves were exported from the island, particularly between 1730 and 1780, despite the fairly continuous demand for coerced laborers to work in the European establishments that dotted the shores of the Indian Ocean. The traffic in captives from Madagascar had always been a minor contributor to the total numbers of enslaved individuals carried by Europeans across the Atlantic or Indian Oceans between 1500 and 1850, but the noticeable decline in the slave trade from the island was particularly striking.[3]

As figure 7.1 illustrates, the numbers of enslaved individuals exported from Madagascar fluctuated wildly between 1640 and 1780, with two noticeable peaks in slaving around 1680 and during the first decades of the eighteenth century. These slaves were sent to the Americas (primarily Barbados, Saint Domingue, and Jamaica, but also to North

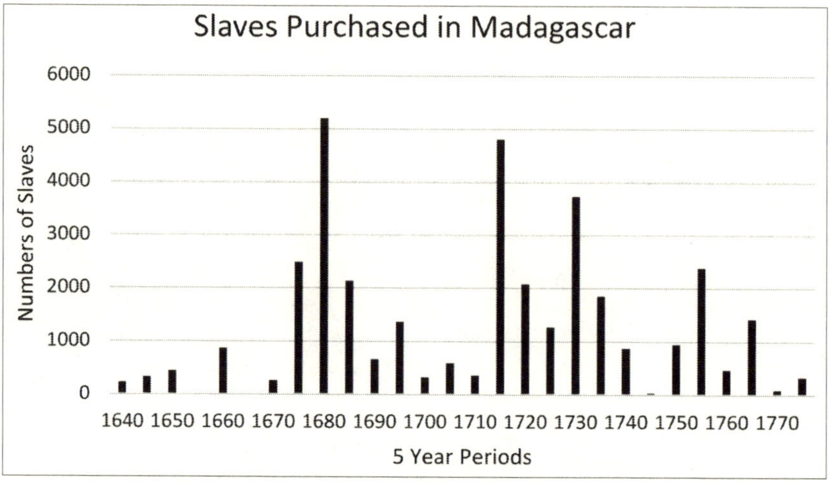


Figure 7.1. Slaves purchased in Madagascar by Europeans, five-year periods, 1640–1780. *Note:* The data come from ship journals and colonial records. Every attempt has been made to record the numbers of slaves loaded in Madagascar, as well as the year of purchase on the island, but this was not possible for all voyages. There were far more voyages that bought slaves from Madagascar not included in this representation; the chart uses information from the voyages for which I found evidence for numbers of slaves from Madagascar (preferably purchased, sometimes unloaded at the destination). *Sources: See appendix for full documentation.*

America) as well as to European outposts in Asia and southern Africa. Outside of these peak years, the successful provisioning stops conducted by hundreds of merchant vessels can be directly contrasted with the many ineffectual attempts by Europeans to set up a traffic in captives from Madagascar. Between 1700 and 1800, for instance, 20 EIC ships stopped for slaves (and food) from Madagascar, while at least 116 EIC ships halted in the ports of the island in search of only provisions during this same period.[4] Throughout this period, the average cargo size for an EIC slaver was only 96 slaves.[5] The English were forced to look elsewhere for laborers to work in their establishments in the Atlantic and Indian Oceans, yet their eighteenth-century provisioning voyages were so successful that Sakalava-dominated ports were used for supplying large fleets of British warships throughout this same period.

Given severe source limitations, the numbers provided in figure 7.1 must be considered provisional at best, but the lull in slaving was also clear in the statements made by slave traders and colonial officials who complained of high prices and low supplies of captives by the mid-eighteenth century.[6] They suggest that the slave trade was perceived as an alternative to the sale of food from the coasts of Madagascar. The increasing exports of rice and cattle from different parts of the island since the mid-seventeenth century meant that intensive agriculture developed in tandem with the export of captive laborers, as it did in many parts of Atlantic Africa.[7] In fact, patterns of European and American slave trading from Madagascar were similar in other ways to those in the Atlantic: European and American slavers had to use certain commodities (chiefly cloth, guns, and currency, in the case of Madagascar) to purchase slaves, they primarily sought young male captives, and slavers maintained strong relationships with coastal merchants and political leaders.[8] The growth of the slaving and provisioning trades went hand-in-hand in both Madagascar and Atlantic Africa, yet the mid-eighteenth-century decline of the slave trade on the shores of Madagascar reflected specific opportunities afforded to those who inhabited this Indian Ocean island. In years of plenty, island merchants were virtually guaranteed purchasers for their rice and cattle, as large numbers of merchants calling at the island were not in search of slaves at all. When facing pressures from challenging environmental conditions or economic competition, coastal groups resorted to selling captives in order to acquire desirable imports. For much of the eighteenth century, the slave trade was supplemental to the commerce in foodstuffs.

This chapter does not attempt to present a comprehensive history of the slave trade from the island.[9] Nor will it provide definitive conclusions about the numbers of people transported from the island during different periods in Madagascar's history. Instead the focus is on understanding major transformations in the eighteenth-century slave traffic, with the sometimes limited data available, in light of the long-running provisioning trade from the island.

## CHALLENGES TO SLAVING

The experience of one Dutch slaving vessel reveals the difficulties that Europeans faced in purchasing slaves from the island by the middle of the eighteenth century, difficulties not usually encountered when they arrived at the island in search of provisions. In 1741, the Dutch ship, the *Brack*, arrived at St. Augustin Bay.[10] After the ship came to anchor, several representatives of the local monarch, "Prins Willem," arrived to welcome the ship. The prince and King "Rammanrasse" of nearby Toliara (later referred to as "Kinnebaba," King Baba) conveyed their greetings to the captain and assured the slave traders that captives would be plentiful and cheap for the merchants.[11]

Despite this warm welcome, trade did not proceed smoothly. The Dutch had their first hint of trouble when negotiations for cattle collapsed. Prince William refused to sell his livestock for cloth and other assorted merchandise, as these goods were, in the prince's words, only valuable for women. The muskets brought by the Dutch were likewise deemed unacceptable, being of poor quality. The islanders demanded fine guns and silver coins in return for cattle. The debates over prices did not end there. King Baba asked for either twenty-five Spanish reales (silver coins) or six muskets, thirty pounds of powder, sixty flints, and ten bullets for each slave. This price shocked the Dutch, who had never used coins for slave trading from St. Augustin Bay previously nor paid such high prices for slaves. The king insisted that the English, French, and Portuguese all used silver coins to purchase slaves from them and the Dutch needed to do likewise. He refused to let the merchants purchase slaves with only their (obviously inadequate) guns, as the Dutch had done on earlier voyages. The Dutch were also told that the guns were useless without supplies of gunpowder and lead, so those items would need to be provided in addition to firearms if they wished to buy slaves. There were protracted negotiations throughout the next two weeks, during which the Dutch attempted to woo the leaders with presents. Finally King Baba agreed to sell the Dutch some slaves in return for a combination of guns, gunpowder, lead, flints, and some silver coins, the actual amount of each to be determined by the age and quality of the enslaved individual.[12]

Shortly after the Dutch had concluded these discussions, the first two captives were delivered to the Dutch ship. "Slapoentje" and "Maleynga" were described as older than the Dutch had wanted, being about thirty-five years old, but the Dutch accepted these two male slaves as they feared they would get few others.[13] These fears were confirmed as the captives slowly arrived at the coast, at most one or two slaves a day. Many of these captives were already in poor condition, being overworked, underfed, and exhausted from their long trip from the interior. The Dutch attempted to encourage trade by giving more presents to the king and his representatives, who continued to demand cloth, gunpowder, yellow beads, and dozens of bottles of alcohol.[14] Whether the king was intentionally delaying the trade to gain the upper hand in negotiations or not, the end result was the same: the Dutch were growing desperate. The crew members on board the ship were becoming impatient and the captain feared trouble if they remained in the port, so he made the decision to shorten their stay on the coast rather than wait, perhaps in vain, for more slaves to be delivered. Twenty-nine days after arriving in St. Augustin Bay, the *Brack* sailed away, its trading representative having dispensed over two hundred liters of arrack and many other valuable goods in return for few slaves.[15]

Before they departed, King Baba accused the Dutch slavers of breaking their trading agreement by leaving so quickly and not agreeing to wait for the slaves to arrive, as they were being held some distance away from the coast. Placated by Dutch promises of returning the following year with guns and silver, the king had the captain write a letter to the Cape governor requesting military assistance to help him triumph over his enemies. In return for this aid, he promised to give the Dutch as many slaves as they could carry. He also asked the Dutch to bring him some large chains so he could more easily transport the slaves from the island's interior. Finally, King Baba told the Dutch that if they brought a large number of small glass beads, necessary for local trade, he would also provide them with plentiful white rice.[16]

The *Brack* sailed to northwestern Madagascar, arriving in the bay of Massaliege in mid-August. During the trip, the Dutch observed that there were three "Arab" ships at anchor in the Bay of Boina, where a Sakalava princess ruled over the trade. The Dutch found the presence of these vessels to be a hopeful sign, particularly after one Arab trader told them two French ships had recently left the northwest coast with 340 slaves on one vessel and 200 on the other.[17] The Dutch also learned that the Sakalava king, the princess's father, was currently living in Marovoay, a nearby town. The captain and trading officials decided to travel to Marovoay to start negotiations for slaves. Upon their arrival, the Dutch were amazed by the king's palatial compound, described as grander than the governor's castle at the Cape, and they enjoyed a meal with the ruler.[18] The king had more than a hundred beautiful guns, an elaborate throne, and the relics of his royal ancestors on display.

Despite the evident sophistication of the king and his followers, the Dutch quickly learned that trading negotiations would not be any easier than they had been in the southwest of the island. The king bragged that he had plenty of slaves but feared that the Dutch ship was not of sufficient size to carry them all. The slave traders then viewed many of the slaves for sale but refused to purchase most of them, as they were either too old or too young to be worth transporting to the Cape. Even worse, the king and his interpreter laughed when the Dutch officials stated their price. The king told them to return to Rammanrasse if they desired better prices, as he was unwilling to waste time negotiating with them.[19] He informed the Dutch that he had to go to war against the "Ambolammois" (Amboalambo) and the "Sehanik" (Sihanaka), two neighboring groups, and did not have time to continue discussions.[20] The Dutch eventually purchased only a few more slaves before returning to the Cape. As some of the elites observed as the Dutch departed, all Europeans were alike in their desperation for slaves—their trading contracts meant nothing and, in the end, they would buy every slave offered, even women, for the price demanded by the king.[21] This comment probably worried the slave traders, as it communicated a clear awareness on the part of the islanders as to their negotiating strength.

The experience of the Dutch traders aboard the *Brack* reveals the challenges faced by Europeans seeking to purchase slaves during the eighteenth century, as prices increased and supplies declined at such rates that the Dutch, English, and French would eventually turn elsewhere for slaves. In fact, the voyage of the *Brack* would have been a complete failure if the Dutch had not succeeded in fulfilling their secondary goal, of acquiring rice to replenish supplies at the Cape. A second Dutch slaving voyage, undertaken the following year, was likewise unproductive in terms of slave purchases, but the merchants once again acquired food during their visit to the island.[22] In short, the rulers were unwilling to bend in their prices for even undesirable slaves, but had little trouble in selling provisions to the same European merchants.

## COMPETITION FOR SLAVES

The experiences of the Dutch point toward at least one reason why few captives were available for purchase from the island: there was considerable competition for slaves, and not just between the Dutch and French. European sources suggest repeatedly that providing slaves to European slavers was not a priority for rulers in the northwestern ports of Madagascar, where African, Arab, and Asian merchants had long dominated trade. In fact, the non-European slave trade was so important during the seventeenth century that Europeans had described hiding their slave purchases while anchored in Massaliege, as slaves were reserved for fulfilling the demands of African and Arab merchants.[23] These merchants remained major players in the slave trade from western Madagascar even after the advent of Sakalava rule.[24] Unlike in West Africa, non-European slaving networks not only drew upon the same supplies of slaves as those demanded by Europeans but frequented the same markets as well. As a result, in 1761 one English slaver visiting northwest Madagascar complained that the "Moor" merchants on board a ship from Surat were able to buy 65 slaves with just cloth, while the English only acquired 34 slaves with their guns during a five-month stay on the island.[25] Sources, such as those provided by traders on the *Brack*, reveal that "Arab" vessels continued to visit the ports of Madagascar, even if Europeans provide us with little information about the numbers of slaves (if any) carried on these ships. By the mid-eighteenth century, Europeans even tried to purchase slaves from Arab, East African, or Comorian merchants residing on the island. A "Johanna [Ndzuwani] man" living in Morondava, described as the wealthiest merchant in the region, sold slaves to European traders on at least one occasion.[26] An "*Arabisch*" merchant supplied the Dutch with slaves on another.[27] By the early nineteenth century, Muslim merchants had even found their way into the far interior markets of the island.[28]

Judging by European observations, rulers on Ndzuwani in the Comoro archipelago were particularly active participants in the slave (and provisioning) trade from Madagascar after 1700.[29] In 1703, an English visitor described one of the leaders of Ndzuwani as possessing at least five dhows, constructed and maintained in Ndzuwani.[30] In times of peace, this sultana sent her ships on frequent trading voyages to northwestern Madagascar. Upon their arrival in the Comoros, dhow captains would stop, unload their cargoes into storehouses near the shore, and purchase more goods before reloading some of the slaves and continuing onward to East Africa. Slaves from Madagascar may have been retained locally in the Comoros for labor and to produce food for export to European vessels. In 1743, the sultan of Ndzuwani reportedly had at least a thousand slaves for his household use, some of them perhaps originating in Madagascar.[31] Thus, as European ships called at Ndzuwani for cattle, coconuts, and other foodstuffs, their crews may have been consuming food that was, either directly or indirectly (via trade from western Madagascar), produced by laborers from Madagascar.[32] The remaining slaves shipped from Madagascar were sold to various East African coastal communities or shipped to ports along the Red Sea and Persian Gulf, particularly Muscat.[33] There was a dramatic expansion in the labor demands of the Omani leadership during the eighteenth century and, while these demands may have been met primarily by East African slaves, Madagascar may have supplied some of these laborers.[34] After all, trade networks connected the islands of the southwestern Indian Ocean to the northern half of the ocean. As evidence of these networks, in 1703, one Ndzuwani "governor" offered to provide visiting European traders with letters of recommendation to "the Arabian king at Muscat."[35]

Given the existence of this commerce, European slavers were frequently at a disadvantage, in more ways than one. Europeans sought to quickly purchase large cargoes of slaves, mostly comprised of young males.[36] Yet there is no indication that coastal rulers made any effort to develop bulking centers for housing captives on the coasts and thus accommodate European demands. As a result, slaving negotiations dragged on as Europeans waited for captives to arrive at their vessels.[37] Large numbers of slaves were not usually available year-round and instead Europeans were frequently urged to return later in the year for slaves.[38] By contrast, when African and Arab traders visited Madagascar, they may have arrived on the monsoonal winds and had several months to wait before they could return, giving time for rulers and merchants to deliver slaves from the interior of the island, where they may have worked in fields and herded cattle, been obtained as war captives, or purchased from neighboring communities (or from tributaries).[39] Even if the traders were simply crossing the Mozambique Channel or sailing from the Comoros, some seasons were more accommodating to this crossing than others, making the timing of their voyages more predictable and reliable. Some of the merchants, as in later years, may have had families on the island or friends with whom they would visit during their stays, more effectively building trust among traders than the many presents Europeans had to give to island rulers.[40]

In spite of logistical challenges, there may have been other explanations for the delays that European slavers faced. The lack of European bargaining power, produced in part by the existence of alternative slave traffics, meant that supplies of slaves may have been intentionally restricted by island rulers. Island leaders thus gained additional leverage over the European visitors who were forced to remain on the shores of Madagascar for months as they sought to fill their cargo holds, increasing the risk of sailors dying and slave revolt. Just as Joseph Miller has suggested for West-Central Africa, it was possible that coastal rulers manipulated Europeans' need to load and leave the island quickly.[41] European desperation enabled rulers to sell slaves, even undesirable ones, for high prices and extort numerous presents, as well as force European slavers to buy large quantities of provisions during their stays. These maneuvers would give them access to the guns and coins they sought without selling valuable captives.

Competition with other merchant networks had existed during the late seventeenth century as well, when European and American slavers were able to acquire thousands of slaves annually from the island, with few major interruptions. Judging from the available records, many of these slaves were purchased at ports in western Madagascar, although some were also dispatched from eastern Madagascar thanks to the presence of Euro-American pirates.[42] The movement of slaves to the Americas between 1690 and 1730 was so large that it temporarily forced the price of slaves from ports throughout Madagascar upwards for all American and European traders.[43] This brief but vigorous trade to the Americas, combined with that of the Dutch, Portuguese, French, and English, was on such a scale that one scholar estimates that somewhere between fifteen and twenty ships visited various parts of Madagascar annually during the late seventeenth century in search of slaves. This number does not include the continued exports of slaves on non-European vessels as well.[44]

European observations suggest that even during this peak period, the slave trade from Madagascar was subject to large fluctuations. For every successful slave-trading venture, there was at least one utter failure when Europeans faced difficulty in obtaining enough slaves. One notable example was an English slave-trading ship in 1682 that spent eighteen months off Massaliege. During this lengthy stay, the English only managed to purchase 130 slaves. Almost all of the crew, aside from seven men, died while the ship was at anchor in Massaliege, thanks to disease and insufficient food supplies. This death toll included three captains.

The crew had to sail to Ndzuwani to purchase food before returning to Massaliege and resuming their attempt to fill the ship with slaves.[45]

The strength of this trade until 1730, despite numerous challenges, reveals that the later decline in slaving was not simply due to regional competition. It seems that other developments were discouraging the slave trade with Europeans by the mid-eighteenth century. Given the presence of an alternative traffic in slaves, a better question to ask would be why the rulers along Madagascar's coastline traded with Europeans at all. The answer can be found in the goods they carried during the eighteenth century: guns and silver coins. Both of these commodities would be more difficult to obtain from non-European trading partners during the eighteenth century, and, as such, gave Europeans an opportunity to enter into the slave trade with merchants and rulers in Madagascar in years during which the sales of cattle and rice faltered.

## A GUN-SLAVE CYCLE?

The slave trade from Madagascar was marked by two major shifts in slave pricing during the eighteenth century. Before 1692, Europeans bought slaves from island ports with an assortment of goods including carnelian and colored glass beads, copper, and some silver (including silver chains and jewelry, as well as coins).[46] After this date, guns were necessary to trade in slaves from ports throughout the island.[47] One English guide written during the 1690s advised slave-trading captains to bring large quantities of firearms to Madagascar: the trading goods that the "natives esteem most are good powder and arms."[48] This was true by the late seventeenth century even in the ports along the northwest coast where the trade had previously been in cloth, beads, and other items.[49] The first appearance of large numbers of guns in Madagascar occurred during the mid-seventeenth century, when the French provided them to their allies in the southern portion of the island, but guns were not in high demand until the end of the century, when the most valued imports became firearms and their accoutrements: gunpowder, flints, and bullets. These goods were used as presents to royalty and merchants, but were also the only commodities that could be used to purchase slaves.[50] As revealed in the account of the *Brack* above, coastal rulers did not just desire guns but were insistent on the type and size of these firearms as well. While these guns were not seen as terribly expensive by Europeans, they were worth more than the beads and other trinkets slavers had preferred to use in previous years, especially after rulers in Madagascar learned to demand high-quality guns.[51]

At first glance, this sudden demand supports the existence of a "gun-slave cycle" such as discussed by a number of historians focusing on West Africa. These historians have described a cycle in which guns used in warfare helped to produce captives who would be sold for more firearms.[52] A few scholars focused on Madagascar have also drawn connections between increased warfare on the island and the growth of the export trade in slaves from both coasts of Madagascar, although frequent battles did not guarantee quick and easy purchases of slaves for Europeans.[53] R. J. Barendse even refers to Boina, the northern Sakalava kingdom, as "the quintessential gunpowder empire," although arguably the state had little in common with the so-called "gunpowder empires" found throughout Asia during this period.[54]

On the face of it, the connection between warfare and enslavement appears credible. After all, one of the first demands for guns in return for slaves was made by a new Sakalava ruler in 1695, in the midst of the Sakalava wars of expansion.[55] These observations, combined with descriptions of the growing popularity of guns on the island in general, might suggest that the Sakalava rulers used guns both to consolidate control on the west coast of Madagascar as well as to continue to acquire slaves for export.[56] Likewise, the development of the Betsimisaraka state coincided with a sudden, strong demand for firearms in return for slaves.[57] Upon closer investigation, however, these importations of firearms were only loosely associated with the expansion of Sakalava and Betsimisaraka power.[58] It is true that the development of these states initially destabilized communities throughout the island and produced a large number of captives for sale in the ports of both coasts. The ability of the Sakalava rulers to dominate ports in the north, for instance, helps to explain the brief but voluminous traffic with European and American slavers in slaves from the northwest ports around the end of the seventeenth century. Wars on the east coast also resulted in plentiful slaves for the French in the 1720s and 1730s, but not in subsequent decades.[59]

This trend, though, could also reflect an overall lack of food for sale as battles disrupted cultivation and harvests, as French observations reveal.[60] Instead of selling food in years of shortages, captives, obtained through warfare or other means, were sold for imports. Furthermore,

more than one European visitor to the island noted that men were frequently killed in battle, with the women and children kept alive and enslaved.[61] While this was not a universal practice, it does suggest, given the potential for sale of male captives to European slavers, a more complicated picture of slave procurement than a simple gun-slave cycle. Perhaps in years of need, instead of being killed, these captives would be retained to be sold to the French or other slave traders. This situation seems to have transformed significantly by the second half of the eighteenth century, when captives were kept to perform agricultural and pastoral work.[62] Furthermore, even with the continued importation of firearms, there was a dramatic reduction in the number of slaves available for sale on both coasts, even as there was evidence of warfare in the interior of the island, at the borders of Sakalava and Betsimisaraka control.[63] For instance, in 1734 an English slaver was told that the king of Toliara was at war and would return shortly with a large number of slaves for sale. The English only managed to purchase twenty-nine before departing several weeks later.[64]

It seems that most islanders were not armed with guns during the early conflicts of state expansion, especially during the initial battles for control. The Sakalava rulers in particular lacked reliable sources for gunpowder and bullets until the second half of the seventeenth century, by which point they had already gained control over most of the western ports on the island. Only during the mid to late eighteenth century does limited evidence surface, such as that described in the visit of the *Brack,* of the use of guns for military purposes. In fact, guns were not responsible for the expansion of warfare on the island, but their amassing was more likely a by-product of state centralization.[65] European observations describe how firearms were symbolic of ritual power in Madagascar, as they were used as early as 1715 in Sakalava royal ceremonies and continued to be a major part of royal funerary rituals throughout the eighteenth century.[66] When Europeans arrived on the shores of Madagascar, they were greeted by rulers accompanied by a large number of men armed with guns, and rulers repeatedly demonstrated their mastery of European weaponry by noting the type and quality of guns they desired.[67] In addition, the most valuable guns on the entire west coast were decorated arms, valued more for their appearance than utility, a fact that backs up Gerald Berg's argument that guns were symbolically powerful in Madagascar.[68] These guns would be used to decorate the walls of a king's palace or to menace enemies, not fired in battle.[69]

It is unclear how many slaves were produced from Madagascar directly through battle, as there were other mechanisms in place to enslave islanders, particularly on the west coast. European observations suggest that people were being enslaved for violating royal injunctions (including those around the killing of livestock, particularly cattle), not seized in war, and transported via long-distance trade routes that moved slaves from the interior of the island.[70] Some may have been enslaved under the suspicion of witchcraft.[71] One late eighteenth-century Frenchman stated that, following the administration of the *tanguin* poison ritual, in which a deadly poison was given to those suspected of crimes, the former dependents of the deceased would be enslaved by the local leader and could be sold to Europeans.[72] Reportedly, only those who owned slaves and cattle in southeastern Madagascar had to participate in the ingesting of tanguin.[73] All of these mechanisms for enslavement point to a more complex path to slavery than suggested by a gun-slave cycle. Indeed, these mechanisms echo social-control practices found elsewhere in Africa, including on the Upper Guinea coast, where the enslavement of suspected witches became more common during this same period.[74]

## SILVER FOR SLAVES

The greatest argument against a gun-slave cycle in Madagascar, however, is the major shift in slave pricing by around the middle of the eighteenth century, as coastal rulers began to demand silver coins, not guns, in return for slaves.[75] The French in particular were shocked by this development, as it dramatically increased the cost of slaving in eastern Madagascar. Gradually this pricing extended to food as well. In 1768, Pierre Poivre began a letter to the French governor-general of the Mascarene Islands, Pierre-Benoît Dumas, by describing the trade at Foulpointe. Having recently become administrator of the islands of Mauritius and Réunion, Poivre observed with surprise that French merchants could no longer make their purchases with cheap guns and poor-quality gunpowder. Instead they had to purchase not only slaves but also provisions with silver coins. He observed that "In all this time, we never traded for cattle and rice at Foulpointe except with trading goods . . . only slaves were purchased with piastres [silver coins]."[76]

Poivre argued that this development had already resulted in a major drain of specie from the French islands and the expense associated with buying food and provisions from Madagascar would only get worse in the future.[77]

French observers traced this dramatic shift to the influence of trade networks throughout the Indian Ocean basin, where silver was already a valued commodity well before the eighteenth century.[78] Certainly, by the mid to late eighteenth century, silver coins were part of the transfer of cloth for slaves on the east coast of Africa, according to historian Pedro Machado.[79] World historians have recently argued that flows of silver from the Atlantic into the Indian Ocean served to create "a highly integrated global economy" as early as the sixteenth century. These historians argue convincingly that silver played a unique role in forging permanent trading connections between the Americas and Asia.[80] In addition to being transported from Peru to China, silver was also widely circulated along the Indian Ocean littoral, from the Middle East to Southeast Asia, by the sixteenth century, and then into East Africa. As Machado argues, the movement of silver into East Africa has been frequently overlooked by scholars interested in the circulation of coins into South Asia, but was important to the expansion of commerce within the region.[81] Likewise, despite living on the fringes of trade networks that crossed the Indian Ocean, communities on Madagascar were also becoming integrated into global markets through the use of silver.

Europeans had been using silver to purchase provisions much earlier in the Comoros archipelago, where Europeans describe "pieces of eight being our best barter" in buying food as early as 1636.[82] By 1700, English and French traders consistently used coins while refreshing their ships at Ndzuwani.[83] During a French visit to the small island in 1767, for instance, a bullock cost five reales, a goat was a single real, and thirty small fowl could be bought with one real.[84] Likewise, the only region where silver coins were routinely accepted in return for slaves during the seventeenth century was in the northwest of Madagascar.[85] In 1676, when a Dutch slaving vessel returned to the Cape from the northwestern bays of "Magelage and Marangaan" with 254 slaves, the slavers on board reported that the "nation is very strict on cash, without which no slave can be obtained there. They only accepted Mexican dollars, which they weigh on receipt, to see whether the weight agrees with their fancy. If not, they reject it, hence, if they [the Dutch officers] had been sufficiently provided with the aforesaid heavy standard coin, they would have been able to buy more slaves."[86]

Despite the early demand for silver in northwestern Madagascar, it was not until around 1750 that silver coins became the primary commodity for purchasing slaves from the opposite coast of the island. In 1748, an English trader complained he could not purchase any slaves on the east coast, as he had "only old trading guns, coarse red & blue Europe cloth . . . & arrack," as would be typical for trading on the island, not the silver coins he was told he had to use in Foulpointe.[87] By 1760, the French likewise reported that leaders from Antongil Bay, Foulpointe, and Nosy Boraha accepted no other commodities for slaves.[88] Even communities to the far southeast of the island, near Taolagnaro, began asking for coins around 1768.[89] Throughout the late eighteenth century, reales were being used within markets on the east coast of Madagascar in purchasing locally produced bark cloth, valued at two or three coins per piece.[90]

The only part of the island in which the demand for firearms, gunpowder, flints, and bullets remained high throughout the entire century—one of frequent warfare—was to the southwest, produced by the continued desire of groups in the interior, such as the Androy, to possess guns. Archeological digs have revealed considerable stores of gun flints in the south of Madagascar, suggesting that rudimentary firearms were used extensively there well into the nineteenth century.[91] Even in Saint Augustin Bay and Toliara, coins were sometimes desired by slave traders, as is clear in the experience of the *Brack*.[92] Further north along the west coast, prices for slaves in Morondava and Mahajanga could be given in either silver coins or a combination of silver and guns. For example, in 1773, the Dutch found that they could buy slaves on the northwest coast using 35 reales, or 20 reales plus some gunpowder, or 15 reales and a single gun.[93] West coast rulers presumably could obtain silver coins (necessary in purchasing goods from Africa and Asia) from other parts of the island, and relied upon Europeans for firearms that would then be sold in the interior in return for food supplies or slaves.[94]

In spite of the intermittent demand for firearms, coins had become important to Sakalava royalty. In 1726, one visitor to Morondava observed that "They put a great value upon their pieces of eight and imperial dollars, and I believe the K[ing of Morondava] has got most of them into his hands, for few of them are to be got but from the King or his people."[95] This description suggests that the circulation of coins throughout the west coast was monopolized by Sakalava royalty and elites beginning in the early eighteenth century. Silver coins were still used for ceremonial purposes in western Madagascar well into the twentieth century.[96] Such practices echo those of Atlantic West Africa, where commodities imported in return for slaves became a "part of the creative appropriation of the foreign," according to historian Lisa Lindsay.[97] Anthropologist Zoë Crossland describes a similar appropriation in the nineteenth-century highlands of Madagascar, where the European presence was co-opted "into strategies of prestige building by indigenous elites."[98] Royal control over silver coins and guns was used to bolster Sakalava political and economic power, just as elites deployed Western dress, language, and titles to maintain dominance over trading rituals. More importantly, silver coins were also used as a form of currency and enabled the rulers to access long-distance exchange networks throughout the island by the mid-eighteenth century.

Slaves were expensive for European slavers not only because they were now calculated in silver coins, but also because the number of coins required for slave purchases increased by the close of the eighteenth century. The price varied somewhat in eastern Madagascar ports from voyage to voyage and port to port, but trading records reveal that the price for a young male slave on the east coast of the island gradually rose from about 10 silver coins in 1765 to 20 in 1774, and finally 52 in 1792.[99] On the northwest coast the price was steadier, ranging from 25 to 35 coins per slave between 1753 and 1775.[100] The price for a slave in northwestern Madagascar closely approximated the amount that the Dutch paid at Kilwa Island off the coast of Africa in 1777: 25 silver coins for an adult male slave.[101]

The rising price for slaves on the east coast of Madagascar may have been driven, at least initially, by high French demand.[102] Given the desperation of the French for food and laborers, coastal rulers knew that they could set high prices for their slaves. During the 1760s, when it became apparent that islanders were uninterested in other commodities, the French were initially happy to acquiesce in providing silver, particularly since they had long worried that the firearms they sold on the island could be turned against them.[103] The flow of silver into the east coast continued unabated throughout this decade, following the sudden increase in slaving from Madagascar after the introduction of royal rule on the Mascarene Islands and the opening of trade to all French nationals in 1769.[104] After this date, fewer slave cargoes arrived in the islands from Madagascar and, more significantly, the cargoes that did arrive were substantially smaller in size than those from East Africa at the close of the eighteenth century.[105] In 1773, following the end of a brief interdiction against the slave trade from Madagascar, the French again provided silver through their slave merchants on the east coast of Madagascar, although frequently they found only a few slaves available for purchase.[106] Note that, as Poivre's complaints attest, throughout this entire period the French were also using silver to buy provisions from eastern Madagascar.

In contrast to rising prices in eastern Madagascar, the similarity of pricing for slaves in western Madagascar and on the east coast of the African continent reveals the convergence of slave values across the Mozambique Channel by the late eighteenth century. European observations note that slaves were being imported into Madagascar from East Africa through the northwest ports by 1774.[107] During this period of "New Slavery," as historian R. J. Barendse describes the late eighteenth century, slave merchants in Madagascar joined those from Oman, the Mascarenes, and southern Africa in purchasing East African laborers.[108] Europeans noted that the importation of "Makoa" and "Mozambique" African slaves into northwestern Madagascar picked up around 1780. By 1807, an estimated one thousand "black Africans" had been brought into the island. Some of these slaves were sold to highland communities, others made their way to French vessels on the east coast, and the remainder stayed in the northwest of Madagascar.[109]

This commerce was enabled by the arrival of new merchant groups on the northwest coast of Madagascar. According to Sakalava traditions, the Sakalava queen Ravahiny, who ruled over Boina, spent the last decades of the eighteenth century ushering in a dramatic increase in trade between northwestern Madagascar and Arabia, East Africa, and the Comoros. In the northwest ports, especially Mahajanga, Karany and Banian merchants from Asia funded and organized trade under the supervision of the Sakalava, as they also financed the expansion of commercial networks crossing the Indian Ocean and the Mozambique Channel.[110] These merchants had connections throughout the ocean, including in East Africa, enabling the flow of East African slave laborers into Madagascar.[111] French observations also suggest that Sakalava rulers and their representatives became more involved in exchanges within the island, including selling cattle and raffia cloth far into the interior of Madagascar, both commodities priced in silver coins.[112] Some Frenchmen believed that merchants in Foulpointe and Taolagnaro were using silver coins to buy cloth from Arab traders, but it seems far more likely they used the coins to purchase goods within Madagascar itself.[113]

There were also dramatic political developments occurring within the interior of Madagascar, although it took Europeans several decades to perceive them, that contributed to the rising desire for silver coins on the east coast and the integration of internal markets throughout the island. Throughout the seventeenth century, the interior was home to several kingdoms. The people in this fertile, rice-producing region had long engaged in regular trade with groups on both coasts, to whom they sold not only rice, cattle, and slaves, but also silk, iron tools, cloth, and jewelry. In fact, some of the leaders in the highlands may have been related, by blood or alliance, to the Sakalava kingdom at Menabe to which they owed tribute payments.[114] Starting around the mid-eighteenth century, these divided kingdoms were uniting into an expansive military state and its rulers would control much of the island's commerce by the middle of the nineteenth century.[115]

In 1777, when the French translator and merchant Nicolas Mayeur visited the "Ancove" kingdom, he discovered that the markets of the interior functioned through the exchange of *vakim-bola* (broken money) made from pieces of French silver coins. The people had developed a highly sophisticated trading system in which pieces of silver coins were weighed with grains of rice, with a whole coin weighing 720 grains of rice, half a coin 360 grains, and so on. Mayeur also noted that all free people were taxed half a silver coin by their king, Andrianamboatsimarofy, annually.[116] As on the west coast, control over the circulation of silver coins was a royal prerogative.[117] The coins contributed to the expansion of a monetary exchange economy dominated by the king, but they were not only used to buy slaves and pay taxes. As Crossland argues, coins also would become symbolically powerful, with uncut coins signifying the unity of the kingdom and the unbroken power of the monarch.[118] It seems unlikely that the increasing power of the highland kingdom and rising prices for slaves in eastern Madagascar were unrelated, particularly as silver was a means to support the kingdom's growing power and slave labor was essential to the transformation of the interior into highly productive rice fields.[119]

Silver had reached the interior highlands of Madagascar from both coasts of the island through the slave trade. Highland slaves were likely sold on the east coast of Madagascar by the early 1760s and this trade continued into the 1770s, with the silver used in purchasing these captives flowing far into the island's interior.[120] In 1817, the British noted that slaves on Mauritius included people from Madagascar who identified as Ambanivolo, Amboalambo, Andrantsay, Antaisaka, Antaloatra, Antanosy, Antatsimo, Betanimena, Maninga, Marvace, and Sakalava.[121] In spite of the challenges posed in deciphering these (adopted or ascribed) identities, their diversity suggests that a variety of groups on the island were vulnerable to enslavement by the early nineteenth century, including those in the highlands.

The economic integration of the island was thus accomplished, at least in part, through the threat of violence. By the time Mayeur returned to the highlands in 1785, the king was using military force to access the coastal commerce previously dominated by the rather weak Betsimisaraka state at Foulpointe. Mayeur described the highland king as commanding an army of at least two thousand armed men who were prepared to pillage villages near the east coast of the island for food and captives.[122] He noted that the highlanders had superior military tactics that contributed to quick victories over coastal populations.[123] By the close of the century, the highland king Andrianampoinimerina had directed his slave exports to Toamasina to circumvent the Betsimisaraka king.[124] His troops were also beginning to encroach upon the border regions of the Sakalava kingdoms, regions that Sakalava leaders relied upon for trade and tribute, as he redirected the trade of the interior away from Sakalava-controlled ports.[125] Yet, despite the constant wars fought in the highlands, the primary commodities traded in the capital, Antananarivo, were silver coins, not guns. While guns were still desired and could be purchased via coastal merchants, silver coins propelled the expansion of these internal long-distance trade routes stretching across Madagascar.[126] Only after considerable training and the importation of more advanced weaponry during the nineteenth century did firearms decisively turn the tide of political power on the island.[127]

Alongside these seismic economic and political shifts, new resident merchants arrived in eastern Madagascar, just as they had on the northwest coast. These merchants were also seeking to expand their trading presence in the southwestern Indian Ocean, with the entire region in the midst of a massive commercial expansion.[128] Unlike on the west coast of Madagascar, the new merchants on the east coast were primarily French, as officials in the Mascarenes attempted once again to provide stability to the slave and provisioning trades from Madagascar. French merchants, in a far less centralized manner than in earlier years, had established trading posts along the east coast, including at Foulpointe, Nosy Boraha, and Teinteingue Point, between 1790 and 1818. They also set up households along the east coast of the island from which they could benefit from ties with local communities and encourage trade.[129] By the close of the eighteenth century, French merchants also explored expanding connections with portions of southwestern Madagascar and began to purchase cattle and rice in St. Augustin Bay.[130] The most significant of these new residents were the French slavers who lived first at Foulpointe and then at Toamasina.[131] They tried to form connections with merchants in the interior of the island, effectively bypassing the Betsimisaraka, who had contributed to commercial instability throughout much of the eighteenth century.[132]

## FOOD, NOT SLAVES

How can these dramatic developments help us make sense of the declining slave trade from Madagascar? Although slave ships had carried away cargoes of several hundred slaves per vessel just years earlier, the slave trade from Madagascar to the Americas and locations within the Indian Ocean plummeted sharply after the 1730s. European sources reveal that the failure of European slaving vessels to fill their holds with enslaved individuals in the ports of Madagascar became especially apparent by the middle of the eighteenth century. Large numbers of captives could be purchased only during periods of major unrest or (likely related) food shortages, but were otherwise increasingly hard to come by and more expensive when they were available. As historian Richard Allen argues, EIC (and other European) officials attempted to maintain "a relatively high level of control" over this trade.[133] European monopoly trading companies proved unresponsive to economic and political changes within Madagascar and urged their ships to frequent the same slaving ports and strike similar deals for slaves, even when prices or supplies had shifted dramatically.[134] Slave traders were ordered to purchase large numbers of slaves during brief stays of only a few months, but they were almost always unable to fill their cargo holds. Most EIC ships, for instance, only managed to buy small cargoes of slaves (many purchasing fewer than fifty slaves per vessel) during the mid-eighteenth century, mostly from St. Augustin Bay, Toliara, Morondava, and Massaliege. Note that these purchases were still made alongside large acquisitions of rice and salted beef.[135] Despite the continued importance of the provisioning trade from western Madagascar, the EIC relied upon supplies of laborers from India and other parts of Asia for their establishments in Asia.[136]

The downturn in the slave trade occurred on both coasts of the island, suggesting that it was not merely that island merchants were redirecting supplies of coerced laborers away from the west and toward the east coast of Madagascar. The large island, as the nearest populated land to the Mascarenes, should have continued to be the primary source of slaves for the French-owned islands, but it was not. During the 1730s, several French trading vessels frequented the east coast every year, visiting especially the port of Foulpointe and others around Antongil Bay, and regularly purchased slaves along with supplies of rice and cattle, but supplies of captives were less available than they were in East Africa.[137] While the average cargo size for French vessels leaving Madagascar was 129 slaves between 1700 and 1770, this estimate included several very large cargos (over 300 slaves) loaded in western Madagascar. It was more usual for French vessels to have fewer than a hundred slaves on their return to the Mascarenes during the mid-eighteenth century.[138]

Supplies of slaves in Madagascar were even more severely restricted by the 1750s, judging by complaints made by French colonial leadership.[139] In 1767, a French governor noted that "The island of Madagascar today furnishes very few slaves" to the colonies.[140] Between 1769 and 1793, a period that J. M. Filliot has labeled "*la grande époque*" of French slave trading, few slaves were brought by the French from Madagascar.[141] The government at Mauritius had developed plans for procuring slaves from East Africa and a merchant named Jean-Vincent Morice concluded a treaty with the Sultan of Kilwa in 1776.[142] French demand contributed to a large slave traffic from East Africa to markets throughout the Indian and the Atlantic Oceans that continued into the nineteenth century.[143] Even as trade revived from eastern Madagascar following the rise of Toamasina as a slaving port, it seems that the sizes of individual cargoes of slaves from Madagascar were decreasing.[144] In 1735, the vast majority of slaves on Réunion were from Madagascar (3,855, compared to 725 Africans, 487 Indians, and 1,503 "creoles"), but this gap had closed slightly by 1765 and then even more dramatically by 1808, when there were almost twice as many slaves from the African continent as from Madagascar.[145]

Why did Europeans look for new sources for slaves and other laborers by the late eighteenth century? While it is true that the distances involved in moving laborers from Madagascar to the Americas were enough to prevent this particular traffic from being profitable, the same is not true for the trade to European establishments located within the Indian Ocean. Given the frequency of European visits to the island, the number of slaves transported from Madagascar should have been much higher, particularly if the slaving vessels dispatched to the island had been more successful in fulfilling their orders. If slaves had been cheap and readily available, there would have been little to prevent English, French, and Dutch traders from obtaining slaves alongside their regular purchases of provisions. Yet, as prices increased and the number of slaves for sale dwindled, Europeans searched for supplies of slaves elsewhere.

The desire for coins was not unrelated to this decline in slaves available for sale. Coastal merchants and leaders in Madagascar had realized that silver could also be acquired through the sale of provisions. Many of the ports of the island had been converted into food supply centers by the mid-eighteenth century and all signs pointed toward a general expansion in the intensified exploitation of land for food production.[146] Europeans described how coerced laborers, islanders as well as East Africans, were commonly engaged in agricultural tasks and cattle herding throughout the island by the close of the eighteenth century. Along the east coast and into the interior, slaves cleared, cultivated, and harvested rice fields.[147] Eighteenth-century Europeans also described how Sakalava rulers kept their "king's slaves," as they were known to the foreign observers, far in the interior, where they were engaged in herding tasks.[148] Ravahiny, the queen at Boina, reportedly owned ten thousand head of cattle, all kept in the interior and maintained by slave workers.[149] The rapid transformation of the interior of Madagascar into higher-yielding rice fields was accomplished through massive inputs of labor.[150] Even after harvest, labor was required to move the grain to the coast.[151] By the close of the eighteenth century, the price of rice was substantially cheaper from Toamasina than from other ports along the east coast of the island, due to the linking of the port with markets around Antananarivo.[152] While it is unclear that the labeling of these individuals as "slaves" was always appropriate, these coerced laborers, both slaves and other unfree laborers, contributed to a revolution in agricultural production within Madagascar in which rice, cattle, and other products were sold to coastal merchants.

The contrast between the availability of food in Madagascar and in East Africa became even more apparent when the French and Dutch turned to the African continent for laborers. As one Dutch captain explained in 1776, "the small number of slaves and the long time that on previous voyages had to be expended to acquire them on the island of Madagascar" encouraged Dutch slavers to visit "the coast of Zanguebar [Zanzibar] . . . [to purchase] a large number [of slaves] at a more reasonable price."[153] Despite this decision, the lack of food on the East African coast remained an important consideration in the pursuit of this new slave trade. A Dutch slave trader concluded in 1777 that East African slaves "are far weaker by nature than those on Madagascar. I believe that the cause of this is that Madagascar is much more plentiful in its foods, such as cattle, which are there in abundance, poultry, rice, and many sorts of good foods. In contrast, the land of Kilwa, where most of these slaves come from, is very bare, because, according to reports of people who have been there it occurs regularly that 200 at once come out of the bush to the government to sell themselves because of the famine."[154] Given this lack of provisions, the Dutch would visit western Madagascar after buying slaves in East Africa so they could obtain large amounts of food to support the crew and slaves. When the Dutch did come to Madagascar for only a few dozen slaves, they still sought to buy sizable supplies of provisions.[155] The French also purchased slaves on the East African coast but then procured provisions from western Madagascar. The slaves that were loaded in eastern Madagascar on French vessels sailed with rice, live cattle, and salted meat. As Allen explains, by the late eighteenth century and into the nineteenth century, the provisioning and slave trades from Madagascar had become "inextricably intertwined."[156]

On Madagascar, unlike in Atlantic Africa, commercial agriculture did not develop as an alternative to the slave trade but preceded and then accompanied this traffic well into the nineteenth century by virtue of the importance the island's productions had assumed in provisioning merchant and naval vessels. It was only during years of food shortages, fairly frequent in a land of cyclones and locust infestations, not to mention frequent warfare, that slave trading became a way of acquiring desirable imports. From this perspective, it is possible to understand the encounter between the French and rulers of eastern Madagascar in 1734. The rulers readily offered up supplies of captives to the French, but the French refused to purchase them as there was no rice available to feed the slaves on board the vessels.[157] It seems that, without food to sell, the leaders believed that selling their dependents would be the best way to obtain firearms.[158]

The desire for imports encouraged conflict between competing leaders and communities, conflict that was more controlled on the west than on the east coast of the island.[159] By the late eighteenth century, the importation of silver coins, necessary to expansion of commercial networks within and from the island, created a situation akin to that described by Joseph Miller in Atlantic Africa: "The quest for imports, once begun, thus tended to gain uncontrollable momentum in these areas, and the rate of importing, while not destroying local production, created a kind of political dependence on foreign trade. It accelerated to the benefit of a few African masters and merchant princes, at the expense of reducing many people to resettlement and dependency in Africa and of sending thousands of others each year to death or to enslavement in the Americas."[160] The provisioning trade may have initially enticed European slavers to visit the island, as they learned of the already existing traffic in captives from the north of the island to elsewhere in the Indian Ocean basin, but it also encouraged island leaders to sell their captives in the years when they were unable to produce enough food to sell in return for guns and coins, contributing to an atmosphere of violence and competition within the island.

# EIGHT

## Exporting Violence to the Comoros

A FLEET OF LARGE wooden outrigger canoes with dozens of armed men on each vessel approached the Comoros, just as similar fleets had in recent years. People in the higher portions of the islands had been keeping watch for their arrival, hoping to repulse the attackers. After the *Wabuki* (Malagasy) disembarked at the shores, they unleashed chaos on the islands' villages.[1] The men raided homes and fields. They took away all that they could carry, including food, but also men, women, and children, before burning what remained. After months of prolonged destruction, the Wabuki boarded the canoes again, this time with their captives, and returned to the shores of Madagascar, where they would plan future incursions. The attackers left behind communities in disarray and leaders in the Comoros sought to ransom the hostages before they were sold to slave traders visiting Madagascar's ports.[2]

These attackers arrived at the shores of the Comoro archipelago almost annually between 1790 and 1820, according to Comorian and European accounts. The sizes of their canoe fleets and the regularity of the attacks suggested an extremely high level of coordination and planning. For European observers visiting the waters around western Madagascar and the Comoros, these attacks appeared unprovoked and exceptionally violent. A British naval officer, James Prior, later described the incursions as "very remarkable" from a "nation of savages," meaning the people of Madagascar. That the islanders could launch such devastating attacks was "so strange an event in modern history as scarcely to be believed." He asserted that the British navy should be mortified that they were "excelled, in numbers at least, by African savages!"[3] Decades after the raids had ceased, the people of Madagascar were still known to some visitors as "a race of bloodthirsty and treacherous people," not to be trusted.[4] By contrast, the Ndzuwani sultan and other leaders in the Comoros were now described as "timid," along with their countrymen, who "involuntarily shudder at the name of the enemy."[5] In 1823, an Englishman visiting the Comoro Islands insisted that the islanders did not possess "sufficient courage to defend themselves, as has more than once been evinced by their dastardly conduct when attacked by the Malegash," who they passively allowed to plunder them for several decades.[6]

The raids were acts of almost unthinkable violence, perhaps produced by desperate men in search of captives to sell in return for guns or urged on by "King" Benyowsky.[7] British and French visitors to the Comoros wrote numerous reports about the devastation that the raids had wrought on the islands.[8] The sultan of Ndzuwani loudly complained to the British that many of his people had been carried off into slavery.[9] Nineteenth-century Europeans also described the population of the Comoro Islands as "evidently diminished," based on their (perhaps questionable) population estimates. Even as the French took control of Mayotte in the mid-nineteenth century, they blamed the island's low population density on the incursions.[10]

While guns and slaves may have been part of the story, it seems that the raids were an extension of much older developments, namely the continued integration of Madagascar into the economic, cultural, and political networks of the southwestern Indian Ocean region. The targeting of the Comoros was not accidental but was initially provoked by conflicts between leaders in the archipelago seeking aid from Madagascar. The history of conflict within the Comoros itself was partially rooted in the provisioning trade between Europeans and Comorians, a trade that had kept the leaders in the archipelago in close contact with suppliers of rice and cattle in northern Madagascar. The raids provoked sudden and unprecedented concern from the Portuguese, British, and French who resided in the southwestern Indian Ocean region. Their reactions to the raids were, in turn, indicative of the growing attention paid to maritime violence by European powers and their desire to curtail the activities of non-state actors. By the late eighteenth century, the preservation of peaceful trade in the waters around Madagascar had become essential to the survival of European colonies, although officials were slow to act against this new threat to regional commercial networks.

## COMORIAN PROVISIONING

The Comorian archipelago is made up of four islands located very close together, with Ndzuwani about a hundred kilometers from Mayotte and seventy kilometers from Mwali.[11] During the early nineteenth century, a European ship could travel between Ndzuwani and Mayotte in less than a day, and, on Comorian vessels, the journey was described as lasting only a day or two. Travel to East Africa or Madagascar from any of the Comorian islands only took another few days on European ships, with trips on dhows or canoes likely fairly short as well.[12] Their geographical proximity to both of these larger landmasses allowed communities in the Comoros to act as intermediaries for the frequent traffic in captives and food between East Africa and Madagascar.[13]

The history of political disputes on the four islands paralleled the conflicts that had occurred within Madagascar, as leaders in the Comoros faced similar challenges and opportunities following the introduction of European commerce. The Comoros had become centers for the provisioning trade during the seventeenth and eighteenth centuries, but there were important differences between the environments of the islands, especially in terms of agricultural productivity.[14] Ndzuwani and Mwali offered safe anchorage for large vessels, even though food supplies appeared initially to be scarcer on these two islands.[15] During the sixteenth and seventeenth centuries, Portuguese from Mozambique Island attempted to establish fueling depots in the archipelago. They eventually gave up but continued to engage in regular trade with the islanders.[16] English and French traders initially stopped at Mwali and Mayotte for supplies, but, by the eighteenth century, they relied almost entirely on Ndzuwani for fresh food and water. Their ships would stop after they had passed by Madagascar and before they caught the southern end of the monsoon winds.[17] English and French reliance on Ndzuwani for food exacerbated the differences that already existed among the islands' populations. Ndzuwani became known as a location with supplies of cattle, rice, fruit, and fresh water, all readily available, but in smaller quantities than found in nearby Madagascar. Indeed, some of the food purchased from the Comoros by Europeans had been carried from Madagascar, along with supplies of slave laborers.[18]

Despite European descriptions of their negotiations with single kings or sultans in the Comoros during provisioning visits, there were probably a number of rulers on each island, one of whom may have been paramount, controlled the major port(s), and dominated trading negotiations.[19] As in Madagascar, political disputes were common, although they seldom produced large numbers of slaves for sale.[20] Access to food supplies for export may have led to conflict between leaders on different islands. The rulers of Ndzuwani in particular claimed dominance over the other three islands and encouraged Europeans to view the people of Ndzuwani as superior to other Comorians.[21] As early as 1601, the Dutch were told that one queen on Ndzuwani controlled the other three Comorian islands, although each island had its own sovereigns who ruled through a complex arrangement of alliances.[22] The maintenance of Ndzuwani dominance required frequent military intervention and French and English visitors observed multiple armed clashes between the islands throughout the seventeenth century.[23] For instance, in 1672, John Fryer, an Englishman, wrote about the "continual war" between Ndzuwani and Mwali. The Ndzuwani ruler used to send soldiers in canoes ("planks") to fight at sea with "stones and darts," but now the Ndzuwani soldiers fought with guns obtained through trade with the English. Out of this assistance, the Ndzuwani people had developed a "more than ordinary love of the English."[24] Historians have suggested that the rulers on Ndzuwani used force to monopolize the provisioning trade in the region and discouraged Europeans from visiting other islands in the archipelago.[25] Certainly the people of Ndzuwani benefitted from their military might and managed to dominate trade within the region, much as the Sakalava rulers did on the relatively arid west coast of Madagascar.

During the eighteenth century, English and French traders continued to describe frequent battles between islanders and continual requests for help in these struggles.[26] In 1704, "Myohazeree-Hoosans," a "governor" on Ndzuwani, told the English that the people of Mwali had been his tributaries for the past four hundred years, yet he had not received payments from them recently and planned an attack to reestablish his dominance.[27] In 1736, a ruler on Ndzuwani, "Abdala," told the French that he had regained control of Mayotte but his struggles with Mwali were still ongoing.[28] Prince "Zard Mahomet," uncle to a king on Ndzuwani, told the French in 1743 that he had sent eighteen hundred men in forty vessels to force Mwali to submit but this attack had not succeeded.[29] On multiple occasions, Ndzuwani leaders asked the English for gunpowder and firearms and complained bitterly when this support was not forthcoming.[30] When an unnamed English captain failed to fulfill his promise to transport a company of Ndzuwani soldiers to Mwali, one Ndzuwani king repeatedly complained to future visitors.[31] The king must have eventually found support from the English, as he later described the English as great friends of the Ndzuwani people. He expressed his "gratitude for the effectual assistance they formerly received from them in their wars with [Mwali]."[32]

Throughout the 1780s, these conflicts continued. In 1781, a British visitor to Ndzuwani was told that the Ndzuwani ruler claimed sovereignty over the neighboring islands but he was "sometimes obliged to assert [his power] by the sword." In this year, the ruler was planning an expedition against Mayotte, "which [was] in a state of rebellion." When he was asked about the cause of the war, the sultan replied that "Mayotta [is] like America." He was likely attempting to appeal to British sympathy by referring to Mayotte as a colony of Ndzuwani.[33]

European records suggest that these conflicts were not only between island leaders. When the EIC ship *Walpole* visited Ndzuwani in 1786, the captain noted that there was "a great scarcity of bullocks and poultry owing to the country people having rebelled against the king."[34] One historian has argued that such rebellions, perhaps protesting taxation, occurred frequently throughout the 1770s and 1780s.[35] The clearing of land to expand pasturage for cattle may have further contributed to discontent, as leaders and merchants sought to acquire additional land to produce provisions for export. The expansion of royal control could have contributed to an uprising that historian Malyn Newitt describes as carrying "the hallmark of a bitter class struggle."[36] The revolt was crushed with the help of British forces, as leaders sought assistance from outside forces to resolve internal disputes once again. Even prior to the arrival of forces from Madagascar, the provisioning demands of European ships were already shaping political developments in the Comoros, as they had in neighboring Madagascar.

Eventually it was not only European trading partners, but also those on Madagascar, who were drawn into interisland conflicts. Food and slaves had been imported into the archipelago for centuries from northern Madagascar and it was to this part of the island that sultans in the Comoros turned for military assistance. The mercenaries from Madagascar were promised supplies of slaves in return for their help, or so one Ndzuwani chronicler suggests.[37]

The first raids, starting in the late eighteenth century, targeted Mayotte and Ndzuwani before spreading to the other islands and ending by 1816. According to one Comorian account, the attacks occurred repeatedly throughout these years, perhaps annually.[38] Early nineteenth-century French records note that, starting around October, different kings in Madagascar would gather armed fleets of canoes holding about thirty men each. Fleets from eastern Madagascar would head to the north, where they would recruit more soldiers, before rounding the northern end of Madagascar. The fleets from the east would then meet soldiers arriving from the west coast at Nosy Be. The attacking force was comprised of four or five hundred canoes, for a total of fifteen to eighteen thousand men.[39] The British complained that the soldiers were armed with muskets obtained from French and Arab traders, although the British had long exported guns to Madagascar as well.[40]

Contemporary accounts suggest that the raids were rather decentralized and frequently provide conflicting descriptions of the raiders' identities. One chronicler from Mayotte wrote in 1865 that the attackers were both Sakalava and Betsimisaraka.[41] Other sources identified the attackers as Betsimisaraka, Sakalava, Antankara, and Antavaratra (the latter two being groups from the north of the island).[42] Some historians believe that, given the size of the canoes used in the attacks, the Betsimisaraka of eastern Madagascar were definitely involved, in spite of the distance between the east coast of Madagascar and the Comoros.[43] During the raids, soldiers arrived in large canoes, known as *lakana* or *laka*, fitted with outriggers and perhaps sails.[44] These canoes lacked metal nails but were of "ingenious" construction and could reportedly carry a great deal of weight.[45] The Betsimisaraka, by the middle of the nineteenth century, frequently used similar canoes, measuring roughly 10 by 1.2 meters, for whale fishing.[46] Smaller canoes with both single and double outriggers were also frequently observed in use during the seventeenth and eighteenth centuries in the waters around the Comoros and near the western coast of Madagascar.[47] The canoes used in the raids were described by nineteenth-century Europeans as holding up to sixty men, although Europeans had previously observed canoes capable of carrying fewer than forty men on the east coast of Madagascar.[48] It is certainly possible that Comorians had exaggerated their reports of fleet sizes or that these canoes were of special construction to enable them to transport more passengers.[49] Although the immense number of soldiers reported as attacking the Comoros suggest involvement by the Betsimisaraka in their large canoes, this fact does not preclude Sakalava participation in the raids.[50]

Historians have disagreed over when the raids began, although evidence points to 1792 as the first year of these attacks.[51] A French captain, François Péron, reveals that a Ndzuwani king requested French assistance in his struggles against Mayotte and Mwali in 1791. In return for his assistance, the king promised him ample slaves. The captain agreed to carry three hundred Ndzuwani soldiers on his ship to Mayotte and they sailed alongside a fleet carrying a thousand more soldiers (likely in canoes or small dhows). The attack itself was a disaster, but following his defeat the king of Ndzuwani gave Péron 350 slaves as a reward for his assistance.[52] Following this unsuccessful attack, an Ndzuwani ruler reportedly formed an alliance with the Betsimisaraka for assistance the following year. This date (1792) also coincides with the first formal request for help against the attackers from a leader on Ndzuwani.[53]

In 1796, only a few years later, the eldest son of the sultan of Ndzuwani visited British officials in Bombay. He begged the British government to take control of the island and protect the islanders from "depredations committed by the inhabitants of the northern part of the island of Madagascar." The prince reminded the British of the long and peaceful history of exchanges between the British and the people of Ndzuwani. In return for granting the island to the British, the prince asked for a ship with several hundred guns and instruction on the use of these weapons.[54] After the British failed to accept this proposal, the Ndzuwani ruler again asked for help in 1798 from a British captain to arm his men against the thousands of soldiers who attacked him with French muskets (implying that the attackers were Betsimisaraka obtaining guns from the French on the east coast of the island). The British largely ignored these pleas for assistance, only providing the ruler with a few firearms. This was to become a common British response to Comorian requests.[55]

The raids that occurred between 1800 and 1816 were among the most devastating, as the fleets of canoes began traveling to East Africa and targeting portions of the coast that had historically been trading partners with communities throughout northern Madagascar.[56] It is also worth noting that this was a period of drought and warfare in the Mozambique region (between 1794 and 1802), which may have exacerbated the damage produced by the raids.[57] During these years, Ndzuwani leaders also renewed their appeals for assistance, suggesting that the attacks on the Comoros continued into the nineteenth century.[58]

Portuguese responses to the attacks provide us with some of the most detailed descriptions of the attackers. According to one Portuguese account, three boats carrying about sixty people each arrived on the coast of East Africa in 1800. The "Betsimisaraka" men robbed coastal communities of food and slaves before leaving a few months later.[59] If the soldiers were coming from Madagascar, they had crossed the Mozambique Channel, a wide body of water with unpredictable currents, to locations comparatively distant from the west coast of Madagascar (and even further from Betsimisaraka communities to the east).[60] It may have taken these fleets several weeks to cross the channel, especially if they first halted at the Comoro Islands.[61] It seems unlikely that such a lengthy voyage would have been undertaken without considerable planning and coordination.

In 1805, a fleet of large canoes again encountered Portuguese traders, this time while a merchant ship was visiting Ndzuwani. Twenty-five canoes, each holding about twenty armed men, approached the ship. The Portuguese, believing the men to be friendly, allowed them to board. The men killed many of the Portuguese and stole trading goods from the ship.[62] Portuguese rulers in Mozambique were determined to seek retribution and, the following year, they sent a ship to Ndzuwani and northern Madagascar but failed to find any more canoes.[63]

According to Portuguese records, the most ambitious attack was undertaken in 1808. After leaving Madagascar, a fleet of five hundred boats carrying eight thousand armed men split into multiple groups, with one set of canoes going to the Comoros and another to East Africa.[64] These "Sakalava" canoes landed at villages on the East African coast to the north of Mozambique. At each location, the men began attacking coastal communities, but they made little progress, in part due to an outbreak of smallpox. At Cape Delgado, the attackers "carried away all the blacks, but did not succeed in taking the fort, to which the Portuguese had retired."[65] During their trip to East Africa, the men seized eight hundred Africans and returned with them to Madagascar. Swahili traders later paid ransoms to free some of these captives at the Sakalava trading port of Bombetoc, on the west coast of Madagascar.[66] This hostage-taking mirrors descriptions of earlier actions in the Comoros, but this time the people of western Madagascar are explicitly labeled as the culprits.

In 1812, the governor of Mozambique told a British captain that, during the invasions, the Querimba Islands (to the north of Mozambique Island) had been invaded by people from Madagascar who had destroyed crops and captured slaves. The Portuguese reportedly requested assistance from the British to help defend the coast.[67] The British emphasized the weakness of the Portuguese for doing little to stop these raids, but it appears the Portuguese did try to take action.[68] The Portuguese sent a letter in 1811 to the Sakalava queen Ravahiny requesting that she put a stop to the raids in the region. The queen responded that the Ndzuwani king had provoked the raids by demanding assistance in his attacks on Mwali. Her subjects had been given permission to attack the Comoros but were not acting under her command and hence she was powerless to stop them.[69] Historian Edward Alpers has described a similar, but earlier, exchange, in which the Sakalava queen Ravahiny sent a letter in 1805 to the governor-general of Mozambique warning that a fleet of six hundred canoes had left her coast and was headed to East Africa. She insisted that these ships carried her people but were not under her control.[70]

The Ndzuwani sultan also warned the Portuguese of an imminent attack on Mozambique in 1814.[71] Although his warning proved ungrounded, it suggests that some of the attackers that travelled to East Africa had direct ties to the Comoros. The following year, several "Moors," likely East African traders, told the Portuguese that "Sakalava" soldiers were planning another visit to the coast. The Portuguese confronted the canoes as they arrived at Querimba Island. The men retreated to Madagascar.[72] Two years later, another fleet containing 150 canoes reached East Africa. The Portuguese heard that the fleet was moving south following their attack on the island of Kilwa. The fleet reached Mozambique six months later, but now consisted of seventy-one canoes. The group was led by "Prince Sicandar of Anjouan," who told the Portuguese that he was headed to battle with the shaikh of Sancul, a Swahili sultan living on the African mainland near Mozambique Island. The prince explained that they had simply gotten off-course and they meant no harm to the Portuguese or their subjects. The Portuguese leaders refused to believe him.[73]

The second part of this attacking force, likely separated in the crossing of the channel, consisted of an estimated five hundred canoes. A "Moor" named "Nassiri" commanded this fleet. His force assailed communities on Kilwa before disembarking near Mozambique Island. These men left after the Portuguese refused to abandon their fortress on the island. Later that year, Portuguese colonial officials observed about thirty-eight canoes assaulting villages along the east coast. When the canoes came close to Zanzibar, the sultan sent ships to fight against the "Sakalava" intruders, who were armed with spears. The Zanzibari soldiers fought off the invaders. After their defeat, the leader of the attackers reportedly swore that they would not return and promised they would cease attacking the "Umani [Omani] and Portuguese coasts of East Africa."[74] There were no more recorded incidences of raids on East Africa.

During this era of raids on East Africa, leaders on Ndzuwani resumed their requests for help in this "unjust war" with "the Inhabitants of Madagascar." In 1800, "Alli Abdulla King" of Ndzuwani asked for assistance from the British and offered half his island in return.[75] Only a few years later, the sultan "Syed Abdulle" traveled to Bombay in person to make his case.[76] The sultan repeatedly attempted to cede all four Comoro Islands to the British, but they dismissed his claim to the throne.[77] The British finally provided him firearms but gave no other aid.[78] Ndzuwani leaders also asked the Portuguese and French for help.[79] It appears that, given the lack of requests for help in later years, the attacks ceased in the Comoros, as they had in East Africa, by the first decades of the nineteenth century.[80]

## A PRELUDE TO THE NINETEENTH CENTURY

In the midst of the attacks, European ships continued to visit the Comoro Islands. The records left by their crew members make little or no mention of the raids, suggesting the scale of devastation may have been overstated. Few Europeans observed the attacks themselves, and, when they did mention the raids, they relied upon Comorian descriptions of the violence. For instance, in 1802 the king of Ndzuwani told the British that the people of Madagascar raided his island for slaves annually.[81] However, René-Marie Kermel, a French naval officer, described the people of Ndzuwani as constantly at war with their neighbors during the first decade of the nineteenth century, but never mentioned involvement of people from Madagascar in these conflicts.[82] This is not to say that raids did not occur during the early nineteenth century, but that they may have been more isolated and periodic than the leaders of Ndzuwani suggested in their pleas for assistance.

Furthermore, commerce continued between Madagascar, the Comoros, and East Africa in the years immediately following the raids.[83] Given that trade resumed with little fanfare and there was no mention of new attacks after 1816, were the raids on the Comoros and East Africa significant over the long term? When examined from the perspective of the nineteenth century, the violence and disorder produced in these raids was not comparable to that unleashed later within the island of Madagascar. Yet the raids themselves were a continuation of earlier pressures felt on Madagascar following the expansion of global commerce. It was unsurprising that people in coastal Madagascar tried to secure their own share of profits at the close of the eighteenth century, as markets for food and slave laborers became increasingly integrated across the Mozambique Channel. The expansion of regional networks enabled trans-Channel cooperation but also encouraged political and economic competition.

The violence produced by the Sakalava and Betsimisaraka soldiers was rapidly overshadowed by that created by the emergent Imerina state. In the early nineteenth century, Andrianampoinimerina was urged by the British to put an end to the piracy committed by the coastal populations of Madagascar.[84] When his heir, Radama I, signed a treaty with the British in 1817 agreeing to put an end to the slave trade, the treaty also included a clause in which he promised to "protect the faithful friend and ally of England, the King of Johanna [Ndzuwani], from the predatory attacks to which he has been for many years annually exposed from some of the smaller States of the sea-coast of Madagascar . . . to put a final end to this system of piracy."[85] While the raids appear to have ceased for reasons independent of Radama I's promises, the sudden assertion of control over populations on Madagascar's coasts by a leader from the highlands marked a clear political transition on the island. Radama I was poised to negotiate with European imperial forces and steadily chip away at Betsimisaraka and Sakalava control of coastal commerce. He would oversee invasions that would bring new waves of violence to communities in Madagascar.

The nineteenth century, as many examining the history of the Indian Ocean have argued, was a turning point for many populations along the ocean's littoral. Gwyn Campbell notes the development of a "truly international economy" during this century.[86] During the "steamship era" in the ocean, especially after 1869 and the opening of the Suez Canal, Europeans benefited from increased ease of trade and communication throughout the ocean.[87] Steamships, like European sailing vessels, had specific requirements for refueling and refilling throughout the ocean and fulfilling these needs led to the development of new European fueling stations, such as those in Aden, Karachi, Mombasa, and Bombay.[88] In these ports, smaller ships, such as dhows, helped supply the visiting steamships with not just food but also coal by the end of the century.[89] The use of steamships not only influenced European travel but also enabled cheaper travel throughout the Indian Ocean.[90] The use of the steamship, as historian Erik Gilbert argues, changed the relationship between the coast and interior of East Africa, fueling a "region-wide commercial expansion" that resulted in the export of ivory, slaves, and spices from East Africa and the expansion of plantations in East Africa during the nineteenth century.[91]

The nineteenth century also ushered in a new era for merchants visiting ports in Madagascar.[92] For the first time, a diverse group of merchants, from Europe, North America, Africa, and Asia, established permanent trading posts, negotiated long-lasting treaties, and attempted to directly shape the economic development of the island. The dramatic events of the nineteenth century in Madagascar were influenced by the presence of French and British merchants on the shores of the island, especially after British abolitionist policies began to influence their relationship with island leaders. The British occupied the Cape Colony, formerly a refueling hub for the Dutch East India Company, in 1795, and British control over Mauritius was formalized in the Treaty of Paris in 1814.[93] Given these changes, there were more British ships in the ocean but fewer of them chose to stop in western Madagascar after 1810. Instead they came to the eastern side of the island.

The first hint of a shift in British policy occurred in 1811, when a British fleet arrived and seized control of the French trading fort at Toamasina. Although the presence of British soldiers was short-lived, this attempt to secure resources on the east coast of Madagascar demonstrated how important the island had become to British plans for the Indian Ocean.[94] Only a few years later, the British governor at Mauritius decided to send representatives to discuss the British position against the slave trade with the ruler of Toamasina, Jean-René, and the Betsimisaraka king at Foulpointe, Tsiririlaza.[95] As historian Ranaivo Ratsivalaka has argued, the British constrained their diplomacy to the coast during their initial encounters in Madagascar.[96] It was unsurprising that the British targeted Toamasina, as this had become a major slaving port by the early nineteenth century. In 1817, Radama I's forces descended on Toamasina and shortly thereafter he asserted control of the port. After Radama I sent his own representatives to Mauritius, negotiations began in earnest for a treaty between rulers in Madagascar and the British to suppress slave trading.[97]

Given British investment in the provisioning trade of eastern Madagascar, some expressed a hope that ending the slave trade would provide increased stability to the exports of the island. For example, Samuel Copland wrote in 1822 that "Agriculture is yet in its infancy in Madagascar, notwithstanding it is extensively practised."[98] He blamed the reliance on slave labor, the lack of regular ownership of land, and widespread "civil discord" for the failure of coastal communities to advance in their agricultural practices. He described islanders as simply reacting to external demands for food exports and failing to prepare for the "frequent arrival of ships" by stockpiling provisions.[99] Copland also argued that the slave trade (introduced by the French, he believed) had significantly depressed population sizes on the island, and, hence, the productivity of local communities. The slave trade had "desolated that beautiful country; turning a garden into a wilderness, and the habitations of man into a retreat for wild beasts."[100] The ending of this traffic would return prosperity to island populations, he reasoned, and restore agricultural productivity.

Copland's perceptions of the island hearken back to those of sixteenth- and seventeenth-century Europeans who had viewed Madagascar as an undeveloped Eden, but these hopes for Madagascar were not simply the preserve of European abolitionists. Radama I also proclaimed that he sought help from the governor of Mauritius not only to increase "arts and industry" and provide military aid, but also to "prevent famine, by more extensive cultivation."[101] He continued, "Let my Subjects then who have Slaves, employ them in planting rice and other provisions, and in taking care of their flocks, in collecting bees-wax and gums, and in manufacturing cloths and other articles which they can sell."[102] His words thus echoed those of Copland, expressing a hope that he would be able to encourage the greater production of other commodities, including foodstuffs, for domestic consumption as well as for export.

Despite the challenges that Radama I and future Imerina leaders would face in securing labor to increase production on the island, the export of provisions from Madagascar's shores continued unabated.[103] Toamasina remained a center for commerce on the east coast of Madagascar and, in 1825, Radama I seized control of Mahajanga, the former export center on the northwestern coast.[104] Following the attack, an estimated ten thousand Sakalava and Antaloatra fled in dhows and canoes for the islands of the Comoro archipelago.[105] A fortress was constructed in Mahajanga for the newly appointed Merina governor and his soldiers. Following this military campaign, it was decreed that all export trade from Madagascar was to go through Merina-controlled ports, especially Mahajanga and Toamasina, so the governors could collect trading duties from passing ships.[106] Other merchants in western Madagascar were outlawed from participating in foreign trade, although some small-scale commerce continued, particularly in salted beef and hides, but also provisions.[107]

French officials in Réunion decided to make themselves a permanent presence on Madagascar by colonizing Nosy Boraha in 1818 and seeking to maintain small trading posts on the east coast of the island.[108] The French also took advantage of disorder in the Comoros and northwestern Madagascar to gain control of Mayotte and Nosy Be in 1841.[109] Originally, these French establishments were intended to make it easier and cheaper for the French to secure supplies of food for their settlements on Réunion, as the ports of Mauritius as well as those of Merina-controlled Madagascar taxed provisions at a high rate.[110] French colonists constantly dealt with labor shortages, as early as the 1820s on Nosy Boraha and after 1841 in other colonies.[111] Eventually the French attempted to address the labor shortage by acquiring *engagé* (contract) labor from East Africa, Madagascar, and the Comoro Islands between 1850 and 1880.[112]

Even with the vast changes occurring in and around Madagascar throughout the nineteenth century, the maintenance and growth of trans–Mozambique Channel trade, particularly in slaves, suggest that the impact of these European interventions was only gradually felt in the region, perhaps only by the late nineteenth century, following French conquest. By the mid-nineteenth century, coastal trade shifted to frequent but shorter visits of ships on regular trading missions to supply European colonies, most of which had official trading representatives residing in Madagascar in both Merina-controlled and independent ports. These European, African, Comorian, Arab, and Indian merchants gradually exercised greater influence on the exchanges on the coast of the island, asserting monopolies over exports of both provisions and commodities.[113]

# NINE

## From Feasts to Famine

THE PEOPLE WHO LIVE on the island of Madagascar today are some of the poorest in the world. One of the most pressing issues on the island is that of food insecurity, ironic in a land historically known to be one of plenty. In 2010, researchers from the United Nations Children's Fund (UNICEF) and the World Food Programme (WFP) published a study in which they concluded that more than a third of Malagasy households were "food insecure" and close to half were "vulnerable to food insecurity." Fewer than 20 percent were deemed "food secure," in other words, able to reliably obtain or purchase food throughout the year.[1] Chronic malnutrition impacts almost half of Madagascar's children. Difficulty in obtaining food varies seasonally throughout the island and the UNICEF and WFP study also notes that direct access to food, or the cash to purchase it, is distributed highly unevenly throughout Madagascar, with the populations most vulnerable to food shortages living in the south or southwest. Researchers concluded that as few as 13 percent of people in the far south had access to improved water sources during the dry season.[2] Some coastal communities also struggle to survive in the years when cyclones hit eastern Madagascar.[3] The WFP estimates that more than 70 percent of the island's population lives below the national poverty line and, in 2014, Madagascar ranked 154th out of 188 countries in the United Nations Development Programme's Human Development Index (based on a combination of economic, educational, and medical indicators).[4]

The study suggests that frequent environmental disasters, including droughts, cyclones, and locust invasions, coupled with recurrent political crises, have driven families in Madagascar, many of whom were already suffering from a poor diet, to the brink of starvation in recent years, even while "large areas of Madagascar's fertile lands remain unfarmed."[5] The WFP identifies two chronic challenges for the Malagasy: environmental degradation and political instability. In their discussion of Madagascar's natural disasters, they place much of the blame on impoverished rural Malagasy, citing that "85 percent of Madagascar's rainforest has been lost to logging, charcoal-making and slash-and-burn agriculture."[6] The WFP cites this number, even though many scholars have cast doubt on both the 85 percent figure and simplistic narratives of deforestation that place the blame on the shoulders of rural cultivators, rather than considering the deleterious roles played by other actors, including national and international conglomerates.[7] Blaming contemporary food insecurity on Malagasy land-management techniques is shortsighted. The history of postindependence Madagascar suggests that the second of the two problems described by the WFP, political instability, has truly exacerbated conditions of systemic poverty on the island.

Widespread and chronic food shortages on Madagascar appear to be a relatively late development, although, as this book argues, not all communities on the island consistently produced agricultural surpluses prior to the twentieth century. To the contrary, as eighteenth-century French merchants observed during their visits, many island communities experienced famine in the years following environmental disasters. Enslavement would increase sharply after cyclones had battered the island, as Mascarene slavers bemoaned the lack of food to feed the people they could easily purchase during their visits. Did political conflicts create the food shortages the French found in eastern Madagascar or were the wars in fact struggles over scarce resources in years of environmental crisis? It appears impossible to fully disentangle the relationship between natural disasters, political violence, and food shortages in eighteenth-century Madagascar.

Likewise, French and English settlers discovered that the arid south and southwest portions of the island were not conducive to widespread cultivation of grains except along the banks of certain rivers. Their observations suggest that frequent migration enabled survival in tenuous circumstances, where access to water for livestock and crops could be uncertain. Islanders also consumed roots, locusts, and wild game in challenging years. Even during times of plenty, when communities could produce or purchase ample food, access to a rich and varied diet may have been an elite privilege, as it is today. The sale of food in St. Augustin Bay to passing European vessels does not mean that most of the people of the bay regularly consumed the rice that had to be obtained from a distance in the interior. The annual export of provisions does not mean that subsistence needs were met for all in eighteenth-century Madagascar.

In spite of these caveats, the historical record suggests that food shortages tended to be short-lived and regional during peacetime prior to the twentieth century.[8] Conditions of scarcity, rooted in natural phenomena, were exacerbated by the violence of European imperialism, as they were elsewhere in Africa. Following the imposition of French colonial rule on the island and years of intense resistance, thousands of Malagasy died of disease and famine, even as the exports of agricultural products from Madagascar continued unabated.[9] As the French colonial government sought to expand their dominion over the far south of the island in the early years of the twentieth century, they explored different strategies to create a stable and productive workforce in the region. Several of the colonial leaders identified the widespread adoption of prickly pear cactus as hindering their efforts. This "cactus pastoralism," to borrow Jeffrey Kaufmann's phrasing, enabled cattle herders in the south of the island to develop large stands of cacti that served as fodder and water sources in the arid region.[10] After the arrival of cochineal insects to the island, likely introduced with French assistance, these cactus stands were rapidly wiped out. While scholars may debate the extent of the resulting crisis, the event likely resulted in the death of many cattle and people.[11] In an echo of the years when food shortages drove islanders into slavery, migrants from Antandroy arrived in the French-controlled cities of Toliara and Taolagnaro seeking work and some even traveled as laborers to Réunion.[12] The victims of this environmental disaster were in the south, among the poorest of the poor, highlighting an inequality of access to quality food that continued into the colonial period. Following these challenges, French imperialists continued to implement a series of inept plans aimed at transforming an island of small-scale agriculturalists and herders into productive workers.[13] These efforts coincided with a burgeoning interest in environmentalism that was designed to improve production in Madagascar, but also served to diminish local control and access to land.[14]

The postcolonial state has also struggled with how to deal with unrest in the south, in part provoked by its dry climate, as well as how to grapple with international imaginings of the island and how they contrast with the reality for small landholders on Madagascar.[15] In general, African politics are increasingly shaped by food scarcity and Madagascar is no exception.[16] Rice in particular is an essential part of the livelihoods of so many on the island, where "*vary ny politika*" (rice is politics).[17] For many islanders, rice is not simply a food but a way of life and essential for survival. In fact, Madagascar is one of the highest per capita consumers of rice in the world. By the close of the twentieth century, over half of the agricultural lands on the island grew rice.[18] Yet despite the prevalence of small-scale farming on the island, Madagascar's markets currently sell large amounts of imported Asian rice to feed their populations. Madagascar had been a net exporter of food items throughout the colonial and postcolonial period until 1973. Many economists blame the shift toward nationalization in the 1970s and resulting political crises for the downward spiral in agricultural production on the island, although the international situation of the 1970s and 1980s also made it challenging for the country's economy to recover.[19] Unfortunately, many households lack the income to buy the necessary quantities of rice to make up for shortfalls in production and feed their families. The economic challenges the islanders face are exacerbated by political instability and the related lack of international investment and aid to Madagascar. Postcolonial government attempts at storing a quantity of rice to protect against price fluctuations have been fairly unsuccessful.[20] As a result, when droughts and locust invasions threaten harvests, the infrastructure to identify these crises and distribute aid is lacking, increasing the chances of a small food shortage transforming into widespread famine.[21]

Uncovering the causes of systemic impoverishment and food insecurity are beyond the scope of this project but it is worth noting that the long history of food production and export from the island, shaped by distinct geographies, survival strategies, and the use of unfree labor, has left its imprint on Madagascar. A recent edited collection examining the challenges facing conservation efforts in Madagascar includes a timeline of "significant political and economic events" on the island, but it begins in 1817 with the signing of the treaty between Great Britain and Radama I.[22] What would happen if we looked several centuries earlier (as some of the contributions in the collection do)? If the timeline began with the first major purchase of rice and cattle by Europeans? With the first sale of islanders as slaves? With the importation of East African slaves into the island? Major shifts in land use in reaction to internal developments, including population growth and the adoption of new crops and agricultural practices, and external ones, such as the pressures and opportunities presented by foreign trade, were not nineteenth- or twentieth-century innovations. Nor was the unequal allocation of benefits from the land. Debates over regional inequality in particular have prompted political upheaval at regular intervals in modern Madagascar. As historians Solofo Randrianja and Stephen Ellis argue, "We need to ask whether such regional differences today are greater or smaller than they were in the past."[23] We can only address this issue by looking at the earlier history of land and labor use in Madagascar.

Understandings of land in Madagascar are increasingly linked to complicated international attitudes toward conservation and development, attitudes that are often constructed at a great distance from the island itself. As Ivan Scales argues, the importance to the island of these "global political and economic processes" is only growing.[24] A 1990–2000 maize boom, for instance, contributed to forest clearance around Toliara following high demand for the crop from Réunion. As in earlier centuries, migrant labor was essential in producing a deforested landscape and the expansion in cultivation around Toliara. Even after the downturn in demand for maize, the linking of southwestern Madagascar to national and international commodity markets had a lasting impact on economic processes in the area, just as the pressures to produce food for export had marked the land in earlier centuries.[25] It makes sense to look at the roots of these interactions, which serve as a reminder that responsiveness to external changes is not new, even in seemingly isolated Madagascar.

The long history of provisioning also reminds us that, despite current conditions of scarcity, the island was once a center of rice and cattle exports in the Indian Ocean. But Madagascar was far from the only exporter of food items intended to feed sailors and slaves on board transoceanic vessels. For every ship that came to anchor off Madagascar's shoreline, several others called at Ndzuwani, St. Helena Island, and the Cape of Good Hope. During the seventeenth century, these locations became centers for producing and selling specific food items that kept well at sea and effectively powered the bodies of maritime laborers. While certainly less noticeable in metropolitan records than the valuable purchases of silks and cloves, access to the right provisions meant life or death for many sailors and slaves. The resources that went into fueling long-distance trade have largely gone unnoticed by historians, despite a growing interest in the global exchange of commodities and the environmental ramifications of their production. If the annual visits of several European vessels to the island of Madagascar had an impact on coastal communities there, how did the people of Cape Town, Jakarta, or Colombo deal with the arrival of a dozen or more such ships a year? How was food produced or obtained? Whose labor was necessary to produce supplies for the European merchant fleets that connected the globe during the seventeenth and eighteenth centuries? Each location likely had different strategies for securing the bread and rice sought after by Europeans, but, in each case, the arrival of trading vessels introduced new pressures and opportunities for coastal communities and their leaders. Only by addressing these questions can historians fully understand the scale and impact of commerce during the years that first brought people living along the shores of the Atlantic and Indian Oceans into direct and frequent contact.

# Appendix

## *Sources for Figures*

### Figure 2.1: Dutch VOC ships visiting Madagascar, by decade, 1590–1780

From Nationaal Archief, The Hague: VOC 1.04.02/2217; VOC 1.04.02/4280; VOC 1.04.02/4245; VOC 1.04.02/10811.

From Archives of the Western Cape: C 2338; C 2247; C 2248; C 2250; C 2251; C 2253; C 2254; C 2255; C 551.

Leibbrandt: *Precis . . . Riebeeck's Journal,* 56, 207; *Precis . . . Letters Dispatched, 1696,* 5–6, 34, 65, 119–21, 266, 278, 318; *Precis . . . Letters Received, 1695,* 24; *Precis . . . Journal, 1662,* 85, 127–29, 196–200, 238–39; *Precis . . . Journal, 1671,* 98, 116–17, 301.

*COACM,* 3:191, 197, 203–6, 382; 5:15; Heeringa, "De Nederlanders," 885; Armstrong, "Madagascar and the Slave Trade," 215–31; Bruijn, Gaastra, and Schöffer, *Dutch-Asiatic Shipping,* 2:2–11, 14–19, 26–39, 42–43, 58–59, 80–81, 96–97, 114–15, 158–59, 176–77, 196–97, 206–9, 218–21, 344–45, 420–21, 540–41, 712–13; 3:10–11, 16–17, 26–29, 34–35, 66–67, 70–71; Armstrong and Worden, "Slaves," 114–19; van Duivenvoorde, *Dutch East India Company Shipbuilding,* 198–99.

### Figure 2.3: French visits to Madagascar, by decade, 1600–1700

From Archives nationales, Paris: COL C/5A/1; COL C/2/2; COL C/2/3; MAR 4JJ/86; MAR B/4/4; MAR 4JJ/90; MAR 4JJ/125; COL C/3/3; MAR 4JJ/88.

Galaisière, *Voyage,* 373, 376, 383; Lougnon, *Correspondance,* 1:13, 161; 2:20, 67, 69–70, 110, 141–45, 147, 155, 320; Flacourt, *Histoire,* 266–74, 279–85; Ames, *Colbert,* 9, 35–37, 90–98; Allen, *European Slave Trading,* 32–60, 72–87.

### Figure 2.4: English East India Company visits to Madagascar, by decade, 1600–1700

From British Library: IOR/E/3/1; IOR/L/MAR/A/VI; IOR/L/MAR/A/XIX; IOR/L/MAR/A/XX; IOR/L/MAR/A/XXI; IOR/L/MAR/A/XVIII; IOR/L/MAR/A/XXXIV; IOR/L/MAR/A/XLII; IOR/L/MAR/A/L; IOR/L/MAR/A/XLIV; IOR/L/MAR/A/XLVI; IOR/L/MAR/A/XLIX; IOR/L/MAR/A/LVI; IOR/L/

MAR/A/XLI; IOR/L/MAR/A/XLIX; IOR/E/14; IOR/L/MAR/A/LX; IOR/L/MAR/A/LXII; IOR/L/MAR/A/LXIV; Add MS 14037; IOR/L/MAR/A/LXVII; IOR/E/3/20; IOR/B/23; IOR/E/3/22; IOR/L/MAR/A/LXVIII; IOR/E/3/86; Sloane MS 3672; IOR/L/MAR/A/CVIII; IOR/L/MAR/A/CVI; IOR/L/MAR/A/CXXIV; IOR/L/MAR/A/CL; Add MS 25496; IOR/E/3/98; Add MS 25497; IOR/E/3/99.

See also Bodleian Library, Rawlinson MS A 334. Other voyages (that lack written records) are listed in The National Archives, British Library online catalog.

### Figure 6.1: British and French visits to Madagascar, by decade, 1700–1780

*Note:* The voyages include British merchant and admiralty vessels, and French merchant and naval vessels, but exclude pirate or interloper ships, as well as ships sailing to the Americas.

From British Library: IOR/L/MAR/B/402 B; Add MS 25502; IOR/L/MAR/B/605 B; IOR/L/MAR/B/656 E-G; IOR/L/MAR/B/654 B; IOR/L/MAR/B/324 E; Dean, *Narrative;* IOR/L/MAR/B/642 C; IOR/L/MAR/B/622 A; IOR/L/MAR/B/164 C; IOR/L/MAR/B/617 I; IOR/L/MAR/B/617 K; IOR/L/MAR/B/478 A; IOR/L/MAR/B/616 A; IOR/L/MAR/B/235 H; IOR/L/MAR/B/438 F; IOR/L/MAR/B/549 A; IOR/L/MAR/B/613 D; IOR/L/MAR/B/605 G; IOR/L/MAR/B/475 B; IOR/L/MAR/B/478 C; IOR/L/MAR/B/602 H; IOR/L/MAR/B/385 A; IOR/L/MAR/B/568 D; IOR/L/MAR/B/571 A; IOR/L/MAR/B/601 B; IOR/L/MAR/B/617 K-L; IOR/L/MAR/B/588 B; IOR/L/MAR/B/322 B; IOR/L/MAR/B/535 A; IOR/L/MAR/B/558 A; IOR/L/MAR/B/582 A; IOR/L/MAR/B/607 C; IOR/L/MAR/B/619 B; IOR/L/MAR/B/4 C; IOR/L/MAR/B/598 D; IOR/L/MAR/B/606 C; IOR/L/MAR/B/285 HH; IOR/L/MAR/B/438 H; IOR/L/MAR/B/599 C; IOR/L/MAR/B/507 A; IOR/L/MAR/B/593 F; IOR/L/MAR/B/594 H; IOR/L/MAR/B/614 C; IOR/L/MAR/B/800 B; IOR/L/MAR/B/1 A; IOR/L/MAR/B/4 D; IOR/L/MAR/B/404 H; IOR/L/MAR/B/525 A; IOR/L/MAR/B/590 B; IOR/L/MAR/B/596 E; IOR/L/MAR/B/598 E; IOR/L/MAR/B/458 B; IOR/L/MAR/B/603 D; IOR/L/MAR/B/620 A; IOR/L/MAR/B/551 A; IOR/L/MAR/B/610 G; IOR/L/MAR/B/320 D-E; IOR/L/MAR/B/325 G; IOR/L/MAR/B/456 D; IOR/L/MAR/B/486 A-B; IOR/L/MAR/B/579 A; IOR/L/MAR/B/390 A; IOR/L/MAR/B/481 A; IOR/L/MAR/B/553 A; IOR/L/MAR/B/272 E; IOR/L/MAR/B/554 C; IOR/L/MAR/B/561 A; IOR/L/MAR/B/591 A-B; IOR/L/MAR/B/597 B; IOR/L/MAR/B/645 A; IOR/L/MAR/B/541 G-H; IOR/L/MAR/B/472 C; IOR/L/MAR/B/488 F-G; IOR/L/MAR/B/474 B; IOR/L/MAR/B/483 B, D; IOR/L/MAR/B/464 B-D; IOR/L/MAR/B/508 B; IOR/L/MAR/B/472 D; IOR/L/MAR/B/480 D; IOR/L/MAR/B/555 A; IOR/L/MAR/B/86 A; IOR/L/MAR/B/140 C; IOR/L/MAR/B/410 A.

From British National Archives: ADM: 1/160; 51/723; 52/675; 52/696; 52/696; 1/161; 1/162; 1/163.

From Archives nationales, Paris: MAR 4JJ/88; MAR 4JJ/111; MAR 4JJ/91; MAR 4JJ/112; MAR B/3/295; MAR 4JJ/144 C; COL C/3/5; MAR 4JJ/74; MAR 4JJ/95; MAR 4JJ/96; COL C/3/7; COL C/4/2; MAR 4JJ/97; MAR 4JJ/98;

MAR 4JJ/114; MAR 4JJ/126; MAR 4JJ/76; MAR 4JJ/115; MAR 4JJ/144 O; COL C/2/27; COL C/3/8; MAR 4JJ/99; COL C/4/3; MAR 4JJ/100; MAR 4JJ/131; COL C/4/4; MAR 4JJ/116; MAR 4JJ/144 B; MAR 4JJ/144 D; MAR 4JJ/101; COL C/4/5; COL C/2/33; COL C/4/6; MAR 4JJ/77; MAR 4JJ/102; COL C/4/8; COL C/3/11; COL C/4/9; MAR 4JJ/78; MAR 4JJ/127; MAR 4JJ/87; MAR 4JJ/104; MAR 4JJ/89; COL C/4/10; MAR 4JJ/105; COL C/4/11; COL C/5B/1; COL C/4/12; MAR 4JJ/79; COL C/4/13; MAR 4JJ/80; COL C/4/14; MAR 4JJ/81; COL C/4/16; MAR 4JJ/106; MAR 4JJ/107; COL C/4/17; COL C/4/18; COL C/4/19; MAR 4JJ/92; COL C/4/22; COL C/5A/2; MAR 4JJ/82; MAR 4JJ/83; MAR 4JJ/121; COL C/4/24; COL C/4/25; COL C/4/28; COL C/4/32; COL C/4/34; COL C/4/36.

Allen, *European Slave Trading*, 32–60, 72–87.

The National Archives, British Library online catalog.

### Figure 7.1: Slaves purchased in Madagascar by Europeans, five-year periods, 1640–1780

*Note:* The data comes from ship journals and colonial records. Every attempt has been made to record the numbers of slaves loaded in Madagascar, as well as the year of purchase on the island, but this was not possible for all voyages. There were far more voyages that bought slaves from Madagascar not included in this representation; the chart uses information from the voyages for which I found evidence for numbers of slaves from Madagascar (preferably purchased, sometimes unloaded at the destination).

From British Library: IOR/E/3/98; Add MS 25497; IOR/E/3/99; IOR/L/MAR/B/402 B; Add MS 25502; IOR/L/MAR/B/605 B; IOR/L/MAR/B/656 E-G; IOR/L/MAR/B/654 B; IOR/L/MAR/B/324 E; Dean, *Narrative;* IOR/L/MAR/B/642 C; IOR/L/MAR/B/622 A; IOR/L/MAR/B/164 C; IOR/L/MAR/B/617 I; IOR/L/MAR/B/617 K; IOR/L/MAR/B/478 A; IOR/L/MAR/B/616 A; IOR/L/MAR/B/235 H; IOR/L/MAR/B/438 F; IOR/L/MAR/B/549 A; IOR/L/MAR/B/613 D; IOR/L/MAR/B/605 G; IOR/L/MAR/B/475 B; IOR/L/MAR/B/478 C; IOR/L/MAR/B/602 H; IOR/L/MAR/B/385 A; IOR/L/MAR/B/568 D; IOR/L/MAR/B/571 A; IOR/L/MAR/B/601 B; IOR/L/MAR/B/617 K-L; IOR/L/MAR/B/588 B; IOR/L/MAR/B/322 B; IOR/L/MAR/B/535 A; IOR/L/MAR/B/558 A; IOR/L/MAR/B/582 A; IOR/L/MAR/B/607 C; IOR/L/MAR/B/619 B; IOR/L/MAR/B/4 C; IOR/L/MAR/B/598 D; IOR/L/MAR/B/606 C; IOR/L/MAR/B/285 HH; IOR/L/MAR/B/438 H; IOR/L/MAR/B/599 C; IOR/L/MAR/B/507 A; IOR/L/MAR/B/593 F; IOR/L/MAR/B/594 H; IOR/L/MAR/B/614 C; IOR/L/MAR/B/800 B; IOR/L/MAR/B/1 A; IOR/L/MAR/B/4 D; IOR/L/MAR/B/404 H; IOR/L/MAR/B/525 A; IOR/L/MAR/B/590 B; IOR/L/MAR/B/596 E; IOR/L/MAR/B/598 E; IOR/L/MAR/B/458 B; IOR/L/MAR/B/603 D; IOR/L/MAR/B/620 A; IOR/L/MAR/B/551 A; IOR/L/MAR/B/610 G; IOR/L/MAR/B/320 D-E; IOR/L/MAR/B/325 G; IOR/L/MAR/B/456 D; IOR/L/MAR/B/486 A-B; IOR/L/MAR/B/579 A; IOR/L/MAR/B/390 A; IOR/L/MAR/B/481 A; IOR/L/MAR/B/553 A; IOR/L/MAR/B/272 E; IOR/L/MAR/B/554 C; IOR/L/

MAR/B/561 A; IOR/L/MAR/B/591 A-B; IOR/L/MAR/B/597 B; IOR/L/MAR/B/645 A; IOR/L/MAR/B/541 G-H; IOR/L/MAR/B/472 C; IOR/L/MAR/B/488 F-G; IOR/L/MAR/B/474 B; IOR/L/MAR/B/483 B, D; IOR/L/MAR/B/464 B-D; IOR/L/MAR/B/508 B; IOR/L/MAR/B/472 D; IOR/L/MAR/B/480 D; IOR/L/MAR/B/555 A; IOR/L/MAR/B/86 A; IOR/L/MAR/B/140 C; IOR/L/MAR/B/410 A.

From Archives nationales, Paris: COL C/5A/1; COL C/2/2; COL C/2/3; MAR 4JJ/86; MAR B/4/4; MAR 4JJ/90; MAR 4JJ/125; COL C/3/3; MAR 4JJ/88; MAR 4JJ/111; M 1025; MAR 4JJ/91; MAR 4JJ/112; MAR B/3/295; MAR 4JJ/144 C; COL C/3/5; MAR 4JJ/74; MAR 4JJ/95; MAR 4JJ/96; COL C/3/7; COL C/4/2; MAR 4JJ/97; MAR 4JJ/98; MAR 4JJ/114; MAR 4JJ/126; MAR 4JJ/76; MAR 4JJ/115; MAR 4JJ/144 O; COL C/2/27; COL C/3/8; MAR 4JJ/99; COL C/4/3; MAR 4JJ/100; MAR 4JJ/131; COL C/4/4; MAR 4JJ/116; MAR 4JJ/144 B; MAR 4JJ/ 144 D; MAR 4JJ/101; COL C/4/5; COL C/2/33; COL C/4/6; MAR 4JJ/77; MAR 4JJ/102; COL C/4/8; COL C/3/11; COL C/4/9; MAR 4JJ/78; MAR 4JJ/127; MAR 4JJ/87; MAR 4JJ/104; MAR 4JJ/89; COL C/4/10; MAR 4JJ/105; COL C/4/11; COL C/5B/1; COL C/4/12; MAR 4JJ/79; COL C/4/13; MAR 4JJ/80; COL C/4/14; MAR 4JJ/81; COL C/4/16; MAR 4JJ/106; MAR 4JJ/107; COL C/4/17; COL C/4/18; COL C/4/19; MAR 4JJ/92; COL C/4/22; COL C/5A/2; MAR 4JJ/82; MAR 4JJ/83; MAR 4JJ/121; COL C/4/24; COL C/4/25; COL C/4/28; COL C/4/32; COL C/4/34; COL C/4/36.

From Nationaal Archief, The Hague: VOC 1.04.02/2217; VOC 1.04.02/4280; VOC 1.04.02/4245; VOC 1.04.02/10811.

From Archives of the Western Cape: C 2338; C 2247; C 2248; C 2250; C 2251; C 2253; C 2254; C 2255; C 551.

*COACM*, 1:76–80, 280–84, 290, 402; 3:191, 197, 203–6, 382; 5:15.

Leibbrandt: *Precis . . . Riebeeck's Journal*, 56, 207; *Precis . . . Letters Despatched, 1696*, 5–6, 34, 65, 119–21, 266, 278, 318; *Precis . . . Letters Received, 1695*, 24; *Precis . . . Journal, 1662*, 85, 127–29, 196–200, 238–39; *Precis . . . Journal, 1671*, 98, 116–17, 301.

Heeringa, "De Nederlanders," 885; Lougnon, *Correspondance*, 1:13, 161; 2:20, 67, 69–70, 110, 141–45, 147, 155, 320; Armstrong, "Madagascar and the Slave Trade," 215–31; Bruijn, Gaastra, and Schöffer, *Dutch-Asiatic Shipping*, 2:2–11, 14–19, 26–39, 42–43, 58–59, 80–81, 96–97, 114–15, 158–59, 176–77, 196–97, 206–9, 218–21, 344–45, 420–21, 540–41, 712–13; 3:10–11, 16–17, 26–29, 34–35, 66–67, 70–71; Armstrong and Worden, "Slaves," 114–19; Flacourt, *Histoire*, 266–74, 279–85; Allen, *European Slave Trading*, 32–60, 72–87; McDonald, *Pirates*, 41, Appendix 1: 132–40, Appendix 2: 141–43; Trans-Atlantic Slave Trade Database.

# Notes

## CHAPTER 1: FEASTS AND VIOLENCE

1. O. L. Hemmy, "Journaal . . . de *Brack* [*Brak*]," 1741, VOC 1.04.022585, 95, records of the Dutch East India Company (hereafter cited as VOC 1.04.02), National Archives of the Netherlands (NA). A French translation can be found in Alfred Grandidier et al., eds., *Collection des ouvrages anciens concernant Madagascar*, vol. 6 (Paris: Comité de Madagascar, 1913), 52–191. The king's name is given as both "King Baba" and "Rammanrasse" in the source. All translations herein are my own unless otherwise noted.

2. Hemmy, "Journaal . . . de *Brack*," 79, 81. James was described as capable of reading, writing, and speaking English well.

3. Ibid., 81.

4. Ibid., 81–82.

5. Ibid., 82–83.

6. Ibid., 91.

7. Ibid., 95.

8. The numbers are derived from estimates provided by Pier M. Larson, *Ocean of Letters: Language and Creolization in an Indian Ocean Diaspora* (Cambridge: Cambridge University Press, 2009), 41, table 1.2, and calculations from Voyages: The Trans-Atlantic Slave Trade Database, http://www.slavevoyages.org. Note that I have omitted voyages that appear to be repeated in the database from the calculations. For more on these numbers, see Jane Hooper and David Eltis, "The Indian Ocean in Transatlantic Slavery," *Slavery & Abolition* 34, no. 3 (2013): 361. Other recent evaluations of the Indian Ocean slave trade include Pier M. Larson, "Enslaved Malagasy and 'Le Travail de la Parole' in the Pre-Revolutionary Mascarenes," *Journal of African History* 48, no. 3 (2007): 457–79; Richard B. Allen, "The Constant Demand of the French: The Mascarene Slave Trade and the Worlds of the Indian Ocean and Atlantic during the Eighteenth and Nineteenth Centuries," *Journal of African History* 49, no. 1 (2008): 43–72; Gwyn Campbell,

"Slave Trades and the Indian Ocean World," in *India in Africa, Africa in India: Indian Ocean Cosmopolitanisms*, ed. John C. Hawley (Bloomington: Indiana University Press, 2008), 17–51; Thomas Vernet, "Slave Trade and Slavery on the Swahili Coast, 1500–1750," in *Slavery, Islam and Diaspora*, ed. Paul Lovejoy, Behnaz A. Mirzai, and Ismael M. Montana (Trenton, NJ: Africa World Press, 2009), 37–76; Henri Médard, "La traite et l'esclavage en Afrique orientale et dans l'océan Indien: Une historiographie éclatée," in *Traites et esclavages en Afrique orientale et dans l'océan Indien*, ed. Henri Médard et al. (Paris: Karthala, 2013), 31–63; Richard B. Allen, *European Slave Trading in the Indian Ocean, 1500–1850* (Athens: Ohio University Press, 2015).

9. On global developments, see Joseph C. Miller, "A Theme in Variations: A Historical Schema of Slavery in the Atlantic and Indian Ocean Regions," *Slavery & Abolition* 24, no. 2 (2003): 172–76; C. A. Bayly, *The Birth of the Modern World, 1780–1914: Global Connections and Comparisons* (Malden, MA: Blackwell, 2004), 52–60; Paul Lovejoy, *Transformations in Slaves: A History of Slavery in Africa*, 3rd ed. (Cambridge: Cambridge University Press, 2011), 18–23.

10. I have records for 294 English voyages (by the English East India Company, the Courteen Association, the South Sea Company, and the British Admiralty, as well as Anglo-American vessels listed in Voyages: The Trans-Atlantic Slave Trade Database) between 1600 and 1800. Of these, 87 indicate they were slaving voyages (almost 30 percent of the total). I have found records of 379 French voyages, most from the eighteenth century, held in the records of the French Compagnie des Indes, that include both naval and merchant vessels. At least a hundred of these were intended to purchase slaves from Madagascar (roughly 26 percent). In my research in the Western Cape Archives and the National Archives of the Netherlands, as well as the list of voyages in Jaap R. Bruijn, Femme S. Gaastra, and Ivo Schöffer, *Dutch-Asiatic Shipping in the 17th and 18th Centuries*, 3 vols. (The Hague: Martinus Nijhoff, 1979–87) and from the database, The Dutch East India Company's Shipping between the Netherlands and Asia 1595–1795, Historici.nl: http://resources.huygens.knaw.nl/das/detailVoyage/91055. I have found 116 voyages of the Dutch East India Company stopping at Madagascar, and at least 50 of these bought slaves from the island (about 43 percent). These numbers are likely to underestimate provisioning voyages, as slaving vessels tended to preserve more detailed records and additional merchant vessels may have made brief stops at the ports of Madagascar, although it is possible that there was some (perhaps illicit) additional slave trading on a small scale on provisioning vessels. Note that I am counting visits to Madagascar in different years as distinct voyages, even if they were undertaken by the same vessel and captain.

11. On feasting as an "inherently political" activity and instrument of political relations, as well as a summary of the recent scholarship on feasting in Africa, see Michael Dietler, "Theorizing the Feast: Rituals of Consumption, Commensal Politics, and Power in African Contexts," in *Feasts: Archaeological and Ethnographic Perspectives on Food, Politics, and Power*, ed. Michael Dietler and Brian Hayden (Tuscaloosa: University of Alabama Press, 2010), 65–114. See also Jeffrey M. Pilcher, *¡Que Vivan Los Tamales!: Food and the Making of Mexican Identity* (Albuquerque: University of New Mexico Press, 1998), 2–6; Arnold J. Bauer, *Goods, Power, History: Latin America's Material Culture* (Cambridge: Cambridge University Press, 2001), 1–2, 87–88; Judith A. Carney, *Black Rice: The African Origins of Rice Cultivation in the Americas* (Cambridge, MA: Harvard University Press, 2001), 165–68; Linda A. Newson and Susie Minchin, "Diets, Food Supplies, and the African Slave Trade in Early Seventeenth-Century Spanish America," *Americas* 63, no. 4 (2007): 549–50; Jeffrey Fleisher, "Rituals of Consumption and the Politics of Feasting on the Eastern African Coast, AD 700–1500," *Journal of World Prehistory* 23, no. 4 (2010): 198–202; Monique Chastanet et al., eds., "Eating and Drinking in Africa before the 20th Century: Cuisines, Exchanges, Social Constructions," special issue, *Afriques: Débats, méthodes et terrains d'histoire*, no. 5 (2014), http://afriques.revues.org/1346. These elaborate meals also echo the food rituals in early Greece. See Pauline Schmitt-Pantel, "Greek Meals: A Civic Ritual," in *Food: A Culinary History from Antiquity to the Present*, ed. Jean-Louis Flandrin and Massimo Montanari (New York: Columbia University Press, 1999), 90–92.

12. Some historians label this period as early modern, although there are considerable debates around the use of the term to describe the years roughly spanning 1500 to 1800 CE. See esp. Jack A. Goldstone, "The Problem of the 'Early Modern' World," *Journal of the Economic and Social History of the Orient* 41, no. 3 (1998): 249–84; Randolph Starn, "The Early Modern Muddle," *Journal of Early Modern History* 6, no. 3 (2002): 296–307; Jeroen Duindam, "Early Modern Europe: Beyond the Strictures of Modernization and National Historiography," *European History Quarterly* 40, no. 4 (2010): 606–23. Some scholars, including Subrahmanyam and Lieberman, have argued convincingly that using the term "early modern" to only describe developments in Western Europe privileges European ideas of progress and modernity. Instead, they draw upon connected and comparative histories in order to describe similarities across much of Eurasia during these centuries. See Sanjay Subrahmanyam, "Connected Histories: Notes towards a Reconfiguration of Early Modern Eurasia," *Modern Asian Studies* 31, no. 3 (1997): 735–62; Victor Lieberman, *Strange Parallels: Southeast Asia in Global Context, c. 800–1830*, vol. 1, *Integration on the Mainland* (New York: Cambridge University Press, 2003); Victor Lieberman, *Strange*

*Parallels: Southeast Asia in Global Context, c. 800–1830*, vol. 2, *Mainland Mirrors: Europe, Japan, China, South Asia, and the Islands* (Cambridge: Cambridge University Press, 2009). Other scholars eschew the label entirely. See, for instance, essays in Rila Mukherjee, ed., *Networks in the First Global Age, 1400–1800* (Delhi: Primus Books, 2011); Gwyn Campbell, "Africa, the Indian Ocean World, and the 'Early Modern': Historiographical Conventions and Problems," in *Africa, Empire, and Globalization: Essays in Honor of A. G. Hopkins*, ed. Toyin Falola and Emily Brownell (Durham, NC: Carolina Academic Press, 2011), 81–92.

13. Recent discussions of the interactions between the European newcomers and communities in Africa and Asia include Michael N. Pearson, *The Indian Ocean* (London: Routledge, 2003), 159–89; Sugata Bose, *A Hundred Horizons: The Indian Ocean in the Age of Global Empire* (Cambridge, MA: Harvard University Press, 2006), 19–21; R. J. Barendse, *Arabian Seas, 1700–1763* (Leiden: Brill, 2009), 1:4–8; Tonio Andrade, "Beyond Guns, Germs, and Steel: European Expansion and Maritime Asia, 1400–1750," *Journal of Early Modern History* 14, no. 1 (2010): 168–70; Edward A. Alpers, *The Indian Ocean in World History* (Oxford: Oxford University Press, 2014), 69–97.

14. One important exception here is Auguste Toussaint, *History of the Indian Ocean*, trans. June Guicharnaud (Chicago: University of Chicago Press, 1966), 109, 144–46. On the important roles played by communities in Madagascar in early trade in the ocean and throughout the early modern period, see also Michael N. Pearson, *Port Cities and Intruders: The Swahili Coast, India, and Portugal in the Early Modern Era* (Baltimore: Johns Hopkins University Press, 1998), 36–38; Edward A. Alpers, *East Africa and the Indian Ocean* (Princeton, NJ: Markus Wiener, 2009), vii–viii; Gwyn Campbell, "The Role of Africa in the Emergence of the 'Indian Ocean World' Global Economy," in *Eyes across the Water: Navigating the Indian Ocean*, ed. Pamila Gupta, Isabel Hofmeyr, and Michael N. Pearson (Pretoria: Unisa Press, 2010), 170–96; Abdul Sheriff, *Dhow Cultures of the Indian Ocean: Cosmopolitanism, Commerce and Islam* (New York: Columbia University Press, 2010), esp. 20–22. For a discussion along similar lines about the limitations of area studies for the history of Northeast Africa, see Jonathan Miran, *Red Sea Citizens: Cosmopolitan Society and Cultural Change in Massawa* (Bloomington: Indiana University Press, 2009), 5–9.

15. On early Madagascar and nearby East Africa, see esp. Philippe Beaujard, *Les mondes de l'océan Indien*, 2 vols. (Paris: Armand Colin, 2012).

16. Others have made similar comments. For instance, McDonald describes Madagascar as a link connecting the "Indo-Atlantic world" during the late seventeenth century: Kevin P. McDonald, *Pirates, Merchants,*

*Settlers, and Slaves: Colonial America and the Indo-Atlantic World* (Berkeley: University of California Press, 2015), 2–3. On the goal of placing maritime Africa in global history, see Patrick Manning, "African and World Historiography," *Journal of African History* 54, no. 3 (2013), esp. 329.

17. Thanks to the growing power of the Merina state, two ports on the island, Toamasina (visited by British and French merchants, especially those from the Mascarenes) and Mahajanga (largely monopolized by American merchants), became dominant in regional trade from Madagascar. By contrast, innovations in transportation ensured that transoceanic voyages were faster and less dependent on frequent refueling stops within the ocean. See, for instance, Colette Dubois, "The Red Sea Ports during the Revolution in Transportation, 1800–1914," in *Modernity and Culture: From the Mediterranean to the Indian Ocean*, ed. Leila Tarazi Fawaz and C. A. Bayly (New York: Columbia University Press, 2002), 62; Pearson, *Indian Ocean*, 190–201; Bose, *A Hundred Horizons*, 273. Scholars examining similar trends in the Atlantic, with ramifications for African history, include Martin Lynn, "From Sail to Steam: The Impact of the Steamship Services on the British Palm Oil Trade with West Africa, 1850–1890," *Journal of African History* 30, no. 2 (1989): 227–45; Martin Lynn, "Technology, Trade and 'A Race of Native Capitalists': The Krio Diaspora of West Africa and the Steamship, 1852–95," *Journal of African History* 33, no. 3 (1992): 421–40; Klas Rönnbäck, "The Speed of Ships and Shipping Productivity in the Age of Sail," *European Review of Economic History* 16, no. 4 (2012): 469–89.

18. Manning, *Slavery and African Life: Occidental, Oriental, and African Slave Trades* (Cambridge: Cambridge University Press, 1990), 8. For a review of earlier scholarship, see Paul E. Lovejoy, "The Impact of the Atlantic Slave Trade on Africa: A Review of the Literature," *Journal of African History* 30, no. 3 (1989): 365–94. Some of the more prominent advocates of this viewpoint include J. E. Inikori, "The Import of Firearms into West Africa 1750–1807: A Quantitative Analysis," *Journal of African History* 18, no. 3 (1977): 339–68; Warren Whatley and Rob Gillezeau, "The Fundamental Impact of the Slave Trade on African Economies," in *Economic Evolution and Revolution in Historical Time*, ed. Paul W. Rhode, Joshua L. Rosenbloom, and David F. Weiman (Stanford, CA: Stanford University Press, 2011), 86–110. See also Whatley, "The Gun-Slave Cycle in the 18th Century British Slave Trade in Africa," *Munich Personal RePEc Archive (MPRA)*, December 2012, http://mpra.ub.uni-muenchen.de/44492/1/MPRA_paper_44492.pdf. Note that Inikori presents a more nuanced argument on the impact of the slave trade on African economic development in *Africans and the Industrial Revolution in England: A Study in International Trade and Economic Development* (New York: Cambridge University Press, 2002), esp. 481–82.

19. On the slave trade and accompanying shifts in agricultural production in Atlantic Africa, see Walter Hawthorne, *Planting Rice and Harvesting Slaves: Transformations along the Guinea-Bissau Coast, 1400–1900* (Portsmouth, NH: Heinemann, 2003), 177–78; Kristin Mann, *Slavery and the Birth of an African City: Lagos, 1760–1900* (Bloomington: Indiana University Press, 2007), 1–3; Edda L. Fields-Black, *Deep Roots: Rice Farmers in West Africa and the African Diaspora* (Bloomington: Indiana University Press, 2008), 5–11; Philip Misevich, "The Sierra Leone Hinterland and the Provisioning of Early Freetown, 1792–1803," *Journal of Colonialism and Colonial History* 9, no. 3 (2008), doi:10.1353/cch.0.0032; Rebecca Shumway, *The Fante and the Transatlantic Slave Trade* (Rochester, NY: University of Rochester Press, 2011), 2–3; Philip J. Havik and Toby Green, "Introduction: Brokerage and the Role of Western Africa in the Atlantic World," in *Brokers of Change: Atlantic Commerce and Cultures in Precolonial Western Africa*, ed. Toby Green (Oxford: Oxford University Press, 2012), 1–24; Michael W. Tuck, "Everyday Commodities, the Rivers of Guinea, and the Atlantic World: The Beeswax Export Trade, c. 1450–c. 1800," in *Brokers of Change*, 285–303; James D. La Fleur, *Fusion Foodways of Africa's Gold Coast in the Atlantic Era* (Leiden: Brill, 2012), 3–12; Toby Green, *The Rise of the Trans-Atlantic Slave Trade in Western Africa, 1300–1589* (Cambridge: Cambridge University Press, 2012), 3; David Eltis, "The Slave Trade and Commercial Agriculture in an African Context," in *Commercial Agriculture, the Slave Trade and Slavery in Atlantic Africa*, ed. Robin Law, Suzanne Schwarz, and Silke Strickrodt (Woodbridge, Suffolk: James Currey, 2013), 28–53.

20. J. Cameron Monroe, *The Precolonial State in West Africa: Building Power in Dahomey* (Cambridge: Cambridge University Press, 2014), 220. See also W. A. Richards, "The Import of Firearms into West Africa in the Eighteenth Century," *Journal of African History* 21, no. 1 (1980): 43–59; Robin Law, *The Slave Coast of West Africa, 1550–1750: The Impact of the Atlantic Slave Trade on an African Society* (Oxford: Oxford University Press, 1991); James F. Searing, *West African Slavery and Atlantic Commerce: The Senegal River Valley, 1700–1860* (Cambridge: Cambridge University Press, 1993). Other historians have focused on the slave trade among decentralized communities, including Martin A. Klein, "The Slave Trade and Decentralized Societies," *Journal of African History* 42, no. 1 (2001): 49–65; Shumway, *Fante*, 4–9. On the domination of trade by trusted merchant elites, see Paul E. Lovejoy and David Richardson, "Trust, Pawnship, and Atlantic History: The Institutional Foundations of the Old Calabar Slave Trade," *American Historical Review* 104, no. 2 (1999): 333–55.

21. Despite the similar demand for slaves, the conduct of the slave trade was vastly different between European and non-European slavers. Gwyn Campbell describes the major differences between slavery and the slave

trade in the Atlantic versus the Indian Ocean World: Campbell, "Introduction: Slavery and Other Forms of Unfree Labour in the Indian Ocean World," in *The Structure of Slavery in Indian Ocean Africa and Asia*, ed. Gwyn Campbell (London: Frank Cass, 2004), vii–xxiv.

Comparing the competition for slaves within the same ports to different conditions of competition in Atlantic Africa, see Green, *Rise*, 16, 33–34. See also David Northrup, "The Growth of Trade among the Igbo before 1800," *Journal of African History* 13, no. 2 (1972): 225–27.

22. As it did within West Africa. James Searing, for instance, describes "Atlantic commerce," rather than simply the slave trade, as transforming West Africa: Searing, *West African Slavery*, 1. Northrup argues that most historians would agree that "African traders and rulers expected to benefit from these [slaving] transactions and worked hard to ensure they did." David Northrup, *Africa's Discovery of Europe, 1450–1850*, 2nd ed. (New York: Oxford University Press, 2009), 55.

23. See, for example, K. N. Chaudhuri, *Trade and Civilisation in the Indian Ocean: An Economic History from the Rise of Islam to 1750* (Cambridge: Cambridge University Press, 1985), 189; Chaudhuri, *Asia before Europe: Economy and Civilisation of the Indian Ocean from the Rise of Islam to 1750* (Cambridge: Cambridge University Press, 1990), 151–52, 156. Two examples of these maps: Chaudhuri, *Trade and Civilisation*, 130, map 13; Milo Kearney, *The Indian Ocean in World History* (London: Routledge, 2004), 111, fig. 6.1.

24. Jerry Bentley argues that oceanic histories present challenges to historians seeking to understand regional interactions: Bentley, "Sea and Ocean Basins as Frameworks of Historical Analysis," *Geographical Review* 89, no. 2 (1999): 220. For this reason, Sugata Bose describes the Indian Ocean as an "interregional arena of economic and cultural interaction." Bose, *A Hundred Horizons*, 21. For a regionally focused history within the ocean, see Sunil S. Amrith, *Crossing the Bay of Bengal: The Furies of Nature and the Fortunes of Migrants* (Cambridge, MA: Harvard University Press, 2013).

25. Pearson, *Indian Ocean*, 85–86; see also Sheriff, *Dhow Cultures*, 7. According to Philip D. Curtin, one of the major incentives to trade in Africa was "differing resource endowments," including in food. Curtin, *Cross-Cultural Trade in World History* (Cambridge: Cambridge University Press, 1984), 16. For two examples of the possibilities presented by this research topic, see Kenneth R. Hall, "Local and International Trade and Traders in the Straits of the Melaka Region: 600–1500," *Journal of the Economic and Social History of the Orient* 47, no. 2 (2004): 251–53; Thomas Vernet, "Avant le giroflier: Esclavage et agriculture sur la côte swahili, 1590–1812," in Médard et al., *Traites et esclavages*, 245–306.

26. Notable exceptions for both the pre-1498 and post-1498 periods include Sinnappah Arasaratnam, "The Rice Trade in Eastern India, 1650–1740," *Modern Asian Studies* 22, no. 3 (1988): 531–32; Mark Horton, *Shanga: The Archaeology of a Muslim Trading Community on the Coast of East Africa* (London: British Institute in Eastern Africa, 1996), 60; Chapurukha Makokha Kusimba, *The Rise and Fall of Swahili States* (Walnut Creek, CA: Alta Mira, 1999), 74, 129; Mark Horton and John Middleton, *The Swahili: The Social Landscape of a Mercantile Society* (Oxford: Blackwell, 2000), esp. 89–91; Kenneth McPherson, "Port Cities as Nodal Points of Change: The Indian Ocean, 1890s–1920s," in Fawaz and Bayly, *Modernity and Culture*, 79; Philippe Beaujard, "East Africa, the Comoros Islands and Madagascar before the Sixteenth Century: On a Neglected Part of the World System," *Azania* 42, no. 1 (2007): 22–26.

27. For example, see Toussaint's focus on spices: Toussaint, *History*, 117–18.

28. Chaudhuri, *Trade and Civilisation*, 23, 189, 192–93; Chaudhuri, *Asia before Europe*, 151–52, 156.

29. Jack Turner, *Spice: The History of a Temptation* (New York: Alfred A. Knopf, 2004), xvii.

30. I am agreeing with the criticisms presented by Jeremy Prestholdt that modern understandings of commerce tend to marginalize Africans. Prestholdt, *Domesticating the World: African Consumerism and the Genealogies of Globalization* (Berkeley: University of California Press, 2008), 3–5.

31. Judith A. Carney and Richard Nicholas Rosomoff, *In the Shadow of Slavery: Africa's Botanical Legacy in the Atlantic World* (Berkeley: University of California Press, 2009), 46–64. See also various essays in Kenneth F. Kiple and Kriemhild Coneè Ornelas, eds., *The Cambridge World History of Food* (Cambridge: Cambridge University Press, 2000), esp. James L. Newman, "Africa South from the Sahara," in ibid., 2:1330–39; Kenneth F. Kiple, *A Movable Feast: Ten Millennia of Food Globalization* (Cambridge: Cambridge University Press, 2007), 144–49.

32. Provisioning is most extensively discussed in Malyn Newitt, "The Southern Swahili Coast in the First Century of European Expansion," *Azania* 13, no. 1 (1978): 121–23; Malyn Newitt, "The Comoro Islands in Indian Ocean Trade before the 19th Century," *Cahiers d'études africaines* 23, nos. 89–90 (1983): 153–55; Edward A. Alpers, "The Western Indian Ocean as a Regional Food Network in the Nineteenth Century," in Alpers, *East Africa and the Indian Ocean*, 23–38. There are also references to rice production and sale from the Bay of Bengal, esp. Arasaratnam, "Rice Trade"; Amrith, *Crossing*, 54–55.

33. See, for example, Mark Kurlansky, *Cod: A Biography of the Fish that Changed the World* (New York: Penguin, 1998), 27–29; Brian Fagan,

*Fish on Friday: Feasting, Fasting, and the Discovery of the New World* (New York: Basic Books, 2006), xviii. On provisioning in West Africa, see Hawthorne, *Planting Rice*, 154; Fields-Black, *Deep Roots*, 5–10; Stephen D. Behrendt, "Seasonality in the Trans-Atlantic Slave Trade," 2008, at Voyages: The Trans-Atlantic Slave Trade Database, http://www.slavevoyages.org/assessment/essays#.

34. On the influence of Mediterranean trading practices in the Atlantic, see Alison Games, *The Web of Empire: English Cosmopolitans in an Age of Expansion, 1560–1660* (Oxford: Oxford University Press, 2008), 47.

35. Some of these foods, albeit in reduced quantities, were also sought by Indian Ocean sailors. See Pearson, *Indian Ocean*, 57.

36. Sarah C. Walshaw, "Converting to Rice: Urbanization, Islamization and Crops on Pemba Island, Tanzania, AD 700–1500," *World Archaeology* 42, no. 1 (2010): 137–54; Kenneth R. Hall, *A History of Early Southeast Asia: Maritime Trade and Societal Development, 100–1500* (Lanham, MD: Rowman & Littlefield, 2011), 4–9, 48–49.

37. For an example of shipments of Asian rice, see Arasaratnam, "Rice Trade," 535–38.

38. See Jonathan Curry-Machado, "Global Histories, Imperial Commodities, Local Interactions: An Introduction," in *Global Histories, Imperial Commodities, Local Interactions*, ed. Jonathan Curry-Machado (New York: Palgrave Macmillan, 2013), 1–14.

39. The need to understand the connections between the coast and interior is highlighted in various works by Michael N. Pearson, including "Littoral Society: The Case for the Coast," *Great Circle* 7, no. 1 (1985): 1–8; "Littoral Society: The Concept and the Problems," *Journal of World History* 17, no. 4 (2006): 353–73; "The Idea of the Ocean," in Gupta et al., *Eyes across the Water*, 7–12. On the links between agricultural production and coastal trading centers in premodern Southeast Asia, see Anthony Reid, "The Structure of Cities in Southeast Asia, Fifteenth to Seventeenth Centuries," *Journal of Southeast Asian Studies* 11, no. 2 (1980): 247; Hall, *History of Early Southeast Asia*, esp. 112–13, 335–36. Likewise, port cities can be seen as "frontier spaces," to borrow Jonathan Miran's phrasing, for the intersection of land- and sea-based concerns. See Miran, *Red Sea Citizens*, 35; Pedro Machado, *Ocean of Trade: South Asian Merchants, Africa and the Indian Ocean, c. 1750–1850* (Cambridge: Cambridge University Press, 2014), esp. 183–200.

40. John F. Richards, *The Unending Frontier: An Environmental History of the Early Modern World* (Berkeley: University of California Press, 2003); Edmund Burke III, "The Big Story: Human History, Energy Regimes, and the Environment," in *The Environment and World History*, ed. Edmund Burke III and Kenneth Pomeranz (Berkeley: University of California Press, 2009), esp. 40–42.

European vessels also carried products in demand by markets throughout Europe and Asia, such as rare hardwoods, yet these products were difficult to acquire without harming local ecosystems or being moved long distances. R. J. Barendse, *The Arabian Seas: The Indian Ocean World of the Seventeenth Century* (Armonk, NY: M. E. Sharpe, 2002), 13–70; McPherson, "Port Cities," 78–81; Michel Tuchscherer, "Trade and Port Cities in the Red Sea–Gulf of Aden Region in the Sixteenth and Seventeenth Century," in Fawaz and Bayly, *Modernity and Culture*, 30–33. See also Henk Driessen, "Mediterranean Port Cities: Cosmopolitanism Reconsidered," *History and Anthropology* 16, no. 1 (2005): 129–41. For a look at the environment at the end of this period, see N. Thomas Håkansson, "The Human Ecology of World Systems in East Africa: The Impact of the Ivory Trade," *Human Ecology* 32, no. 5 (2004): 561–91; Gwyn Campbell, "Forest Depletion in Imperial Madagascar, c. 1790–1861," in *Contest for Land in Madagascar: Environment, Ancestors and Development*, ed. Sandra J. T. M. Evers, Gwyn Campbell, and Michael Lambek (Leiden: Brill, 2013), 64–67.

41. See, for example, Arasaratnam, "Rice Trade," 532–34, 540–43.

42. Richard H. Grove, *Ecology, Climate and Empire: Colonialism and Global Environmental History, 1400–1940* (Cambridge, UK: White Horse, 1997), 37–43.

43. C. R. Boxer, *The Portuguese Seaborne Empire, 1415–1825* (London: Hutchinson, 1969); Holden Furber, *Rival Empires of Trade in the Orient, 1600–1800* (Minneapolis: University of Minnesota Press, 1976). For a critique of this earlier work, see Sanjay Subrahmanyam, "Introduction: The Indian Ocean between Empire and Nation," in *Maritime India*, ed. Sanjay Subrahmanyam (New Delhi: Oxford University Press, 2004), xi–xvii. For more recent discussions, see also Andrade, "Beyond Guns," 172–73; Antoni Picazo Muntaner, "Ports and Commercial Networks in the Indian and Pacific Oceans: Models and Flows of Capitalism," in Mukherjee, *Networks in the First Global Age*, 35–44.

44. These foods would include those exported from Madagascar and imported into East Africa, the Comoro Islands, and the Mascarene Islands. Even visits to St. Helena Island or Indonesia would mean the consumption of food produced by slaves from Madagascar. On trade routes, see esp. Malyn Newitt, *A History of Portuguese Overseas Expansion, 1400–1668* (London: Routledge, 2005), 207; Jean Sutton, *The East India Company's Maritime Service, 1746–1834: Masters of the Eastern Seas* (Rochester, NY: Boydell, 2010), 14.

45. See Malyn Newitt, "Mozambique Island: The Rise and Decline of a Colonial Port City," in *Portuguese Colonial Cities in the Early Modern World*, ed. Liam Matthew Brockey (Burlington, VT: Ashgate, 2008), 109–11; Alpers, "Western Indian Ocean"; Eugénia Rodrigues, "Eating and

Drinking at the Royal Hospital of Mozambique Island: Medicine and Diet Change between the End of the 18th and the Early 19th Century," *Afriques: Débats, méthodes et terrains d'histoire*, no. 5 (2014), http://afriques.revues.org/1553. On Portuguese routes and establishments in the Indian Ocean, see V. Magelhães Godinho, "The Portuguese and the 'Carreira da India,' 1497–1810," in *Ships, Sailors and Spices: East India Companies and Their Shipping in the 16th, 17th and 18th Centuries*, ed. Jaap R. Bruijn and Femme S. Gaastra (Amsterdam: NEHA, 1993), 1–47. For the history of the Portuguese in the Indian Ocean more generally, see esp. Pearson, *Merchants and Rulers in Gujarat: The Response to the Portuguese in the Sixteenth Century* (Berkeley: University of California Press, 1976); C. R. Boxer, *Portuguese Conquest and Commerce in Southern Asia, 1500–1750* (London: Variorum Reprints, 1985); James C. Boyajian, *Portuguese Trade in Asia under the Habsburgs, 1580–1640* (Baltimore: Johns Hopkins University Press, 1993), esp. xii–xiv, 3; Pearson, *Port Cities*; Liam Matthew Brockey, "Introduction: Nodes of Empire," in Brockey, *Portuguese Colonial Cities*, 8–9; Stuart B. Schwartz, "The Economy of the Portuguese Empire," in *Portuguese Oceanic Expansion, 1400–1800*, ed. Francisco Bethencourt and Diogo Ramada Curto (Cambridge: Cambridge University Press, 2007), 32; A. R. Disney, *A History of Portugal and the Portuguese Empire* (Cambridge: Cambridge University Press, 2009), 2:137–49; Sanjay Subrahmanyam, *The Portuguese Empire in Asia, 1500–1700: A Political and Economic History*, 2nd ed. (West Sussex, UK: Wiley-Blackwell, 2012), 81–116.

46. On competition for spices, see Newitt, *History of Portuguese Overseas Expansion*, 203–4; P. J. Moree, *A Concise History of Dutch Mauritius, 1598–1710: A Fruitful and Healthy Land* (London: Kegan Paul International, 1998), 7–8. On struggles with the Portuguese, see Boyajian, *Portuguese Trade*, 123–47. Histories of the VOC, EIC, and French trading companies include various essays in Bruijn and Gaastra, *Ships, Sailors and Spices*; Om Prakash, *Precious Metals and Commerce: The Dutch East India Company in the Indian Ocean Trade* (Aldershot: Variorum, 1994); Glenn Joseph Ames, *Colbert, Mercantilism, and the French Quest for Asian Trade* (DeKalb: Northern Illinois University Press, 1996); Jocelyn Chan Low, *"La VOC, t'Eylandt Mauritius et Rodrigues": Avec le voyage de Wolfert Harmensz vers les Îles Rodrigues et Maurice, 1601* (Port-Louis, Mauritius: National Library, 2001); Philippe Haudrère, *La compagnie française des Indes au XVIIIe siècle*, 2nd ed. (Paris: Les Indes savantes, 2005), esp. 1:13–33 and 2:751–70; various works by Markus Vink, esp. "A Match Made in Heaven? World-Systems Analysis and Dutch Indian Ocean Studies," in *Rivalry and Conflict: European Traders and Asian Trading Networks in the 16th and 17th Century*, ed. Leonard Blusse and Ernst van Veen (Leiden: CNWS, 2005), 267–314; Donald C. Wellington,

*French East India Companies: A Historical Account and Record of Trade* (Lanham, MD: Hamilton Books, 2006); Games, *Web of Empire*, 290–98; Kerry Ward, *Networks of Empire: Forced Migration in the Dutch East India Company* (Cambridge: Cambridge University Press, 2009); Barendse, *Arabian Seas, 1700–1763*, 1:33–46; Philip J. Stern, "Soldier and Citizen in the Seventeenth-Century English East India Company," *Journal of Early Modern History* 15, no. 1 (2011): 83–104; Emily Erikson, *Between Monopoly and Free Trade: The English East India Company, 1600–1757* (Princeton, NJ: Princeton University Press, 2014); Philip Lawson, *The East India Company: A History* (New York: Routledge, 2014). There were other, less well known players in the Indian Ocean, including the Danish East India Company, the Swedish East India Company, and the Ostend East-India Company. Some of their vessels appear to have stopped at Madagascar, in addition to frequenting the Cape, St. Helena, and the Comoro Islands. See E. Gøbel, "Danish Companies' Shipping to Asia, 1616–1807," in Bruijn and Gaastra, *Ships, Sailors and Spices*, 99–120; C. Koninckx, "The Swedish East India Company (1731–1807)," ibid., 121–38; K. Degryse and J. Parmentier, "Maritime Aspects of the Ostend Trade to Mocha, India and China (1715–1732)," ibid., 139–75.

47. For discussions of nineteenth-century networks of trade and migration that support this argument, that commerce remained strong through the late precolonial period, see Edward Alpers, "The Somali Community at Aden in the Nineteenth Century," *Northeast African Studies* 8, nos. 2–3 (1986): 143–68; Linda Boxberger, *On the Edge of Empire: Hadhramawt, Emigration, and the Indian Ocean, 1880s–1930s* (Albany: State University of New York Press, 2002); Anne K. Bang, *Sufis and Scholars of the Sea: Family Networks in East Africa, 1860–1925* (London: RoutledgeCurzon, 2003); Engseng Ho, *The Graves of Tarim: Genealogy and Mobility across the Indian Ocean* (Berkeley: University of California Press, 2006); Machado, *Ocean of Trade*.

48. On these interactions, see esp. Janet J. Ewald, "Crossers of the Sea: Slaves, Freedmen, and other Migrants in the Northwestern Indian Ocean, c. 1750–1914," *American Historical Review* 105, no. 1 (2000): 69–91; Sugata Bose, "Space and Time on the Indian Ocean Rim: Theory and History," in Fawaz and Bayly, *Modernity and Culture*, 372; Francisco Bethencourt, "Political Configurations and Local Powers," in Bethencourt and Curto, *Portuguese Oceanic Expansion*, 199.

49. On the issue of competition, see esp. Sanjay Subrahmanyam, "Of Imarat and Tijarat: Asian Merchants and State Power in the Western Indian Ocean, 1400 to 1750," *Comparative Studies in Society and History* 37, no. 4 (1995): 750–80; Bose, *A Hundred Horizons*, 12–15. See also Om Prakash, "Cooperation and Conflict among European Traders in the Indian Ocean

in the Late Eighteenth Century," in *Land, Politics, and Trade in South Asia*, ed. Sanjay Subrahmanyam (Delhi: Oxford University Press, 2004), 20–43; Alpers, *Indian Ocean*, 69–97; Adam Clulow, *The Company and the Shogun: The Dutch Encounter with Tokugawa Japan* (New York: Columbia University Press, 2014), 255–62.

50. On the older literature over continuity versus rupture, see John E. Wills Jr., "Maritime Asia, 1500–1800: The Interactive Emergence of European Domination," *American Historical Review* 98, no. 1 (1993), 83–105. More recently, see Bayly, *Birth of the Modern World*, 1–3; H. V. Bowen, *The Business of Empire: The East India Company and Imperial Britain, 1756–1833* (Cambridge: Cambridge University Press, 2005), esp. 23; Bose, *A Hundred Horizons*, 377–81; Thomas R. Metcalf, *Imperial Connections: India in the Indian Ocean Arena, 1860–1920* (Berkeley: University of California Press, 2007), esp. 9; David Armitage and Sanjay Subrahmanyam, "Introduction: The Age of Revolutions, c. 1760–1840," in *The Age of Revolutions in Global Context, c. 1760–1840*, ed. David Armitage and Sanjay Subrahmanyam (London: Palgrave MacMillan, 2010), xii–xxvi.

51. Only a portion of the ship records and logs from ships visiting Madagascar are still available. I consulted 128 English ship logs, primarily left by the EIC, 84 French ship logs left by both merchant and naval vessels, and 19 Dutch logs that all recorded stops at the island of Madagascar. The remainder of the ship logs I studied included visits to other portions of the southwestern Indian Ocean (the Mascarenes, Comoros, or Mozambique).

52. Examples include Leif Svalesen, *The Slave Ship Fredensborg*, trans. Pat Shaw and Selena Winsnes (Bloomington: Indiana University Press, 2000); Bruce L. Mouser, ed., *A Slaving Voyage to Africa and Jamaica: The Log of the Sandown, 1793–1794* (Bloomington: Indiana University Press, 2002); Hendrik Frappé and Willem van der Lint, *Slawehandel met Madagaskar: Die joernale van die Kaapse slaweskip Leijdsman, 1715*, ed. Piet E. Westra and James C. Armstrong (Cape Town: Africana Uitgewers, 2006); Robert Harms, *The Diligent: A Voyage through the Worlds of the Slave Trade* (New York: Basic Books, 2002); Thomas Vernet, "La première traite française à Zanzibar: Le journal de bord du vaisseau *l'Espérance*, 1774–1775," in *Civilisations des mondes insulaires*, ed. Chantal Radimilahy and Narivelo Rajaonarimanana (Paris: Karthala, 2011), 477–521. For evidence of growing interest in the human experience onboard slave vessels, see Marcus Rediker, *The Slave Ship: A Human History* (New York: Viking Penguin, 2007).

53. As a reviewer of *The Diligent* argues: David Barry Gaspar, review of *The Diligent: A Voyage through the Worlds of the Slave Trade*, by Robert Harms, *American Historical Review* 109, no. 1 (2004): 145.

54. Stephanie E. Smallwood, *Saltwater Slavery: A Middle Passage from Africa to American Diaspora* (Cambridge, MA: Harvard University Press, 2007), 1–4.

55. On the use of European records to understand economic innovations in the Indian Ocean, see the work of C. G. Brouwer, including Brouwer, "Non-Western Shipping Movements in the Red Sea and Gulf of Aden during the 2nd and 3rd Decades of the 17th Century, according to the Records of the Dutch East India Company," pts. 1 and 2, *Die Welt des Islams* 31, no. 2 (1991): 105–67, and 32, no. 1 (1992): 6–40; Brouwer, *Al-Mukha: Profile of a Yemeni Seaport as Sketched by Servants of the Dutch East India Company (VOC), 1614–1640* (Amsterdam: D'Fluyte Rarob, 1997). See also R. J. Barendse, "Slaving on the Malagasy Coast, 1640–1700," in *Cultures of Madagascar: Ebb and Flow of Influences*, ed. Sandra Evers and Marc Spindler (Leiden: International Institute for Asian Studies, 1995), 137–56; Yvette Ranjeva-Rabetafika, René Baesjou, and Natalie Everts, "Of Paper and Men: A Note on the Archives of the VOC as a Source for the History of Madagascar," *Itinerario* 24, no. 1 (2000): 45–67.

56. Aside from occasional (failed) settlements on the island and the presence of pirates at the turn of the eighteenth century, few merchants remained on the island before the late eighteenth century. To contrast this situation with the Atlantic, see Rebecca Shumway, "Castle Slaves of the Eighteenth-Century Gold Coast (Ghana)," *Slavery & Abolition* 35, no. 1 (2014): 84–98; Pernille Ipsen, *Daughters of the Trade: Atlantic Slavers and Interracial Marriage on the Gold Coast* (Philadelphia: University of Pennsylvania Press, 2015).

57. Alfred Grandidier et al., eds., *Collection des ouvrages anciens concernant Madagascar*, 9 vols. (Paris: Comité de Madagascar, 1903–20) (hereafter cited as *COACM*).

58. For a critique of the sources in *COACM*, see Stephen Ellis, "Un texte du XVIIe siècle sur Madagascar," *Omaly sy anio* (Université d'Antananarivo) 9 (1979): 151. See also Vernet, "Slave Trade," 37–38. On the use of sources outside of the COACM collection, see Stephen Ellis, "The History of Sovereigns in Madagascar: New Light from Old Sources," in *Madagascar revisitée: En voyage avec Françoise Raison-Jourde*, ed. Didier Nativel and Faranirina V. Rajaonah (Paris: Karthala, 2009), 406–8.

59. James C. Armstrong, "Madagascar and the Slave Trade in the Seventeenth Century," *Omaly sy anio* (Université d'Antananarivo) 17–20 (1983): 211–33; Barendse, "Slaving."

60. Most of the English East India Company documents we have are held in India Office records (IOR) currently found in the Asian and African Studies Reading Room of the British Library, which also holds a few more in its rare manuscripts collection (Add MS). Journals of EIC ships can be

found at IOR/L/MAR/A–B. There are also a few sources in the Bodleian Library at Oxford University and the National Maritime Museum in Greenwich. The ship logs of British naval vessels are collected in the Records of the Admiralty (ADM) at the British National Archives in Kew. Logs of Compagnie des Indes ships are held at the Archives nationales (MAR 4JJ), Paris, as well as in their various Fonds des Colonies microfiche collections (COL). Most of the ship logs of the Dutch East India Company (including the *Dagregisters* used primarily here) are held in The Hague, in the Nationaal Archief (VOC 1.04.02), but a few are also found in the Archives of the Western Cape in Cape Town, South Africa (C). Note that there are multiple records available for some ships, sometimes kept by different officials on board (particularly for Dutch vessels). See the bibliography for additional information on archives.

A few of these ship logs have been published: see Robert Ross, ed., "The Dutch on the Swahili Coast, 1776–1778: Two Slaving Journals," pts. 1 and 2, *International Journal of African Historical Studies* 19, no. 2 (1986): 305–60, and 19, no. 3 (1986): 479–506; Stephen Ellis and Solofo Randrianja, "Les archives de la Compagnie néerlandaise des Indes orientales et l'histoire de Madagascar: L'expédition du navire de la V.O.C. le *Schuylenburg*, septembre 1752," in *La route des esclaves: Système servile et traite dans l'est malgache*, ed. Ignace Rakoto (Paris: Harmattan, 2000), 47–73; Frappé and Lint, *Slawehandel met Madagaskar*; Vernet, "La première traite française." There are likely more ship logs to be found in private collections and public archives, such as the "Journal and Logbook of an anonymous Scotch sailor, 1726–1729," from a slave-trading voyage that included Madagascar, HC 363/129, Hispanic Society of America.

61. For examples of how Portuguese sources can be used to study the history of Madagascar, see Edward Alpers, "Madagascar and Mozambique in the Nineteenth Century: The Era of the Sakalava Raids (1800–1820)," *Omaly sy anio* (Université d'Antananarivo) 5–6 (1977): 37–53; Vernet, "Slave Trade."

62. Michael H. Fisher, "Working across the Seas: Indian Maritime Labourers in India, Britain, and in between, 1600–1857," in "Coolies, Capital, and Colonialism," supplement, *International Review of Social History* 51, no. S14 (2006): 22; see also Marcus Rediker, *Between the Devil and the Deep Blue Sea: Merchant Seamen, Pirates and the Anglo-American Maritime World, 1700–1750* (Cambridge: Cambridge University Press, 1989), 39–41.

63. On differences in access to food on board vessels, see Pearson, *Indian Ocean*, 187–88.

64. Given the multitude of names for each location and the irregular use of geographical descriptions, the identification of specific ports will not always be possible. Modern-day spelling will be used whenever possible,

as place names tended to change over time and spellings differed from one European language to another. Alternative spellings for locations found in the sources will be given at their first mention.

65. National Archives, British Library, Asian and African Studies, India Office Records, Maritime Department Records, Ships' Journals, IOR/L/MAR/A–B.

## CHAPTER 2: "THE RICHEST AND MOST FRUITFUL ISLAND IN THE WORLD"

1. Walter Hamond, *Madagascar, the Richest and Most Fruitful Island in the World* (London, 1643); Walter Hamond, *A Paradox: Prooving, That the Inhabitants of the Isle Called Madagascar, or St. Laurence, (in Temporall Things) Are the Happiest People in the World* (London, 1640). See also William Foster, "An English Settlement in Madagascar in 1645–6," *English Historical Review* 27, no. 106 (1912): 241. Some quotations and titles have been altered to reflect modern spelling.

2. J. Megiser, description of Madagascar, 1609, in Alfred Grandidier et al., eds., *Collection des ouvrages anciens concernant Madagascar*, 9 vols. (Paris: Comité de Madagascar, 1903–20) (hereafter cited as *COACM*), 1:425.

3. See, for instance, Sébastien Munster, "Cosmographia," 1572, ibid., 1:113; François de Belleforest, 1575, ibid., 1:136.

4. On contemporary fascination with Indian Ocean islands, see David Picard, "Cultivating Human Gardens: Tropical Island Tourism in the South-Western Indian Ocean," in *Eyes across the Water: Navigating the Indian Ocean*, ed. Pamila Gupta, Isabel Hofmeyr, and Michael N. Pearson (Pretoria: Unisa Press, 2010), 32–36.

5. William Davenant, *Madagascar, with Other Poems* (London, 1638), frontispiece; see also Foster, "English Settlement," 241; Alison Games, *The Web of Empire: English Cosmopolitans in an Age of Expansion, 1560–1660* (Oxford: Oxford University Press, 2008), 186–87.

6. Translated quotation from Dirk Boogaart, VOC slave trader on the *Soldaat*, 1697, in R. J. Barendse, "Slaving on the Malagasy Coast, 1640–1700," in *Cultures of Madagascar: Ebb and Flow of Influences*, ed. S. Evers and M. Spindler (Leiden: International Institute for Asian Studies, 1995), 139.

7. Memoir, 1665, COL C/5A/1. See also Gabriel Dellon, *A Voyage to the East-Indies* (London, 1698), 14.

8. Europeans confused Madagascar with East Africa, thanks to the description of "Mogdoxo" provided by Marco Polo: André Thevet, 1538, described in *COACM*, 1:108nn1–2; Sebastien Munster, 1572, ibid., 1:113; Porcacchi, 1572, ibid., 1:115–16; Jean Hughes de Linschot, 1583, ibid., 1:143.

9. On the use of the terms foreland and hinterland, see Michael N. Pearson, *Port Cities and Intruders: The Swahili Coast, India, and Portugal in the Early Modern Era* (Baltimore: Johns Hopkins University Press, 1998), 67.

10. Étienne de Flacourt, *Histoire de la Grande Isle Madagascar*, ed. Claude Allibert (Paris: Karthala, 1995), 126.

11. On the early Mediterranean and the use of islands, see Lincoln Paine, *The Sea and Civilization: A Maritime History of the World* (New York: Knopf, 2013), 79–136.

12. T. Bentley Duncan, *Atlantic Islands: Madeira, the Azores, and the Cape Verdes in Seventeenth-Century Commerce and Navigation* (Chicago: University of Chicago Press, 1972), 1.

13. In West Africa, the Portuguese first dealt primarily with coastal or offshore locations. See Herbert S. Klein, *The Atlantic Slave Trade*, 2nd ed. (Cambridge: Cambridge University Press, 2010), 10, 51–52.

14. Memoir on Madagascar, 1664, COL C/5A/1.

15. Powle Waldegrave, *An Answer to Mr Boothbies Book, of the Description of the Island of Madagascar* (London, 1649), 6, 21. Waldegrave was writing in response to Richard Boothby, *A Briefe Discovery or Description of the Most Famous Island of Madagascar or St. Laurence in Asia Neare unto East-India* (London, 1646).

16. Robert Hunt, *The Island of Assada, Neere Madagascar Impartially Defined: Being a Succint, Yet Plenary Discription of the Situation, Fertility and People Therein Inhabiting* (London, 1650), 3–4. See also French memoir, 1664, COL C/5A/1.

17. See Jean-Michel Racault, "Les premières tentatives coloniales à Madagascar (XVIIe–XVIIIe siècles): Échos dans la fiction," in *Idées et représentations coloniales dans l'océan Indien*, ed. Norbert Dodille (Paris: Presses de l'Université Paris-Sorbonne, 2009), 285–98.

18. Margarette Lincoln, *British Pirates and Society, 1680–1730* (London: Ashgate, 2014), 153.

19. For example, see the French memoir written in about 1789 citing Flacourt when describing the people living in Antananosy, COL C/5A/9.

20. The island was also targeted for settlement and the slave trade by others, including a plan proposed to the Brandenburg Company and the Swedes. See Arne Bialuschewski, "Thomas Bowrey's Madagascar Manuscript of 1708," *History in Africa* 34 (2007): 41.

21. Discovery of Madagascar by Diaz, in *COACM*, 1:3–4; see also Pier M. Larson, "Colonies Lost: God, Hunger, and Conflict in Anosy (Madagascar) to 1674," *Comparative Studies of South Asia, Africa and the Middle East* 27, no. 2 (2007): 345.

22. Mike Parker Pearson, "Close Encounters of the Worst Kind: Malagasy Resistance and Colonial Disasters in Southern Madagascar," *World Archaeology* 28, no. 3 (1997): 395.

23. On Portuguese shipwrecks, see Larson, "Colonies Lost," 349–50.

24. J. R. E. Lutjeharms, *The Agulhas Current* (New York: Springer, 2006), 1–5; Michael N. Pearson, *The Indian Ocean* (London: Routledge, 2003), 24–25. See also Alexander George Findlay, *A Directory for the Navigation of the Indian Ocean*, 3rd ed. (London: Richard Holmes Laurie, 1876), 421. The Portuguese named the southern entrance into the channel Cabo das Correntes due to the "violent current of water which often endangers ships there." Manuel de Faria e Sousa, *Asia Portuguesa*, book 1, 1666, in *Records of South-Eastern Africa Collected in Various Libraries and Archive Departments in Europe*, ed. George McCall Theal, 9 vols. (Cape Town: Printed for the Government of the Cape Colony, 1898–1903), 1:12.

25. "Letter from Father Manuel Fernandes to Father Mirão," 6 August 1555, in *Documents on the Portuguese in Mozambique and Central Africa, 1497–1840*, 9 vols. (Lisbon: National Archives of Rhodesia and Nyasaland, Centro de Estudos Históricos Ultramarinos, 1962–89), 7:307.

26. V. Magelhães Godinho, "The Portuguese and the 'Carreira da India,' 1497–1810," in *Ships, Sailors and Spices: East India Companies and Their Shipping in the 16th, 17th and 18th Centuries*, ed. Jaap R. Bruijn and Femme S. Gaastra (Amsterdam: NEHA, 1993), 29.

27. Pearson, *Indian Ocean*, 19–20; Edward A. Alpers, *The Indian Ocean in World History* (Oxford: Oxford University Press, 2014), 7.

28. On the frequency of cyclones, see Edward A. Alpers, "Littoral Society in the Mozambique Channel," in Alpers, *East Africa and the Indian Ocean* (Princeton, NJ: Markus Wiener, 2009), 170–71.

29. "Letter from Père Ferreira Fogaca, Captain of Kilwa, to the King," 22 December 1506, in *Documents on the Portuguese*, 1:12–19; "Letter from Afonso de Albuquerque to the King," 5 February 1507, ibid., 2:113; Portuguese description, 1506, in Anne Molet-Sauvaget, ed., *Documents anciens sur les îles Comores: 1591–1800, Supplément / II* (Paris: Institut national des langues et civilisations orientales, 1996), 1–2. Recent work on the Portuguese Empire describes how Portuguese colonists and traders had to contend with strong local rulers. See Pearson, *Port Cities*, 20–21, 131–32; Pearson, *Indian Ocean*, 126–27; Kenneth R. Hall, "Local and International Trade and Traders in the Straits of the Melaka Region: 600–1500," *Journal of the Economic and Social History of the Orient* 47, no. 2 (2004): 253; Francisco Bethencourt and Diogo Ramada Curto, "Introduction," trans. Neil Safier, in *Portuguese Oceanic Expansion, 1400–1800*, ed. Francisco Bethencourt and Diogo Ramada Curto (Cambridge: Cambridge University Press, 2007), 1–3; Michael N. Pearson, "Markets and Merchant Communities in

the Indian Ocean: Locating the Portuguese," in Bethencourt and Curto, *Portuguese Oceanic Expansion*, 97–98; A. R. Disney, *A History of Portugal and the Portuguese Empire* (Cambridge: Cambridge University Press, 2009), 2:146–49; Sanjay Subrahmanyam, *The Portuguese Empire in Asia, 1500–1700: A Political and Economic History*, 2nd ed. (West Sussex, UK: Wiley-Blackwell, 2012), 194–204.

30. "Description of the Situation, Customs and Produce of some Places of Africa," 1518, in *Documents on the Portuguese*, 5:371. See also "Relation de Castanheda," in *COACM*, 1:34.

31. "Letter from Afonso de Albuquerque to the King," 6 February 1507, in *Documents on the Portuguese*, 2:121, 123; see also "Letter from Lourenço Moreno to the King," 30 November 1513, ibid., 3:489–91.

32. In the encounter, the Portuguese had been shown cloves and the islander, when asked where they were from, responded by pointing to the interior of the island, far from a sure identification. "Letter from Afonso de Albuquerque to the King," 6 February 1507, ibid., 2:123. Vernet suggests that cloves grew in East Africa in 1812, so it is unlikely cloves were found in Madagascar during the sixteenth century. Thomas Vernet, "Avant le giroflier: Esclavage et agriculture sur la côte swahili, 1590–1812," in *Traites et esclavages en Afrique orientale et dans l'océan Indien*, ed. Henri Médard et al. (Paris: Karthala, 2013), 245.

33. "Summary by António Carneiro, secretary of state, of a letter from Afonso de Albuquerque to the King," 10 November 1507, in *Documents on the Portuguese*, 2:219; see also the "Letter from the King to the Archbishop of Braga," 19 June 1508, ibid., 2:273; "Letter from Antonio Peal to Afonso de Albuquerque," 1512, ibid., 3:395–97.

34. "Letter from Sebastião de Sousa to the King," 17 September 1521, ibid., 6:67.

35. "Extracts from the Book called Lendas da India," 1528, in Theal, *Records of South-Eastern Africa*, 2:51.

36. For these reasons, Newitt states that while the food export trade had already existed, with the arrival of the Portuguese it reached a new level of importance: Malyn Newitt, "The Southern Swahili Coast in the First Century of European Expansion," *Azania* 13, no. 1 (1978): 121–23.

37. "List of maintenance payments for May 1506 in the Fortress of Kilwa," 1 May 1506, in *Documents on the Portuguese*, 1:501–2.

38. Malyn Newitt, "Mozambique Island: The Rise and Decline of a Colonial Port City," in *Portuguese Colonial Cities in the Early Modern World*, ed. Liam Matthew Brockey (Burlington, VT: Ashgate, 2008), 112–14.

39. "Lendas da India," in Theal, *Records of South-Eastern Africa*, 2:51.

40. See Robert E. Dewar and Henry T. Wright, "The Culture History of Madagascar," *Journal of World Prehistory* 7, no. 4 (1993): 431; Henry

T. Wright et al., "The Evolution of Settlement Systems in the Bay of Boeny and the Mahavavy River Valley, North-Western Madagascar," *Azania* 31, no. 1 (1996): 47. Beaujard sees the creation of port cities close to the Comoro Islands as part of a thrust of Arab-Swahili influence or settlers into the Comoros and northwestern Madagascar: Philippe Beaujard, "East Africa, the Comoros Islands and Madagascar before the Sixteenth Century: On a Neglected Part of the World System," *Azania* 42, no. 1 (2007): 21–22. See also Solofo Randrianja and Stephen Ellis, *Madagascar: A Short History* (Chicago: University of Chicago Press, 2009), 23–24.

41. On various locations visited by Arab sailors in Madagascar, see the remarks of Tibbetts in Ahmad ibn Majid al-Najdi, *Arab Navigation in the Indian Ocean before the Coming of the Portuguese*, ed. G. R. Tibbetts (London: Royal Asiatic Society of Great Britain and Ireland, 1972), 432–35. On identifying these ports, see Jean-Claude Hébert, "Sur des ports esclavagistes de la côte nord-ouest de Madagascar dont le nom est devenu obsolète: Maringado ou Moringambo et Lulangani/Langany/Morumgany," in *Navires, ports, itinéraires*, ed. Claude Allibert (Paris: Institut national des langues et civilisations orientales, 1999), 11–60; Thomas Vernet, "Slave Trade and Slavery on the Swahili Coast, 1500–1750," in *Slavery, Islam and Diaspora*, ed. Paul Lovejoy, Behnaz A. Mirzai, and Ismael M. Montana (Trenton, NJ: Africa World Press, 2009), 42.

42. See the records of Jesuit missionaries Freire and Mariano to Madagascar, 1613–14, in *COACM*, 2:13–17.

43. See Chantal Radimilahy, *Mahilaka: An Archaeological Investigation of an Early Town in Northwestern Madagascar* (Uppsala: Department of Archaeology and Ancient History, Uppsala University, 1998), 203–11.

44. "Description of the Situation, Customs and Produce of some Places of Africa," 1518, in *Documents on the Portuguese*, 5:371. See also Manoel Teles de Meneces, 1506, in *COACM*, 1:13; Barros, 1506, ibid., 1:30; A. Corsali, "Des moeurs de ses habitants et de l'île d'Oetabacam," 1514, ibid., 1:51; Ramusio, 1550, ibid., 1:101–4; see also Newitt, "Southern Swahili Coast," 120. On cloth exports, perhaps from the twelfth century, to the Middle East, see John Baldry, *Textiles in Yemen: Historical References to Trade and Commerce in Textiles in Yemen from Antiquity to Modern Times* (London: British Museum, 1982), 17–18. On the linkages with elsewhere in Madagascar, see Henry T. Wright and Jean-Aimé Rakotoarisoa, "The Rise of Malagasy Societies: New Developments in the Archaeology of Madagascar," in *The Natural History of Madagascar*, ed. Steven M. Goodman and Jonathan P. Benstead (Chicago: University of Chicago Press, 2006), 114; Pierre Vérin, *The History of Civilisation in North Madagascar*, trans. David Smith (Rotterdam: A. A. Balkema, 1986), 145–51. On timber in Madagascar to Mozambique, see Manoel Barretto, "Report upon the

State and Conquest of the Rivers of Cuama," 1667, in Theal, *Records of South-Eastern Africa*, 3:465.

45. Vernet, "Avant le giroflier," 252. See also Wright and Rakotoarisoa, "Rise of Malagasy Societies," 114–18; Philippe Beaujard, *Les mondes de l'océan Indien* (Paris: Armand Colin, 2012), 1:552–60, 2:369; Nicole Boivin et al., "East Africa and Madagascar in the Indian Ocean World," *Journal of World Prehistory* 26, no. 3 (2013): 266–67.

46. "Letter from Afonso de Albuquerque to the King," 6 February 1507, in *Documents on the Portuguese*, 2:123.

47. Ibid., 2:121.

48. Tristan da Cunha, 1506, in *COACM*, 1:15; see also Manoel Barreto, 1667, ibid., 3:339; "Letter from Sebastiao de Sousa to the King," 17 September 1521, in *Documents on the Portuguese*, 6:67; "Letter from Afonso de Albuquerque to the King," 6 February 1507, ibid., 2:121.

49. Portuguese sources from the sixteenth and especially seventeenth century describe dhows carrying about one thousand to five thousand slaves from the northwestern ports annually. Based on these observations, historians have postulated that two hundred thousand slaves were exported from Madagascar on non-European vessels between 1500 and 1800. It seems probable that the Portuguese writers did not actually observe the loading of slaves onto dhows. Instead, these numbers may have been "more a reflection of capacity than actual exports." Pier M. Larson, "Enslaved Malagasy and 'Le Travail de la Parole' in the Pre-Revolutionary Mascarenes," *Journal of African History* 48, no. 3 (2007): 459n1.

Furthermore, many ports probably attracted only two or three dhows a year after the peak period during the early eighteenth century, but it is hard to be certain. For instance, one French source from 1664 states that two or three large dhow ships of four hundred tons visited the northwest ports for slaves annually. See the memoir, 1664, in COL C/5A/1. The largest slave trading dhows were described by Europeans as carrying up to two hundred slaves each, although it was likely fewer, as they typically transported supplies of rice and cattle as well. In 1734, a dhow from northwest Madagascar carried a hundred slaves ("*captifs*") to Ndzuwani. See the ship journal of the *Chauvelin*, 1734, MAR 4JJ/98.

Finally, the trade was likely subject to frequent disruption both at sea and land. The Portuguese were openly hostile to "Moor" slave traders operating in the ports of Madagascar and tried to interfere with this traffic whenever possible. In 1676, for instance, one Portuguese slave trader ransacked the northwest port of "New Massaliege" and stole slaves from dhows anchored in the harbor. See Barendse, "Slaving," 137.

For all of these reasons, I tend to agree with Vernet that the most likely number of slaves exported during the seventeenth-century peak was between two and three thousand a year. See Vernet, "Slave Trade," 60. It is hard to believe that the merchants in the northwestern ports could have exported more than five thousand slaves annually on non-European dhows between 1600 and 1800, especially because, after 1506, ports in northwestern Madagascar were supplying both European and non-European traders, further lowering the supply of slaves for sale to just Arab and African traders. European slave traders, after all, rarely purchased more than two thousand slaves a year from the entire island of Madagascar, not just the northwestern ports, even during the peak of the slave trade in the late seventeenth and early eighteenth centuries. See Stephen Ellis, "The History of Sovereigns in Madagascar: New Light from Old Sources," in *Madagascar revisitée: En voyage avec Françoise Raison-Jourde*, ed. Didier Nativel and Faranirina V. Rajaonah (Paris: Karthala, 2009), 409–10.

50. See Walter Peyton, 1614, in *COACM*, 2:84; Jean de la Roque, *A Voyage to Arabia Felix*, trans. Dominique de Moulins (New York: Oleander, 2004), 8. During the seventeenth century, Malagasy slaves were frequently sent to the Lamu archipelago off East Africa. See Vernet, "Slave Trade," 44. Vernet uses Portuguese documents to compile a list of major slave trading ports of the seventeenth century, including Mocha (al-Mukha), Aden, al-Shihr, and Kishn, with each one importing and exporting slaves via East Africa and the Comoros, with a significant number sold out of Boeny (near Massaliege). Ibid., 45.

51. Regarding this annual movement of bodies and goods, see "A Voyage in ye ship *Frances* from Mossambique for St. Lawrence," 1640, Rawlinson MS A 334, fols. 54–57; reproduced in Stephen Ellis, "Un texte du XVIIe siècle sur Madagascar," *Omaly sy anio* (Université d'Antananarivo) 9 (1979): 155–57. See also the comments of Jesuit priests Freire and Mariano, 1613–14, in *COACM*, esp. 2:13–14; records left by the French colonist François Martin, 1665–68, ibid., 9:555–57.

52. On the use of cloth and silver in the region, see, for instance, "Relâche du capitaine Christophe Newport," 1613, ibid., 1:491; letter of Père Luis Mariano, July 1616, ibid., 2:214.

53. See the account of van der Meersch, c. 1645, in *COACM*, 3:198. The Portuguese bought slaves from other northwestern ports, including Ampasindava and Manambolo: Jean-Michel Filliot, *La traite des esclaves vers les Mascareignes au XVIIIe siècle* (Paris: ORSTOM, 1974), 115.

54. As suggested by various documents in *COACM*. See also Henri Daniel Liszkowski, *Mayotte et les Comores: Escales sur la route des Indes aux XVe et XVIIe siècles* (Mamoudzou, Mayotte: Baobab, 2000), 123.

55. For more details on later Portuguese slave trading within the Indian Ocean, particularly between Mozambique and India, see Pedro Machado, "A Forgotten Corner of the Indian Ocean: Gujarati Merchants, Portuguese

India and the Mozambique Slave-Trade, c. 1730–1830," *Slavery & Abolition* 24, no. 2 (2004): 17–32; Richard B. Allen, *European Slave Trading in the Indian Ocean, 1500–1850* (Athens: Ohio University Press, 2015), 8–9.

56. Barretto, "Report," in Theal, *Records of South-Eastern Africa*, 3:465.

57. On the locations of these ports, see Hébert, "Sur des ports esclavagistes."

58. "Letter from Afonso de Albuquerque to the King," 6 February 1507, in *Documents on the Portuguese*, 2:121–22.

59. For example, in 1577: "History of the Dominicans in the Possessions of Portugal," 1585, in Theal, *Records of South-Eastern Africa*, 1:387–89. See also Larson, "Colonies Lost," 357. For more details on how these hostilities shaped Portuguese and East African relations, see Pearson, *Port Cities*, 58, 142; Giancarlo Casale, *The Ottoman Age of Exploration* (Oxford: Oxford University Press, 2010), 163–75. See also G. S. P. Freeman-Grenville, ed., *The Mombasa Rising against the Portuguese, 1631: From Sworn Evidence* (London: Oxford University Press for the British Academy, 1980).

60. Malyn Newitt, *A History of Mozambique* (Bloomington: Indiana University Press, 1995), 172.

61. "Histoire de la révolte des Musulmans de Madagascar contre les Portugais, et martyre du P. Thomas," 1587, in *COACM*, 1:153–59; Manuel de Faria e Sousa, "Asia Portuguesa," 1674, vol. 3, in Theal, *Records of South-Eastern Africa*, 1:33.

62. These complaints were made by a Genoese Jesuit, Luigi Mariana (Mariano) who visited Madagascar in 1619: *COACM*, 2:319–21. More evidence for Portuguese interference with trade in the region is found in a Hadhrami chronicle. Around 1533, two vessels from "al-Sawahil" arrived in the port al-Shihr on the Arabian Peninsula. While they were at anchor, the Portuguese arrived and the merchants were forced to hand over their passengers and part of the cargo. R. B. Serjeant, *The Portuguese off the South Arabian Coast: Hadrami Chronicles, with Yemeni and European Accounts of Dutch Pirates off Mocha in the Seventeenth Century* (Oxford: Clarendon, 1963), 68. The Portuguese also described the constant wars within Madagascar as hampering the mission: Mariano, 1616, *COACM*, 2:218–222.

63. For a description of the people who lived in Antanosy in southeastern Madagascar, see Larson, "Colonies Lost," 349.

64. On later attempts to convert the people in the region, see ibid., 350–57.

65. The English report states that the feast was seven years earlier: Ellis, "Un texte," 158. The Portuguese source is Mariano, letter, 9 September 1640, in *COACM*, 2:431–432.

66. Ellis, "Un texte," 157n26. The king's name and location are given in Mariano, in *COACM*, 2:431.

67. Ellis, "Un texte," 158; Mariano, in *COACM*, 2:431.

68. Ellis, "Un texte," 158–59.

69. Ibid., 159.

70. "Relâche aux îles Comores de l'Amiral G. Spilberg," 1601–2, in *COACM*, 1:314.

71. On the use of Portuguese by rulers in the Comoros, see the report of the *Ascension*, 1608, in Anne Molet-Sauvaget, ed., *Documents anciens sur les îles Comores: 1591–1810* (Paris: Institut national des langues et civilisations orientales, 1994), 9. Portuguese was understood by interpreters throughout the Comoros. See the first visit of the English, 1591, in *COACM*, 1:160–61; an early French voyage in 1602, ibid., 1:284–86.

72. "Relâche," *COACM*, 1:315. For more examples, see the observation of a ship in Mwali that was leaving Madagascar with an "Arab" pilot speaking Portuguese: "Relation de Thomas Rhoe," 1614, ibid., 2:89; a Dutch observation of slaves from Madagascar in Ndzuwani, before being sent to Arabia: Pieter van den Broeke, 1614, ibid., 2:90. Such vessels are described in Newitt, *History of Mozambique*, 172–73.

73. Barendse, "Slaving," 140; Disney, *History of Portugal*, 2:178–79.

74. João dos Santos, "Ethiopia Oriental," 1609, in Theal, *Records of South-Eastern Africa*, 7:332.

75. Disney, *History of Portugal*, 2:179. For additional descriptions of this trade, see "Twelfth Voyage of the East India Company, in 1613, by Captain Christopher Newport," in *A General History and Collection of Voyages and Travels*, ed. Robert Kerr (Edinburgh: W. Blackwood, 1824), 9:140. In practice, this trade was subject to seizure by Portuguese officials. See Glenn J. Ames, "An African Eldorado? The Portuguese Quest for Wealth and Power in Mozambique and the Rios de Cuama, c. 1661–1683," *International Journal of African Historical Studies* 31, no. 1 (1998): 91–92.

76. On the Portuguese focus on continental East Africa (particularly in pursuit of gold), see Disney, *History of Portugal*, 2:134–144; Pearson, *Port Cities*, 131–33. Rodrigues argues that the influence of Goa encouraged rice consumption on Mozambique Island: Eugénia Rodrigues, "Eating and Drinking at the Royal Hospital of Mozambique Island: Medicine and Diet Change between the End of the 18th and the Early 19th Century," *Afriques: Débats, méthodes et terrains d'histoire*, no. 5 (2014), http://afriques.revues.org/1553.

77. Newitt argues that during the course of the eighteenth century the Portuguese focused on encouraging agricultural development in East Africa and were less reliant on the trade with the Comoros and Madagascar. Newitt, *History of Mozambique*, 140.

78. "Description of the Situation, Customs and Produce of Various Places of Africa," 1518 in *Documents on the Portuguese*, 5:381.

79. Barretto, "Report," in Theal, *Records of South-Eastern Africa*, 3:465. Similar fears were expressed a few decades earlier in a letter from the Portuguese king Philip II to the Viceroys of India, 24 February 1635, ibid., 4:256.

80. Newitt, *History of Mozambique*, 29, 172.

81. For instance, there are fewer mentions of Portuguese vessels on the Malagasy coastline in English, French, and Dutch sources by about 1676. See also the conclusions of James C. Armstrong, "Madagascar and the Slave Trade in the Seventeenth Century," *Omaly sy anio* (Université d'Antananarivo) 17–20 (1983): 216–17; Glenn J. Ames, *Colbert, Mercantilism, and the French Quest for Asian Trade* (DeKalb: Northern Illinois University Press, 1996), 6.

82. On the first Dutch voyage by the ship *Amsterdam*, 1595, see "Details of voyage 0001.1 from Texel to Engano," short description found in the online database, The Dutch East India Company's Shipping between the Netherlands and Asia 1595–1795, Historici.nl: http://resources.huygens.knaw.nl/das/detailVoyage/91055. This database has summaries of Dutch voyages, including details about their itineraries and voyage outcomes. See also the list of voyages in Jaap R. Bruijn, Femme S. Gaastra, and Ivo Schöffer, *Dutch-Asiatic Shipping in the 17th and 18th Centuries*, 3 vols. (The Hague: Martinus Nijhoff, 1979–87).

83. M. N. Pearson, *Indian Ocean*, 145.

84. The ship *Banda*, 1606, "Details of Voyage 0107.1 from Texel to Goa," http://www.historici.nl/Onderzoek/Projecten/DAS/DAS/detailVoyage/91161; the ship *Hollandia*, 1607, "Details of Voyage 0125.2 from Texel to Goa," http://www.historici.nl/Onderzoek/Projecten/DAS/DAS/detailVoyage/91179.

85. Orginally written in 1598: Jan Huygen van Linschoten, *The Voyage of John Huyghen van Linschoten to the East Indies*, ed. P. A. Tiele, vol. 2 (London, 1885), 22.

86. For example, Auguste Toussaint, *History of the Indian Ocean*, trans. June Guicharnaud (Chicago: University of Chicago Press, 1966), 120. See also a popular history of these conflicts, Giles Milton, *Nathaniel's Nutmeg* (London: Hodder & Stoughton, 2012). Historians who have focused on the Dutch in Asia include George D. Winius and Marcus P. M. Vink, *The Merchant-Warrior Pacified: The VOC (the Dutch East India Company) and Its Changing Political Economy in India* (Delhi: Oxford University Press, 1991); Tonio Andrade, *How Taiwan Became Chinese: Dutch, Spanish, and Han Colonization in the Seventeenth Century* (New York: Columbia University Press, 2007); Adam Clulow, *The Company and the Shogun: The*

*Dutch Encounter with Tokugawa Japan* (New York: Columbia University Press, 2014).

87. The *Amsterdam*, in Bruijn, Gaastra, and Schöffer, *Dutch-Asiatic Shipping*, 2:2–3. See also Robert Parthesius, *Dutch Ships in Tropical Waters: The Development of the Dutch East India Company (VOC) Shipping Network in Asia 1595–1660* (Amsterdam: Amsterdam University Press, 2010), 32–33.

88. Pearson, *Indian Ocean*, 23; Parthesius, *Dutch Ships*, 51. On the dangers of sailing in this part of the ocean, see Jaap R. Bruijn, *Commanders of Dutch East India Ships in the Eighteenth Century* (Woodbridge, Suffolk: Boydell, 2011), 260.

89. See itineraries of ships in Bruijn, Gaastra, and Schöffer, *Dutch-Asiatic Shipping*, 2:2–29. See also K. Heeringa, "De Nederlanders op Mauritius en Madagascar," in *De Indische gids*, ed. C. E. van Kesteren, R. A. van Sandick, and J. E. de Meyier (Amsterdam: J. H. de Bussy, 1895), 864–92. Note that European ship logs frequently listed the names of the bays or rivers of Madagascar, such as Antongil Bay, St. Augustin Bay, or Boina Bay, and used them to identify major regions of the island.

90. See the description of the region near the bay provided by three anthropologists in Chantal Radimilahy and Barthélémy Manjakahery, "Archaeology of St. Augustine's Bay, Lower and Middle Onilahy Valley, Southwestern Madagascar," in *The African Archaeology Network: Research in Progress*, Studies in the African Past 5 (Dar es Salaam: Dar es Salaam University Press, 2006), 61–63.

91. The ship also spent time in "Mosselbaai" in southern Africa and "Ampalazabaai." The ship *Amsterdam*, 1595, "Details of Voyage 0001.1 from Texel to Engano," http://www.historici.nl/Onderzoek/Projecten/DAS/DAS/detailVoyage/91055; see also Dutch account of visiting Madagascar, 1593, in *COACM*, 1:166–86.

92. The ship *Leeuw*, 1598, "Details of Voyage 0008.1 from Veere to Atjeh," http://www.historici.nl/Onderzoek/Projecten/DAS/DAS/detailVoyage/91062.

93. The ship *Mauritius*, 1598, "Details of Voyage 0010.1 from Texel to Engano," http://www.historici.nl/Onderzoek/Projecten/DAS/DAS/detailVoyage/91064.

94. When visiting Antongil, many ships also halted at the island of Nosy Boraha.

95. Jan van Riebeeck, *Journal of Jan van Riebeeck*, ed. Hendrik Bernardus Thom, trans. W. P. L. van Zyl, C. K. Johnman, A. Ravenscroft, J. Smuts, van Oordt, vol. 1 (Cape Town: Van Riebeeck Society, 1952), 191.

96. For instance, see "Premier atterrissage des hollandais à Madagascar, lors du voyage de l'amiral Cornelis de Houtman aux Indes orientales

(1595)," in *COACM*, 1:218. On archeological finds in eastern Madagascar, see Boivin et al., "East Africa and Madagascar," 266–67; Beaujard, *Les mondes*, 1:552–60, 2:369.

97. See the account of Admiral van Neck, 1598, in *COACM*, 6:1–14; Claude Allibert, "Les Hollandais et Madagascar," in Evers and Spindler, *Cultures of Madagascar*, 89.

98. See the account of François Martin, 1665–68, in *COACM*, 9:460–63, 556, 561–62. See also letter from MM. de la Faye and Caron, directors of the former Compagnie des Indes, 1667, COL C/5A/1.

99. Heeringa, "De Nederlanders," 865. See also the ship *Langebark*, 1601, "Details of Voyage 0047.2 from Zeeland to Atjeh," http://www.historici.nl/Onderzoek/Projecten/DAS/DAS/detailVoyage/91101.

100. For instance, the ship *Wassende Maan*, 1599, "Details of Voyage 0028.1 from Texel to Bantam," http://www.historici.nl/Onderzoek/Projecten/DAS/DAS/detailVoyage/91082.

101. Wendy van Duivenvoorde, *Dutch East India Company Shipbuilding: The Archaeological Study of Batavia and Other Seventeenth-Century VOC Ships* (College Station: Texas A&M University Press, 2015), 198–99. See also the account of refreshing, presumably on Nosy Boraha, in Willem Ysbrantsz Bontekoe, *Memorable Description of the East Indian Voyage, 1618–25*, trans. C. B. Bodde-Hodgkinson and Pieter Geyl (London: RoutledgeCurzon, 2005), 34–37.

102. P. J. Moree, *A Concise History of Dutch Mauritius, 1598–1710: A Fruitful and Healthy Land* (London: Kegan Paul International, 1998), 3; Jocelyn Chan Low, *"La VOC, t'Eylandt Mauritius et Rodrigues": Avec le voyage de Wolfert Harmensz vers les Îles Rodrigues et Maurice, 1601* (Port-Louis, Mauritius: National Library, 2001), 5–7; Allibert, "Les Hollandais et Madagascar," 91.

103. Megan Vaughan, *Creating the Creole Island: Slavery in Eighteenth-Century Mauritius* (Durham, NC: Duke University Press, 2005), 4–5.

104. Ibid., 11, 52. See also Huguette Ly-Tio-Fane Pineo, "Food Production and Plantation Economy of Mauritius," in *Slavery in South West Indian Ocean*, ed. U. Bissoondoyal and S. B. C. Servansing (Moka, Mauritius: Mahatma Gandhi Institute, 1989), 210–22.

105. Vaughan, *Creating the Creole Island*, 8. On the distance between Madagascar and the Mascarenese, see, for instance, the voyages of the *Duc d'Anjou*, 1737, to and from Île de France (Mauritius) and eastern Madagascar in only a few weeks, MAR 4JJ/74.

106. Treaty between Portugal and the Netherlands, 12 June 1641 (ratified by the Portuguese king on 18 November 1641 and the Dutch Estates General, 22 February 1642), in Theal, *Records of South-Eastern Africa*, 1:407. See also Armstrong, "Madagascar and the Slave Trade," 216–23.

107. The voyages of van der Stel, in *COACM*, 3:31–33.

108. Moree, *Concise History*, 31.

109. Treaty of 8 March 1642 with Adrien van der Stel, second governor of Dutch Mauritius, *COACM*, 6:19–21. See also Chan Low, *La VOC*, 38.

110. Sateeanund Peerthum, "Resistance against Slavery," in Bissoondoyal and Servansing, *Slavery in South West Indian Ocean*, 125; Vaughan, *Creating the Creole Island*, 9. For more on the long history of maroonage in the Mascarenes, see Richard B. Allen, *Slaves, Freedmen, and Indentured Laborers in Colonial Mauritius* (Cambridge: Cambridge University Press, 1999), 35–51.

111. On the impact of Dutch forestry, see Richard Grove, "Conserving Eden: The (European) East India Companies and Their Environmental Policies on St. Helena, Mauritius and in Western India, 1660 to 1854," *Comparative Studies in Society and History* 35, no. 2 (1993): 329–30.

112. Flacourt states that a dozen Dutch were living at Antongil during this century: Flacourt, *Histoire*, 131–32.

113. Chan Low, *La VOC*, 39; Moree, *Concise History*, 32; Armstrong, "Madagascar and the Slave Trade," 223. On the trading connections across the north of the island, see René Battistini and Pierre Vérin, "Irodo et la tradition Vohémarienne: Les découverts d'Irodo et les civilisations du nord-est," *Revue de Madagascar* 36 (1966): 27; Vérin, *History of Civilisation*, 151–69.

114. Van der Meersch, 1646, in *COACM*, 3:191, 197.

115. Peerthum, "Resistance," 125.

116. Chan Low, *La VOC*, 39–40.

117. On this period on the island, see Moree, *Concise History*, 19, 76–78; Vaughan, *Creating the Creole Island*, 18–19. See also Daniel Sleigh, "The Economy of Mauritius during the Second Dutch occupation (1664–1710)," in *Globalisation and the South-West Indian Ocean*, ed. Sandra Evers and V. Y. Hookoomsingh (Réduit: University of Mauritius and International Institute for Asian Studies, 2000), 51–56.

118. Jaap R. Bruijn, "Between Batavia and the Cape: Shipping Patterns of the Dutch East India Company," *Journal of Southeast Asian Studies* 11, no. 2 (1980): 253.

119. On the procurement of food at the Cape, see Leonard Guelke, "Frontier Settlement in Early Dutch South Africa," *Annals of the Association of American Geographers* 66, no. 1 (1976): 25–42; John F. Richards, *The Unending Frontier: An Environmental History of the Early Modern World* (Berkeley: University of California Press, 2003), 274–302; Kerry Ward, *Networks of Empire: Forced Migration in the Dutch East India Company* (Cambridge: Cambridge University Press, 2009), 129–31.

120. Bruijn, "Between Batavia and the Cape," 256. The Dutch also wanted to import Malagasy cattle to breed with their own: Barendse, "Slaving," 141.

121. Chan Low, *La VOC*, 41.

122. van Riebeeck, *Journal of Jan van Riebeeck*, 1:191.

123. The VOC ships included the *Delft*, *Nieu Delf*, *Tulp*, *Roode Vose*, *Arnhem*, *Erasmus*, *Postiljon*, *Waterhoen*, *Lansmeer*, *Poelsnip*, *Ijsvolgel*, and *Westwout*.

124. Jan van Riebeeck, entry from 12 December 1653, in H. C. V. Leibrandt, ed., *Precis of the Archives of the Cape of Good Hope, December 1651–December 1653: Riebeeck's Journal, &c*, pt. 1 (Cape Town: W. A. Richards & Sons, 1897), 207. See also James C. Armstrong and Nigel A. Worden, "The Slaves, 1652–1834," in *The Shaping of South African Society, 1652–1840*, ed. Richard Elphick and Hermann Giliomee (Middletown, CT: Wesleyan University Press, 1988), 111.

125. The ship *Tulp*, 1653, "Details of Voyage 0785.1 from Texel to the Cape," http://www.historici.nl/Onderzoek/Projecten/DAS/detailVoyage/91902.

126. Jan van Riebeeck, entry from 9 February 1656, in H. C. V. Leibrandt, ed., *Precis of the Archives of the Cape of Good Hope: January 1656–December 1658: Riebeeck's Journal, &c*, pt. 2 (Cape Town: W. A. Richards & Sons, 1897), 7–8.

127. Letter, 5 May 1662, in H. C. V. Leibrandt, ed., *Precis of the Archives of the Cape of Good Hope: Letters Despatched from the Cape, 1652–1662*, vol. 3 (Cape Town: W. A. Richards & Sons, 1900), 236.

128. Letter, 9 April 1662, ibid., 214.

129. Jan van Riebeeck, various entries from 1662, in H. C. V. Leibrandt, ed., *Precis of the Archives of the Cape of Good Hope: Journal, 1662–1670* (Cape Town: W. A. Richards & Sons, 1901), 53–56, 84–85, 129.

130. Kevin P. McDonald, *Pirates, Merchants, Settlers, and Slaves: Colonial America and the Indo-Atlantic World* (Berkeley: University of California Press, 2015), 41.

131. Armstrong, "Madagascar and the Slave Trade," 226.

132. Armstrong and Worden, "Slaves," 114.

133. Armstrong, "Madagascar and the Slave Trade," 225–27.

134. The ship *Elisabeth*, 1678, in "Details of Voyage 1362.1 from Texel to Batavia," http://www.historici.nl/Onderzoek/Projecten/DAS/detailVoyage/91591.

135. The Dutch also benefited from the stops of English and French slave ships at the Cape throughout the late seventeenth and well into the eighteenth century to purchase additional slaves. Armstrong and Worden, "Slaves," 117–18.

136. Armstrong, "Madagascar and the Slave Trade," 222. For examples, see description of the Dutch slave trade, in *COACM*, 3:334–36; J. C. Hoffmann, ibid., 3:370–72; description of slaves for the Americas, ibid., 3:381; the Dutch slave trade, ibid., 3:382.

137. Armstrong and Worden, "Slaves," 113–14.

138. Allen, *European Slave Trading*, 16, table 1. The table also lists smaller quantities of slaves imported into Ceylon and Sumatra. See Markus Vink, "'The World's Oldest Trade': Dutch Slavery and Slave Trade in the Indian Ocean in the Seventeenth Century," *Journal of World History* 14, no. 2 (2003): 131–77.

139. Rafolo Andrianaivoarivony, "Regards furtifs sur les poteries importées à Madagascar avant l'arrivée des Portugais (VIIIe–début XVIe siècle après J.-C.)," in *Civilisations des mondes insulaires*, ed. Chantal Radimilahy and Narivelo Rajaonarimanana (Paris: Karthala, 2011), 337–55; Beaujard, *Les mondes*, 2:474, 480–84. On Chinese immigrants, see Guido Schreurs et al., "The Rasikajy Civilization in Northeast Madagascar: A Pre-European Chinese Community?" *Études océan Indien*, nos. 46–47 (2011): 107–32.

140. Augustin de Beaulieu, *Mémoires d'un voyage aux Indes Orientales, 1619–1622: Un marchand normand à Sumatra*, ed. Denys Lombard (Paris: École française d'Extrême-Orient; Maisonneuve & Larose, 1996), 52. On the history of French commerce in the region, see Ames, *Colbert*, 7; Donald C. Wellington, *French East India Companies: A Historical Account and Record of Trade* (Lanham, MD: Hamilton Books, 2006), 3–10. See also Toussaint, *History*, 124–26; Filliot, *La traite des esclaves*, 21–27; Philippe Haudrère, *La compagnie française des Indes au XVIIIe siècle*, 2nd ed. (Paris: Les Indes savantes, 2005), 1:13–29. There are also various documents on the early history of the French trading companies in COL C/5A/1 and COL C/3/1.

141. Toussaint, *History*, 126; Larson, "Colonies Lost," 354–57.

142. Bontekoe, *Memorable Description*, 139–40.

143. See 1664 memoir, COL C/2/2; "ces notes tout extraites de l'histoire des voyages," 1701, COL C/3/1. See also Wellington, *French East India Companies*, 8; Larson, "Colonies Lost," 358. Note that Pronis was originally accompanied by Sieur Fouqembourg, who left in 1646 and died shortly thereafter: Flacourt, *Histoire*, 269–70.

144. In the southeast of Madagascar, near Taolagnaro, sixteenth- and seventeenth-century European descriptions mention local mythologies that defined the divisions that existed between the "*fotsy*" (white) leadership, with their foreign origins, and their "*mainty*" (black) followers. For a discussion of these histories, see Françoise Raison-Jourde, ed., *Les souverains de Madagascar: L'histoire royale et ses résurgences contemporaines* (Paris: Karthala, 1983), 18–26; Larson, "Colonies Lost," 348–50. See also Abdul Sheriff, *Dhow Cultures of the Indian Ocean: Cosmopolitanism, Commerce and Islam* (New York: Columbia University Press, 2010), 207–9. On the sorabe traditions, see Jacques Dez, "De l'influence arabe à Madagascar à

l'aide de faits de linguistique," in *Arabes et Islamisés à Madagascar et dans l'océan Indien*, ed. Jean-Aimé Rakotoarisoa (Antananarivo: Revue de Madagascar, distributed by Hachette-Madagascar, 1967), 4; Gabriel Ferrand, *Les musulmans à Madagascar et aux îles Comores,* vol. 1 (Paris: Ernest Leroux, 1891), 36.

145. For instance, see discussion of the "Ombiasse" in a letter from Father Nacquart, 5 February 1650, quoted by Claude Allibert, "Présentation de l'oeuvre d'Étienne de Flacourt," in Flacourt, *Histoire*, 70–71.

146. Flacourt, *Histoire*; see also Dellon, *Voyage to the East-Indies*, 19–20; Alexis-Marie de Rochon, *A Voyage to Madagascar and the East Indies* (London: G. G. J. and J. Robinson, 1792; originally published in French in 1791), 29–35.

147. Flacourt, *Histoire*, 179, 273. The local people also threatened to kill the French on several occasions: ibid., 276.

148. "Relation de l'établissement de la compagnie française," n.d., COL C/2/2.

149. Flacourt, *Histoire*, 268–72.

150. "Relation de l'établissement," COL C/2/2.

151. Examples of the impact of Flacourt's writing include "Extrait des voyages de M. Le Gentil: Voyage à Madagascar (1761–1763)," COL C/5A/2; Sieur Siette de la Rousse, memoir about Madagascar, 16 August 1783, COL C/5A/8; de la Serre (?) memoir, c. 1789, COL C/5A/9.

152. Ames, *Colbert*, 22–28.

153. Ibid., 31.

154. Memoir, 1664, COL C/2/2; see also notes from French voyages, COL C/3/1.

155. De la Haye's description of the island, 1670, COL C/5A/1.

156. Rochon, *Voyage to Madagascar,* 6. Rochon visited the island during the 1770s.

157. Dellon, *Voyage to the East-Indies*, 23.

158. Ibid., 12–13; see also Aniruddha Ray, "French Colonial Policy in Seventeenth Century Madagascar: François Martin's Account," *Archipel* 17 (1979): 85.

159. See extract of a letter from MM. de Faye and Caron, the general directors of the former Compagnie des Indes, 14 October 1667, COL C/5A/1; extract of a letter by M. de Mondervageue to the company, 26 February 1668, COL C/5A/1; Dellon, *Voyage to the East-Indies*, 18, 25–26.

160. MM. de Faye and Caron, COL C/5A/1. Ames states that the colonists had been "spread out haphazardly throughout the huge island in a vain search for the easy wealth that Charpentier's polemic had promised." Ames, *Colbert*, 35.

161. "Relation de l'établissement," COL C/2/2.

162. Martin's description of his time on the east coast in *COACM*, 9:429–62; see also Ray, "French Colonial Policy," 84–97.

163. See esp. Martin, in *COACM*, 9:464–47, 503, 509–13, 566–67, 572–81.

164. See, for example, Dellon, *Voyage to the East-Indies*, 20; M. Caron, letter, 15 October 1666, COL C/5A/1; "Mémoire sur l'état présent de l'isle Dauphine," 1668, COL C/5A/1; "Observations sur les ppaux [principaux] havres et mouillages de l'isle Dauphine et isles adjacentes," 22 February 1670, COL C/5A/1.

165. "Relation de l'établissement," COL C/2/2.

166. Rochon, *Voyage to Madagascar*, 90–92.

167. Ibid., 95.

168. Ibid., 96–97.

169. Ibid., 100–103; see also Carpeau du Saussay, *Voyage de Madagascar* (Paris, 1722), 67–73.

170. "Relation de l'établissement," COL C/2/2; Dellon, *Voyage to the East-Indies*, 16.

171. "Relation de l'établissement," COL C/2/2.

172. For the Arabico-Malagasy documents, see Emile-Félix Gautier and Henri Froidevaux, *Un manuscrit arabico-malgache sur les campagnes de La Case dans l'Imoro de 1659 à 1663* (Paris: Imprimerie nationale, 1907).

173. Rochon, *Voyage to Madagascar*, 65–111.

174. Martin, in *COACM*, 9:457.

175. Dellon, *Voyage to the East-Indies*, 23.

176. Extracts from visits, COL C/3/1.

177. Larson, "Colonies Lost," 360.

178. De Faye, directeur de la Compagnie des Indes orientales, letter, 21 February 1668, COL C/5A/1: "le plus méchant pays du monde."

179. De Mondevergue, Baron de Barles, gouverneur des îles Dauphine et de Bourbon, extracts of letters, 1669, COL C/5A/1; journal of Sieur du Tremblay, commissaire of the fleet, 19 February 1671, MAR B/4/4.

180. Filliot, *La traite des esclaves*, 24; Wellington, *French East India Companies*, 11–30. See the French orders of 4 February 1672, 9 March 1673, 26 April 1673, and 16 January 1674 about relocating the colony to Surat, COL C/5A/1.

181. Philippe Haudrère, "The 'Compagnie des Indes' and Maritime Matters (c. 1725–1770)," in Bruijn and Gaastra, *Ships, Sailors and Spices*, 81.

182. See various documents, 1687–88, COL C/2/6.

183. The ship journal of the *Royalle*, 1682, MAR 4JJ/90; ship journal of the *Président*, 1684, visiting Ndzuwani, MAR 4JJ/93. On routes, see also the memoir of the Compagnie des Indes orientales, 30 March 1694, COL C/2/7; Haudrère, "'Compagnie des Indes,'" 94.

184. For example, see de Mondevergue, Baron de Barles, gouverneur des îles Dauphine et de Bourbon, extracts of letters, 1669, COL C/5A/1. In 1698, a French merchant urged the resettlement of Madagascar: Dellon, *Voyage to the East-Indies*, 42. See also various seventeenth- and eighteenth-century memoirs in the Archives nationales collection in Paris, especially those in COL F/3/49.

185. Gautier and Froidevaux, "Un manuscrit," 139–40. The use of the term "whites" is presumably a reference to the Frenchmen (*vazaha*), not the "white" (*fotsy*) island leaders who lived in Madagascar.

186. Ibid., 147–50. The documents were likely recopied during the nineteenth century.

187. Ibid., 150–51. The editors provide the following French translation: "Je vais aller voler, parce que le peuple meurt de faim." The original Malagasy (transcribed from Arabico-Malagasy script) reads: "zaho hanafiky fa iñy Jamaa lainy [lany?] ny iñy mosare" (ibid., 135).

188. Games, *Web of Empire*, 181–216; Emily Erikson, *Between Monopoly and Free Trade: The English East India Company, 1600–1757* (Princeton, NJ: Princeton University Press, 2014), esp. 81, 112, 123, 137–39, 187–89.

189. Games, *Web of Empire*, 6.

190. For the accounts that provide evidence for this section, see the ship journal of the *Hector*, recorded by John Munden, mate, 1613–14, IOR/L/MAR/A/XX; the ship journals of the *New Year's Gift*, *Hector*, *Solomon*, and *Hope*, 1613, IOR/L/MAR/A/XIX; the ship journal of the *New Year's Gift*, 1614, IOR/L/MAR/A/XXI. See also the accounts of Nicholas Downton and Thomas Elkington, in *COACM*, 2:80–81, and the orders given by Captain Downton, commander of the *New Year's Gift*, before leaving England, IOR/G/40/25(1), fol. 50. The *Hector* had previously visited Madagascar in 1602, although no records remain from this voyage. We lack records for many of the early voyages of EIC vessels. See also Hamond, *Madagascar*, 9; various EIC letters recounting their stays in St. Augustin Bay in Frederick Charles Danvers, ed., *Letters Received by the East India Company from Its Servants in the East*, vol. 1 (London: Sampson Low, Marston & Company, 1896), 215, 252–53.

191. For more on the environment of the island, see M. R. Jury, "The Climate of Madagascar," in Goodman and Benstead, *Natural History of Madagascar*, 78–79.

192. "Relâche de François Martin de Vitre à la Baie de Saint-Augustin et à Mohely," 1602, and "Relâche à Saint-Augustin de David Middleton, Commandant le *Consent*," 1607, in *COACM*, 1:284, 299, and 403.

193. Manoel Barretto, "Report upon the State and Conquest of the Rivers of Cuama, Supplement to the above Report," 1667, in Theal, *Records of South-Eastern Africa*, 3:503.

194. Samuel Squire, letter to Sir Thomas Smythe, 7 March 1613, in William Foster, ed., *Letters Received by the East India Company from Its Servants in the East*, vol. 3 (London: Sampson Low, Marston, 1899), 46–47.

195. Glass beads were likely already exchanged in southwestern Madagascar: Radimilahy and Manjakahery, "Archaeology of St. Augustine's Bay," 68; Mike Parker Pearson, *Pastoralists, Warriors and Colonists: The Archaeology of Southern Madagascar* (Oxford: Archaeopress, 2010), 167–70.

196. For discussions of the wind patterns by seventeenth-century English captains, see, for instance, the ship journal of the *Lion*, 1616, IOR/L/MAR/A/XVIII. See also the discussion of winds in John Thornton, *The English Pilot: The Third Book*, 1703, Maps 22.d.30, Maps Reading Room, British Library.

197. The ship journal of the *Hector*, 1615, IOR/L/MAR/A/XX.

198. Letters of John Sandcrofte to the East India Company, 29 November 1614, and Ralph Preston to the East India Company, 1 January 1614, both in William Foster, ed., *Letters Received by the East India Company from Its Servants in the East*, vol. 2 (London: Sampson Low, Marston, 1897), 212, 255.

199. See the first letter book of the EIC merchants, in George Birdwood and William Foster, eds., *The Register of Letters etc. of the Governour and Company of Merchants of London Trading into the East Indies, 1600–1619* (London, Quartich, 1893), 118.

200. McDonald, *Pirates*, 28–31.

201. For examples of early trading, see the ship journal of the *Hector* and letter, John Sandcroft to the East India Company, 29 November 1614, both in Foster, *Letters Received*, vol. 2, 212, 250, 255; report from the ship the *Hector*, 1608, IOR/E/3/1. See also "An account of the present comodityes that are imported & exported at Madagascarr and the manner of dealing with the natives," Rawlinson MS A 334, fols. 61–62. There are mentions of "Androa," "Dian," and "Andria" as prefixes for leaders' names. See various letters, 1646, IOR/E/3/20. It is perhaps significant to note that "andriana" was translated as "king" in the nineteenth-century translation of "Tantaran'ny Andriana" [History of the Kings]: François Callet, ed., *Histoire des rois, traduction du "Tantaran'ny Andriana,"* 5 vols. (Antananarivo: Académie Malgache, 1953–78).

202. For such an appeal for help, see the documents in Captain John Smart, "A Booke of Consultations belonging to the Plantation of Madagascar," 1643–46, Add MS 14037. This manuscript is a collection of letters and orders given by Smart, the leader of the colony. See also Boothby, *A Briefe Discovery*, 11; see also Foster, "English Settlement," 241–43. For the French interference in local politics in Anosy, see various colonial archives,

esp. "Relation de ce qui s'est passé à l'île Dauphin depuis le 1er mars 1668," COL C/5A/1.

203. On the French desire to send a representative to St. Augustin, see, for example, "Extrait du règlement de la compagnie établie en France pour le commerce de l'isle St Laurences dite de Madagascar du 27 Octobre 1664," COL C/5A/1.

204. Boothby, *A Briefe Discovery*, 61–66; Waldegrave, *An Answer*, 4–26. On the history of the Courteen Association that financed these colonies, see Foster, "English Settlement," 240; reports to the Courteen Association, 1646, IOR/E/3/20, fols. 25–32. Courteen had trouble settling his debts with the English East India Company following the failure of the plantation: details of the hearing, 1650, IOR/B/23. A short tract was written in defense of the plans, describing how the East India Company thwarted the St. Augustin Bay colony: John Darell, *Strange News from th' Indies* (London, 1652). See also Alfred Grandidier and Guillaume Grandidier, *Les Anglais à Madagascar au XVIIe siècle* (Paris: G. de Malherbe, 1903), 8–10; Games, *Web of Empire*, 181–216.

205. Boothby, *A Briefe Discovery*, 5–7; Hunt, *Island of Assada*, 1650, ibid., 3:264–65. See also McDonald, *Pirates*, 68–77.

206. Radimilahy and Manjakahery, "Archaeology of St. Augustine's Bay," 64.

207. Visit to St. Augustin Bay, 1646, IOR/E/3/20. These challenges securing cattle are reminiscent of those facing early Dutch settlers at the Cape: Ward, *Networks of Empire*, 137–39.

208. Journal by Captain Jeremy Blackman, in "Booke of Consultations," 1645, fol. 17.

209. Consultation at Augustine Bay, 15 May 1646, in "Booke of Consultations," fol. 23.

210. Waldegrave, *An Answer*, 4.

211. James Berblocks (Bearblocke), journal entry from 6 October 1650, found in "Account, from his journal, of James Bearblock's voyage from Assada to Bantam in the *Supply*," IOR/E/3/22, fols. 29–36. Also written Bearblocke.

212. Berblocks, journal entry from 9 October 1650, ibid. A similar report is given by Charles Wilde, who was carrying additional colonists in 1650 to Assada, although it is unclear what happened to the Englishmen he deposited in Assada. Charles Wilde, "Jornal kept by mee Charles Wilde purser in Shipp 'Bonitto,'" 1650, in *COACM*, 3:276. He reported that "the king of the country had traitorously murdered the colonel, the *commissaire*, and nine sailors or colonists"; ibid., 267–70. Wilde left a letter at Ndzuwani, likely read by Berblocks.

213. Berblocks, journal entry from 3 November 1650, found in "Account . . . of James Bearblock's voyage." Another report from 1653 suggested that

the people were killed for selling "falce Ryalls [reales]" to the king there. Nicholas Buckeridge, letter from Johanna, 1653, in Nicholas Buckeridge, *Journal and Letter Book of Nicholas Buckeridge, 1651–1654*, ed. John R. Jenson (Minneapolis: University of Minnesota Press, 1973), 67.

214. Berblocks, journal entry from 16 and 18 November 1650, found in "Account . . . of James Bearblock's voyage,"

215. "An account of the present comodityes," fols. 61–62.

216. Molet-Sauvaget, *Documents anciens . . . Supplément / II*, 37–38. Richard B. Allen notes that an EIC captain bought eighteen slaves from the Portuguese at Mwali in 1637: Allen, *European Slave Trading*, 31. In both cases, these slaves may have originated in Madagascar, judging by European observations.

217. Letter, 1650, IOR/B/22, fol. 232.

218. Proposal made by Mr Aaron Baker, 1645, IOR/B/21, fol. 131.

219. "Commission and instructions," 1663, IOR/E/3/86, fol. 154.

220. For more on this slave trade and use of slaves from Madagascar by the British in Asia, see Janet J. Ewald, "African Bondsmen, Freedmen, and the Maritime Proletariats of the Northwestern Indian Ocean World, c. 1500–1900," in *Indian Ocean Slavery in the Age of Abolition,* ed. Robert Harms, Bernard K. Freamon, and David W. Blight (New Haven: Yale University Press, 2013), 204–5; Allen, *European Slave Trading*, 32–47.

221. An exception to this focus on luxury goods, Michael N. Pearson discusses the trade not only in gold and ivory, but in food and other necessities along the East African coast. Pearson–, *Port Cities*, 46–50.

222. See "The Dutch were not interested in the large neighbouring island of Madagascar, which produced neither pepper nor spices, except as a place from which to procure slaves." Toussaint, *History*, 120.

223. See Randrianja and Ellis, *Madagascar*, 90.

224. See especially the descriptions of the north provided by Freire and Mariano, 1613–14, in *COACM*, 2:7–10. For "rangoe" beads described by the English colonial leaders in St. Augustin, see Account of Captain Blackman at Augustine Bay, 18 August 1645, in "Booke of Consultations," fol. 13. On the eighteenth-century wearing of beads on the west coast, see "Journal and Logbook of an anonymous Scotch sailor, 1726–1729," HC 363/129, Hispanic Society of America.

225. On the early settlement of the island and trade, see Robert E. Dewar, "Of Nets and Trees: Untangling the Reticulate and Dendritic in Madagascar's Prehistory," *World Archaeology* 26, no. 3 (1995): 313–14; David A. Burney et al., "A Chronology for Late Prehistoric Madagascar," *Journal of Human Evolution* 47, nos. 1–2 (2004): 30, 34; Robert E. Dewar, "Early Human Settlers and Their Impact on Madagascar's Landscapes," in *Conservation and Environmental Management in Madagascar*, ed. Ivan R.

Scales (New York: Routledge, 2014), 54. Traditions around migration and settlement have been recorded for different parts of the island (particularly involving the *tompon-tany* (the original inhabitants of the island) and *vazimba* (the foreigners who arrived at the island)). See especially the discussions in Ramilisonina, "Topographies religieuse d'un terroir et relations entre vivants et ancêtres à Madagascar: Les Bezanozano Zanadroandrena et Tsimifahy (Mandialaza-Moramanga)," in *Ancestralité et Identité à Madagascar*, Études océan Indien 30 (Paris: Institut national des langues et civilisations orientales, 2001), 100; Sandra J. T. M. Evers, *Constructing History, Culture, and Inequality: The Betsileo in the Extreme Southern Highlands of Madagascar* (Leiden: Brill, 2002), 28–30; Charlotte Liliane Rabesahala-Randriamananoro, *Ambohimanga-Rova: Approche anthropologique de la civilisation merina (Madagascar)* (Paris: Publieur, 2005), 30–35; Radimilahy and Manjakahery, "Archaeology of St. Augustine's Bay," 63–64.

226. On early trade, urbanization, and centralization, see Radimilahy, *Mahilaka*, 198, 205–6; Wright and Rakotoarisoa, "Rise of Malagasy Societies," 117; Randrianja and Ellis, *Madagascar*, 85; Beaujard, *Les mondes*, 2:334.

227. Wright and Rakotoarisoa, "Rise of Malagasy Societies," 116.

228. Robert E. Dewar, "Processual Assessment of Population Changes in Western Avaradrano," in *Early State Formation in Central Madagascar: An Archaeological Survey of Western Avaradrano*, ed. Henry Tutwiler Wright (Ann Arbor: Museum of Anthropology, University of Michigan, 2007), 101–3.

229. Dewar argues that there was agricultural development to support population growth after 1500, perhaps contributing to upheaval during this "momentous and in some ways calamitous period of growth": Dewar, "Early Human Settlers," 53–54.

230. This debate is laid out in Sheriff, *Dhow Cultures*, 4–5; see also Sanjay Subrahmanyam, "Of Imarat and Tijarat: Asian Merchants and State Power in the Western Indian Ocean, 1400 to 1750," *Comparative Studies in Society and History* 37, no. 4 (1995): 753–56; Sugata Bose, *A Hundred Horizons: The Indian Ocean in the Age of Global Empire* (Cambridge, MA: Harvard University Press, 2006), 14–15; Clulow, *The Company and the Shogun*, 3–10.

231. On alternative trade networks, see, for instance, Sebouh Aslanian, *From the Indian Ocean to the Mediterranean: The Global Trade Networks of Armenian Merchants from New Julfa* (Berkeley: University of California Press, 2011); Tonio Andrade, "Beyond Guns, Germs, and Steel: European Expansion and Maritime Asia, 1400–1750," *Journal of Early Modern History* 14, no. 1 (2010): 168–70; Sanjay Subrahmanyam, *The Portuguese Empire in Asia, 1500–1700: A Political and Economic History*, 2nd ed. (West Sussex, UK: Wiley-Blackwell, 2012), 30–31, 116; Alpers, *Indian Ocean*, 79–80.

## CHAPTER 3: THE SAKALAVA

1. John Dean, "Narrative of One of the Crew Belonging to the Ship *Sussex*," 1738, MSS Eur. B2 / K11, British Library. Upon Dean's return and report, the deserting officers were punished. The other ship was the *Winchester*: the ship journal of the *Winchester*, 1736, IOR/L/MAR/B/643A.

2. Dean, "Narrative," 1–10.

3. Ibid., 25. He described himself as king of "Rambour."

4. Ibid., 10–35. He was picked up by the *Prince William*: the ship journal of the *Prince William*, 1738–39, IOR/L/MAR/B/324E, vol. 1.

5. Dean, "Narrative," 23.

6. Ibid., 29–30. They did the same on the return journey through the town; ibid., 31.

7. Robert Drury, *The Adventures of Robert Drury* (London, 1729; reprint, Hull: Stodart and Craggs, 1807); page references are to the 1807 edition. Drury was shipwrecked in southern Madagascar in 1701. He published his narrative in 1729 and it has been through several reprints. As an individual with fluency in the local language, his account provides a fairly reliable description of the islanders he encountered.

Some scholars, most notably Molet-Sauvaget, have argued that this book was the work of a novelist, perhaps Daniel Defoe, along with the narrative of another shipwrecked sailor, Robert Everard. See Anne Molet-Sauvaget, "La *Relation de Robert Everard*, ébauche probable du *Journal de Robert Drury* de Daniel Defoe," *Studies on Voltaire and the Eighteenth Century*, no. 241 (1986): 1–28. Arguments that Drury's narrative is entirely fictitious have been put to rest (in my mind) in Mike Parker Pearson, "Reassessing 'Robert Drury's Journal' as a Historical Source for Southern Madagascar," *History in Africa* 23 (1996): 233–56; Mike Parker Pearson and Karen Godden, *In Search of the Red Slave: Shipwreck and Captivity in Madagascar* (Stroud, UK: Sutton, 2002). Even if Defoe or another writer assisted in the writing of the book, it appears that "to have written such a convincing book someone must have spent a long time out there in southern Madagascar": Parker Pearson and Godden, *In Search of the Red Slave*, 206.

8. Drury, *Adventures*, 423.

9. See esp. ibid., 390–91.

10. Drury provides lengthy descriptions of these rituals. For example, one "ambassador" licked the king and asked that the "Supreme God bless the Progeny of Dean Lohefute." Ibid., 434. Also, the entire population ruled by the king had to shave their heads after the king's brother had died in battle.

11. See French reflections on warfare in southeast Madagascar. Gabriel Dellon, *A Voyage to the East-Indies* (London, 1698), 19. Flacourt's map notes the west-central portion of Madagascar was "very fertile, abandoned

and ruined by the wars." Alfred Grandidier et al., eds., *Collection des ouvrages anciens concernant Madagascar*, 9 vols. (Paris: Comité de Madagascar, 1903–20) (hereafter cited as *COACM*), vol. 8, frontispiece, map of Madagascar, 1656.

12. "Slave-trader kings": Solofo Randrianja and Stephen Ellis, *Madagascar: A Short History* (Chicago: University of Chicago Press, 2009), 99.

13. See, for instance, Ramusio, 1550, *COACM*, 1:99; "Account of an expedition of the Portuguese from India to Madagascar in 1613," in Robert Kerr, ed., *A General History and Collection of Voyages and Travels* (Edinburgh, 1824), 7:4. See the definition for "Buki" provided in Charles Sacleux, *Dictionnaire Swahili-Français, Tome 1* (Paris: Institut d'Ethnologie, 1939), 117. Sacleux's Swahili-French dictionary defines "Buki" as a word that appears to be neither Malagasy nor Sakalava in origin. The term, used to denote the west coast of Madagascar, first was found in the words of Diego de Couto in 1557. The editors of *COACM* claim that the Malagasy lacked a name for the entire island, instead having names for various provinces, and that the name "Bouky" was given to the island by Africans and Comorians. *COACM*, 2:6n1.

14. "Kaffirs who could not understand those from the land of Sam Louremço." "Letter from Afonso de Albuquerque to the King," 6 February 1507, in *Documents on the Portuguese in Mozambique and Central Africa, 1497–1840*, 9 vols. (Lisbon: National Archives of Rhodesia and Nyasaland, Centro de Estudos Históricos Ultramarinos, 1962–89), 2:121.

15. "A Voyage in ye ship *Frances* from Mossambique for St. Lawrence," 1640, reproduced in 1700?, Rawlinson MS A 334, fols. 54–57.

16. On minor differences in language, see Drury, *Adventures*, 372. On the "country of Saccalauvor," ibid., 364, 366; "Merfaughla," ibid., 82; "Anterndroea," ibid., 71.

17. Ibid., 391.

18. Examples include reference to "Succulava slaves" in "Journal and Logbook of an anonymous Scotch sailor, 1726–1729," HC 363/129, Hispanic Society of America; the ship journal of the *Vierge de Grace*, 1732, visiting "Seclaver," MAR 4JJ/74; references to the Sakalava king in Morondava in the ship journal of the *Delaware*, 1752, IOR/L/MAR/B/322B; the visit to the "rade des Selaves" by the *Phalyspeaux*, 1756, MAR 4JJ/87. Benyowsky refers consistently to the northwestern kingdom of the "Seclaves," also known as "Boyana." Maurice-Auguste Benyowsky, *Voyages et mémoires de Maurice-Auguste, Comte de Benyowsky* (Paris, 1791), 2:386.

19. On Sakalava as an ethnonym, see Randrianja and Ellis, *Madagascar*, 107–11.

20. Charles Guillain, *Documents sur l'histoire, la géographie et le commerce de la partie occidentale de Madagascar* (Paris: Imprimerie Royale,

1845), 7–31. In addition to Guillain's reports, see also André Dandouau, *Contes populaires des Sakalava et des Tsimihety de la région d'Analalava* (Algiers: Jules Carbonel, 1922); Emil Birkeli, *Folklore Sakalava, recueilli dans la région de Morondava* (Antananarivo: Imp. G. Pitot de la Beaujardière, 1924); originally published in *Bulletin de l'Académie Malgache*, n.s., 6 (1922–23): 185–417. Historians who cite Guillain include Dandouau, *Contes populaires*; Raymond K. Kent, "Madagascar and Africa: II. The Sakalava, Maroserana, Dady and Tromba before 1700," *Journal of African History* 9, no. 4 (1968): 517–46; Raymond K. Kent, *Early Kingdoms in Madagascar, 1500–1700* (New York: Holt, Rinehart and Winston, 1970), esp. 160–64; Jean François Baré, *Sable rouge: Une monarchie du nord-ouest malgache dans l'histoire* (Paris: L'Harmattan, 1980); Sophie Blanchy, *Karana et Banians: Les communautés commerçantes d'origin indienne à Madagascar* (Paris: Harmattan, 1995); Marie-Pierre Ballarin, *Les reliques royales à Madagascar: Source de légitimation et enjeu de pouvoir, XVIIIe-XXe siècles* (Paris: Karthala, 2000). Guillain's writings were also very influential among nineteenth-century visitors to Madagascar, including Lyons McLeod, *Madagascar and Its People* (New York: Negro Universities Press, 1969; originally published 1865); Joseph Mullens, *Twelve Months in Madagascar* (New York: Robert Carter & Brothers, 1875).

21. For a discussion of these developments, see Gillian Feeley-Harnik, *A Green Estate: Restoring Independence in Madagascar* (Washington, DC: Smithsonian Institution Press, 1991), 64. For a look at Merina oral traditions, see Pier M. Larson, "Multiple Narratives, Gendered Voices: Remembering the Past in Highland Central Madagascar," *International Journal of African Historical Studies* 28, no. 2 (1995): 295–325.

22. See, for instance, the General Report on the Colony, 1910, F/12/6190, in Section Moderne, Administration générale de la France, Commerce et industrie, Archives nationales.

23. One such attempt is Barthelemy Huet de Froberville, "Index de la géographie de Madagascar," 1816, Add MS 18132, British Library, see esp. fols. 4–88.

24. For other discussions of the Sakalava identity, see esp. Sophie Goedefroit, *À l'ouest de Madagascar: Les Sakalava du Menabe* (Paris: Karthala, 1998), 52–53, 79; Michael Lambek, "Reflections on the 'Ethno-' in Malagasy Ethnohistory," *Ethnohistory* 48, nos. 1–2 (2001): 301–4; essays in Françoise Raison-Jourde and Solofo Randrianja, eds., *La nation malgache au défi de l'ethnicité* (Paris: Karthala, 2002).

25. Drury has a lengthy description of burial practices in the southwest of the island: Drury, *Adventures*, 223–31. For more on burial practices and beliefs, see Chantal Radimilahy, "Sacred Sites in Madagascar," in *Sacred Sites, Sacred Places*, ed. David L Carmichael et al. (London: Routledge,

1994), 84; Sophie Goedefroit and Jacques Lombard, *Andolo: L'art funéraire Sakalava à Madagascar* (Paris: Biro, 2007). The practice of guarding and worshiping royalty at tombs increased even further during the twentieth century. Françoise Raison-Jourde, "Introduction," in *Les souverains de Madagascar: L'histoire royale et ses résurgences contemporaines*, ed. Françoise Raison-Jourde (Paris: Karthala, 1983), 50–51.

26. On these ceremonies and the history of their practice in different parts of the island, see esp. Bernard Schlemmer, "La domination royal au Menabe: Détournement colonial, survivance et décomposition," in Raison-Jourde, *Les souverains*, 402; Suzanne Chazan-Gillic, "Le fitampoha de 1968 ou l'efficacité symbolique du mythe de la royauté Sakalava dans l'actualité politique et économique malgache," in Raison-Jourde, *Les souverains*, 467; Michael Lambek, "The Sakalava Poiesis of History: Realizing the Past through Spirit Possession in Madagascar," *American Ethnologist* 25, no. 2 (1998): 106–27; Pier M. Larson, "A Cultural Politics of Bedchamber Construction and Progressive Dining in Antananarivo: Ritual Inversions during the *Fandroana* of 1817," in *Ancestors, Power and History in Madagascar*, ed. Karen Middleton (Leiden: Brill, 1999), 37–70.

27. Gillian Feeley-Harnik, "The King's Men in Madagascar: Slavery, Citizenship and Sakalava Monarchy," *Africa: Journal of the International African Institute* 52, no. 2 (1982): 34; see also Goedefroit, *À l'ouest*, 96.

28. Rita Astuti, *People of the Sea: Identity and Descent among the Vezo of Madagascar* (Cambridge: Cambridge University Press, 1995), 74–75. See also Gillian Feeley-Harnik, "Sakalava Royal Work: A Study of Aesthetics in Labor and Government" (PhD diss., New York University, 1976), 146–47.

29. For example, see Jacob Granaet, description of war at St. Augustin Bay, 1666, *COACM*, 3:334; Jean Ovington, description of Madagascar and Ndzuwani, mentioning warfare in northwestern Madagascar, 1690, *COACM*, 3:457.

30. The town was described by the Portuguese as located at the mouth of the Manambolo River, which would place it approximately sixty miles north of Morondava. Of course, we cannot be certain that the "Suculambes" were the Sakalava, although the name is comparable. It is perhaps more important that the region was described as subject to "continual" wars during the early seventeenth century. The priest, Mariano, describes the Sakalava making defensive preparations, building forts, and losing many men in the battles. If this were the case, it would suggest that the early buildup of the Sakalava military was for defensive, not offensive reasons. Luis Mariano, letter, 22 October 1616, in *COACM*, 2:224–26.

31. For instance, the ship journal of the *Barneveld*, 1719, includes a description of a visit to "Macalena Nova" and Sakalava conflicts with other groups on the island, in *COACM*, 5:23.

32. It is difficult to pin down the start of the original Sakalava Maroserana dynasty: Jacques Lombard, *Le royaume Sakalava du Menabe, 17è–20è: Essai d'analyse d'un système politique à Madagascar* (Paris: Editions de l'ORSTOM, 1988), 16–22. See also Guillain, *Documents*, 7. Wright dates the period of the Sakalava state from 1660 to 1720: Henry T. Wright, "Early State Dynamics as Political Experiment," *Journal of Anthropological Research* 62, no. 3 (2006): 309.

33. Birkeli, "Folklore Sakalava," 186. The southeast and the western regions were linked through a variety of religious practices and beliefs, including that of divination: Pierre Vérin and Narivelo Rajaonarimanana, "Divination in Madagascar: The Antemoro Case and the Diffusion of Divination," in *African Divination Systems: Ways of Knowing*, ed. Philip M. Peek (Bloomington: Indiana University Press, 1991), 54–56. Drury appears to describe these practices in late-seventeenth-century Madagascar: Drury, *Adventures*, 100, 113, 224–27.

34. For a description of the river, see the ship journal of the *Ilchester*, 1750, IOR/L/MAR/B/601B.

35. George Herbert Smith, *Among the Menabe; or, Thirteen months on the West Coast of Madagascar* (London: Society for Promoting Christian Knowledge, 1896), 5–6; see also Vincent Noël, *Île de Madagascar: Recherches sur les Sakkalava* (extrait du *Bulletin de la Société de Géographie*, 1843) (Paris: Bourgogne et Martinet, 1844), 5.

36. Wright, "Early State Dynamics," 309.

37. Discussed at length in Ballarin, *Les reliques royales*, 53–86. Wright states that, according to traditional histories, the first Sakalava capital was at Bengy, on the tributary of the Mangoky River: Wright, "Early State Dynamics," 309.

38. For the best presentation of this myth, see Birkeli, "Folklore Sakalava,"171–92. Kent insisted on the Bantu origins of Sakalava divine kingship: Kent, "Madagascar and Africa," 545–46. Some Sakalava founding myths can be compared to Merina oral traditions: François Callet, ed., *Histoire des rois, traduction du "Tantaran'ny Andriana,"* 5 vols. (Antananarivo: Académie Malgache, 1953–78), 1:8.

39. The term means, roughly, medicine. Birkeli, "Folklore Sakalava,"190.

40. According to Noël, the region was previously known as "Ansakouabe." Noël, *Île de Madagascar*, 18. On the color red, see Arthur Leib, "The Mystical Significance of Colours in the Life of the Natives of Madagascar," *Folklore* 57, no. 3 (1946): 131.

41. The tradition is recounted in Sherry Olson, "Red Destinies: The Landscape of Environmental Risk in Madagascar," *Human Ecology* 15, no. 1 (1987): 68.

42. Guillain, *Documents*, 13.

43. Ibid., 391.

44. See description of the fati-dra in Birkeli, "Folklore Sakalava," 174. The French called the ceremony *serment du sang.* Ceremonies were also practiced in East Africa to create "fictive kinship" bonds, although with some clear differences: Mark Horton, *Shanga: The Archaeology of a Muslim Trading Community on the Coast of East Africa* (London: British Institute in Eastern Africa, 1996), 413; Mark Horton and John Middleton, *The Swahili: The Social Landscape of a Mercantile Society* (Oxford: Blackwell, 2000), 145–46. The fati-dra was described as a "blood-covenant" by an English missionary visiting Menabe during the nineteenth century. Smith stated that it was "an absolute guarantee for safety and assistance from the king or chief with whome it is made." Smith, *Among the Menabe,* 22–23.

45. Guillain, *Documents*, 17; see also Ballarin, *Les reliques royales*, 16. Drury referred to these original inhabitants as *Vazimba* (*tompon-tany*, the "original land owners"). He also describes the "Virzimbers" as having very different customs from other Malagasy, in addition to speaking their own dialect. Drury, *Adventures*, 376.

46. As described in French colonial correspondence, 1713, COL C/3/3–4.

47. Astuti, *People of the Sea*, 74.

48. On the expansion of the non-European slave trade, see Thomas Vernet, "Le commerce des esclaves sur la côte Swahili, 1500–1750," *Azania* 38 (2003): 75–88.

49. François Martin, French colonist in east-central Madagascar, 1665–68, *COACM*, 9:557. Some of this disorder was also caused by the constant French raids throughout the entire east coast for cattle and slaves.

50. Mariano and Freire, letter from 1613, *COACM*, 2:28.

51. Drury, *Adventures*, 367.

52. Ibid., 391. Note that he describes the country as "Saccalauvor." Ellis suggests that highland communities were trying to protect themselves from the slave trade: Stephen Ellis, "The History of Sovereigns in Madagascar: New Light from Old Sources," in *Madagascar revisitée: En voyage avec Françoise Raison-Jourde*, ed. Didier Nativel and Faranirina V. Rajaonah (Paris: Karthala, 2009), 416.

53. For a description of cattle and slaves being seized in battles and redistributed to followers in the southwest, see Drury, *Adventures*, 275–76; gifts of cattle and slaves to the Sakalava king's subjects, ibid., 391.

54. Manoel de la Cerda, report, 1527, in *COACM*, 1:58.

55. Mariano, letter, 1613–14, in *COACM*, 2:28. Mariano does not describe the king as Sakalava, but his name is recorded in Sakalava royal histories. See Ballarin, *Les reliques royales*, 32.

56. Mariano, letter, 1613–14, in *COACM*, 2:12. Could "mungo" be manioc, as the Kiswahili term for manioc/cassava was *muhogo*? Mungo might refer to *Vigna mungo*, a bean grown on the Indian subcontinent and perhaps carried by merchants to Madagascar where it is grown now: V. Heuzé, G. Tran, and M. Boval, "Black Gram (Vinga Mungo)," in *Feedipedia, a Programme by INRA, CIRAD, AFZ and FAO*, last modified 30 March 2016, http://www.feedipedia.org/node/236.

It seems unlikely it was manioc, but, by the late eighteenth century, growing drought-tolerant crops such as maize, manioc, and sweet potatoes would lead to increased food security for communities in west-central Madagascar, as it did elsewhere in Africa. Mabrouk A. El-Sharkawy, "Drought-Tolerant Cassava for Africa, Asia, and Latin America," *BioScience* 43, no. 7 (1993): 443–45; Mary Karasch, "Manioc," in Kenneth F. Kiple and Kriemhild Coneè Ornelas, eds., *The Cambridge World History of Food* (Cambridge: Cambridge University Press, 2000), 1:181–87. The editors of *COACM* suggest that manioc was introduced to Mauritius during the mid-eighteenth century: *COACM*, 5:178n2. Jones also describes the introduction of manioc to the East African coast and the Mascarenes in the early to mid-eighteenth century: William O. Jones, *Manioc in Africa* (Stanford, CA: Stanford University Press, 1959), 81. Kent suggests, based on sixteenth and seventeenth-century descriptions in *COACM*, that manioc was introduced much earlier: Raymond Kent, "Note sur l'introduction et la propagation du manioc à Madagascar," *Terre Malgache*, 5 (1969) 178–79. By contrast, Raison agrees with Jones that the date was likely much later: Jean-Pierre Raison, "L'introduction du manioc à Madagascar: Un problème non résolu," *Terre Malgache* 13 (1972) 225–27. Karasch, however, suggests the Portuguese brought in manioc before 1740 to the East African coast. She also dates the arrival of manioc in Mauritius as 1736: Karasch, "Manioc."

Manioc was certainly cultivated throughout Madagascar before the early nineteenth century: see anonymous source in Froberville, "Index de la geographie," 202. The Sakalava were later described feeding their families manioc, maize, beans, and milk, reserving rice and beef for religious ceremonies, royal consumption, and export to passing European merchants. Gwyn Campbell, "The Structure of Trade in Madagascar, 1750–1810," *International Journal of African Historical Studies* 26, no. 1 (1993): 116–19. Manioc and other American crops were also popular in the Comoros: see Claude Chanudet and Jean-Aimé Rakotoarisoa, *Mohéli: Une île des Comores à la recherche de son identité* (Paris: L'Harmattan, 2000), 24.

On the impact of new world crops elsewhere in sub-Saharan Africa, see Joseph Calder Miller, *Way of Death: Merchant Capitalism and the Angolan Slave Trade, 1730–1830* (Madison: University of Wisconsin Press, 1988),

19–21; James C. McCann, *Maize and Grace: Africa's Encounter with a New World Crop, 1500–2000* (Cambridge, MA: Harvard University Press, 2005).

57. Drury, *Adventures*, 423.

58. The principal herdsman was "as grand a figure as a king." Ibid., 386.

59. Mariano and Freire, letter, 1613–14, *COACM*, 2:25–26. Drury describes kings having hundreds of their own slaves: Drury, *Adventures*, 392.

60. Drury, *Adventures*, 391.

61. Feeley-Harnik, "The King's Men," 45. On the use of slaves to farm in southern Madagascar, see Drury, *Adventures*, 68, 110–11. Drury describes headmen in Menabe tending to their own rice: ibid., 395. This labor was also described by Dutch slave traders visiting southwestern Madagascar: R. J. Barendse, "Slaving on the Malagasy Coast, 1640–1700," in *Cultures of Madagascar: Ebb and Flow of Influences*, ed. S. Evers and M. Spindler (Leiden: International Institute for Asian Studies, 1995), 146.

62. Ellis, "History of Sovereigns," 418.

63. Originally, he installed the capital at Maneva, to the southeast, but later moved to this more profitable location. See various descriptions of Sakalava kings and their descendants at Mahabo in Dominique Ranaivoson, *Madagascar: Dictionnaire des personnalités historiques* (Saint-Maur-des-Fossés, France: Sépia, 2005), 8, 37, 42, 122.

64. For example, see Dean, "Narrative," 29–30.

65. Martin, in *COACM*, 9:479–80.

66. Ibid., 9:480.

67. Ibid., 9:514–16.

68. Ibid., 9:514.

69. Ibid., 9:515–16.

70. Ibid., 9:605–6.

71. In 1632 and 1683. James C. Armstrong, "Madagascar and the Slave Trade in the Seventeenth Century," *Omaly sy anio* (Université d'Antananarivo) 17–20 (1983): 219, table 1.

72. Drury repeats a history of Sakalava expansion that he heard from another European in Madagascar, but does not provide any dates: Drury, *Adventures*, 390. See also the ship journal of the *Discovery*, 1700, IOR/L/MAR/A/CL. Guillain states that the name Andriamagnéti-Arivou was this king's posthumous name (Sakalava rulers received a new name after death): Guillain, *Documents*, 14. He was perhaps preceded by his father, named Andriamaneniarivo. Robert Jaovelo-Dzao, *Mythes, rites et transes à Madagascar* (Paris: Karthala, 1996), 392.

73. Dutch observations suggest that there were battles between the rulers in St. Augustin Bay and "Lahafoutis" (Andriandahifotsy) in 1663. See the "Dagregister *I. Blanck*," 1663, VOC 1.04.02, 3998. On earlier cattle raids, see Walter Hamond, *Madagascar, the Richest and Most Fruitful Island in*

*the World* (London, 1643), 7. Drury describes a land already devastated by the time he arrived there: Drury, *Adventures*, 207.

74. Drury, *Adventures*, 349–56. Drury mentions three groups—those of the Mahafaly, Antandroy, and Sakalava—fighting in the region; ibid., 311–12, 316.

75. Drury describes a meeting with some "Amboer-lambo" ambassadors in Mahabo who told him that before the Sakalava had dominated the importation of firearms in the region, the people of the mountains in the interior were more powerful than the coastal peoples. Ibid., 395–97.

76. Around this period, Drury reports a shortage of goods for export in St. Augustin Bay: Drury, *Adventures*, 328–29, 363. He describes a peace between the Sakalava and the ruler of "Feraignher" in order to battle against the Mahafaly attacking to the south.

77. The earliest references to trade in Toliara that I can find include a description found in the ship journal of the *Bedford*, 1698, IOR/L/MAR/A/CXXIV; a very brief mention in the ship journal of the *Little Josiah*, 1692, Rawlinson MS A 334, fols. 58–60.

78. Ship journal of HMS *Stately*, kept by C. P. Beaver, 1796, RUSI 180/2, National Maritime Museum.

79. The English who frequented southwestern Madagascar always used these names to refer to the rulers, while the French and Dutch occasionally used what appear to be proper names instead. The French also referred to King Baba as "Baby": the ship journal of the *Royal Philippe*, 1733, MAR 4JJ/88. A nineteenth-century visitor to the bay also describes the names: Pascoe Grenfell Hill, *Fifty Days on Board a Slave-Vessel in the Mozambique Channel, in April and May, 1843* (London: John Murray, 1844), 12. Terms such as "king" and "prince" are found in French, English, and Dutch sources. For instance, Dutch traders visiting Toliara in 1741 overheard Malagasy children greeting the ruler with the shout, "Ha kinne baba," despite the ruler giving his name to the traders as "Rammanrasse" previously. Ship journal of the *Brack*, 1741, in *COACM*, 6:80. I am not aware of any Malagasy words that relate to "kinne" as a title for a political leader, as the Malagasy typically used the terms *andriana*, *ra*, or *mpanjaka* to indicate elites or rulers, suggesting the term was used to echo the English title of "king." The French also referred to the Sakalava trading representatives in the northwest ports during the eighteenth century as "Baba." This king was known as "Andrian Baba," Andriana being a Malagasy word used for lord or king. The ship journal of the *Hirondelle*, 1731, MAR 4JJ/86. A leader on Nosy Boraha in 1745 was also named "Andrian Baba" according to an account by Grenville de Forval, 1801, in *COACM*, 5:238. Drury makes no mention of either title during his visit in the early years of the eighteenth century.

80. There is no mention of these titles in Sakalava oral traditions, but the sources tend to focus on the Menabe and Boina regions: Guillain, *Documents*, 7–35.

81. Jeremy Prestholdt, *Domesticating the World: African Consumerism and the Genealogies of Globalization* (Berkeley: University of California Press, 2008), 13; on the use of English titles, see ibid., 20.

82. See, for instance, the comments of the king reported to the slave traders on board the *Brack* in 1741, in *COACM*, 6:86–94.

83. On gun flints, see Mike Parker Pearson, *Pastoralists, Warriors and Colonists: The Archaeology of Southern Madagascar* (Oxford: Archaeopress, 2010), 456.

84. The circulation of beads and guns suggests they were being used in trading. Drury, for instance, describes the use of guns to purchase slaves by rulers in the southwest: Drury, *Adventures*, 205–6.

85. Slaving ships would stop in St. Augustin and Toliara for provisions, before continuing along the west coast. See, for instance, the ship journal of the *Onslow*, 1741, IOR/L/MAR/B/164C.

86. One example is the ship journal of the *Dragon*, 1753, IOR/L /MAR/B/598D.

87. On the possibility of fortifications around the bay, see Chantal Radimilahy and Barthélémy Manjakahery, "Archaeology of St. Augustine's Bay, Lower and Middle Onilahy Valley, Southwestern Madagascar," in *The African Archaeology Network: Research in Progress*, Studies in the African Past 5 (Dar es Salaam: Dar es Salaam University Press, 2006), 70.

88. As mentioned in the ship journal of *L'Astrée*, 1735, MAR 4JJ/86. Drury describes conflict between the Mahafaly and others in the southwest of the island: Drury, *Adventures*, 359–60. See also Guillain, *Documents*, 335.

89. See, for instance, the ship journal of the *Northington*, 1770, IOR/L /MAR/B/483B.

90. Note that this trend toward more defensive postures and "progressively isolated" communities may have begun even earlier in the far south of the island: Parker Pearson, *Pastoralists*, 213, 254, 258–59, 531–36.

91. By the nineteenth century, the people around St. Augustin Bay and Toliara were described as Masikoro and King Baba as the ruler of the Masikoro. They were seen as Sakalava, but distinct from the Vezo coastal population (also described as Sakalava). See, for instance, the account of Rev. A. Walen, N.M.S., "Two Years among the Sakalava (Part I)," *Antananarivo Annual and Madagascar Magazine*, no. 5 (1881): 10.

92. Guillain, *Documents*, 19.

93. See, for instance, Drury, *Adventures*, 375–78. There is one brief account of attacks on the king of Toliara by the Sakalava to north in "Journal and Logbook," HC 363/129.

94. Ellis, "History of Sovereigns," 418–19.

95. Guillain, *Documents*, 19–21. Drury describes his march to the north: Drury, *Adventures*, 390–91. See also Ballarin, *Les reliques royales*, 36; Wright, "Early State Dynamics," 311.

96. Birkeli, "Folklore Sakalava," 192; see also Ballarin, *Les reliques royales*, 44.

97. Ranaivoson, *Madagascar*, 34. In 1718, according to Ballarin, *Les reliques royales*, 32.

98. For Mahajanga's founding myth, see Dandouau, *Contes populaires*, 339.

99. Guillain, *Documents*, 33–34; see also Lombard, *Le royaume Sakalava*, 32–35.

100. As suggested by Ellis, "History of Sovereigns," 419. See also Guillain, *Documents*, 19–21.

101. Armstrong cites the visit of a Dutch ship in 1686 to the northwest coast during which the captain found "Magelagie" destroyed in war with the "Sacalave." Armstrong, "Madagascar and the Slave Trade," 215.

102. Report of Jeremias Brons ter Leede, on board the *Standvastigheid*, 14 January 1695, in H. C. V. Leibrandt, ed., *Precis of the Archives of the Cape of Good Hope: Letters Received, 1695–1708* (Cape Town: W. A. Richards & Sons, 1896), 28–31.

103. Liliana Mosca, "La traite à Madagascar dans la seconde moitié du XVIIe siècle à la lumière de quelques documents anglo-américains," in *La route des esclaves: Système servile et traite dans l'est Malgache*, ed. Ignace Rakoto (Paris: L'Harmattan, 2000), 84.

104. Letters of 30 June 1697 and 8-9 March 1698 in H. C. V. Leibrandt, ed., *Precis of the Archives of the Cape of Good Hope: Letters Despatched, 1696–1708* (Cape Town: W. A. Richards & Sons, 1896), 45, 70.

105. R. J. Barendse, *Arabian Seas, 1700–1763* (Leiden: Brill, 2009), 3:1239.

106. The ship journal of the *Fly*, 1763, IOR/L/MAR/B/597B.

107. For example, see Barendse, "Slaving," 151.

108. In 1752, one EIC merchant in Massaliege described meeting with the "Moorman husband to the Queen and Governor of this place." The ship journal of the *Delaware*, 1752, IOR/L/MAR/B/322-B. A decade later, the English described the queen as named Salima and married to a King "Chilavan." She was a "Moor woman," speaking the Moor's tongue, and sold slaves to Moors from Surat. See the ship journal of the *Diligent*, 1761, IOR/L/MAR/B/320E. Her husband may have been Swahili: see Thomas Vernet, "Slave Trade and Slavery on the Swahili Coast, 1500–1750," in *Slavery, Islam and Diaspora*, ed. Paul Lovejoy, Behnaz A. Mirzai, and Ismael M. Montana (Trenton, NJ: Africa World Press, 2009), 56.

109. As detailed in Baré, *Sable rouge*, 41.

110. Map of "Insula S. Laurentii, vulgo Madagascar," 1665, Amsterdam, map collection, Northwestern University Library, http://hdl.library.northwestern.edu/2166.DL/inu-afrmap-4264860-recto-ah.

111. The oral traditions recorded by Guillain barely mention the development of Sakalava control over the northeast of Madagascar: Guillain, *Documents*, 36–52.

112. The ruler at Cap Saint-Sebastien in northern Madagascar described himself as a relative of the Sakalava king of Boina and sold slaves to Arabs. The ship journals of the *Charles* and *Elisabeth*, 1742–43, MAR 4JJ/144-D.

113. See, for instance, the letter on the succession to the Sakalava throne, about eastern Malagasy rulers desiring Sakalava blood in their lineage, n.d., in "Mémoires pour servir à l'histoire de l'isle de Madagascar," ed. M. de Froberville, 2 vols., folio, 1809, 1:127, Add MS 18128–18129, British Library.

114. Ibid., 1:294; see also Dumaine, "Voyage à la côte de l'ouest," 1793, ibid., 1:296 and the description of Lamboine: Guillain, *Documents*, 369–70.

115. Benyowsky, "memoir on the establishment," 1776, M 1031, Archives nationales.

116. Mayeur, 1774, trip to the north of the island, in "Mémoires pour servir," 1:29.

117. Dumaine, "Voyage à la côte de l'ouest," 1793, ibid., 1:294–96; see also Desroches, "Notes sur Madagascar," March 15 1816, in "Memoirs and Papers Relating to Madagascar," ed. M. de Froberville, Add MS 18135, fol. 36; Benyowsky, memoir, in M 1031. By the mid-nineteenth century, leaders in the north in ports such as Vohémar and Diego Suarez identified themselves as "Sakalava" without any hesitation. Descriptions of the Sakalava in the north, 1843, in MAD14/28–29, Archives nationales d'outre-mer (henceforth ANOM); M. Goudon, "Naturalisés sur Madagascar," 183, in "MAD15/30," ANOM; Buisson, 22 November 1880, notes on Vohémar, MAR 3JJ/351.

118. Benyowsky, *Voyages*, 2:386.

119. Karen Middleton, "Power and Meaning on the Periphery of a Malagasy Kingdom," *Ethnohistory* 48, nos. 1–2 (2001): 175.

120. Maurice Bloch, "The Ethnohistory of Madagascar," *Ethnohistory* 48, nos. 1–2 (2001): 297.

121. Middleton, "Power and Meaning," 194.

122. See, for instance, references to wars of succession producing slaves for sale in Young Owl in the ship journal of the *Hertford*, 1734, IOR/L/MAR/B/656E–G.

123. Kottak describes the Merina as not only a state but an empire by the mid-nineteenth century, after developing a strong commercial network,

trade, manufacturing, and control over labor. Conrad P. Kottak, "The Process of State Formation in Madagascar," *American Ethnologist* 4, no. 1 (1977): 141; cf. Randrianja and Ellis, *Madagascar*, 108: "In view of the nature of the social units that had formed in Madagascar over time, it seems misleading to refer to the Sakalava construction as the island's 'first empire,' as some historians have done."

124. Miller argues that rulers in West-Central Africa restricted the distribution of imports to help them retain their value: Miller, *Way of Death*, 125–26.

125. Ellis, "History of Sovereigns," 426. Ellis also suggests strong connections between the rulers of states on the west coast of the island and the interior.

126. Drury, *Adventures*, 371.

## CHAPTER 4: THE BETSIMISARAKA, PIRATE KINGS

1. Portions of this chapter are from Jane Hooper, "Pirates and Kings: Power on the Shores of Early Modern Madagascar and the Indian Ocean," *Journal of World History* 22, no. 2 (2011): 215–42.

2. See various discussions of the pirates, esp. "Advices from India regarding Pirates . . . ," 1697, IOR/H/36, pp. 434–35; see also the encounter with Captain Kidd in the ship journal of the *Madras Merchant*, 1695–96, IOR/L/MAR/A/CVI.

3. For a discussion of piracy in the Atlantic, see Peter Linebaugh and Marcus Rediker, *The Many-Headed Hydra: Sailors, Slaves, Commoners, and the Hidden History of the Revolutionary Atlantic* (Boston: Beacon Press, 2000), esp. 159–60.

4. On this history, see Michael N. Pearson, *The Indian Ocean* (London: Routledge, 2003), 56; Roxani Eleni Margariti, "Mercantile Networks, Port Cities, and 'Pirate' States: Conflict and Competition in the Indian Ocean World of Trade before the Sixteenth Century," *Journal of the Economic and Social History of the Orient* 51, no. 4 (2008): 543–77; Sebastian R. Prange, "A Trade of No Dishonor: Piracy, Commerce, and Community in the Western Indian Ocean, Twelfth to Sixteenth Century," *American Historical Review* 116, no. 5 (2011): 1269–93; Gwyn Campbell, "Piracy in the Indian Ocean World," *Interventions* 16, no. 6 (2014): 775–94.

5. See esp. Anne Pérotin-Dumon, "The Pirate and the Emperor: Power and the Law on the Seas, 1450–1850," in *The Political Economy of Merchant Empires: State Power and World Trade, 1350–1750*, ed. James D. Tracy (Cambridge: Cambridge University Press, 1991), 214–20.

6. Edward A. Alpers, *The Indian Ocean in World History* (Oxford: Oxford University Press, 2014), 86. On shifting definitions of piracy, see Lakshmi

Subramanian, "Of Pirates and Potentates: Maritime Jurisdiction and the Construction of Piracy in the Indian Ocean," in *Cultures of Trade: Indian Ocean Exchanges*, ed. Devleena Ghosh and Stephen Muecke (Newcastle: Cambridge Scholars Publishing, 2007), 25–27. These conflicts were not restricted to the Indian Ocean basin. On the interactions between maritime violence in the East Asia waters and European merchants, see Tonio Andrade, "The Company's Chinese Pirates: How the Dutch East India Company Tried to Lead a Coalition of Pirates to War against China, 1621–1662," *Journal of World History* 15, no. 4 (2004): 415–44; Adam Clulow, "The Pirate and the Warlord," *Journal of Early Modern History* 16, no. 6 (2012): 523–42.

7. Margarette Lincoln, *British Pirates and Society, 1680–1730* (London: Ashgate, 2014), 11–22.

8. See, for instance, Hubert Jules Deschamps, *Les pirates à Madagascar aux XVIIe et XVIIIe siècles* (Paris: Berger-Levrault, 1949); Robert C. Ritchie, *Captain Kidd and the War against the Pirates* (Boston: Harvard University Press, 1989); Kevin P. McDonald, *Pirates, Merchants, Settlers, and Slaves: Colonial America and the Indo-Atlantic World* (Berkeley: University of California Press, 2015).

9. For example, Auguste Toussaint, *History of the Indian Ocean*, trans. June Guicharnaud (Chicago: University of Chicago Press, 1966), 144–46.

10. For more, see Arne Bialuschewski, "Daniel Defoe, Nathaniel Mist, and the 'General History of the Pyrates,'" *Papers of the Bibliographical Society of America* 98, no. 1 (2004): 21–38.

11. McDonald, *Pirates*, 1–3.

12. Jane Hooper and David Eltis, "The Indian Ocean in Transatlantic Slavery," *Slavery & Abolition* 34, no. 3 (2013): 357–59.

13. On Philipse's endeavors in Madagascar, in particular, see the collection HCA 1/98, Records of the High Court of Admiralty and colonial Vice-Admiralty courts, British National Archives. For examples of several of the voyages he sponsored, see Liliana Mosca, "La traite à Madagascar dans la seconde moitié du XVIIe siècle à la lumière de quelques documents anglo-américains," in *La route des esclaves: Système servile et traite dans l'est Malgache*, ed. Ignace Rakoto (Paris: L'Harmattan, 2000), 82–85. For more on Philipse and his activities, see Jacob Judd, "Frederick Philipse and the Madagascar Trade," *New York Historical Society Quarterly* 55, no. 4 (1971), 354–74; McDonald, *Pirates*, 47–53.

14. Hooper and Eltis, "Indian Ocean in Transatlantic Slavery," 258; McDonald, *Pirates*, 118–20.

15. On pirates as cultural brokers, see Michael N. Pearson, "Connecting the Littorals: Cultural Brokers in the Early Modern Indian Ocean," in *Eyes across the Water: Navigating the Indian Ocean*, ed. Pamila Gupta, Isabel Hofmeyr, and Michael N. Pearson (Pretoria: Unisa Press, 2010), 32–36.

16. McDonald, *Pirates*, 9.

17. For example, despite fears over pirates, the captain of the *King George* directed his ship to Nosy Boraha in 1719 because many of his crewmembers were sick with scurvy: the ship journal of the *King George*, 1719, IOR/L/MAR/B/402B.

18. Wright dates the Betsimisaraka Confederation as ruling between 1720 and 1760, although the rulers dominated east coast trade from Foulpointe until most export trade shifted to Toamasina under the control of Jean René, a ruler of Franco-Malagasy descent, by the 1810s. Henry T. Wright, "Early State Dynamics as Political Experiment," *Journal of Anthropological Research* 62, no. 3 (2006): 311.

19. McDonald, *Pirates*, 28–29. There was an earlier wave of English pirates starting in 1635: Pearson, *Indian Ocean*, 126.

20. The ship journal of the *Duchess*, 1655, COL C/5A/1.

21. Letter of M. Caron, 15 October 1666, COL C/5A/1.

22. See the comments of traders in COL C/3/1. Martin describes famine and widespread warfare in the region during the 1660s: François Martin, "Mémoires," in Alfred Grandidier et al., eds., *Collection des ouvrages anciens concernant Madagascar*, 9 vols. (Paris: Comité de Madagascar, 1903–20) (hereafter cited as *COACM*), 9:469. These wars were perhaps due to the destabilizing influence of the French and Dutch in the region.

23. Alpers, *Indian Ocean*, 86–87.

24. Robert Blackborne, letter to Capt. Thomas Warren, 1697, IOR /H/36, 309.

25. See descriptions in HCA 1/98.

26. Robert Blackborne, letter, IOR/H/36, 317. Nutting argues that the colonists in North America, following the passage of the Navigation Acts, required cheap goods by the 1690s. P. Bradley Nutting, "The Madagascar Connection: Parliament and Piracy, 1690–1701," *American Journal of Legal History* 22, no. 3 (1978): 204. He also states that "efforts against the Madagascar pirates promised to dovetail with the policy of the newly created Board of Trade (established in 1696) to achieve greater political and economic consolidation of the colonial empire." Ibid., 206.

27. Judd, "Frederick Philipse," 354–74.

28. McDonald, *Pirates*, 85.

29. In later years, women received the honored title of *vadim-bazaha*, or wife of a white man, which they could retain even after their husbands left the island. Their children inherited the prestige attached to having a *vazaha* (foreign) father. G. A. Rantoandro, "Hommes et réseaux Malata de la côte orientale de Madagascar à l'époque de Jean René (1773–1825)," *Annuaire des pays de l'Océan Indien* 17 (2001–2): 109–11.

30. McDonald, *Pirates*, 85.

31. On other merchants, see ibid., 51–56.

32. Some of the trading records, including the one describing this shipment of slaves, can be found in HCA 1/98. For more descriptions of Baldridge's activities, see Mosca, "La traite," 85–86.

33. McDonald, *Pirates*, 89.

34. Ibid., 119–20.

35. On the EIC response, see Nutting, "Madagascar Connection," 204–9.

36. According to "Mémoire sur les forbans qui sont dans les mers des Indes," 29 November 1707, COL C/2/12. In addition, former pirates appear to have been used as sailors in the Indian Ocean, at least during the 1720s: Holden Furber, *Rival Empires of Trade in the Orient, 1600–1800* (Minneapolis: University of Minnesota Press, 1976), 144–45, 217.

37. Letter, 9 February 1698, COL C/2/8; Charles F. Noble, Account of Island of Bourbon, 1756, printed in Alexander Dalrymple, "Geographical collections of Alexander Dalrymple" on Mauritius, Island of Bourbon, Madagascar, and Diego Rayes, 1808, Add MS 33765, fol. 13. See also Jocelyn Chan Low, *"La VOC, t'Eylandt Mauritius et Rodrigues": Avec le voyage de Wolfert Harmensz vers les Îles Rodrigues et Maurice, 1601* (Port-Louis, Mauritius: National Library, 2001), 75–78.

38. Arne Bialuschewski, "Thomas Bowrey's Madagascar Manuscript of 1708," *History in Africa* 34 (2007): 35–36; Lincoln, *British Pirates*, 90–91; McDonald, *Pirates*, 60.

39. Welch is described as a replacement for Baldridge in HCA 1/98. A French ship in 1708 dealt with the trading representative, "M. Waliche," until his death: MAR 4JJ/88. There is, of course, no proof this is the very same Welch described in HCA 1/98, although the evidence points toward the two being the same man. An Edward Welsh was also mentioned at Nosy Boraha in 1698. See the records of the Dutch ship *Tamboer*, 1698, in *COACM*, 6:44.

40. For references to Kidd and the Comoros, see the ship journal of the *Madras Merchant*, 1696.

41. Bialuschewski, "Thomas Bowrey's Madagascar Manuscript," 35; see also Malyn Newitt, "The Comoro Islands in Indian Ocean Trade before the 19th Century," *Cahiers d'études africaines* 23, nos. 89–90 (1983): 158; David Wilson, "Piracy, Patronage & Political Economy: Captain Kidd and the East India Trade," *International Journal of Maritime History* 27, no. 1 (2015): 31.

42. K. N. Chaudhuri, "The English East India Company's Shipping (c. 1660–1760)," in *Ships, Sailors and Spices: East India Companies and Their Shipping in the 16th, 17th and 18th Centuries*, ed. Jaap R. Bruijn and Femme S. Gaastra (Amsterdam: NEHA, 1993), 65.

43. Likely in the Mozambique Channel, although the exact itineraries and dates are not indicated: K. Degryse and J. Parmentier, "Maritime Aspects of the Ostend Trade to Mocha, India and China (1715–1732)," in Bruijn and Gaastra, *Ships, Sailors and Spices*, 156.

44. R. J. Barendse, *Arabian Seas, 1700–1763* (Leiden: Brill, 2009), 3:1246–47.

45. See letter from Réunion, 1723, COL C/3/3–4; "Journal and Logbook of an anonymous Scotch sailor, 1726–1729," HC 363/129, Hispanic Society of America. See also Hendrik Frappé and Willem van der Lint, *Slawehandel met Madagaskar: Die joernale van die Kaapse slaweskip Leijdsman, 1715*, ed. Piet E. Westra and James C. Armstrong (Cape Town: Africana Uitgewers, 2006), 99.

46. Robert Drury, *The Adventures of Robert Drury* (London, 1729; reprint, Hull: Stodart and Craggs, 1807), 381–82; page references are to the 1807 edition.

47. "The deposition of George Reevelly(?) taken December the 18th, 1698," HCA 1/98.

48. Drury, *Adventures*, 432; see also Noble, Account of Island of Bourbon, 18.

49. Clement Downing, *A Compendious History of the Indian Wars* (London, 1737), 81.

50. The ship journal of the *King George*, 1719.

51. Bialuschewski, "Thomas Bowrey's Madagascar Manuscript," 38–40.

52. Alexis-Marie de Rochon, *A Voyage to Madagascar and the East Indies* (London: G. G. J. and J. Robinson, 1792, originally published in French in 1791), 205–6.

53. Arne Bialuschewski, "*A True Account of the Design, and Advantages of the South-Sea Trade*: Profits, Propaganda, and the Peace Preliminaries of 1711," *Huntington Library Quarterly* 73, no. 2 (2010): 280–81.

54. Hooper and Eltis, "Indian Ocean in Transatlantic Slavery," 358.

55. Letter of Desforges-Boucher, 1724, on the pirates in Madagascar, COL C/3/3–4.

56. Letters from Réunion, 1723–24, COL C/3/3–4. See French worries illuminated in a letter written by Desforges-Boucher, 30 November 1725, COL C/3/3–4. The French government had given the French colonies permission to eliminate piracy: Pérotin-Dumon, "The Pirate and the Emperor," 219.

57. Toussaint, *History*, 146.

58. On pirates during this time, see the ship journal of the *Greenwich*, 1720, IOR/L/MAR/B/488A; the ship journal of the *Prince Frederick*, 1722, IOR/L/MAR/B/663C; the ship journal of the *Duke of York*, 1723, IOR/L/

MAR/B/94B–C. On "Angria" pirates, see the instructions given to English ships in 1737, IOR/E/3/107, fols. 115, 282.

59. The ship journal of the *Duc d'Anjou*, 1736–37, MAR 4JJ/76.

60. The ship journal of *Le Héron*, 1733, MAR 4JJ/91; the ship journal of the *Hirondelle*, 1733, MAR 4JJ/86. A few years later, a French captain noted his ship going past "Île aux Baldrige," and later traders referred to the entrance into Antongil Bay as "Baldrige Point": the ship journal of *L'Astrée*, 1734, MAR 4JJ/86.

61. The ship journal of the *Duc d'Anjou*, 1738.

62. According to Sylla, the term *Malata* is a "déformation malgache" of the French word *mulâtre* (mulatto): Yvette Sylla, "Les Malata: Cohésion et disparité d'un 'groupe,'" *Omaly sy anio* 21–22 (Université d'Antananarivo) (1985): 19. *Zana* roughly translates as children. See Wendy Wilson-Fall, "Women Merchants and Slave Depots: Saint-Louis, Senegal, and St. Mary's, Madagascar," in *Paths of the Atlantic Slave Trade: Interactions, Identities, and Images*, ed. Ana Lucia Araujo (Amherst, NY: Cambria Press, 2011), 273–89. Note that the term is found in archival sources at the close of the eighteenth century, usually in reference to individuals of mixed Mascarene (French) and Malagasy descent.

63. The ship journal of *Le Héron*, 1733; see also Downing, *Compendious History*, 93.

64. See also Rochon, *Voyage to Madagascar*, 232–33 for a similar, if later, description.

65. The EIC first ordered a slave trading ship to visit Foulpointe to procure slaves in 1737: "Orders and Instructions to Captain George Bagwell and Chief Mate Henry Wilson of the Resolution about the purchase of slaves in Madagascar," IOR/E/3/107, fol. 115. The French regularly visited this port throughout the eighteenth century, especially during wartime: see various ship journals, 1747–49, MAR 4JJ/77.

66. Most histories of Ratsimilaho rely upon the French translator and slave trader Mayeur's "Histoire de Ratsimila-hoe," in "Mémoires pour servir à l'histoire de l'isle de Madagascar," ed. M. de Froberville, 2 vols., folio, 1809, 2:183–300, Add MS 18128–18129, British Library. See also Dalrymple, "Geographical Collections," 18. For a discussion of Mayeur's history about Ratsimilaho, see Stephen Ellis, "Tom and Toakafo: The Betsimisaraka Kingdom and State Formation in Madagascar, 1715–1750," *Journal of African History* 48, no. 3. (2007): 447–48. McDonald argues that Tom Tew was likely not the father: McDonald, *Pirates*, 94.

67. Rochon, *Voyage to Madagascar*, 214–15.

68. "Histoire de Ratsimila-hoe," in "Mémoires pour servir," 2:218.

69. Guillaume Joseph Galaisière, *Voyage dans les mers de l'Inde*, vol. 2 (Paris, 1781), 526.

70. Stephen Ellis, "The History of Sovereigns in Madagascar: New Light from Old Sources," in *Madagascar revisitée: En voyage avec Françoise Raison-Jourde*, ed. Didier Nativel and Faranirina V. Rajaonah (Paris: Karthala, 2009), 420–21.

71. Berg, using the history of Ratsimilaho recorded by Mayeur, describes the Betsimisaraka as uniting to seize coastal trade from the Betanimena decades earlier, around 1712–16. This rivalry seems likely and may have been the initial incentive for the Betsimisaraka alliance, although contemporary French sources seem to make no mention of these battles. For more details, see Gerald M. Berg, "The Sacred Musket: Tactics, Technology, and Power in Eighteenth-Century Madagascar," *Comparative Studies in Society and History* 27, no. 2 (1985): 265–67. See also McDonald, *Pirates*, 93–94.

72. See evidence of expanding trade in Pierre Vérin, *The History of Civilisation in North Madagascar*, trans. David Smith (Rotterdam: A. A. Balkema, 1986), 142–56, 209–80.

73. Regarding the attempt of the French to colonize the island of "Anjou" in Antongil Bay and their asking the king of "Massaly" for permission, the first mention is in a letter from Réunion, 1732, COL C/3/6. A description of this voyage to the northwest coast can be found in the ship journal of the *Hirondelle*, 1732; see also letter, 5 January 1733, COL C/3/7; letter to the king of Massaly from the captain d'Hermitte, 23 October 1732, COL C/4/1; letter, 20 Dec 1732, reporting the taking possession of the island, COL C/4/1. See descriptions from various letters from January 1733, COL C/3/7. The colony failed within a few months after its founding: "Projet d'établissement à Madagascar," 1749, COL C/5A/1.

74. The culprits are not named as Sakalava, but rather those acting on behalf of the "king of Massaily." See the ship journal of *L'Astrée*, 1734. These battles were likely fought using primarily spears, but occasionally the use of firearms was also needed: Berg, "Sacred Musket," 266.

75. The French seemed a bit confused by the different alliances: see the ship journal of the *Duc d'Anjou*, 1737. One history recorded in the 1760s notes that after the king defended the people of the east coast against the "Betanimenes," they formed a republic to protect themselves, the Betsimisaraka Confederation. Galaisière, *Voyage*, 527.

76. On the defeat of the attackers, see the ship journal of the *Meduze*, 1733, MAR 4JJ/76.

77. The ship journal of *L'Amphitrite*, 1738–39, ibid. Sources imply ties between Ratsimilaho and the Sakalava Empire as early as 1715: Ellis, "Tom and Toakafo," 451. One source describes a ruler visiting the northwest coast named "Andian Simonalij" or "Simialoe": see Frappé and Lint, *Slawehandel met Madagaskar*, 95. If this was the case, it placed Ratsimilaho in

an even stronger position to mediate between the people of Antongil Bay and the Sakalava.

78. Ellis, "Tom and Toakafo," 442. On the marriage, see Mayeur, "Voyage au pays des Seclaves," 1774, in "Mémoires pour servir," 1:127; see also Mayeur, "Histoire de Ratsimila-hoe," in "Mémoires pour servir,", 2:297.

79. Wright, "Early State Dynamics," 311–12.

80. Galaisière, *Voyage*, 429.

81. Antongil Bay was still visited frequently (129 visits to the bay and Nosy Boraha between 1600 and 1800), in part due to the ability of the bay to hold large numbers of French naval vessels that would visit before continuing on to the northern Indian Ocean. Smaller vessels would be sent to fetch food from Nosy Boraha and Foulpointe and then return to the larger ships at anchor in the bay.

82. Galaisière, *Voyage*, 510–11.

83. See, for example, the evidence sent to French officials in Mauritius in 1768, COL C/5A/2. Descriptions of some of these merchants can be found in Yves Banallec and Jean-Yves Le Lan, "La Compagnie des Indes et la traite des noirs," in *Idées et représentations coloniales dans l'océan Indien*, ed. Norbert Dodille (Paris: Presses de l'Université Paris-Sorbonne, 2009), 38–39.

84. See, for instance, Martin, in *COACM*, 9:469.

85. Galaisière, *Voyage*, 429–30, 527; Rochon, *Voyage to Madagascar*, 345.

86. Ranaivo Ratsivalaka identifies the interior of Ambanivolo as the rice-producing region from which rice was exported to Foulpointe: Ranaivo G. Ratsivalaka, *Les Malgaches et l'abolition de la traite européenne des esclaves (1810–1817): Histoire de la formation du Royaume de Madagascar* (Antananarivo: Hery Arivo, 1999), 46–47.

87. Galaisière, *Voyage*, 518.

88. In 1750, Béti signed a treaty with the French in which she is identified as "Béti, daughter and heir of the kingdom and all the rights of the deceased Tamsimalo, her father, during his lifetime king of Foulpointe and all other countries on the east coast of Madagascar." Treaty in COL C/5A/1(2); copy in B.-F. Leguével de Lacombe, *Voyage à Madagascar et aux îles Comores (1823 à 1830)*, vol. 2 (Paris: Louis Desessart, 1840): 357–64. See Rochon, *Voyage to Madagascar*, 215. Rochon reported that La Bigorne, a former French translator who supposedly had a relationship with Béti, was responsible for fomenting violence against "John Harre": ibid., 243. Béti was also described as Tom Similo's sister: see Noble, Account of Island of Bourbon, 18.

89. Richard B. Allen, *Slaves, Freedmen, and Indentured Laborers in Colonial Mauritius* (Cambridge: Cambridge University Press, 1999), 85–86.

90. Superior council letter, 30 May 1758, COL C/4/10.

91. See various letters about Jean Hard's death around 1768, COL C/5A/2.

92. Galaisière, *Voyage*, 529.

93. Ibid., 541–75. The battle was against a neighboring king, "Silouloute." On Galaisière's voyage, see also "Extrait des voyages de M. Le Gentil: Voyage à Madagascar (1761–1763)," COL C/5A/2.

94. According to Rochon, Andrianjanahary died in 1767 and Yavi was his son: Rochon, *Voyage to Madagascar*, 249.

95. As described in Mayeur, "Voyage au pays des Seclaves," 1774, in "Mémoires pour servir," 1:98.

96. In 1774, after the French angered the Sakalava, the king of Boina dispatched 250 cattle to buy the assistance of a Sakalava-appointed king near Antongil Bay. Mayeur, "Histoire de Ratsimila-hoe," in "Mémoires pour servir," 2:280.

97. On the later trade of the French, see esp. Pier Larson, "The Route of the Slave from Highland Madagascar to the Mascarenes: Commercial Organization, 1770–1820," in Rakoto, *La route des esclaves*, 145–48.

98. Wright, "Early State Dynamics," 311–12.

99. Ibid., 314.

100. See, for instance, Pierre Sonnerat, *A Voyage to the East-Indies and China*, trans. Francis Magnus, vol. 3 (Calcutta, 1789), 35–39.

101. Ibid., 42–43.

102. On the continuation of these wars, see "Rédaction par Modave d'un journal relatant les évènements survenus à Fort Dauphin du 5 septembre 1768 au 11 decembre suivant," COL C/5A/2.

103. Galaisière, *Voyage*, 372.

104. The ship journal of the *Harrington*, 1736, IOR/L/MAR/B/654B; "Journal and Logbook," HC 363/129.

105. Galaisière, *Voyage*, 524.

106. See "Rédaction par Modave."

107. Ellis, "History of Sovereigns," 423.

## CHAPTER 5: RITUALS OF CONSUMPTION, RITUALS OF DOMINATION

1. The ship journal of the *Swallow*, 1749–50, IOR/L/MAR/B/385A. See also "William Purser, the interpreter" described by Robert Drury, *The Adventures of Robert Drury* (London, 1729; reprint, Hull: Stodart and Craggs, 1807), 332–33; page references are to the 1807 edition. Prince Will and King Baba appear to have been described by the Dutch traders who visited Toliara in 1715 as "king Demonaji" and "viceroy Bevaha."

Hendrik Frappé and Willem van der Lint, *Slawehandel met Madagaskar: Die joernale van die Kaapse slaweskip Leijdsman, 1715*, ed. Piet E. Westra and James C. Armstrong (Cape Town: Africana Uitgewers, 2006), 67. The titles are also listed by the French in the journal of the *Royal Philippe*, 1733, MAR 4JJ/88.

2. The ship journal of the *St. Charles*, 1742, MAR 4JJ/74; see also the ship journal of *L'Astrée*, 1737, MAR 4JJ/86. See also John Dean, "Narrative of One of the Crew Belonging to the Ship *Sussex*," 1738, MSS Eur. B2/K11, British Library, 8–9.

3. Noble states that only Arabian navigators knew how to pilot the coast between northwest Madagascar, the Comoro Islands, and East Africa: Charles F. Noble, Account of Island of Bourbon, 1756, printed in Alexander Dalrymple, "Geographical collections of Alexander Dalrymple" on Mauritius, Island of Bourbon, Madagascar, and Diego Rayes, 1808, Add MS 33765, fol. 13, 18. Machado makes a similar comment for East Africa: Pedro Machado, *Ocean of Trade: South Asian Merchants, Africa and the Indian Ocean, c. 1750–1850* (Cambridge: Cambridge University Press, 2014), 76–77.

4. For example, see the ship journal of the *Caesar*, 1747, IOR/L/MAR/B/235H.

5. "When you come upon the coast of Madagascar and begin to draw near any bay or river where ships commonly touch at for slaves or provisions, you must spread your ensign, and if you are afraid of rocks or shoals and can't discover the proper anchoring place, . . . [ask] if there be any white men upon the place, and canoes to come off." From "An account of the present comodityes that are imported & exported at Madagascarr and the manner of dealing with the natives," Rawlinson MS A 334, 61.

6. Noble, Account of Island of Bourbon, 18v.

7. On the dangers of St. Augustin Bay, see the ship journal of the *Marquis*, 1769, MAR 4JJ/83. For observations of Nosy Boraha in 1847, see MAR 5/JJ/436; see the chart of Boteler's River in western Madagascar made under the orders of the British captain W. F. W. Owen in 1824, G251:18/11, National Maritime Museum.

8. The ship journal of the *Reine*, 1734, MAR 4JJ/91. In at least one instance, Captain Bush also presented himself as an influential king at Morondava: the ship journal of the *Hertford*, 1734, IOR/L/MAR/B/656F. The Dutch referred to elites in St. Augustin Bay and Toliara as "Ryks Bestierder" and "Croon Prins." "Dagregister *Drie Heuvelen*," 1753, VOC 1.04.02, 4193, 4018. For a discussion of the Dutch rituals in Madagascar in particular, see Andrew Alexander, "Negotiation, Trade and the Rituals of Encounter: An Examination of the Slave-Trading Voyage of *De Zon*, 1775–1776," *Itinerario* 31, no. 3 (2007): 39–58.

9. Drury suggested that William Purser learned English from pirates. Drury, *Adventures*, 332–33.

10. The ship journal of *La Conde*, 1733, MAR 4JJ/97. There were also French interpreters at Taolagnaro, such as "Paul Nègre," in 1737: the ship journal of the *Duc d'Anjou*, 1737, MAR 4JJ/76. In 1796, a British captain observed that "Most of the natives [of Saint Augustin Bay] speak English and many of them French, and in their language they have incorporated many Portuguese words. They are remarkably attached to the former of these nations, and singularly averse to the latter." The ship journal of HMS *Stately*, kept by C. P. Beaver, 1796, RUSI 180/2, National Maritime Museum.

11. The ship journal of *L'Astrée*, 1734.

12. "Dagregister *Binnenwisent*," 1732, VOC 1.04.02, 2217, 6983.

13. The ship journal of the *Lys*, 1713, MAR 4JJ/94.

14. The ship journal of the *Reine*, 1735; the ship journal of the *Sirène*, 1729, MAR 4JJ/112; the ship journal of the *Brack*, 1741, in Alfred Grandidier et al., eds., *Collection des ouvrages anciens concernant Madagascar*, 9 vols. (Paris: Comité de Madagascar, 1903–20) (hereafter cited as *COACM*), 6:62.

15. The ship journal of *L'Astrée*, 1733; see also the ship journal of the *Hertford*, 1734.

16. The ship journal of *L'Astrée*, 1734.

17. Translators were murdered on the *Delaware* in 1752 and the *Meermin* in 1766: Dan Sleigh and Piet Westra, *The Taking of the Slaver Meermin, 1766* (Cape Town: Africana, 2013), 31; the *Zon* in 1775: Andrew Alexander, "Shipboard Slave Uprisings on the Malagasy Coast: The '*Meermin*' (1766) and '*De Zon*' (1775)," *Kronos*, no. 33 (2007): 103–4. On the Atlantic, see Emma Christopher, *Slave Ship Sailors and Their Captive Cargoes, 1730–1807* (New York: Cambridge University Press, 2006), 64–66.

18. Drury describes elites as "ambassadors": Drury, *Adventures*, 202.

19. The ship journal of the *Onslow*, 1741 IOR/L/MAR/B/164C. See also the ship journal of the *Reine*, 1732; the ship journal of the *Chauvelin*, 1734, MAR 4JJ/98.

20. The ship journal of the *Onslow*, 1741 IOR/L/MAR/B/164C. See also description of Prince "Ouil" and his messenger: the ship journal of *L'Astrée*, 1735.

21. The ship journal of the *Salisbury*, 1742, IOR/L/MAR/B/478A; the ship journal of the *Swallow*, 1749–50. At Young Owl, a parallel procedure took place: upon the arrival of a European ship, the king's messenger came to assist with the movement of his present twelve to fifteen leagues up the Morondava River to the king's palace in the town of Mahabo. The ship journal of the *Delaware*, 1752, IOR/L/MAR/B/322B; observations of a French captain, the ship journal of the *St. Charles*, 1742.

22. The ship journal of *L'Astrée*, 1734.

23. "An account of the present comodityes," 61.

24. See, for instance, the ship journal of the *Hertford*, 1734.

25. The ship journal of the *Delaware*, 1752; "Dagregister *Binnenwisent*," 1732, 6987–89; the ship journal of the *Hirondelle*, 1731, MAR 4JJ/86; the ship journal of the *Ilchester*, 1750, IOR/L/MAR/B/601B.

26. "Dagregister gehou aan boord die *Neptunus*," 1760, C 2250, 102.

27. The ship journal of the *Haeslingfield*, 1739, IOR/L/MAR/B/642C; the ship journal of the *Duke of York*, 1723, IOR/L/MAR/B/94C.

28. The ship journal of the *Caesar*, 1747.

29. The ship journal of the *Warren*, 1749–50, IOR/L/MAR/B/571A. For example, when the *Sussex* went missing in 1738, the captain of the *Prince William* heard a rumor that the Malagasy had seized and enslaved the entire crew at Massaliege. The ship journal of the *Prince William*, 1738, IOR/L/MAR/B/324E. In 1740, the EIC officers commanded the captain of the *Onslow* to touch at Madagascar "in her outward bound passage in order to enquire further after the ship *Sussex*," as well as purchase supplies for their voyage to India. "Orders and Instructions, to Cap John Balchen Commander and Ralph Congreve Chief Mate of the *Onslow*," 1740, IOR/E/3/108, 164. When the ship arrived, "James Martin," one of the messengers, informed the captain that the Malagasy had not seized the crew of the *Sussex* and instead they had been castaways on the coast of Madagascar. Another English ship had been in the bay the previous year and received one of the surviving sailors of the *Sussex*, John Dean, as well as a letter left with King Baba by another survivor. The ship journal of the *Onslow*, 1741. For the full story, see Dean, "Narrative." On rescuing some of the crew, see the ship journal of the *Winchester*, 1736, IOR/L/MAR/B/643A. On "Prince Martin," see the ship journal of *L'Astrée*, 1735.

30. For instance, see the ship journal of the *Dragon*, 1753, IOR/L/MAR/B/598D.

31. "Mémoire de M. Parat sous l'isle de Madagascar," 1714, COL C/3/3–4.

32. The ship journal of the *Diligent*, 1761, IOR/L/MAR/B/320E.

33. "Journal and Logbook of an anonymous Scotch sailor, 1726–1729," HC 363/129, Hispanic Society of America.

34. The ship journal of the *Brack*, 1741, in *COACM*, 6:55.

35. For such exchanges at Nosy Boraha, see the ship journal of *Le Héron*, 1733, MAR 4JJ/91.

36. In St. Augustin Bay in 1733, see the ship journal of the *Philibert*, 1733, MAR 4JJ/114; the ship journal of the *Delaware*, 1752; Silas James, *A Narrative of a Voyage to Arabia, India, &c.* (London, 1797), 140–41.

37. The ship journal of the *Houghton*, 1746, IOR/L/MAR/B/438F.

38. The ship journal of *L'Amphitrite*, 1734, MAR 4JJ/126; see also the ship journal of the *Philibert*, 1733, MAR 4JJ/114; the ship journal of the *Onslow*, 1741.

39. James, *Narrative of a Voyage*, 140.

40. The ship journal of *Le Héron*, 1733, at Nosy Boraha.

41. For example, see the ship journal of the *Grantham*, 1750, IOR/L /MAR/B/617K; the ship journal of the *Dragon*, 1753.

42. Paul E. Lovejoy and David Richardson, "Trust, Pawnship, and Atlantic History: The Institutional Foundations of the Old Calabar Slave Trade," *American Historical Review* 104, no. 2 (1999): 350–54.

43. "Dagregister *Drie Heuvelen*," 1753, 4020; "Dagregister gehou aan boord die *Neptunus*," 1760. In Ndzuwani, European traders frequently faced challenges in trading in the midst of disputes between rulers on Ndzuwani and the other islands. The ship journal of the *Penthéière*, 1743, MAR 4JJ/116.

44. The ship journal of the *Duc d'Anjou*, 1736–37; the ship journal of the *Hirondelle*, 1734; the ship journal of *L'Astrée*, 1734.

45. On trade in Antongil, see esp. the ship journal of *L'Astrée*, 1737; the ship journal of the *Comte d'Argenson*, 1765, MAR 4JJ/92.

46. See various letters of "Jean Hard" and trade in Foulpointe, COL C/5A/2.

47. The ship journal of the *Hirondelle*, 1732; the ship journal of the *St. Louis*, 1746, MAR 4JJ/92. See also the instructions for Sr Gosse embarked on the ship *La Paix* going to trade at Foulpointe, 1750, COL C/4/6.

48. The ship journal of the *Minotaure*, 1758, MAR 4JJ/105, and complaints of 1759, COL C/4/12, following several years of very frequent trade between the Mascarenes and eastern/southern Madagascar. For earlier disputes, see the ship journal of the *Courrier*, 1721, MAR 4JJ/75; the ship journal of *L'Astrée*, 1734; the ship journal of the *Edgebaston*, 1740, IOR/L/MAR/B/622A.

49. The Dutch and French both set up informal trading posts in a few Malagasy ports during the latter half of the eighteenth century, although the English do not appear to have done likewise. For instance, around 1762, the French had left trading representatives in Foulpointe and Taolagnaro to try to coordinate trade. See Guillaume Joseph Galaisière, *Voyage dans les mers de l'Inde*, vol. 2 (Paris, 1781), 374, 378.

50. The ship journal of the *Hardwicke*, 1751, IOR/L/MAR/B/568D; see also the ship journal of the *Pitt*, 1759, IOR/L/MAR/B/525A; the ship journal of the *Grantham*, 1743, IOR/L/MAR/B/617I; the ship journal of the *Grantham*, 1750, IOR/L/MAR/B/617K.

51. James, *Narrative of a Voyage*, 146. See also the ship journal of the *London*, 1767, IOR/L/MAR/B/1E. These names were repeated by Dr.

Edward Ives, "A voyage to India in the year 1754," in *COACM*, 5:255. At Young Owl, various headmen and "captains" boarded along with the Sakalava king. The ship journal of the *Haeslingfield*, 1739.

52. The ship journal of the *Dragon*, 1758, IOR/L/MAR/B/598E.

53. Even in Taolagnaro, "we have had many kings aboard the ship, always wanting to drink eau de vie." The ship journal of *L'Astrée*, 1734.

54. J. Cameron Monroe and Anneke Janzen, "Le festin dahoméen: Femmes du palais, politiques internes et pratiques culinaires en Afrique de l'Ouest au XVIIIe–XIXe siècle," *Afriques: Débats, méthodes et terrains d'histoire*, no. 5 (2014), https://afriques.revues.org/1632.

55. On ceremonial feasting, see Pierre Sonnerat, *A Voyage to the East-Indies and China*, trans. Francis Magnus, vol. 3 (Calcutta, 1789), 40–41. For one description of a funeral for Prince William involving firearms and the distribution of a large amount of arrack, the ship journal of the *Oxford*, 1751, IOR/L/MAR/B/588B. The ship journal of the *Barneveld* describes a funeral in "Sadian Bon Porte" (along the west-central coast of Madagascar) at which a number of cattle were killed and their heads placed around the tomb, in *COACM*, 5:27–28.

56. The ship journal of the *St. Charles*, 1742; the ship journal of the *Duke of Albany*, 1764, IOR/L/MAR/B/553A.

57. The ship journal of the *Oxford*, 1751. On the importance of alcohol consumption in East African feasting, see Michael Dietler, "Theorizing the Feast: Rituals of Consumption, Commensal Politics, and Power in African Contexts," in *Feasts: Archaeological and Ethnographic Perspectives on Food, Politics, and Power*, ed. Michael Dietler and Brian Hayden (Tuscaloosa: University of Alabama Press, 2010), 96–97. Similar goods were required for trade with elites in parts of West Africa. See Rebecca Shumway, *The Fante and the Transatlantic Slave Trade* (Rochester, NY: University of Rochester Press, 2011), 7.

58. The ship journal of the *Héron*, 1733.

59. Furthermore, once visitors came aboard European ships, they usually drank "a good deal of brandy." The ship journal of the *Diligent*, 1761.

60. The ship journal of the *Prince Henry*, 1761, IOR/L/MAR/B/325G.

61. The ship journal of the *Dragon*, 1753.

62. The ship journal of the *Brack*, 1741, in *COACM*, 6:112–18.

63. For a discussion of toaka, see Drury, *Adventures*, esp. 239–40, about "toak" and circumcision ceremonies in the south; see also Robert Everard, "A Relation of Three Years Sufferings of Robert Everard," in *A Collection of Voyages and Travels*, vol. 6, ed. Awnsham Churchill and John Churchill (London, 1732), 263.

64. The ship journal of the *Haeslingfield*, 1739; on the use of alcohol to keep up the sailors' "spirits," see the ship journal of the *Warren*, 1749–50.

Dellon describes the sailors who drank excessively as prone to "colicks" while visiting Madagascar: Gabriel Dellon, *A Voyage to the East-Indies* (London, 1698), 230–31.

65. For a detailed list of presents to the king and "crown prince," see, for example, the "Dagregister *Drie Heuvelen*," 1753, 4019.

66. The ship journal of the *St. Charles*, 1742.

67. Ibid.; the ship journal of the *Onslow*, 1741.

68. The ship journal of the *Swift*, 1742, IOR/L/MAR/B/616A.

69. The ship journal of the *Dragon*, 1753.

70. John Kelly Thornton, *Africa and Africans in the Making of the Atlantic World, 1400–1800*, 2nd ed. (Cambridge: Cambridge University Press, 1998), 67–68. See also David Northrup, *Africa's Discovery of Europe, 1450–1850*, 2nd ed. (New York: Oxford University Press, 2009), 62–63.

71. The ship journal of the *Swift*, 1741–42, IOR/L/MAR/B/616-A.

72. The coat was of such poor quality that it was said to have been the property of the cabin boy, not the captain. James, *Narrative of a Voyage*, 146. In 1749, an English captain gave the king of Massaliege a "scarlet gold laced cloak" and a "gold laced . . . hat." The ship journal of the *Swallow*, 1749–50.

73. The ship journal of the *Oxford*, 1751.

74. The ship journal of *L'Astrée*, 1737. One exception was in 1742 when King Baba desired beads as a present, as the Dutch lacked proper guns for gifts: the ship journal of the *Brack*, in *COACM*, 1741, 6:72–74.

75. The ship journal of the *Swallow*, 1749.

76. The ship journal of the *Stormont*, 1759, IOR/L/MAR/B/458B; see also the ship journal of the *Hertford*, 1734; the ship journal of the *Chesterfield*, 1748, IOR/L/MAR/B/507A; the ship journal of the *Houghton*, 1748.

77. The ship journal of the *Prince Henry*, 1761; the ship journal of the *Onslow*, 1741.

78. For instance: the ship journal of the *Onslow*, 1741; in the case of Massaliege, ruled by a queen, the ship journal of the *Delaware*, 1752. On gifts to women, see also the ship journal of the *Philibert*, 1733, MAR 4JJ/97.

79. The ship journal of the *Grantham*, 1743, IOR/L/MAR/B/617I.

80. The ship journal of the *Dragon*, 1753.

81. The ship journal of the *Beckenham*, 1764, IOR/L/MAR/B/561A.

82. In 1733, St. Augustin Bay, the ship journal of the *Philibert*, MAR 4JJ/97.

83. "Dagregister gehou aan boord die *Schuijlenburg*," 1775–76, C 2249, 24–25. In some parts of the island, the ruler asked a diviner for the most auspicious day to start trade. Solofo Randrianja and Stephen Ellis, *Madagascar: A Short History* (Chicago: University of Chicago Press, 2009), 103.

84. The ship journal of the *Philibert*, 1736, MAR 4JJ/86.

85. See, for instance, the French visit to Massaly: the ship journal of the *Griffon*, 1735, MAR 4JJ/144C.

86. The ship journal of the *Diligent*, 1761. Without fixed weights (prior to the Merina Empire and the creation of a rice-based weight measurement), the debates over the size of a "gamelle" of rice or a "bamboo" of gunpowder became quite heated: the ship journal of *L'Astrée*, 1737. By the end of the eighteenth century, the French tried to fix the size of a "gamelle" more firmly: Jean Valette, "Le Commerce de Madagascar vers les Mascareignes au XVIIIe siècle," *La revue de Madagascar* 33 (1966): 38–39.

87. The ship journal of the *Oxford*, 1751.

88. "Journal and Logbook," HC 363/129.

89. See, for instance, the letter in 1733, COL C/3/7.

90. The ship journal of the *Dragon*, 1753. Most likely because guns were the preferred commodity for trade in the south of Madagascar: Mike Parker Pearson, *Pastoralists, Warriors and Colonists: The Archaeology of Southern Madagascar* (Oxford: Archaeopress, 2010), 456–63.

91. Mayeur, 1774, trip to the north of the island, in "Mémoires pour servir à l'histoire de l'isle de Madagascar," ed. M. de Froberville, 2 vols., folio, 1809, 1:19, Add MS 18128–18129, British Library.

92. "Dagregister gehou aan boord die *Schuijlenburg*", 1755, 25–30; see also R. J. Barendse, "Slaving on the Malagasy Coast, 1640–1700," in *Cultures of Madagascar: Ebb and Flow of Influences*, ed. S. Evers and M. Spindler (Leiden: International Institute for Asian Studies, 1995), 152.

93. Thornton, *Africa and Africans*, 67–68.

94. "Dagregister *Brak*," 1742, C 2247, Archives of the Western Cape, 202–4.

95. Robert Ross, ed., "The Dutch on the Swahili Coast, 1776–1778: Two Slaving Journals," pt. 1, *International Journal of African Historical Studies* 19, no. 2 (1986): 357; see also Barendse, "Slaving," 151–52; Ranaivo G. Ratsivalaka, *Les Malgaches et l'abolition de la traite européenne des esclaves (1810–1817): Histoire de la formation du Royaume de Madagascar* (Antananarivo: Hery Arivo, 1999), 37–38, 42–43.

96. The ship journal of the *Fly*, 1764, IOR/L/MAR/B/597B.

97. "Dagregister *Zon*," 1775, C 2255, Archives of the Western Cape, 73. For more about "Arabs" in northwestern Madagascar, see also "Dagregister van de *Soldaat*," 1696–97, VOC 1.04.02, 10811, 2–3; "Dagregister *Binnenwisent*," 1732, 7043.

98. "Journal and Logbook," HC 363/129.

99. Frequently called a "palisade" in southern Madagascar: the ship journal of the *Duc d'Anjou*, 1736–37.

100. Mayeur defines *marmittes*: "On appelle Marmittes ceux des naturels de Madagascar qui habitant sur les bords de la mer, s'offrent aux

européennes à leur arrive, pour commissaires, pour guides, pour pilotes, pour la traite, la conduite, et le soin des bœufs, tant à terre qu'à bord des vaisseaux." In effect, the French on the east coast came to refer to hired laborers as marmittes (usually hired through a king hiring out his slaves/workers). "Notes et éclaircissements," 1774, in "Mémoires pour servir," 1:60. The term may have been derived from a Malagasy word meaning cooking pot, according to McDonald. He has identified a man named "Marramitta" who was employed as a cook by Euro-American pirates: Kevin P. McDonald, *Pirates, Merchants, Settlers, and Slaves: Colonial America and the Indo-Atlantic World* (Berkeley: University of California Press, 2015), 103–5. Drury referred to slaves who worked for the French as the "mauromínters." Drury, *Adventures*, 103.

101. "An account of the present comodityes," 61.

102. The ship journal of the *Atalante*, 1732, MAR 4JJ/96.

103. The ship journal of the *Discovery*, 1700, IOR/L/MAR/A/CL. See also the later description of cattle loading in Gwyn Campbell, *David Griffiths and the Missionary "History of Madagascar"* (Leiden: Brill, 2012), 450–51.

104. In 1734, three tents were erected at St. Augustin Bay: the ship journal of the *Philibert*, MAR 4JJ/97; see also "An account of the present comodityes," 62; the ship journal of the *Onslow*, 1741.

105. There are many examples, but one clear description of this wait can be found in the ship journal of the *Edgebaston*, 1740.

106. Suggested most strongly in the ship journal of the *Astrée*, 1734, MAR 4 JJ/86; the ship journal of the *Duc d'Anjou*, 1736–37. During one visit, King Baba suggested that he could send his men in search of rice and slaves for sale: the ship journal of the *Brack*, 1741, in *COACM*, 6:93–94.

107. Such as in the case of the *Lys*: the ship journal of the *Lys*, 1735, MAR 4JJ/144C.

108. The ship journal of the *Hertford*, 1734.

109. The ship journal of the *Delaware*, 1752; see also "Journal and Logbook," HC 363/129.

110. Barendse, "Slaving," 143–44.

111. The ship journal of the *Penthéière*, 1743. It was also known to be dangerous to sleep ashore in Madagascar. In a nineteenth-century American description of visiting Nosy Boraha, the author identifies the danger as malaria: Charles Nordhoff, *Whaling and Fishing* (New York: Dodd, Mead, 1855), 213.

112. The ship journal of the *Beckenham*, 1764.

113. The ship journal of the *Delaware*, 1752.

114. Stephen D. Behrendt, "Crew Mortality in the Transatlantic Slave Trade in the Eighteenth Century," in *Routes to Slavery: Direction, Ethnicity*

*and Mortality in the Atlantic Slave Trade*, ed. David Eltis and David Richardson (London: Frank Cass, 1997), 49–65.

115. The ship journal of the *Prince Henry*, 1761. A similar encounter occurred during a French stopover in Zanzibar during the 1750s: the ship journal of the *Gloire*, 1757, MAR 4JJ/87.

116. See, for instance, the ship journal of the *Prince Henry*, 1761; the ship journal of the *Delaware*, 1752. On the use of pawns in West Africa, see Lovejoy and Richardson, "Trust, Pawnship, and Atlantic History."

117. James, *Narrative of a Voyage*, 150–53.

118. The ship journal of the *Delaware*, 1752.

119. One clear case of such exchanges is the ship journal of the *Duke of Albany*, 1764.

120. James, *Narrative of a Voyage*, 145.

121. For examples of runaways in Madagascar, see the ship journal of the *Northington*, 1777, IOR/L/MAR/B/483D; the ship journal of the *Godfrey*, 1778, IOR/L/MAR/B/464D; the ship journal of the *Egmont*, 1770, IOR/L/MAR/B/535F. Christopher describes a desire for food, as well as women, encouraging desertion in the Atlantic: Christopher, *Slave Ship Sailors*, 132.

122. For a later example of desertion, see Nordhoff, *Whaling and Fishing*, 217. Nordhoff deliberated where best to escape from his ship, eventually choosing to desert while visiting the Seychelles.

123. As suggested in the ship journal of the *Dragon*, 1758. For pirate sightings during the eighteenth century, see the ship journal of the *Curieux*, 1708, MAR 4JJ/88. See also the ship journal of the *King George*, 1718, IOR/L/MAR/B/402B.

124. The ship journal of the *Dragon*, 1758.

125. The ship journal of the *Delaware*, 1752.

126. The ship journal of the *Onslow*, 1741; the ship journal of the *Haeslingfield*, 1739.

127. The ship journal of the *Durrington*, 1748, IOR/L/MAR/A/613D; the runaways of the *Tilbury* also stole a long boat: the ship journal of the *Tilbury*, 1757, IOR/L/MAR/B/551A.

128. As was the case on the *Durrington:* ship journal of the *Durrington*, 1748.

129. The challenges the British faced are outlined in Michael H. Fisher, "Working across the Seas: Indian Maritime Labourers in India, Britain, and in Between, 1600–1857," in "Coolies, Capital, and Colonialism," supplement, *International Review of Social History* 51, no. S14 (2006): 24–27.

130. The ship journal of the *Houghton*, 1748; see also the ship journal of the *Ajax*, 1759, IOR/L/MAR/B/620A.

131. The ship journal of the *Talbot*, 1769, IOR/L/MAR/B/474B. On lascars, see Janet J. Ewald, "Crossers of the Sea: Slaves, Freedmen, and

other Migrants in the Northwestern Indian Ocean, c. 1750–1914," *American Historical Review* 105, no. 1 (2000): 69–91; Fisher, "Working across the Seas," 23–27.

132. James, *Narrative of a Voyage*, 170–73.

133. The ship journal of the *Delaware*, 1752.

134. The ship journal of the *Oxford*, 1751.

135. "Journal and Logbook," HC 363/129. Drury was allowed to leave Morondava after he promised the ruler that he would return with a ship to trade there. Drury, *Adventures*, 235–37.

136. The ship journal of the *Chesterfield*, 1748.

137. The ship journal of the *Devonshire*, 1764, IOR/L/MAR/B/272E. On one occasion, an English captain learned of three English sailors on board a Dutch ship anchored in Toliara, where the Dutch were engaged in buying slaves. The Dutch captain refused to return the English sailors, as the sailors said they were not interested in boarding the English ship. A fourth man changed his mind about leaving Madagascar on either ship and ran away into the country. The ship journal of the *Sandwich*, 1753, IOR/L/MAR/B/606C.

138. Peter Linebaugh and Marcus Rediker, *The Many-Headed Hydra: Sailors, Slaves, Commoners, and the Hidden History of the Revolutionary Atlantic* (Boston: Beacon Press, 2000), esp. 154–62; Niklas Frykman et al., "Mutiny and Maritime Radicalism in the Age of Revolution: An Introduction," in "Mutiny and Maritime Radicalism in the Age of Revolution: A Global Survey," supplement, *International Review of Social History* 58, no. S21 (2013): 1–14.

139. Although Drury was enslaved after his ship wrecked in southern Madagascar, Dean did not face enslavement on the west-central coast of the island. He was actively discouraged from seeking passage on an EIC ship when he sought to leave the island and faced occasional challenges in procuring enough food: Dean, "Narrative," 34–35. In general, the rulers on the west coast were perceived to be "kind and humane," as well as "generous," according to one English sailor who survived a shipwreck near Toliara in 1792: John Dale, *Narrative of the Loss of the Winterton East Indiaman* (London: Tegg & Castleman, 1802), 14, 26.

140. In addition, more than a hundred English and French vessels visited Ndzuwani and Mwali during the eighteenth century.

141. For example, see the "Dagregister gehou aan boord die *Schuijlenburg*," 1755.

142. For one such voyage, see "Dagregister *Drie Heuvelen*," 1753, VOC 1.04.02, 4193.

143. In reference to this early trade, see the letter from de Nyon of Mauritius, 29 April 1723, and the letter from M. Le Noir, governor of Pondichery, 1726, both in COL C/4/1.

144. As discussed earlier and in Jeremy Prestholdt, *Domesticating the World: African Consumerism and the Genealogies of Globalization* (Berkeley: University of California Press, 2008), 13–32.

145. See, for instance, Lovejoy and Richardson, "Trust, Pawnship, and Atlantic History," 339–46. See also the diary of one of these elites, Stephen D. Behrendt, A. J. H. Latham, and David Northrup, eds., *The Diary of Antera Duke, an Eighteenth-Century African Slave Trader* (Oxford: Oxford University Press, 2010).

## CHAPTER 6: EUROPEAN WARFARE AND IMPERIALISM

1. Portions of this chapter are from Jane Hooper, "*Flux du sang et sauterelles:* How the People and Environment of Madagascar Thwarted French Commercial Expansion," *Proceedings of the Western Society for French History* 37 (2009): 49–60.

2. Desforges-Boucher, 6 March 1760, COL C/4/12.

3. Magon, journal, 6 October 1757, COL C/4/10.

4. Desforges-Boucher, 6 March 1760, COL C/4/12; see also various letters in COL C/4/13.

5. The term Mascarene Islands also refers to the French possession of Île de Rodrigues. On the early history of Rodrigues, see "Une note pour l'île Rodrigue," 1692, COL C/3/1.

6. Transforming the ocean into a "British Lake": Edward A. Alpers, *The Indian Ocean in World History* (Oxford: Oxford University Press, 2014), 98. Recent perspectives on the impact of 1757 on the Indian Ocean include H. V. Bowen, *The Business of Empire: The East India Company and Imperial Britain, 1756–1833* (Cambridge: Cambridge University Press, 2005), 23; Sugata Bose, *A Hundred Horizons: The Indian Ocean in the Age of Global Empire* (Cambridge, MA: Harvard University Press, 2006), 7–10, 20–22; Thomas R. Metcalf, *Imperial Connections: India in the Indian Ocean Arena, 1860–1920* (Berkeley: University of California Press, 2007), 9; Markus P. M. Vink, "Indian Ocean Studies and the 'New Thalassology,'" *Journal of Global History* 2, no. 1 (2007): 57; Ghulam A. Nadri, *Eighteenth-Century Gujarat: The Dynamics of Its Political Economy, 1750–1800* (Leiden: Brill, 2009), 151–52; R. J. Barendse, *Arabian Seas, 1700–1763* (Leiden: Brill, 2009), 1:4; Alpers, *Indian Ocean*, 98–99.

7. For details on conflict in India, see esp. S. P. Sen, *The French in India: 1763–1816*, 2nd ed. (New Delhi: Munshiram Manoharlal, 1971); Stewart Gordon, *The Marathas: 1600–1818* (Cambridge: Cambridge University Press, 1993); Anil Athale, *Struggle for Empire: Anglo-Maratha Wars, 1679–1818* (New Delhi: Reliance, 2001); Aniruddha Ray, *Trade, Politics, and Plunder: The Marathas at Cambay, c. AD 1725–1825* (New Delhi: Munshiram

Manoharlal, 2006). For a traditional history of British and French conflict in India, see Alfred Thayer Mahan, *The Influence of Sea Power upon History, 1660–1783* (Boston: Little, Brown, 1890), 273–311.

8. For a description of the East African region as a periphery, see Barendse, *Arabian Seas, 1700–1763*, 1:8.

9. Important recent discussions of the EIC establishments in Asia during the seventeenth-century include Philip J. Stern, "Soldier and Citizen in the Seventeenth-Century English East India Company," *Journal of Early Modern History* 15, no. 1 (2011): 85–95; Emily Erikson, *Between Monopoly and Free Trade: The English East India Company, 1600–1757* (Princeton, NJ: Princeton University Press, 2014), esp. 4–6, 51–76.

10. Anne E. C. McCants, "Exotic Goods, Popular Consumption, and the Standard of Living: Thinking about Globalization in the Early Modern World," *Journal of World History* 18, no. 4 (2007): 460–61.

11. Auguste Toussaint, *History of the Indian Ocean*, trans. June Guicharnaud (Chicago: University of Chicago Press, 1966), 134–39; Philippe Haudrère, *La compagnie française des Indes au XVIIIe siècle*, 2nd ed. (Paris: Les Indes savantes, 2005), 1:202; Holden Furber, *Rival Empires of Trade in the Orient, 1600–1800* (Minneapolis: University of Minnesota Press, 1976), 177.

12. See esp. Toussaint, *History*, 157; Jean Sutton, *The East India Company's Maritime Service, 1746–1834: Masters of the Eastern Seas* (Rochester, NY: Boydell, 2010), 6–10.

13. Chris Nierstrasz, *In the Shadow of the Company: The Dutch East India Company and Its Servants in the Period of Its Decline (1740–1796)* (Leiden: Brill, 2012), 1–4; see also Om Prakash, "Cooperation and Conflict among European Traders in the Indian Ocean in the Late Eighteenth Century," in *Land, Politics, and Trade in South Asia*, ed. Sanjay Subrahmanyam (Delhi: Oxford University Press, 2004), 20–22.

14. On the development of the imperial networks that connected these two corners of the ocean, see Kerry Ward, *Networks of Empire: Forced Migration in the Dutch East India Company* (Cambridge: Cambridge University Press, 2009), esp. 55–64. See also Barendse, *Arabian Seas, 1700–1763*, 1:35–38. The Dutch formally withdrew from Mauritius by 1707: Jocelyn Chan Low, *"La VOC, t'Eylandt Mauritius et Rodrigues": Avec le voyage de Wolfert Harmensz vers les Îles Rodrigues et Maurice, 1601* (Port-Louis, Mauritius: National Library, 2001), 79; P. J. Moree, *A Concise History of Dutch Mauritius, 1598–1710: A Fruitful and Healthy Land* (London: Kegan Paul International, 1998), 93.

15. Femme S. Gaastra and Jaap R. Bruijn, "The Dutch East India Company's Shipping, 1602–1795, in a Comparative Perspective," in *Ships, Sailors and Spices: East India Companies and Their Shipping in the 16th, 17th*

*and 18th Centuries*, ed. Jaap R. Bruijn and Femme S. Gaastra (Amsterdam: NEHA, 1993), 192.

16. Femme S. Gaastra, "Soldiers and Merchants: Aspects of Migration from Europe to Asia in the Dutch East India Company in the Eighteenth Century," in *Migration, Trade, and Slavery in an Expanding World: Essays in Honor of Pieter Emmer*, ed. Wim Klooster (Leiden: Brill, 2009), 106–9.

17. James C. Armstrong and Nigel A. Worden, "The Slaves, 1652–1834," in *The Shaping of South African Society, 1652–1840*, ed. Richard Elphick and Hermann Giliomee (Middletown, CT: Wesleyan University Press, 1988), 115–17. Most of these visits were by VOC ships sent from the Cape to get food and slaves, but the number also includes emergency stops by VOC ships in desperate need of water or food.

18. Edward A. Alpers, "The Western Indian Ocean as a Regional Food Network in the Nineteenth Century," in Alpers, *East Africa and the Indian Ocean* (Princeton, NJ: Markus Wiener, 2009), 28–38; Barendse, *Arabian Seas, 1700–1763*, 3:1242. On the ivory trade, see esp. Edward Alpers, *Ivory and Slaves: Changing Pattern of International Trade in East Central Africa to the Later Nineteenth Century* (Berkeley: University of California Press, 1975).

19. Eugénia Rodrigues, "Eating and Drinking at the Royal Hospital of Mozambique Island: Medicine and Diet Change between the End of the 18th and the Early 19th Century," *Afriques: Débats, méthodes et terrains d'histoire*, no. 5 (2014), http://afriques.revues.org/1553.

20. This may have also coincided with greater availability of food: Pier Larson, "The Route of the Slave from Highland Madagascar to the Mascarenes: Commercial Organization, 1770–1820," in Rakoto, *La route des esclaves*, 133–35.

21. The ship journal of the *Houghton*, 1748, IOR/L/MAR/B/438F.

22. Compare this success to the failures of the *Beckenham* visiting during the hotter months. The ship journal of the *Beckenham*, 1764, IOR/L/MAR/B/561A.

23. On purchasing these goods in the bay, see also the ship journal of the *Winchelsea*, 1743, IOR/L/MAR/B/4C.

24. See, for instance, Lt. Colpoy, report, 1772, ADM 1/160. British ships bought cattle and rice on the east coast in 1751 but had trouble getting water and had to return to the Cape of Good Hope. The ship journal of the *Ruby*, 1751, ADM 52/696.

25. Edward Bosawen, letter, 17 October 1748, ADM 1/160.

26. The ship journal of the *Harrington*, 1736, IOR/L/MAR/B/654B. They stayed for about three months and purchased 165 slaves from Taolagnaro, Matitanana, and Nosy Boraha. When they visited Foulpointe, they met Ratsimilaho but "durst not stay the season being far spent." See

a similar experience described in "Journal and Logbook of an anonymous Scotch sailor, 1726–1729," HC 363/129, Hispanic Society of America. The French merchant Jean-Vincent Morrice also contrasted supplies on the west and east coast of Madagascar at the close of the eighteenth century: G. S. P. Freeman-Grenville, ed., *The French at Kilwa Island: An Episode in Eighteenth-Century East African History* (Oxford: Clarendon, 1965), 164–65.

27. See, for instance, the voyages of the *Duc d'Anjou*, 1737–38, to and from Mauritius, Taolagnaro, and Antongil Bay, MAR 4JJ/74. During the nineteenth century, Nordhoff describes three days from Port Louis to Toamasina and then 17 days on the return voyage: Charles Nordhoff, *Whaling and Fishing* (New York: Dodd, Mead, 1855), 277–79. Allen concludes that it took about 23 days for ships to sail from Madagascar's east coast to Mauritius or Réunion. Richard B. Allen, *European Slave Trading in the Indian Ocean, 1500–1850* (Athens: Ohio University Press, 2015), 79.

28. Orders to take control of Île Maurice, 1 March 1716, MAR B/1/14, 31.

29. Philippe Haudrère, "The 'Compagnie des Indes' and Maritime Matters (c. 1725–1770)," in Bruijn and Gaastra, *Ships, Sailors and Spices*, 82–83, 94.

30. The initial need for slaves was for Réunion. See the proposal for a colony in Madagascar in order to purchase slaves, 1697, MAR B/3/98, 320. So desperate was the need for slaves that the French openly traded with the pirates of east Madagascar during the early part of the eighteenth century. Desforges-Boucher, 30 November 1725, COL C/3/3–4. See also Jean-Michel Filliot, *La traite des esclaves vers les Mascareignes au XVIIIe siècle* (Paris: ORSTOM, 1974), 56–58.

31. Antoine Davelu, "Notes historiques sur l'isle de Bourbon," n.d., COL F/3/1.

32. On the use of slave labor on Mauritius during the mid-eighteenth century, see esp. Megan Vaughan, *Creating the Creole Island: Slavery in Eighteenth-Century Mauritius* (Durham, NC: Duke University Press, 2005), 39–51. For more on nineteenth-century sugar production and the use of slave labor, see Vijaya Teelock, *Bitter Sugar: Sugar and Slavery in 19th Century Mauritius* (Moka, Mauritius: Mahatma Gandhi Institute, 1998), esp. 21–45.

33. For the chronology of the slave trade to the Mascarenes, see Allen, *European Slave Trading*, 72–82.

34. For the history of this provisioning trade at the close of the eighteenth century, see Jean Valette, "Le Commerce de Madagascar vers les Mascareignes au XVIIIe siècle," *La revue de Madagascar* 33 (1966): 36–52.

35. See, for instance, the ship journal of the *Griffon*, 1735, MAR 4JJ/144C; the ship journal of the *Fulvy*, 1742, MAR 4JJ/144B.

36. Jean-Michel Filliot, "La traite vers l'Île de France," in U. Bissoondoyal and S. B. C. Servansing, eds., *Slavery in South West Indian Ocean* (Moka, Mauritius: Mahatma Gandhi Institute, 1989), 86.

37. For one example, see the ship journal of the *Sirène*, 1729–30, MAR 4JJ/112.

38. Letter, 9 August 1741, COL C/3/8. See also the instructions to the captain of the *Jupiter*, 1725, COL C/2/27; orders from the council of Île de France, 1744 and 1745, COL C/2/31; Diore, letter, 30 March 1728, COL C/3/5. The French also desired slaves from Senegal: David, letter, 25 October 1749, COL C/4/6.

39. These issues and crop failures are especially well laid out in Davelu, "Notes historiques sur l'isle de Bourbon," n.d., COL F/3/1. Davelu was a priest on Réunion during the late eighteenth century. See also various letters and reports from the colonial government in COL C/3 and COL C/4. These problems are also described in Anthony Cheke and Julian Hume, *Lost Land of the Dodo: The Ecological History of Mauritius, Réunion, and Rodrigues* (New Haven, CT: Yale University Press, 2010), 92–94. There were also periodic attempts to get the needed food from wild game; ibid., 91–99.

40. There is a discussion of maroonage in Charles F. Noble, Account of Island of Bourbon, 1756, printed in Alexander Dalrymple, "Geographical collections of Alexander Dalrymple" on Mauritius, Island of Bourbon, Madagascar, and Diego Rayes, 1808, Add MS 33765, fol. 13, 10; see also Richard B. Allen, *Slaves, Freedmen, and Indentured Laborers in Colonial Mauritius* (Cambridge: Cambridge University Press, 1999), 42–55; Vaughan, *Creating the Creole Island*, 172–77.

41. A letter written by Jean Marchand on the ship *Vierge de Grace* discussed getting slaves from Madagascar to grow manioc, 1733, COL C/5A/1. In 1771, a law was passed obligating plantation owners to plant a certain amount of manioc per slave per year and rations were typically fixed in manioc, rice, or beans for slaves. Jean Valentin Payet, *Histoire de l'esclavage à l'Île Bourbon (Réunion)* (Paris: L'Harmattan, 1990), 27.

42. Desforges-Boucher, letter noting the arrival of the *Ruby*, 1723, COL C/3/3–4.

43. Lenoir, letter, 1726, COL C/4/1. In 1734, the company decided they needed six hundred cows and bulls to be purchased for Mauritius: orders given to Bourdonnais, 11 December 1734, COL C/4/2.

44. Memoir, n.d., COL F/3/1. In 1737, the crops again failed due to a cyclone and the French sent ships to Madagascar for food and slaves: Bourdonnais, letter, 1 December 1737, COL C/4/2.

45. Ahuja describes crises around 1728 and 1736: Ravi Ahuja, "State Formation and 'Famine Policy' in Early Colonial South India," in *Land, Politics, and Trade in South Asia*, ed. Sanjay Subrahmanyam (Delhi: Oxford University Press, 2004), 156.

46. Deliberations of the Compagnie des Indes, 4 March 1733, COL C/3/7; letter, 7 February 1731, COL F/3/46–48.

47. Dumas, letter, 15 March 1733, COL C/3/7. This failed colony is also mentioned in Yves Banallec and Jean-Yves Le Lan, "La Compagnie des Indes et la traite des noirs," in *Idées et représentations coloniales dans l'océan Indien*, ed. Norbert Dodille (Paris: Presses de l'Université Paris-Sorbonne, 2009), 39.

48. See the French complaint about St. Augustin Bay: Desforges-Boucher, letter, 1760, COL C/4/12; see also the proposal for a French establishment in Madagascar, 1749, COL C/5A/1; Bellecombe, journal and notes, 10 September to 31 October 1776, COL C/5A/7. These complaints were not just made about Madagascar. See also comments about the disruption posed by wars in the Comoro Islands: the ship journal of the *Penthéière*, May 1743, MAR 4JJ/116; the ship journal of the *Warren*, 1749–50, IOR/L/MAR/B/571A; the ship journal of the *Walpole*, 1786, IOR/L/MAR/B/293O.

49. Ahuja suggests, for example, that the heightened demand for food may have contributed to the great famine of 1781–83: Ahuja, "State Formation," 161–63.

50. Curtis Barnett, letter, 9 October 1744, ADM 1/160.

51. Given the shortage in healthy sailors, the captains also tried to hire any "lascars, Portuguese, Dutch, or any sort of people we think can be of service to us." Griffin, 23 October, 1746, ADM 1/160.

52. Barnett, letter, 9 October 1744, ADM 1/160.

53. Ibid; the ship journal of the *Pearl*, 1745, ADM 51/723.

54. Barnett, letter, 9 October 1744, ADM 1/160.

55. Albert, letter, October 1747, COL C/2/33; the ship journal of the *Anglesea*, 1748, MAR 4JJ/77; the ship journals of the *Argonaut*, *Brilland*, *Lis* (*Lys*), and *Leside*, 1736, MAR 4JJ/102.

56. David, letter, December 1747, COL C/4/5. Additionally, the French bought 320 cattle from Taolagnaro in 1757, in the midst of a drought in southern Madagascar: Magon, journal, 14 December 1757, COL C/4/10.

57. David, letter, 28 February 1749, COL C/4/6.

58. Described repeatedly in various letters written by David in 1749–50, ibid. Similarly, when English merchant ships lay at anchor off Madagascar, the officers ordered a cow to be killed every two to three days for consumption by the crew. See "Journal and Logbook," HC 363/129.

59. On the use of lemons, limes and vinegar, see Gabriel Dellon, *A Voyage to the East-Indies* (London, 1698), 228–29. See also letters in COL C/4/18.

60. For example, see Poivre, letter, 1767, COL C/4/18. On the destruction of tortoise and turtle populations on Rodrigues due to the demands of French ships and their "scurvy sufferers," see Cheke and Hume, *Lost Land*, 110–11. According to one estimate, 280,000 animals were taken from the island between 1735 and 1771: ibid., 114, citing Alfred North-Coombes. The

consumption of tortoise meat not just on Rodrigues, but also on Mauritius, Réunion, the Seychelles, and Madagascar, probably forced several species of tortoises into extinction. For instance, tortoises on Réunion were scarce by 1728: ibid., 104.

61. Lilian Berthelot, *La petite Mascareigne: Aspects de l'histoire de Rodrigues* (Port-Louis, Mauritius: Centre Culturel Africain, 2002), 1–12.

62. David, letter, 28 February 1749, COL C/4/6.

63. Edward Boscawen, letter, 17 October 1748, ADM 1/160. See also the ship journal of the *Ruby*, 1751. An expedition to gather intelligence about the islands was discussed by the English in 1761: Cornish, letter, 6 December, 1761, ADM 1/162. On the surveillance, see George Pocock, reports on French ships, 1757–59, ADM 1/161; Robert Harland, 26 December 1769, ADM 1/163. Other valuable information on French activities was obtained from passing Portuguese ships and by questioning locals. For instance, see the ship journal of the *Haeslingfield*, 1739, IOR/L/MAR/B/642B. See also the description in [Dugald Carmichael], *Account of the Conquest of Mauritius* (London: T. Egerton, 1811), 26.

64. Bourdonnais had previously been in charge of the taking of Mahé on the coast of India in 1724 and then became governor-general of Mauritius in 1735.

65. See Bourdonnais, letter from Madagascar, 1746, in Charles Grant, ed., *The History of Mauritius, or the Isle of France, and the Neighbouring Islands* (London: W. Bulmer, 1801), 242–43. See also the accounts of some of the ships in the fleet: the *Achille*, 1746, MAR 4JJ/101; the *Neptune*, MAR 4JJ/117; the *Achille*, 1746, MAR 4JJ/144/O.

66. Bourdonnais, letter from Madagascar, 1746, in Grant, *History of Mauritius*, 243–44.

67. Ibid., 244–45. For an English account of this history, see [Carmichael], *Account of the Conquest*, 25–26.

68. COL C/4/20; see also description in Alfred Grandidier et al., eds., *Collection des ouvrages anciens concernant Madagascar*, 9 vols. (Paris: Comité de Madagascar, 1903–20) (hereafter cited as *COACM*), 3:313; COL C/5A/2; David, orders, 1750, COL C/4/6;Vignol, "project of the establishment in Madagascar," 1749, COL C/5A/1.

69. Stories of this "princess" come primarily from the early nineteenth century, when she was described as the sister of Ratsimilaho and reportedly was married to a Frenchman. See André Coppalle, *Voyage dans l'intérieur de Madagascar et à la capitale du roi Radama Ier: Un peintre découvre la Grande Île, 1825–1826* (Besançon: La lanterne magique, 2006), 49 (footnote by editor).

70. A copy of the treaty is found in COL C/5A/1. Her position in terms of signing this treaty is unclear. According to later French reports,

Ratsimilaho had also agreed to give the French the island. Note that the French continued to return to this treaty as evidence for their right to occupy the small island during the nineteenth century. See Antoine Marrier Unienville, *Statistique de l'Île Maurice et ses dépendances, suivie d'une notice historique sur cette colonie et d'un essai sur l'île de Madagascar* (Paris: Gustave Barba, 1838), 307.

71. See the ship journal of the *Princesse Emilie*, 1751, MAR 4JJ/86; Unienville, *Statistique*, 308.

72. Detailed by Legentil, memoir, 1761, Fonds ministériels, Dépôt fortifications colonial, Sainte Marie de Madagascar, XVII/mémoires/88, Archives nationales d'outre-mer (henceforth ANOM).

73. Guillaume Joseph Galaisière, *Voyage dans les mers de l'Inde*, vol. 2 (Paris, 1781), 452. The attacks were reportedly organized by Ratsimilaho's wife (the Queen Mother), who accused the French of disturbing her husband's remains on Nosy Boraha. French colonial officials dispatched a warship and brought Béti back to Mauritius to stand trial. She later cleared her name. See ibid., 533–34.

74. The community of Foulpointe, a major trading partner for the French, came under attack from their neighbors, the "Betalimenes," who pillaged the port in 1754. Letter from Mauritius, 20 January 1753, COL C/4/153. Ratsivalaka suggests there was frequent conflict between different kings for control over trade, particularly by the latter half of the eighteenth century: Ranaivo G. Ratsivalaka, *Les Malgaches et l'abolition de la traite européenne des esclaves (1810–1817): Histoire de la formation du Royaume de Madagascar* (Antananarivo: Hery Arivo, 1999), 44–46.

75. Magon, journal, 6 October 1757, COL C/4/10.

76. On the history of these trading representatives, see Banallec and Le Lan, "La Compagnie," 39.

77. Allen, *European Slave Trading*, 13.

78. D'Aché, letter to Magon, written off the coast of Madagascar, 31 July 1759, COL C/4/11. See also comments about prices in David, letter discussing trade in Madagascar, 1750, COL C/2/35–36; Brenier, letter, 19 October 1755, COL C/3/11.

79. Magon, journal, 12 December 1756, COL C/4/9.

80. Memoir on the commerce of the Indies, around 1766, COL C/4/16; memoir on the financial difficulties on the islands, 1767, COL C/4/19. The governors of the Mascarene Islands later came under investigation for their expenditure of large amounts of silver during the last few years of the war.

81. On problems getting food throughout the 1760s, see Desforges-Boucher, letter, 1 December 1761, COL C/4/13; the visits of French ships to Madagascar detailed in the ship journals of the *Bertin*, *Valliant*, and *Comte d'Artois*, 1761–62, all in MAR 4JJ/80; the ship journal of the *Comte de*

*Provence*, 1763, MAR 4JJ/81. On further disruptions at Foulpointe, see the ship journal of the *Comte d'Argenson*, 1765, MAR 4JJ/92. On the trade being ruined, see Poivre, letter, 15 January 1768, COL C/4/22.

82. Desforges-Boucher, 6 March 1760, COL C/4/12.

83. Desforges-Boucher, journal, 31 December 1759, COL C/4/12.

84. Desforges-Boucher, letter, 18 January 1762, COL C/4/14.

85. Huguette Ly-Tio-Fane Pineo, "Food Production and Plantation Economy of Mauritius," in Bissoondoyal and Servansing, *Slavery in South West Indian Ocean*, 212. See also Poivre, letter, 30 November 1767, COL C/4/18.

86. Cornish, letter, 19 December 1759, ADM 1/162. See also the records of EIC merchant ships visiting Madagascar and successfully obtaining food during this period: the ship journal of the *Royal Duke*, 1756, IOR/L/MAR/B/614 A–D; the ship journal of the *London*, 1767, IOR/L/MAR/B/1E. Despite British successes, the French complained in 1759 that they could not get any rice in St. Augustin Bay, perhaps due to the time of year: Desforges-Boucher, journal, 28 November 1759, COL C/4/12.

87. Jonathan R. Dull, *The French Navy and the Seven Years' War* (Lincoln: University of Nebraska Press, 2005), 141.

88. Mahan, *Influence of Sea Power*, 309–10.

89. Dull, *French Navy*, 170–73. Actions in the Seven Years' War in the Indian Ocean essentially ended in 1761.

90. Memoir on trade in the Indies, 1785?, COL C/2/113–14. For a similar view, see the late eighteenth-century document on Madagascar's role in trade, "sous la république," in MAD 150/207, ANOM.

91. Alexis-Marie de Rochon, *A Voyage to Madagascar and the East Indies* (London: G. G. J. and J. Robinson, 1792, originally published in French in 1791), 10.

92. See the French "essai sur le commerce de l'Inde," 1770?, COL C/2/107; Laval is also described in Galaisière, *Voyage*, 459.

93. Galaisière, *Voyage*, 461–62.

94. Ibid., 480.

95. Dumas, letter, 26 July 1768, COL C/4/20; Dumas and Poivre, correspondence about the necessity for a colony in Madagascar, 17 March and 3 June 1768, COL C/5A/2.

96. "Rédaction par Modave d'un journal relatant les évènements survenus à Fort Dauphin du 5 septembre 1768 au 11 decembre suivant," COL C/5A/2.

97. Modave, letter asking for reinvestment in a French colony at Taolagnaro, 28 August 1770, COL C/5A/3.

98. See the work of Karen Middleton and Jeffrey Kaufmann on the prickly pear cactus: Karen Middleton, "Who Killed 'Malagasy Cactus'?

Science, Environment and Colonialism in Southern Madagascar (1924–1930)," *Journal of Southern African Studies* 25, no. 2 (1999): 215–48; Jeffrey C. Kaufmann, "Prickly Pear Cactus and Pastoralism in Southwest Madagascar," *Ethnology* 43, no. 4 (2004): 345–61.

99. Madeleine Ly-Tio-Fane, "Problèmes d'approvisionnement de l'Île de France au temps de l'Intendant Poivre," *Proceedings of the Royal Society of Arts and Sciences of Mauritius* 3, pt. 1 (1968): 104–5.

100. Larson, "Route of the Slave," 138–40; Allen, *European Slave Trading*, 72–73.

101. On the continuation of the illegal trade despite the restrictions, see des Roches, letter, 16 September 1770, COL C/4/26.

102. Cremont, letter, 3 July 1771, COL C/3/13; de Ternay, letter, 23 February 1773, COL C/4/33.

103. Maillart Dumesle, letter, 17 October 1773, COL C/4/34; Percheron, letter, 7 February 1775, COL C/5B/1; Provost de la Croix, letter, 16 March 1775, MAR B/3/618, 214. See also Ly-Tio-Fane, "Problèmes d'approvisionnement," 110–11.

104. De Boyner, letter to Benyowsky, 19 March 1773, M 1031.

105. Benyowsky first arrived in Mauritius in 1772: letter, 1772, MAR G/222; notes of Chevalier des Roches, 20 March 1772, COL C/5A/3. On his life, see Miklós Molnár, "Héros ou imposteur? Un aventurier au XVIIIe siècle," *Revue européenne des sciences sociales* 27, no. 85 (1989): 80.

106. Letter, c. 1773, COL C/4/33. On his arrival, see letter, 13 October 1773, and letter, 7 February 1774, both in COL C/4/31; see also letters in COL C/5A/3. See also letter, Maillart, 1773, COL C/4/34.

107. Orders for the colony, COL C/5A/3. For English information about Benyowsky as the colony was founded, see J. Clavering, report, 18 July 1774, IOR/H/116, 201–2.

108. His relation of his time on Madagascar can be found in Maurice-Auguste Benyowsky, *Voyages et mémoires de Maurice-Auguste, Comte de Benyowsky* (Paris, 1791), 2:211–472. Many details from his account have been shown to be incorrect: Molnár, "Héros," 79.

109. Letter of Benyowsky, undated, COL C/5A/4. These included Nicolas Mayeur, who assisted Benyowsky and left the first records of the interior of the island: Gilbert Ratsivalaka, "Éléments de biographie de Nicolas Mayeur (1747–1809)," *Omaly sy anio* (Université d'Antananarivo) 5–6 (1977): 80–83.

110. See various letters written by Benyowsky, n.d., COL/C/5A/4.

111. M. de Kerguelen, report, n.d., COL/C/5A/5; the reports of captains in the letters of de Ternay, including those from 14 December 1774, 10 February 1775, and 29 July 1775, COL C/4/35.

112. Letter of Benyowsky, 1 September 1774, COL C/5A/4.

113. Letter, December 1775, COL/C/5A/5; letter, 22 September 1776, COL C/5A/7.

114. Report from Kerguelen, COL/C/5A/5.

115. This title has been translated by at least one historian as "Emperor of Madagascar." Eufrosina Dvoichenko-Markov, "Benjamin Franklin and Count M. A. Benyowski," *Proceedings of the American Philosophical Society* 99, no. 6 (1955): 406.

116. Letter from Benyowsky, 20 March 1775; letter from 23 September 1776, both in M 1031.

117. Benyowsky, "memoir on the establishment," September 1776, M 1031.

118. On sending expeditions to the Cape, see Benyowsky to the ministry, letter, 13 May 1776, COL C/5A/6. On slave exports in 1776, see the ship journal of the *Étoile* describing the arrival of the *Belle Arture* with slaves at the Cape, 1776, MAR 4JJ/144/D. See also various correspondence in COL C/5A/5.

119. Letter of Benyowsky, 2 October 1776, COL/C/5A/5.

120. Letter, 8 January 1777, COL C/5A/8.

121. Report in COL C/5A/8; see also Dvoichenko-Markov, "Benjamin Franklin," 413; Molnár, "Héros," 90.

122. Vaughan, *Creating the Creole Island*, 34.

123. For examples of French plans for the Indies, see Montigny, letter, 30 June 1782, COL C/2/166–167; Soulliac, letter, 8 July 1785, COL C/2/169. Naval fleets and soldiers increased once again at the turn of the century, during the era of the Napoleonic wars.

124. See, for instance, Harland, letters 9 October 1771 and 9 January 1773, ADM 1/163.

125. Allen, *European Slave Trading*, 68–69, table 9.

126. Haudrère, *La compagnie française*, esp. 2:751–70; see also Furber, *Rival Empires*, 177, 201; Donald C. Wellington, *French East India Companies: A Historical Account and Record of Trade* (Lanham, MD: Hamilton Books, 2006), 9–28.

127. Eighteenth-century sea wars have been described as "struggles of endurance," as banking and credit became crucial to success: Paul Kennedy, *The Rise and Fall of the Great Powers: Economic Change and Military Conflict from 1500 to 2000* (New York: Random House, 1987), 76; see also Mahan, *Influence of Sea Power*, 225–30; Dull, *French Navy*, 10–35.

128. For example, a collection focusing on French Indian Ocean commerce examines interactions between French and Indian trade networks: Indrani Ray, *The French East India Company and the Trade of the Indian Ocean: A Collection of Essays by Indrani Ray*, ed. Lakshmi Subramanian (New Delhi: Munshiram Manoharlal, 1999). The same is true for studies of

the English East India Company that focus on the influence of India on EIC policies, for example, Bowen, *Business of Empire.*

129. Wellington, *French East India Companies*, 10.

130. See, for instance, Mahan, *Influence of Sea Power*, 42–43; Haudrère, *La compagnie française*, 1:203.

131. As outlined in Ly-Tio-Fane, "Problèmes d'approvisionnement," 101–15.

132. On these events, see esp. Davelu, "Notes historiques sur l'isle de Bourbon," n.d., COL F/3/1.

133. Edward R. Cook et al., "Asian Monsoon Failure and Megadrought during the Last Millennium," *Science*, n.s., 328, no. 5977 (23 April 2010): 487.

134. Christopher V. Hill, *River of Sorrow* (1997), quoted in Richard H. Grove, "The Great El Niño of 1789–93 and Its Global Consequences: Reconstructing an Extreme Climate Event in World Environmental History," *Medieval History Journal* 10, nos. 1–2 (2007): 79.

135. Sunil S. Amrith, *Crossing the Bay of Bengal: The Furies of Nature and the Fortunes of Migrants* (Cambridge, MA: Harvard University Press, 2013), 67.

136. Mike Davis, *Late Victorian Holocausts: El Niño Famines and the Making of the Third World* (London: Verso, 2001).

137. Grove, "Great El Niño," 88–91.

138. For an example of this focus on Asia, see Cook et al., "Asian Monsoon Failure." Research suggests that crop failures did not necessarily occur in both Madagascar and India at the same time: David J. Nash et al., "Tropical Cyclone Activity over Madagascar during the Late Nineteenth Century," *International Journal of Climatology* 35, no. 11 (2015): 3249–61, published online 13 November 2014.

139. On the purchase of slaves in the midst of the late eighteenth-century famine in India, see Allen, *European Slave Trading*, 77, 98; see also ibid., 123–26, on earlier famines driving many into slavery.

## CHAPTER 7: SLAVING FAILURES

1. For more on the early importance of Madagascar in the slave trade within the Indian Ocean as well as in the Atlantic during the sixteenth and seventeenth centuries, see Thomas Vernet, "Slave Trade and Slavery on the Swahili Coast, 1500–1750," in *Slavery, Islam and Diaspora*, ed. Paul Lovejoy, Behnaz A. Mirzai, and Ismael M. Montana (Trenton, NJ: Africa World Press, 2009), 42–43; Jane Hooper and David Eltis, "The Indian Ocean in Transatlantic Slavery," *Slavery & Abolition* 34, no. 3 (2013): 353–75.

2. The phrase comes from R. J. Barendse, "Slaving on the Malagasy Coast, 1640–1700," in *Cultures of Madagascar: Ebb and Flow of*

*Influences*, ed. S. Evers and M. Spindler (Leiden: International Institute for Asian Studies, 1995), 137. For an overview of this later slave trade, see esp. Gwyn Campbell, "Madagascar and Mozambique in the Slave Trade of the Western Indian Ocean, 1800–1861," in *The Economics of the Indian Ocean Slave Trade in the Nineteenth Century*, ed. William Gervase Clarence-Smith (London: Frank Cass, 1989), 166–93.

3. Recent publications covering the topic of the eighteenth- and nineteenth-century Indian Ocean slave trade include Henri Médard, "La traite et l'esclavage en Afrique orientale et dans l'océan Indien: Une historiographie éclatée," in *Traites et esclavages en Afrique orientale et dans l'océan Indien*, ed. Henri Médard et al. (Paris: Karthala, 2013), 31–63; essays in Robert Harms, Bernard K. Freamon, and David W. Blight, eds., *Indian Ocean Slavery in the Age of Abolition* (New Haven: Yale University Press, 2013); Alessandro Stanziani, *Sailors, Slaves, and Immigrants: Bondage in the Indian Ocean World, 1750–1914* (New York: Palgrave Macmillan, 2014); Richard B. Allen, *European Slave Trading in the Indian Ocean, 1500–1850* (Athens: Ohio University Press, 2015).

4. In addition, a number of slaving ships from the South Sea Company came to Madagascar in the first few decades of the eighteenth century, likely along with illicit slaving vessels that were loaded by pirates before sailing to the Americas. There were also an equivalent number of EIC vessels stopping at Ndzuwani for food, while some of the vessels included in the count stopped at both Madagascar and the Comoro Islands.

5. For calculations of the EIC trade, see the sources for fig. 7.1 in the appendix. The overall slave trade from Madagascar was dominated by a few vessels from Europe and the Americas, not EIC vessels, that carried extremely large cargos of slaves from the island.

6. The hurdles to quantitative analysis of the slave trade from Madagascar, at least prior to the late eighteenth century, are too great for anything approaching precision. I do not seek to minimize the benefits of this sort of analysis, but rather point to source difficulties even more challenging than those described for early western Africa: see Toby Green, *The Rise of the Trans-Atlantic Slave Trade in Western Africa, 1300–1589* (Cambridge: Cambridge University Press, 2012), 4–9. Despite this caveat, archival documents do allow us to reach some limited conclusions about the general magnitude of the trade. As Allen suggests for European slaving within the Indian Ocean, the actual figures were likely higher: Allen, *European Slave Trading*, 24.

7. See, for instance, Edda L. Fields-Black, *Deep Roots: Rice Farmers in West Africa and the African Diaspora* (Bloomington: Indiana University Press, 2008), 162–70; Walter Hawthorne, *From Africa to Brazil: Culture, Identity, and an Atlantic Slave Trade, 1600–1830* (Cambridge: Cambridge

University Press, 2010), 77–80; David Eltis, "The Slave Trade and Commercial Agriculture in an African Context," in *Commercial Agriculture, the Slave Trade and Slavery in Atlantic Africa*, ed. Robin Law, Suzanne Schwarz, and Silke Strickrodt (Woodbridge, Suffolk: James Currey, 2013), 28–31.

8. On pricing in the Atlantic, for instance, see Herbert S. Klein, *The Atlantic Slave Trade*, 2nd ed. (Cambridge: Cambridge University Press, 2010), 109–11.

9. Refer instead to various works by Gwyn Campbell, esp. Campbell, "Madagascar and the Slave Trade, 1810–1895," *Journal of African History* 22, no. 2 (1981): 203–27; James C. Armstrong, "Madagascar and the Slave Trade in the Seventeenth Century," *Omaly sy anio* (Université d'Antananarivo) 17–20 (1983): 211–33; Barendse, "Slaving"; Pier M. Larson, "Enslaved Malagasy and 'Le Travail de la Parole' in the Pre-Revolutionary Mascarenes," *Journal of African History* 48, no. 3 (2007): 457–79; essays in Ignace Rakoto, ed., *La route des esclaves: Système servile et traite dans l'est malgache* (Paris: Harmattan, 2000); Vernet, "Slave Trade."

10. The ship journal of the *Brack*, 1741, in Alfred Grandidier et al., eds., *Collection des ouvrages anciens concernant Madagascar*, 9 vols. (Paris: Comité de Madagascar, 1903–20) (hereafter cited as *COACM*), 6:62. See also the description in the opening of chapter 1.

11. Ibid., 1741, *COACM*, 6:53.

12. Ibid., 1741, 6:54–77.

13. Ibid., 1741, 6:78. In the Dutch records, names are occasionally provided for enslaved individuals, information typically absent in English and French accounts of slaving.

14. Ibid., 1741, 6:87.

15. Ibid., 1741, 6:93.

16. Ibid., 1741, 6:105.

17. Ibid., 1741, 6:176. One of these ships was likely the *Fulvy*, which delivered 362 slaves from western Madagascar to the Mascarenes in 1740. The other ship may have been the *Subtile*, which was to visit western Madagascar and Mozambique, but never returned to the Mascarenes: Bourdonnais, letter, 1740, COL C/4/4.

18. Ibid., 1741, *COACM*, 6:115.The Dutch describe meeting Danish traders who had had a factory in the village for the past four years. Marovoay is currently a town just to the interior of Mahajanga, along the Betsiboka River.

19. Ibid., 1741, 6:129.

20. Ibid., 1741, 6:142.

21. Ibid., 1741, 6:186. The slaves purchased on this trip tried to rebel, and three of the culprits were shot and thrown into the ocean. The slaves from Toliara renounced those from the northwest as responsible.

22. The records for the second voyage of the ship: "Dagregister *Brak*," 1742, C 2247, Archives of the Western Cape. On 26 May, the *Brak* [*Brack*] sailed into St. Augustin Bay, where they met a French ship from Mauritius carrying slaves from Mozambique. After negotiations with both Prince William and Rammanrasse, they purchased some slaves and food items for "*reelen*" (silver coins) and a combination of flints and gunpowder. Next, they sailed to Massaliege, where they likewise bought goods. They purchased, in all, 19 male slaves, 3 adolescents ("*half wasse*"), and 6 girls, for a total of 28 slaves.

23. In "Account . . . of James Bearblock's voyage," taken out of his journal, IOR/E/3/22, fols. 29–36. This seventeenth-century incident can be compared to the experience of the Dutch, who also needed to hide their slave purchases in Zanzibar during the 1777: Robert Ross, ed., "The Dutch on the Swahili Coast, 1776–1778: Two Slaving Journals," pt. 2, *International Journal of African Historical Studies* 19, no. 3 (1986): 479–506.

24. European visitors to Madagascar frequently noted the presence of African and Asian slaving ships along the coast of Madagascar. For instance, in 1734, a dhow from northwest Madagascar carried a hundred slaves ("*captifs*") to Ndzuwani. The ship journal of the *Chauvelin*, 1734, MAR 4JJ/98.

25. See the ship journal of the *Beckenham*, 1764, IOR/L/MAR/B/561A.

26. The "Johanna" man also provided the English with "diamonds." See "Journal and Logbook of an anonymous Scotch sailor, 1726–1729," HC 363/129, Hispanic Society of America.

27. "Dagregister *Zon*," 1775, C 2255, Archives of the Western Cape, 76.

28. James Hastie noted the arrival in Antananarivo of Islamic merchants from Boina in 1817, cited in Ranaivo G. Ratsivalaka, *Les Malgaches et l'abolition de la traite européenne des esclaves (1810–1817): Histoire de la formation du Royaume de Madagascar* (Antananarivo: Hery Arivo, 1999), 84.

29. There were suggestions that Comorian rulers were involved much earlier as well: Pieter van den Broeke, 1614, in *COACM*, 2:93.; Vernet, "Slave Trade," 43. See also R. J. Barendse, *Arabian Seas, 1700–1763* (Leiden: Brill, 2009), 3:1237–38.

30. James Pyke, "Voyages and Travels: to Muscat and India," 1704–5, Add MS 24931; see also the similar document "Voyages and Travels: Journal of Voyage by Capt. F. Stanes, from England to Msucat in Arabia and back," 1704, Sloane MS 3145.

31. The ship journal of the *Penthéière*, 1743, MAR 4JJ/116.

32. On slavery and the slave trade within this region, see Vernet, "Slave Trade," 43; Gill Shepherd, "The Comorians and the East African Slave Trade," in *Asian and African Systems of Slavery*, ed. James L. Watson

(Berkeley: University of California Press, 1980), 75–80. These slaves were more frequently East Africans, not Malagasy, by the early nineteenth century: ibid., 84–92.

33. See, for instance, the records of Sir Henry Middleton, 1610, in *COACM*, 1:473; records of Pieter van den Broeke, 1614, ibid., 2:93; ship journal of the *Barneveld*, 1719, ibid., 5:33. Vernet suggests that the earlier traffic in slaves from Madagascar to East Africa and the northern Indian Ocean was not sustained at such high levels through the eighteenth century: Vernet, "Slave Trade," 56–57.

34. See, for instance, one description of this trade in Jean de la Roque, *A Voyage to Arabia Felix*, trans. Dominique de Moulins (New York: Oleander, 2004), 8–9. The slave trade between East Africa and the Persian Gulf region likely began much earlier: J. C. Wilkinson, "Oman and East Africa: New Light on Early Kilwan History from the Omani Sources," *International Journal of African Historical Studies* 14, no. 2 (1981): 278–79.

35. Pyke, "Voyages and Travels," Add MS 24931, 114. These letters of recommendation may have been welcome, given that there was "fierce" competition between different principalities in the Gulf for control over trade: Patricia Risso, "Cross-Cultural Perceptions of Piracy: Maritime Violence in the Western Indian Ocean and Persian Gulf during a Long Eighteenth Century," *Journal of World History* 12, no. 2 (2001): 306. The sultan of Ndzuwani also stated he was a dependent of the king of Persia. See the ship journal of the *Lys*, 1713, MAR 4JJ/94.

36. On the impact of this gendered preference on labor, see Pier M. Larson, *History and Memory in the Age of Enslavement: Becoming Merina in Highland Madagascar, 1770–1822* (Portsmouth, NH: Heinemann, 2000), 124–31.

37. On travel into the interior of the west coast, note the challenges encountered in Mayeur, "Mémoires pour servir à l'histoire de l'isle de Madagascar," ed. M. de Froberville, 2 vols., folio, 1809, 1:98–101, Add MS 18128–18129, British Library. This is likely why much trade was riverine.

38. For example, Captain George Bagwell was told in 1734 that the king of Morondava had been at war and had a great many slaves for sale, after killing three of his brothers, but almost two weeks later the captain had only managed to purchase seven slaves. The ship journal of the *Hertford*, 1734, IOR/L/MAR/B/656F. See also the ship journal of the *Swift*, 1741–42, IOR/L/MAR/B/616A; the ship journal of the *Brack*, 1741, in *COACM*, 6:125–35. The challenges in crossing the island must have been even greater once East African slaves were being transported from the west to the east coast of Madagascar: Pier Larson, "The Route of the Slave from Highland Madagascar to the Mascarenes: Commercial Organization, 1770–1820," in Rakoto, *La route des esclaves*, 128.

39. Slave-trading kings gave a variety of explanations for the delay in delivering slaves, usually describing a need to fetch or capture slaves in the interior. Drury describes agricultural work done by slaves around St. Augustin Bay, although the slaves who worked in distant plantations were always vulnerable to slaving raids: Robert Drury, *The Adventures of Robert Drury* (London, 1729; reprint, Hull: Stodart and Craggs, 1807), 68, 306, 322; page references are to the 1807 edition. For another description of slaves cultivating rice and other foods, see "Journal and Logbook," HC 363/129. The king at Toliara told the captain of the *Swift* to wait two or three months for a hundred slaves: the ship journal of the *Swift*, 1741–42. Mayeur describes the use of slaves as laborers (and hence not sold to the French): Mayeur, trip to the north, in "Mémoires pour servir," 1:62. See also Barendse, "Slaving," 146.

40. On the residence of Islamic traders in the north of the island during the nineteenth century, see Sophie Blanchy, *Karana et Banians: Les communautés commerçantes d'origin Indienne à Madagascar* (Paris: Harmattan, 1995), esp. 88–103. See also Ratsivalaka, *Les Malgaches*, 42–43.

41. Miller describes port authorities in Angola deliberately forcing some ships to spend longer than others in ports: Joseph Calder Miller, *Way of Death: Merchant Capitalism and the Angolan Slave Trade, 1730–1830* (Madison: University of Wisconsin Press, 1988), 358–59.

42. A list of slaving voyages from Madagascar to the Americas can be obtained from Voyages: The Trans-Atlantic Slave Trade Database. Note that in my own estimates and remarks I have omitted several voyages that appear to be repeated in the database. McDonald notes these instances: Kevin P. McDonald, *Pirates, Merchants, Settlers, and Slaves: Colonial America and the Indo-Atlantic World* (Berkeley: University of California Press, 2015), Appendix A. On the trade to the Americas, see also Liliana Mosca, "La traite à Madagascar dans la seconde moitié du XVIIe siècle à la lumière de quelques documents anglo-américains," in Rakoto, *La route des esclaves*, 75–90.

43. Barendse, "Slaving," 154.

44. Ibid., 138. Note that some of the later slaves may have originally been from East Africa.

45. The ship journal of the *Royalle*, 1682, MAR 4JJ/90. Note that this was likely prior to the arrival of the Sakalava rulers at the northwest ports. In another example, in 1695 the Dutch only managed to purchase 35 slaves from northwestern Madagascar: see "Dagregister op't jacht de *Tamboer*," 1695, VOC 1.04.02, 1544, 1058.

46. Letter of Père Luis Mariano, July 1616, in *COACM*, 2:214; also voyages of van der Stel, 1644, in *COACM*, 3:31. The Dutch also used copper in Madagascar: see description from 1666, in *COACM*, 3:334–35. Compare

this trade to assortment bartering in West Africa: Philip D. Curtin, *Economic Change in Precolonial Africa: Senegambia in the Era of the Slave Trade* (Madison: University of Wisconsin Press, 1975), 247–53.

47. One trading manual explained that, while traders demanded guns on the east coast, on the west coast they asked for guns as well as "some powder and flints, or some other thing that they want." From "An account of the present comodityes that are imported & exported at Madagascarr and the manner of dealing with the natives," Rawlinson MS A 334, fol. 61 verso.

48. Ibid., fol. 61. Other examples of prices of slaves include those in Taolagnaro, where the French bought slaves for a combination of gunpowder and guns: the ship journal of *L'Astrée*, 1734, MAR 4JJ/86.

49. For example, see "Dagregister op't jacht de *Tamboer*," 1032; "Dagregister van de Soldaat," 1696–97, VOC 1.04.02, 10811, 2, 8. This trade in guns continued in Taolagnaro: see the ship journal of *L'Astrée*, 1734.

50. On the demand for firearms, see Barendse, "Slaving," 148. Regarding the hope expressed by the Dutch of using these trading goods on the Northwest coast: "Dagregister *Drie Heuvelen*," 1753, VOC 1.04.02, 4193, 4018.

51. An example: the ship journal of the *Brack*, 1741, in *COACM*, 6:54–77.

52. For overviews of the debates about this gun-slave cycle, see Gerald M. Berg, "The Sacred Musket: Tactics, Technology, and Power in Eighteenth-Century Madagascar," *Comparative Studies in Society and History* 27, no. 2 (1985): 261–62nn1–3; John Lamphear, introduction to *African Military History*, ed. John Lamphear (Burlington, VT: Ashgate, 2007), xix-xxi; Warren Whatley, "The Gun-Slave Cycle in the 18th Century British Slave Trade in Africa," *Munich Personal RePEc Archive (MPRA)*, December 2012, http://mpra.ub.uni-muenchen.de/44492/1/MPRA_paper_44492.pdf.

53. See, for instance, Jean-Michel Filliot, *La traite des esclaves vers les Mascareignes au XVIIIe siècle* (Paris: ORSTOM, 1974), 117.

54. Barendse, *Arabian Seas, 1700–1763*, 3:1260.

55. Report of Jeremias Brons ter Leede, on board the *Standvastigheid*, 14 January 1695, in H. C. V. Leibrandt, ed., *Precis of the Archives of the Cape of Good Hope: Letters Received, 1695–1708* (Cape Town: W. A. Richards & Sons, 1896), 28–31.

56. On the popularity of guns, see the observations of Drury, *Adventures*.

57. See, for instance, the ship journal of *L'Astrée*, 1734.

58. As, indeed, importations of firearms likewise had little to do with expansion of the Merina Empire in the interior of the island, according to Berg, "Sacred Musket."

59. On the overall flow of slaves on the east coast, see Albert Lougnon, ed., *Correspondance du conseil supérieur de Bourbon et de la Compagnie des Indes*, 2 vols. (Paris: Ernest Leroux, 1933–34), 1:130, 2:221, 320.

60. For example, see Poivre, letter, 30 November 1767, COL C/4/18; the ship journal of the *Dragon*, 1758, IOR/L/MAR/B/598E. In many of these years, in eastern Madagascar food was plentiful but not slaves. See, for example, M. de Lozier Bouvet, letter, 4 November 1754, COL C/4/8.

61. Drury, *Adventures*, 391; "Journal and Logbook," HC 363/129.

62. See Mayeur, trip to the north of the island, 1774, in "Mémoires pour servir," 1:62. Captives would also be exchanged after the end of conflict. The picture was likely far different during the nineteenth century, as suggested by Pier Larson's arguments about enslavement in nineteenth-century highland Madagascar: Larson, *History and Memory*, 119–23.

63. On continued warfare on the west coast, see commentary by Barendse in "Slaving," 146–47; on the east coast, see Ratsivalaka, *Les Malgaches*, 44–47.

64. The ship journal of the *Hertford*, 1734. See also the ship journal of the *Brack*, 1741, in *COACM*, 6:124–25.

65. As argued in Berg, "Sacred Musket," 265.

66. On the ceremonial use of guns, see John Dean, "Narrative of One of the Crew Belonging to the Ship *Sussex*," 1738, MSS Eur. B2/K11, British Library, 29–31; the ship journal of the *Dragon*, 1753, IOR/L/MAR/B/598D; Hendrik Frappé and Willem van der Lint, *Slawehandel met Madagaskar: Die joernale van die Kaapse slaweskip Leijdsman, 1715*, ed. Piet E. Westra and James C. Armstrong (Cape Town: Africana Uitgewers, 2006), 63. This was later the case in Imerina as well: Berg, "Sacred Musket," 273–75.

67. See, for example, the distinction made between "half" and "whole" buccaneer guns and trading pistols: the ship journal of the *Swallow*, 1749, IOR/L/MAR/B/385A; the ship journal of the *Dragon*, 1758; the ship journal of the *Diligent*, 1761, IOR/L/MAR/B/320E.

68. Berg, "Sacred Musket," esp. 265.

69. As seen in the ship journal of the *Brack*, 1741, in *COACM*, 6:54–56.

70. On the sale of criminals, see the ship journal of the *Dragon*, 1758.

71. Stephen Ellis, "The History of Sovereigns in Madagascar: New Light from Old Sources," in *Madagascar revisitée: En voyage avec Françoise Raison-Jourde*, ed. Didier Nativel and Faranirina V. Rajaonah (Paris: Karthala, 2009), 424–25.

72. Pierre Sonnerat, *A Voyage to the East-Indies and China*, trans. Francis Magnus, vol. 3 (Calcutta, 1789), 44–45.

73. Ibid., 44.

74. Hawthorne, *From Africa to Brazil*, 81–90.

75. Filliot dates this shift to around 1740, although it does not appear to be universal in the ports of the east coast until the 1750s and 1760s: Filliot, *La traite des esclaves*, 210.

76. Letter from Poivre to Dumas, 18 May 1768, COL C/5A/2.

77. For more on Poivre and the need for provisions on Mauritius, see Madeleine Ly-Tio-Fane, "Problèmes d'approvisionnement de l'Île de France au temps de l'Intendant Poivre," *Proceedings of the Royal Society of Arts and Sciences of Mauritius* 3, pt. 1 (1968): 101–15.

78. On the use of silver in the Indian Ocean, see esp. Barendse, *Arabian Seas, 1700–1763*, 3:1013; Pedro Machado, *Ocean of Trade: South Asian Merchants, Africa and the Indian Ocean, c. 1750–1850* (Cambridge: Cambridge University Press, 2014), 210–11.

79. Machado, *Ocean of Trade*, 3.

80. On the global silver trade, see esp. Dennis O. Flynn and Arturo Giráldez, "Cycles of Silver: Global Economic Unity through the Mid-Eighteenth Century," *Journal of World History* 13, no. 2 (2002): 391–427; Dennis O. Flynn and Arturo Giráldez, "Globalization Began in 1571," in *Globalization and Global History*, ed. Barry K. Gills and William R. Thompson (New York: Routledge, 2012), 232–47; Alejandra Irigoin, "The End of a Silver Era: The Consequences of the Breakdown of the Spanish Peso Standard in China and the United States, 1780s–1850s," *Journal of World History* 20, no. 2 (2009): 207–44. Note that several scholars have expressed doubt that silver was essential to the Chinese economy, including William S. Atwell, "Another Look at Silver Imports into China, ca. 1635–1644," *Journal of World History* 16, no. 4 (2005): 467–89; Kent G. Deng, "Miracle or Mirage? Foreign Silver, China's Economy and Globalization from the Sixteenth to the Nineteenth Centuries," *Pacific Economic Review* 13, no. 3 (2008): 320–57.

81. Machado, *Ocean of Trade*, 210. The focus has been, for the most part, on the importations of silver into the Middle East and Asia, with far less attention paid to the use of precious metals as currency in the southwestern Indian Ocean region. See K. N. Chaudhuri, *Trade and Civilisation in the Indian Ocean: An Economic History from the Rise of Islam to 1750* (Cambridge: Cambridge University Press, 1985), 95–97; Genevieve Bouchon and Denys Lombard, "The Indian Ocean in the Fifteenth Century," in *India and the Indian Ocean, 1500–1800*, ed. Ashin Das Gupta and Michael N. Pearson (Calcutta: Oxford University Press, 1987), 66–67; Michel Tuchscherer, "Trade and Port Cities in the Red Sea–Gulf of Aden Region in the Sixteenth and Seventeenth Century," in Fawaz and Bayly, *Modernity and Culture*, 29–30; Michael N. Pearson, *The Indian Ocean* (London: Routledge, 2003), 84–85; Najaf Haider, "The Network of Monetary Exchange in the Indian Ocean Trade, 1200–1700," in *Cross Currents and*

*Community Networks: The History of the Indian Ocean World*, ed. Himanshu Prabha Ray and Edward A. Alpers (New York: Oxford University Press, 2007), 181–205.

82. "Relation 21: Journal of a Voyage of a Fleet Consisting of Four Ships and Two Pinnaces," 1636, Rawlinson MS A 315, fols. 116–17.

83. Sources include the ship journal of the *Deux Couronner*, 1715, MAR 4JJ/111; the ship journal of the *Duc de Chartres*, 1734, MAR 4JJ/89; the ship journal of the *Warren*, 1749–50, IOR/L/MAR/B/571A.

84. The ship journal of the *Paix*, 1767, MAR 4JJ/107. By the late eighteenth century, the Malagasy may have been using silver coins to purchase goods from Ndzuwani as well. Guillaume Joseph Galaisière, *Voyage dans les mers de l'Inde*, vol. 2 (Paris, 1781), 576–77.

85. Silver chains and bracelets were also used in trading during the seventeenth century throughout much of the island. See Pier M. Larson, "Colonies Lost: God, Hunger, and Conflict in Anosy (Madagascar) to 1674," *Comparative Studies of South Asia, Africa and the Middle East* 27, no. 2 (2007): 354. Silver "manillas" were popular as bracelets by the eighteenth century: "Journal and Logbook," HC 363/129.

86. The description of the voyage of the *Voorhout*, returned to the Cape 29 November 1676, in H. C. V. Leibrandt, ed., *Precis of the Archives of the Cape of Good Hope: Journal, 1671–1674, & 1676* (Cape Town: W. A. Richards & Sons, 1902), 301.

87. The ship journal of the *Lapwing*, 1748, IOR/L/MAR/B/475B.

88. The ship journal of the *Duc de Chartres*, visiting Foulpoint in 1754, MAR 4JJ/144/B. For complaints about Foulpointe, see letter, 8 November 1768, COL C/4/21; see also Modave's description of the use of piastres in Taolagnaro, 1768, COL C/5A/2; Benyowsky's letter to Île de France, 1774, COL C/4/37.

89. Modave, journal, 1768–70, COL C/5A/2.

90. Galaisière, *Voyage*, 551.

91. On the demand for guns among the Androy, see Mike Parker Pearson, *Pastoralists, Warriors and Colonists: The Archaeology of Southern Madagascar* (Oxford: Archaeopress, 2010), 455–56. On the exchange of guns, powder, and bullets for cattle in Taolagnaro, see Jean Valette, "Le Commerce de Madagascar vers les Mascareignes au XVIIIe siècle," *La revue de Madagascar* 33 (1966): 41–42.

92. The ship journal of the *Brack*, 1741, in *COACM*, 6:54, 64, 71. In some cases, guns and other goods would be accepted and food could usually still be purchased without using coins. "Dagregister *Binnenwisent*," 1732, VOC 1.04.02, 2217, 6993. On the use of guns in the northwest and elsewhere on the island, see also "Dagregister *Huis ten Donck*," 1732–33, VOC 1.04.02, 2266, 5189. See also Claude Allibert, "Les Hollandais et

Madagascar," in Evers and Spindler, *Cultures of Madagascar*, 93–95; Barendse, "Slaving," 148.

93. The ship journal of the *Snelheid*, 1773, C 2253, 47.

94. On the continued demand for guns, see, for instance, the ship journal of the *Hector*, 1761, IOR/L/MAR/B/486A; William MacIntosh, *Travels in Europe, Asia, and Africa,* vol. 2 (London, 1782), 394. There is even evidence of the Sakalava king at Boina taking in silver coins as tribute from the Amboalambo in 1752: Ellis, "History of Sovereigns," 424.

95. "Journal and Logbook," HC 363/129.

96. Lambek explores the connection between gold and silver minted coins and royal ancestor ceremonies in contemporary western Madagascar: Michael Lambek, "The Value of Coins in a Sakalava Polity: Money, Death, and Historicity in Mahajanga, Madagascar," *Comparative Studies in Society and History* 43, no. 4 (2001): 735–62.

97. Lisa A. Lindsay, "Extraversion, Creolization, and Dependency in the Atlantic Slave Trade," *Journal of African History* 55, no. 2 (2014): 144.

98. Zoë Crossland, *Ancestral Encounters in Highland Madagascar: Material Signs and Traces of the Dead* (Cambridge: Cambridge University Press, 2014), 10–11.

99. Mayeur, trip to the north, in "Mémoires pour servir," 1:62; letter, 4 September 1792, COL F/3/23.

100. In 1753, the Dutch slavers on the *Drie Heuvelen* paid 25 reales: "Dagregister *Drie Heuvelen*," 1753, 4023. In 1775, the slavers on the *Zon* paid 35 reales in the same port: "Dagregister van koopman P. J. Truter," 1775, C 2255, 123.

101. The voyage of the *Jagtrust*, in Ross, "The Dutch on the Swahili Coast," pt. 2, 485. The price in 1777 of slaves from Kilwa was 25 reales a head. French merchant Morice managed to contract with the sultan of Kilwa in 1776 for "a thousand blacks," agreeing to pay "20 piastres whether they are men or women. I accept the obligation to pay two piastres on each head of black, or negresses, on the condition they do not sell slaves to any other vessel, whether it be French, English, Dutch, Portuguese, or others; but only to Arabs": G. S. P. Freeman-Grenville, ed., *The French at Kilwa Island: An Episode in Eighteenth-Century East African History* (Oxford: Clarendon, 1965), 70.

102. Slaves were selling for at least twice their original purchasing price in the Mascarenes: Allen, *European Slave Trading*, 86. It became common practice for the colonial authorities to send their *particulier* ships (short-haul ships owned by the colonial governments) to eastern Madagascar. The French also sent ships occasionally to western Madagascar. See the instructions to the captain of the *Jupiter*, 1725, COL C/2/27; orders from the council of Île de France, 1744 and 1745, COL C/2/31; letter, 30 March

1728, COL C/3/5. They also desired slaves from Senegal: David, letter, 25 October, 1749, COL C/4/6.

103. See untitled memoir, n.d. (mid-eighteenth century?), COL C/5A/2.

104. See various letters in COL C/4/10; COL C/4/12; COL C/4/19.

105. Richard B. Allen, "The Constant Demand of the French: The Mascarene Slave Trade and the Worlds of the Indian Ocean and Atlantic during the Eighteenth and Nineteenth Centuries," *Journal of African History* 49, no. 1 (2008): 50, table 1, 54, table 2. Allen suggests that this small cargo size meant that slaves were frequently loaded alongside a variety of provisions; ibid., 56, 65.

106. See various letters in COL C/4/31.

107. Mayeur described traffic in slaves from East Africa to Madagascar, via Ndzuwani, in 1774: Mayeur, trip to the north of the island, in "Mémoires pour servir," 1:48; for connections between trading ports in the region, see also "Dagregister van koopman F. G. Holtzapfel," 1 July 1773–10 March 1774, C 2253, 6–40.

108. Barendse, *Arabian Seas, 1700–1763*, 3:1234.

109. As described in European observations quoted in Ratsivalaka, *Les Malgaches*, 36. See also Campbell, "Madagascar and Mozambique," 166.

110. Mahajanga eclipsed Massaliege as the most important port in northwest Madagascar by the late eighteenth century: Solofo Randrianja and Stephen Ellis, *Madagascar: A Short History* (Chicago: University of Chicago Press, 2009), 106. On this history, see also Blanchy, *Karana et Banians*, 191–92.

111. Dumaine, "Voyage à la côte de l'ouest," 1793, in "Mémoires pour servir," 1:296–97, 302. On some of their activities in East Africa, see also Edward A. Alpers, "Gujarat and the Trade of East Africa, c. 1500–1800," in Alpers, *East Africa and the Indian Ocean* (Princeton, NJ: Markus Wiener, 2009), 20–21; Machado, *Ocean of Trade*, esp. 30–44.

112. Dumaine, "Voyage à la côte de l'ouest," 1793, 1:305.

113. For an example of this belief, see the journal of Comte Dolisie de Modave (Maudave), 9 October 1768, COL C/5A/2, Archives nationales.

114. As suggested in Ratsivalaka, *Les Malgaches*, 67–69.

115. On the early history of these kingdoms, see esp. Gwyn Campbell, *An Economic History of Imperial Madagascar, 1750–1895: The Rise and Fall of an Island Empire* (Cambridge: Cambridge University Press, 2005), 18–58; Charlotte Liliane Rabesahala-Randriamananoro, *Ambohimanga-Rova: Approche anthropologique de la civilisation merina (Madagascar)* (Paris: Publieur, 2005); Henry T. Wright, "Early State Dynamics as Political Experiment," *Journal of Anthropological Research* 62, no. 3 (2006): 313–19.

116. Mayeur, "Voyage au Pays d'Ancove," in "Mémoires pour servir," 1:177–78. See also François Callet, ed., *Histoire des rois, traduction du "Tantaran'ny Andriana,"* 5 vols. (Antananarivo: Académie Malgache, 1953–78), 2:48–49. For a comparative perspective on the importance of coins in the organization of large states and empires in Asia, see Victor Lieberman, *Strange Parallels: Southeast Asia in Global Context, c. 800–1830*, vol. 2, *Mainland Mirrors: Europe, Japan, China, South Asia, and the Islands* (Cambridge: Cambridge University Press, 2009), esp. 87–90.

117. Later, during the nineteenth century, Merina governors in the coastal provinces could reportedly inflict capital punishment for the production of counterfeit money or the burying of money, as it was "the property of the sovereign." Joseph Barlow Felt Osgood, *Notes of Travel; or, Recollections of Majunga, Zanzibar, Muscat, Aden, Mocha, and other Eastern Ports* (Salem, MA: George Creamer, 1854), 14.

118. Crossland, *Ancestral Encounters*, 104–6. Crossland also describes how coins were hoarded, as protection against debt and enslavement, as well as buried in tombs: ibid., 219–22.

119. On the importance of silver in powering transformations in highland Madagascar, likely beginning in the late eighteenth century, see Larson, *History and Memory*, 131–47.

120. Larson, "Route of the Slave," 120. On the impact of this traffic on highland communities, see Pier M. Larson, "Reconsidering Trauma, Identity, and the African Diaspora: Enslavement and Historical Memory in Nineteenth-Century Highland Madagascar," *William and Mary Quarterly* 56, no. 2 (1999): 335–62.

121. Allen, *European Slave Trading*, 73.

122. Mayeur, "Voyage au Pays d'Ancove, 1783," in "Mémoires pour servir," 1:170–208.

123. Citing Mayeur, in Jean Valette, *Études sur le règne de Radama Ier* (Antananarivo: Imprimerie nationale, 1962), 14–16. For more on military tactics, see Berg, "Sacred Musket," 273–74.

124. Ratsivalaka, *Les Malgaches*, 45.

125. Callet, *Histoire des rois*, 2:163–64. He did agree to an alliance with the Sakalava queen of Boina, Ravahiny.

126. On this slave trade, see Larson, "Route of the Slave," 165–67; Pier M. Larson, "A Census of Slaves Exported from Central Madagascar to the Mascarenes between 1769 and 1820," in *L'esclavage à Madagascar: Aspects historiques et résurgences contemporaines: Actes du colloque international sur l'esclavage, Antananarivo (24–28 septembre 1996)*, ed. Ignace Rakoto (Antananarivo: Institut de civilisations, Musée d'art et d'archéologie, 1997), 131–45.

127. Note, too, that the people of the interior were eventually able to manufacture gun parts and even their own gunpowder, although it remained inferior: Berg, "Sacred Musket," 268–71.

128. In part thanks to the "increasingly integrated movement of labor within and between the Indian Ocean and Atlantic worlds," as Allen argues, and through the integration of economic networks existing within the Indian Ocean, as outlined by Machado. See Allen, *European Slave Trading*, 23; Machado, *Ocean of Trade*, 11–17.

129. Various French documents in Madagascar, fonds historique, pièces générales sur Madagascar et fondation des établissements de Sainte-Marie, 1z/1–159, Archives nationales d'outre-mer, and F/5a/10, Archives nationales. For a description of the French post at Foulpointe in 1784, see Jean Valette, "Le Commerce de Madagascar," 37–38.

130. See the account of L'Islet Geffroi, 1787, in "Mémoires pour servir," 1:248.

131. One of the most important being Sylvain Roux. See Ratsivalaka, *Les Malgaches*, 41.

132. For more on late eighteenth-century French slave trading in eastern Madagascar: Larson, *History and Memory*, 65–74.

133. Allen, *European Slave Trading*, 47.

134. For instance, see the orders given to the commander and chief mate of the *Swallow*, 1749, IOR/E/3/110, fol. 172.

135. See, for instance, the description provided of the trade in 1715, IOR/E/3/98, 429; there is a similar list of slave trading in 1717, IOR/E/3/99, 250. As one example of orders, in 1740 the *Edgebaston* was to load 150 slaves "or more"; the captain had considerable difficulty in buying even 109. "Orders and Instructions to Captain Stephen Cobham and Chief Mate Robert Veitch of the Edgbaston," 2 April 1740, IOR/E/3/108, fol. 101; the ship journal of the *Edgebaston*, 1740, IOR/L/MAR/B/622A.

136. On the traffic in slaves from Asia, see esp. Allen, *European Slave Trading*, 108–40.

137. Starting in the 1730s, the French began to explore purchasing slaves in eastern Africa: Edward Alpers, "The French Slave Trade in East Africa (1721–1810)," *Cahiers d'études africaines* 10, no. 37 (1970): 88–91.

138. These estimates were calculated using descriptions of slave arrivals in the various colonial records at the Archives nationales, Paris. The large cargoes included those of French ships in Voyages: The Trans-Atlantic Slave Trade Database, as well as several voyages to the Mascarenes, including the *Méduse* in 1730 and the *Légère* in 1731. Many of these likely visited northwestern Madagascar. Allen estimates the average cargo size as 131 for the slave trade from Madagascar to the Mascarenes (not including those to the Americas) between 1718 and 1766: Allen, *European Slave Trading*, 75, table 10. Note that I have omitted several voyages that appear to be repeated in Voyages: The Trans-Atlantic Slave Trade Database.

139. See, for instance, scattered complaints in the governor's journal describing trade from Mauritius, starting 13 January 1756, COL C/4/9. As

Allen points out, the sources for the period prior to 1767 are more scattered and it is hard to be certain of the extent of slave trading between the Mascarenes and Madagascar. Allen, "Constant Demand," 48. Allen also estimates that the size of slave cargoes from Madagascar declined precipitously throughout the second half of the eighteenth century, to 41 between 1767 and 1799, and then rose slightly to 68 between 1800 and 1809: Allen, *European Slave Trading*, 75, table 10.

140. Poivre, letter, 30 November 1767, COL C/4/18.

141. Filliot, *La traite des esclaves*, 62.

142. On this plan, see Freeman-Grenville, *French at Kilwa Island*, 70–73.

143. This traffic is discussed at length in Alpers, "French Slave Trade," 80–124; Eve Prosper, *Les esclaves de Bourbon, la mer et la montagne* (Paris: Karthala, 2003), 65–68. For a different perspective on the importance of this trade, see Edward A. Alpers and Matthew S. Hopper, "Parler en son nom? Comprendre les témoignages d'esclaves africains originaires de l'océan Indien (1850–1930)," *Annales: Histoire, sciences sociales* 63, no. 4 (2008): 799–828.

144. Allen, *European Slave Trading*, 69, table 9; see also ibid., 75–76.

145. Jean Valentin Payet, *Histoire de l'esclavage à l'Île Bourbon (Réunion)* (Paris: L'Harmattan, 1990), 17.

146. On the spread of irrigated rice production in the highlands especially, see Gerald M. Berg, "Riziculture and the Founding of Monarchy in Imerina," *Journal of African History* 22, no. 3 (1981): 302–7.

147. Mayeur, 1774, trip to the north of the island, in "Mémoires pour servir," 1:62. Sonnerat describes how rice cultivation was left to the slaves, due to the unhealthiness of the marshes: Sonnerat, *Voyage*, 61.

148. Mayeur, 1774, trip to the north of the island, in "Mémoires pour servir," 1:62. On the "king's slaves," see, for example, at Taolagnaro, the ship journal of the *Duc d'Anjou*, 1736–37, MAR 4JJ/76; and along the west coast, the ship journal of the *Onslow*, 1741, IOR/L/MAR/B/164C. Later, slaves owned by the king became part of the royal extended family: Gillian Feeley-Harnik, "The King's Men in Madagascar Slavery, Citizenship and Sakalava Monarchy," *Africa: Journal of the International African Institute* 52, no. 2 (1982): 34–36. See also notes on the geography of Madagascar, 1816, in "Memoirs and Papers Relating to Madagascar," ed. M. de Froberville, Add MS 18135, 77–78; Charles Guillain, *Documents sur l'histoire, la géographie et le commerce de la partie occidentale de Madagascar* (Paris: Imprimerie Royale, 1845), 246, 280.

149. Mayeur, "Voyage au pays des Seclaves," 1774, in "Mémoires pour servir," 1:115–19; Dumaine, "Voyage à la côte de l'ouest," 1793, 1:298.

150. On the use of labor to create irrigated riziculture in the highlands, see Campbell, *Economic History*, 24–28.

151. The ship journal of the *Brack*, 1741, in *COACM*, 6:105; the ship journal of *L'Astrée*, 1737; the ship journal of the *Barneveld*, in *COACM*, 5:44; Frappé and Lint, *Slawehandel met Madagaskar*, 95; Barendse, "Slaving," 153. This appeared particularly true at St. Augustin Bay: see the ship journal of the *Dragon*, 1753; the ship journal of the *Dragon*, 1758; the ship journal of the *Chesterfield*, 1749, IOR/L/MAR/B/507A; the ship journal of the *Prince Henry*, 1761, IOR/L/MAR/B/325G; the ship journal of the *Solebay*, 1764, IOR/L/MAR/B/591A; the ship journal of the *Brack*, 1741, in *COACM*, 6:143–44; Dumaine, "Voyage à la côte de l'ouest," 1793, 1:296.

152. Valette, "Le Commerce de Madagascar," 44, citing Mayeur, 1788.

153. Robert Ross, ed., "The Dutch on the Swahili Coast, 1776–1778: Two Slaving Journals," pt. 1, *International Journal of African Historical Studies* 19, no. 2 (1986): 329.

154. Ross, "The Dutch on the Swahili Coast," pt. 2, 492.

155. See, for example, "Dagregister *Binnenwisent*," 1732. Note that far more Dutch ships came to Madagascar for slaves, given the reliance of the VOC on the Cape for provisioning, and their slaving cargo sizes tended to be larger than either the EIC or the French Compagnie des Indes, averaging 104 slaves per vessel. This higher number might reflect their preference for purchasing slaves on the west coast of the island, where slaves appear to have been more prevalent than on the east coast.

156. Allen, *European Slave Trading*, 97.

157. See the ship journal of *L'Astrée*, 1734.

158. Ratsivalaka makes a similar argument with regard to the trade from Foulpointe in particular: Ratsivalaka, *Les Malgaches*, 46.

159. Ravahiny, for instance, was known to the French as a stabilizing force in the region: Dumaine, "Voyage à la côte de l'ouest," 1793, 1:297–98.

160. Miller, *Way of Death*, 73.

## CHAPTER 8: EXPORTING VIOLENCE TO THE COMOROS

1. On the use of the term *Wabuki*, see Said Bakari bin Sultani Ahmed, *The Swahili Chronicle of Ngazija*, ed. Lyndon Harries (Bloomington: African Studies Program, Indiana University, 1977), 22.

2. This account is a compilation of Comorian and European reports, one written by Said Bakari, son of Sultan Ahmed, a sultan in Grande Comore during the nineteenth century: Ahmed, *Swahili Chronicle*, 100. For European accounts, see Epidariste Colin, *Annales des voyages*, vol. 13, cited in Alfred Gevrey, *Essai sur les Comores* (Pondichery: A. Saligny, 1870), 210–13; James Prior, *Voyage along the Eastern Coast of Africa, to Mosambique, Johanna, and Quiloa; to St. Helena; to Rio de Janeiro, Bahia, and Pernambuco in Brazil, in the Nisus Frigate* (London: Sir Richard Phillips, 1819),

62–63; see also Barbara Dorothy Dubins, "A Political History of the Comoro Islands, 1795–1886" (PhD diss., Boston University, 1972), 6–7, 52–53, 101; Jean Martin, *Comores: Quatre îles entre pirates et planteurs* (Paris: L'Harmattan, 1983), 1:90.

3. Prior, *Voyage*, 58–60.

4. John Ross Browne, *Etchings of a Whaling Cruise, with Notes of a Sojourn on the Island of Zanzibar* (New York: Harper & Brothers, 1846), 218–24. See also Philip H. Colomb, *Slave-Catching in the Indian Ocean: A Record of Naval Experiences* (1873; repr., London: Dawsons of Pall Mall, 1968), 441.

5. Prior, *Voyage*, 63.

6. Thomas Boteler, *Narrative of a Voyage of Discovery to Africa and Arabia* (London: Richard Bentley, 1835), 1:172.

7. On accusations of Benyowsky's involvement, see Prior, *Voyage*, 62; Fressages, cited in Jean Valette, "Quelques textes relatifs aux expéditions Malgaches aux Comores," *Bulletin de Madagascar*, no. 304 (1971): 762. This argument is discounted in Martin, *Comores*, 1:84–85; Jean-Claude Hébert, "Documents sur les razzias Malgaches aux îles Comores et sur la côte orientale africaine," *Études océan Indien*, no. 3 (1983): 8–11; Dubins, "Political History," 62.

8. Frappaz, Colin, and Capmartin, cited in Hébert, "Documents," 28–30; Rondeaux, 1806, cited in Valette, "Quelques textes," 761–64.

9. William Henry Smyth, *The Life and Services of Captain Philip Beaver, Late of His Majesty's Ship Nisus* (London: John Murray, 1829), 253; see also Prior, *Voyage*, 22.

10. Prior, *Voyage*, 53, 58. The French also blamed later Malagasy conflicts for the depopulation: Gevrey, *Essai*, 251.

11. Dubins, "Political History," 8–9.

12. As suggested in Françoise Péron, *Mémoires du Capitaine Péron, sur ses voyages aux côtes d'Afrique, en Arabie, à l'île d'Amsterdam*, vol. 1 (Paris: Brissot-Thivars, 1824), 159.

13. For example, see John-Henry Grose, *A Voyage to the East-Indies, with Observations on Various Parts There* (London, 1757), 25; the ship journal of the *Lelis Brihac*, 1713, MAR 4JJ/94; the ship journal of the *Warren*, 1749–50, IOR/L/MAR/B/571A.

14. Dubins, "Political History," 13–14. For an overview of the region prior to the sixteenth century and archeological findings, see Claude Allibert, *Mayotte: Plaque tournante et microcosme de l'océan Indien occidental: son histoire avant 1841* (Paris: Anthropos, 1984), 13–73.

15. Malyn Newitt, "The Comoro Islands in Indian Ocean Trade before the 19th Century," *Cahiers d'études africaines* 23, nos. 89–90 (1983): 139–40, 151–52.

16. Dubins, "Political History," 42.

17. Ibid., 6–9, 43–50.

18. See description of this commerce in John Fryer, *A New Account of East-India and Persia, in Eight Letters* (London, 1698), 15–16. On trade in food items between the islands, see the ship journal of the *Worcester*, 1767, IOR/L/MAR/B/278D; Claude Chanudet and Jean-Aimé Rakotoarisoa, *Mohéli: Une île des Comores à la recherche de son identité* (Paris: L'Harmattan, 2000), 24–25; Dubins, "Political History," 8. On the slave trade, see Newitt, "Comoro Islands," 153–54.

19. Martin, *Comores*, 1:61–63; Dubins, "Political History," 43.

20. Claude Robineau, "L'Islam aux Comores: Une étude d'histoire culturelle de l'île d'Anjouan," in *Arabes et Islamisés à Madagascar et dans l'océan Indien*, ed. Jean-Aimé Rakotoarisoa (Antananarivo: Revue de Madagascar, distributed by Hachette-Madagascar, 1967), 49; Allibert, *Mayotte*, 101. On later conflict, see Sultan Chouzour, *Le pouvoir de l'honneur: Tradition et contestation en Grande Comore* (Paris: L'Harmattan, 1994).

21. As noted in Grose, *Voyage*, 22; the ship journal of the *Penthéière*, 1743, MAR 4JJ/116; the ship journal of the *Warren*, 1749–50.

22. "Relâche aux îles Comores et Maurice de Jacques van Heemskerk (1601–1602)," in Alfred Grandidier et al., eds., *Collection des ouvrages anciens concernant Madagascar* (Paris: Comité de Madagascar, 1903–20), 1:272; see also "Relâche aux isles Comores de l'Amiral G. Spilberg," 1601–1602, ibid., 1:318–19.

23. John Ovington, *A Voyage to Suratt, in the Year, 1689* (London, 1696), 114–15; the ship journal of the *Royalle*, 1682, MAR 4JJ/90; memoir, 1664, COL/C/5A/1.

24. Fryer, *New Account*, 21.

25. Martin, *Comores*, 1:77–79; Dubins, "Political History," 55.

26. Justin Corfield and Ian Morson, eds., *British Sea-Captain Alexander Hamilton's "A New Account of the East Indies" (17th–18th Century)* (Lewiston, NY: Edwin Mellen, 2001), 31. See the ship journal of the *Pearl*, 1700, and the ship journal of the *Deux Couronner*, 1715, both in MAR 4JJ/111; the ship journal of the *Lis*, 1713, MAR 4JJ/94; the ship journal of the *Appollon*, 1736, MAR 4JJ/98; the ship journal of the *Penthéière*, 1743; Jean de la Roque, *A Voyage to Arabia Felix*, trans. Dominique de Moulins (New York: Oleander, 2004), 13–14. These requests are also mentioned in Newitt, "Comoro Islands," 156–58.

27. James Pyke, "Voyages and Travels: to Muscat and India," 1704–5, Add MS 24931, 90, 113. See also Martin, *Comores*, 1:77–79.

28. The ship journal of the *Appollon*, 1736.

29. The ship journal of the *Penthéière*, 1743.

30. Pyke, "Voyages and Travels," Add MS 24931, 90; Corfield and Morson, *British Sea-Captain*, 31; Roque, *Voyage*, 13.

31. "Voyages and Travels: Journal of Voyage by Capt. F. Stanes, from England to Msucat in Arabia and back," 1704, Sloane MS 3145, 79.

32. Grose, *Voyage*, 40. See also Jeremy Prestholdt, *Domesticating the World: African Consumerism and the Genealogies of Globalization* (Berkeley: University of California Press, 2008), 13–32.

33. Henry Rooke, *Travels to the Coast of Arabia Felix*, 2nd ed. (London, 1784), 43.

34. The ship journal of the *Walpole*, 1786, IOR/L/MAR/B/293O.

35. Martin, *Comores*, 1:53.

36. Newitt, "Comoro Islands," 155.

37. Memoirs describing Saïd Hamza, a claimant to the Ndzuwani throne during the 1830s: Hébert, "Documents," 25–26. Two similar versions of this history of Ndzuwani are cited in ibid.

38. Ahmed, *Swahili Chronicle*, 5, 52–60.

39. Gevrey, *Essai*, 210–12.

40. Prior, *Voyage*, 62.

41. "Chronique de Kadhi Umari," described in Jean-François Gourlet, ed., *Chroniques Mahoraises* (Paris: L'Harmattan, 2001), 35–40.

42. Martin, *Comores*, 1:83. The leader of these raids was "Fohiloha": ibid., 1:89; Ahmed, *Swahili Chronicle*, 100. It has been suggested that he was a celebrated Malagasy soldier: G. S. Chapus and André Dandouau, *Manuel d'histoire de Madagascar* (Paris: Larose, 1961), 22.

43. See, for instance, Gwyn Campbell, *An Economic History of Imperial Madagascar, 1750–1895: The Rise and Fall of an Island Empire* (Cambridge: Cambridge University Press, 2005), 38. Toussaint connects pirate ancestry among the Betsimisaraka to these "minor operations" conducted by Malagasy "pirates" in the Comoros: Auguste Toussaint, *History of the Indian Ocean*, trans. June Guicharnaud (Chicago: University of Chicago Press, 1966), 145–46.

44. Alpers, "Madagascar and Mozambique," 42. Martin implies that they were *lakan-drafitra*, or canoes made of boards found primarily in southern Madagascar. Martin, *Comores*, 1:89.

45. Oscar MacCarthy, "Les Îles Arabes," in *Îles de l'Afrique*, ed. Marie Armand Pascal d'Avezac, part 3 (Paris: Firmin Didot Frères, 1848), 134–35. See also Grose, *Voyage*, 20; Rooke, *Travels*, 46; Fryer, *New Account*, 19–22; see also Dubins, "Political History," 19–20.

46. Campbell, *Economic History*, 38.

47. Vincent Noël, *Île de Madagascar: Recherches sur les Sakkalava* (extrait du *Bulletin de la Société de Géographie*, 1843) (Paris: Bourgogne et Martinet, 1844), 88; Grégoire Avine, "Voyages aux isles de France,

d'Anjouan, de Madagascar, de Mosambique, de Zanzibar, et à la côte Coromandel," in *Les voyages du chirurgien Avine à l'Île de France et dans la mer des Indes au début du XIXe siècle,* ed. Raymond Decary (Paris: G. Durassié, 1961), 26.

48. Gevrey, *Essai*, 106, 212; Péron, *Mémoires*, 117; J. B. Fressanges, cited by Charles Guillain, *Documents sur l'histoire, la géographie et le commerce de la partie occidentale de Madagascar* (Paris: Imprimerie Royale, 1845), 199.

49. Dubins, "Political History," 68. See the report given in Smyth, *Life and Services*, 257.

50. Valette also suggests that the Antaloatra assisted in navigation: Vallet, "Quelques textes," 763, citing Guillain, *Documents*, 199.

51. Hébert, "Documents," 5–6, 20–21. For example, Noël dates them back to 1760–85, likely due to the later Comorian reports: Noël, *Île de Madagascar*, 25. Dubins suggests they began around 1795 but definitely ended by 1820: Dubins, "Political History," 59. Gevrey, based on interviews with Comorians, argues that the raids began centuries earlier: described in Dubins, "Political History," 59–60. A Comorian chronicle describes the earliest invasions from around 1797: Gourlet, *Chroniques Mahoraises*, 40–42. See also Ahmed, *Swahili Chronicle*, 98; Martin, *Comores*, 1:87, 101–3.

52. Péron, *Mémoires*, 133, 141–44, 150–53; see also Hébert, "Documents," 15–19.

53. Hébert, "Documents," 23–25. See also Dubins, "Political History," 64.

54. "Memo Relative to the Offer of the King of Baba to Cede the Island of Johanna to the Company," 1796, IOR/H/511, 1. Dubins describes the visitor as the sultan: Dubins, "Political History," 67.

55. Blankett and Bissel, cited in Hébert, "Documents," 31–32; Dubins, "Political History," 68–69.

56. For more on this trade, see Malyn Newitt, "The Southern Swahili Coast in the First Century of European Expansion," *Azania* 13, no. 1 (1978): 116.

57. Malyn Newitt, *A History of Mozambique* (Bloomington: Indiana University Press, 1995), 253–58.

58. Froberville and Manicacci, cited by Dubins, "Political History," 61–62; Gourlet, *Chroniques mahoraises*, 40–42; Gevrey, *Essai*, 210–11.

59. Alpers, "Madagascar and Mozambique," 38–39; see also Newitt, *History of Mozambique*, 243.

60. On the difficulties in crossing between Madagascar, the Comoros, and East Africa, see Henri Daniel Liszkowski, *Mayotte et les Comores: Escales sur la route des Indes aux XVe et XVIIe siècles* (Mamoudzou, Mayotte: Baobab, 2000), 24–29.

61. See the description of the channel provided in Charles F. Noble, Account of Island of Bourbon, 1756, printed in Alexander Dalrymple, "Geographical collections of Alexander Dalrymple" on Mauritius, Island of Bourbon, Madagascar, and Diego Rayes, 1808, Add MS 33765, fol. 13, 18–19.

62. Ahmed, *Swahili Chronicle*, 99.

63. Alpers, "Madagascar and Mozambique," 40; Martin, *Comores*, 1:87.

64. Newitt, *History of Mozambique*, 243.

65. Letter by J. Tomkinson to Vice Admiral Albemarle Bertie, 7 June 1810, in George McCall Theal, ed., *Records of South-Eastern Africa Collected in Various Libraries and Archive Departments in Europe*, 9 vols. (Cape Town: Printed for the Government of the Cape Colony, 1898–1903), 9:5.

66. Alpers, "Madagascar and Mozambique," 40–41.

67. Letter from the Earl of Caledon to the Right Honourable Nicholas Vansittart, 27 June 1810, in Theal, *Records of South-Eastern Africa*, 9:12–13.

68. Prior, *Voyage*, 38–46.

69. Dubins, "Political History," 82–83, 91–97.

70. Alpers, "Madagascar and Mozambique," 49.

71. Ibid., 41.

72. Ibid., 42–43.

73. Ibid., 43. On political developments in East Africa at this time, see Nancy Jane Hafkin, "Trade, Society, and Politics in Northern Mozambique, c. 1753–1913" (PhD diss., Boston University, 1973), 10–28; Edward Alpers, *Ivory and Slaves: Changing Pattern of International Trade in East Central Africa to the Later Nineteenth Century* (Berkeley: University of California Press, 1975), 108–11.

74. Quotation from Alpers, "Madagascar and Mozambique," 44–45.

75. "Alli Abdulla King, Johanna," letter to the Council of Bombay, 10 July 1800, IOR/H/473, 241–42. See also Guillain, *Documents*, 201; Prior, *Voyage*, 64.

76. East India Company records, 1803, IOR/H/511, 7.

77. Letter on events in Ndzuwani, 1807, ibid., 7.

78. Hébert, "Documents," 39–41; Dubins, "Political History," 80–81. None of this aid reached the island, as the sultan was attacked on his return voyage. There is an alternative account described by Capmartin and Colin, cited in Dubins, "Political History," 77, 87.

79. Hébert, "Documents," 27; Dubins, "Political History," 82.

80. Prior, *Voyage*, 64; see also Smyth, *Life and Services*, 261. Dubins describes another Malagasy attack in 1814: Dubins, "Political History," 86.

81. Dubins, "Political History," 63–64, 69.

82. René-Marie Kermel, "Journal historique de la campagne de l'Inde (1803–1806)," ed. Dast de Boisville, *Bulletin de géographie historique et descriptive*, vol. 13, *Année 1898* (1900): 182.

83. See, for instance, B.-F. Leguével de Lacombe, *Voyage à Madagascar et aux îles Comores (1823 à 1830)*, vol. 2 (Paris: Louis Desessart, 1840), 66, 75–77. No mention is made of any devastation to Ndzuwani in Guillain, *Documents*, 33–34; Lacombe, *Voyage*, 10.

84. Newitt, *History of Mozambique*, 243.

85. "Treaty between Great Britain and Madagascar, signed at Tamatave, 23rd October, 1817," in *Hertslet's Commercial Treaties* (London: Richard Clay & Sons, 1840), 355.

86. Gwyn Campbell, "Servitude and the Changing Face of the Demand for Labor in the Indian Ocean World, c. 1800–1900," in *Indian Ocean Slavery in the Age of Abolition*, ed. Robert Harms, Bernard K. Freamon, and David W. Blight (New Haven: Yale University Press, 2013), 23.

87. Thomas R. Metcalf, *Imperial Connections: India in the Indian Ocean Arena, 1860–1920* (Berkeley: University of California Press, 2007), 14.

88. Erik Gilbert, "Coastal East Africa and the Western Indian Ocean: Long-Distance Trade, Empire, Migration, and Regional Unity, 1750–1970," *History Teacher* 36, no. 1 (2002): 16.

89. Metcalf, *Imperial Connections*, 91; Gilbert, "Coastal East Africa," 17–18.

90. Ulrike Freitag, *Indian Ocean Migrants and State Formation in Hadhramaut: Reforming the Homeland* (Leiden: Brill, 2003), 48–49.

91. Gilbert, "Coastal East Africa," 24–28.

92. This new era was, in part, created by changes within the island itself. According to Randrianja and Ellis, "One way of considering Madagascar's nineteenth century is to see it as the beginning of a gradual convergence between external and internal elements. On the one hand was a European vision of political modernity, projected into the western Indian Ocean with increasing force. On the other hand were Madagascar's historic political cultures." Solofo Randrianja and Stephen Ellis, *Madagascar: A Short History* (Chicago: University of Chicago Press, 2009), 149.

93. For a more in-depth discussion of the British Empire in the Indian Ocean, see Sugata Bose, *A Hundred Horizons: The Indian Ocean in the Age of Global Empire* (Cambridge, MA: Harvard University Press, 2006), 40–71.

94. Ratsivalaka argues that the attempt was part of the British plan to secure the sea lanes of the ocean. Ranaivo G. Ratsivalaka, *Les Malgaches et l'abolition de la traite européenne des esclaves (1810–1817): Histoire de la formation du Royaume de Madagascar* (Antananarivo: Hery Arivo, 1999), 90–92.

95. On Jean-René, see the letter to Farquhar from Jean-René, dated 10 April 1813, in Madagascar, fonds historique, pièces générales sur Madagascar et fondation des établissements de Sainte-Marie, 1z/1–159, Archives nationales d'outre-mer (henceforth ANOM). His father was French and his mother was Malagasy. G. A. Rantoandro, "Hommes et réseaux Malata de la côte orientale de Madagascar à l'époque de Jean René (1773–1825)," *Annuaire des pays de l'Océan Indien* 17 (2001–2): 103–4. See also Randrianja and Ellis, *Madagascar*, 120; Pier M. Larson, "Fragments of an Indian Ocean Life: Aristide Corroller between Islands and Empires," *Journal of Social History* 45, no. 2 (2011): 373–77.

96. Ratsivalaka, *Les Malgaches*, 181–82.

97. Ibid., 185–95.

98. Samuel Copland, *A History of the Island of Madagascar* (London: R. Clay for Burton and Smith, 1822), 23.

99. Ibid., 23–27.

100. Ibid., 40; see also 34–37.

101. "Proclamation of Radama, King of Madagascar, for the Abolition of the Slave Trade, 23rd October, 1817," translated, in *British and Foreign State Papers, 1824–1825*, compiled by the Librarian and Keeper of the Papers, Foreign Office (London: James Ridgway and Sons, 1846), 461.

102. Ibid. For more on this proclamation, see Randrianaja and Ellis, *Madagascar*, 123.

103. On the challenges faced by Radama I following the 1820 treaty, see esp. Campbell, *Economic History*, 69–78.

104. The British appear to have supported, at least tacitly, the attack on the west coast. One British official even urged Radama I to invade the town of "Mazungay" to get rid of this "nest of slave dealers" that included "Arabs, Moors, and Indians." Letter to Secretary Newnham, 27 July 1824, IOR/F/4/905/25664, "Papers regarding the slave trade in the Persian Gulf and on the East Coast of Africa," 77–78.

105. Andriantsoly (Andriantsouli, Tse Levalou), a deposed Sakalava ruler, and Ramanetaka, a former Merina governor, formed alliances with Comorian rulers who begged for Malagasy assistance in their struggles. The two Malagasy battled for control over the islands of Mwali and Mayotte between 1832 and 1836, prompting further disorder throughout the archipelago. These events are mostly clearly outlined in Martin, *Comores*, 1:132–59. See also Sophie Blanchy, *Karana et Banians: Les communautés commerçantes d'origin Indienne à Madagascar* (Paris: Harmattan, 1995), 55–56.

106. The exaction of customs duties is described in Campbell, *Economic History*, 278–80. For more on Mahajanga, see ibid., 170–72.

107. Particularly with American whalers. For more details on American trade and whaling in the region, see firsthand accounts including Browne,

*Etchings* 1846; Charles Nordhoff, *Whaling and Fishing* (New York: Dodd, Mead, 1855); William B. Whitecar Jr., *Four Years Aboard the Whaleship: Embracing Cruises in the Pacific, Atlantic, Indian, and Antarctic Oceans* (Philadelphia: J. B. Lippincott, 1864); William Henry Beehler, *The Cruise of the Brooklyn: A Journal of the Principal Events of a Three Years' Cruise in the U.S. Flag-Ship Brooklyn* (Philadelphia: J. B. Lippincott, 1885). On American merchants, see various documents in Norman R. Bennett and George E. Brooks, eds., *New England Merchants in Africa: A History through Documents, 1802–1865* (Boston: Boston University Press, 1965). On the export of salted beef and hides, see also Guillain, *Documents*, 159, 286, 316, 350–51; Joseph S. Sewell, *The Sakalava: Being Notes of a Journey Made from Antananarivo to Some Towns on the Border of the Sakalava Territory, in June and July, 1875* (Antananarivo: Abraham Kingdon, 1875), 18.

108. On these French settlements, see various documents, 1z/1–159, ANOM. On Nosy Boraha, see the report of the signed treaty provided by the French commercial agent Jean Baptiste Sylvain Roux in 1z/1–159. In the same year, Roux took possession of Point Teintingue. This act is also found in 1z/1–159.

109. Treaty for Mayotte in 1841, in Madagascar, fonds historique, pièces diverses concernant Nossi-Bé, Mayotte et la côte Nord-Ouest de Madagascar, 4z/151–167, ANOM; Gevrey, *Essai*, 227. The treaty was ratified in France in 1843: Martin, *Comores*, 1:148–51.

110. "Précis des avantages d'un établissement à Madagascar," n.d., in "Mémoires sur Madagascar," Add MS 18136, 39–40.

111. On Nosy Boraha, see letters, 1z/1–159, ANOM.

112. Jehanne-Emmanuelle Monnier, *Esclaves de la canne à sucre: Engagés et planteurs à Nossi-Bé, Madagascar 1850–1880* (Paris: L'Harmattan, 2006), see esp. 47–144. They also imported "Makoa" workers, probably from Mozambique: see the list of workers given on 16 October 1867, in 4z/1–13, ANOM.

113. For more, see Guillain's report, 1842, in MAD 14/28–29; Guillain, *Documents*, 196–97, 280, 315; Browne, *Etchings*, 252; Edward A. Alpers, "The Western Indian Ocean as a Regional Food Network in the Nineteenth Century," in Alpers, *East Africa and the Indian Ocean* (Princeton, NJ: Markus Wiener, 2009), 28–29, 30–31.

## CHAPTER 9: FROM FEASTS TO FAMINE

1. United Nations Children's Fund and World Food Programme, "Rural Madagascar Comprehensive Food and Nutrition Security and Vulnerability Analysis," data collected August–September 2010, drafted by WFP Madagascar and UNICEF Madagascar, published November 2011, documents.wfp.org/stellent/groups/public/documents/ena/wfp246796.pdf, 16, 71. For

the basis of these criteria, see ibid., 139–40. Hereafter cited as UNICEF and WFP, "Rural Madagascar."

2. Ibid., 16–18.

3. The study breaks down the island into "eight livelihood zones": ibid., 16–18, 20, table 1.

4. "More than 70 percent of the population lives below the poverty line": "Madagascar: Overview," the World Food Programme, available online at https://www.wfp.org/countries/madagascar/overview (accessed 5 January 2017). The 2014 HDI (Human Development Index) rankings, calculated by the United Nations Development Programme, are available at http://hdr.undp.org/sites/default/files/ranking.pdf (accessed 5 January 2017).

5. UNICEF and WFP, "Rural Madagascar," 24.

6. "Madagascar: Current Issues and What the World Food Programme Is Doing," World Food Programme, available online at http://www.wfp.org/Countries/Madagascar (accessed 5 January 2017). The "Comprehensive Food and Nutrition Security" report, by contrast, focuses instead on the impact of natural disasters, particularly cyclones, and climate change: UNICEF and WFP, "Rural Madagascar," 32–33.

7. See esp. William J. McConnell and Christian A. Kull, "Deforestation in Madagascar: Debates over the Island's Forest Cover and Challenges of Measuring Forest Change," in *Conservation and Environmental Management in Madagascar*, ed. Ivan R. Scales (New York: Routledge, 2014), 84–85.

8. See the discussion of twentieth-century food shortages in Michel Garenne, "An Atypical Urban Famine: Antananarivo, Madagascar, 1985–1986," in *The New Famines: Why Famines Persist in an Era of Globalization*, ed. Stephen Devereux (New York: Routledge, 2006), 180–81.

9. For example, Randrianja and Ellis describe the impact of forced labor regimes leading to food shortages: Solofo Randrianja and Stephen Ellis, *Madagascar: A Short History* (Chicago: University of Chicago Press, 2009), 162–63.

10. Jeffrey Kaufmann has written extensively about cactus pastoralism and French attempts at eradication, including "Forget the Numbers: The Case of a Madagascar Famine," *History in Africa* 27 (2000): 143–57; "*La Question des Raketa*: Colonial Struggles with Prickly Pear Cactus in Southern Madagascar, 1900–1923," *Ethnohistory* 48, nos. 1–2 (2001): 87–121; "Doubting Modernity for Madagascar's Cactus Pastoralists," *History in Africa* 38 (2011): 123–51.

11. For details on the French hand in introducing the insects, see Karen Middleton, "Who Killed 'Malagasy Cactus'? Science, Environment and Colonialism in Southern Madagascar (1924–1930)," *Journal of Southern African Studies* 25, no. 2 (1999): 215–48. The debate over numbers is summarized in Kaufmann, "Forget the Numbers," 152.

12. Kaufmann, "Forget the Numbers," 155.

13. As described in Ivan R. Scales, "The Drivers of Deforestation and the Complexity of Land Use in Madagascar," in Scales, *Conservation and Environmental Management*, 108–9.

14. On the development of conservation in colonial Madagascar, see Ivan R. Scales, "A Brief History of the State and the Politics of Natural Resource Use in Madagascar," in Scales, *Conservation and Environmental Management*, 135–42.

15. For more about the links between famines and political protest in the south, in 1987, for instance, see Christopher B. Barrett, "Understanding Uneven Agricultural Liberalisation in Madagascar," *Journal of Modern African Studies* 32, no. 3 (1994): 456, 463.

16. Lester R. Brown, "The New Geopolitics of Food," *Foreign Policy*, no. 186 (2011): 54–63.

17. Barrett, "Understanding Uneven Agricultural Liberalisation," 452.

18. Ibid. In 2010, Malagasy households spent an average of "32 percent of their total expenditure on rice," except in the south. UNICEF and WFP, "Rural Madagascar," 25. In addition, "households with a borderline food consumption profile" are "more likely to sell micronutrient rich foods such as fruits and vegetables in order to purchase rice and less nutritious foods and non-food items." Ibid., 18.

19. Barrett, "Understanding Uneven Agricultural Liberalisation," 452, table 2. Randrianja and Ellis also point to dramatic population growth encouraging the importation of food: Randrianja and Ellis, *Madagascar*, 198. On some of the challenges rice producers face, see Douglas W. Hume, "Swidden Agriculture and Conservation in Eastern Madagascar: Stakeholder Perspectives and Cultural Belief Systems," *Conservation and Society* 4, no. 2 (2006): 287–303.

20. Barrett, "Understanding Uneven Agricultural Liberalisation," 470–71; see also the discussion of the Antananarivo famine of 1985–86 in Garenne, "An Atypical Urban Famine."

21. For example, the WFP notes: "Recent political instability has underminded government institutional capacity, economic growth and development efforts. It has also reduced people's access to basic services and their ability to prevent and recover from frequent shocks." "Madagascar: Current Issues and What the World Food Programme Is Doing," available at http://www.wfp.org/Countries/Madagascar (accessed 5 January 2017).

22. Ivan R. Scales, "Introduction: Conservation at the Crossroads: Biological Diversity, Environmental Change and Natural Resource Use in Madagascar," in Scales, *Conservation and Environmental Management*, 8, fig. 1.2.

23. Randrianja and Ellis, *Madagascar*, 231.

24. Scales, "Drivers of Deforestation," 120.

25. Ibid., 117–18.

# Bibliography

## ARCHIVAL COLLECTIONS


### *Archives nationales, Paris*

Fonds des Colonies, Correspondance à l'Arrivée, Île Bourbon, COL C/3
Fonds des Colonies, Correspondance à l'Arrivée, Île Maurice, COL C/4
Fonds des Colonies, Correspondance à l'Arrivée, Madagascar, COL C/5A
Fonds des Colonies, Correspondance à l'Arrivée, Cape of Good Hope, COL C/5B
Fonds des Colonies, Divers, Collection Moreau de St Méry, COL F/3
Fonds des Colonies, Missions de Madagascar, des Îles de France (Île Maurice) et Île Bourbon (Réunion), COL F/5a
Séries Marine, Documents Divers, MAR G
Séries Marine, Observations scientifiques et géographiques, MAR 3JJ
Séries Marine, Journaux de bord, MAR 4JJ
Séries Marine, Voyages et missions hydrographiques, MAR 5JJ

### *Archives nationales d'outre-mer, Aix-en-Provence*

Fonds ministériels, Dépôt fortifications colonial, Sainte-Marie de Madagascar, XVII/mémoires/88
Madagascar, fonds historique, pièces générales sur Madagascar et fondation des établissements de Sainte-Marie (1785–1889), 1z
Madagascar, fonds historique, pièces diverses concernant Nossi-Bé, Mayotte et la côte Nord-Ouest de Madagascar (1841–1897), 4z

### *Archives of the Western Cape, Cape Town, South Africa*

Records of the Dutch East India Company, Ship logs and journals, C

### *Bodleian Library, Oxford University*

Rawlinson MS A 315
Rawlinson MS A 334

*British Library, London*

India Office records, African and Asian Studies Reading Room, IOR
Minutes of the East India Company's Directors and Proprietors, IOR/B
East India Company General Correspondence, IOR/E
Records of the Board of Commissioners for the Affairs of India, IOR/F
East India Company Factory Records, IOR/G
Home Miscellaneous, IOR/H
Maritime Department Records, Ships' Journals, IOR/L/MAR/A–B
Manuscript collection, Add MS
Maps Reading Room, Maps

*British National Archives, Kew, London*

Records of the High Court of Admiralty and colonial Vice-Admiralty courts, HCA 1/98
Records of the Admiralty, East Indies, ADM

*Hispanic Society of America, New York*

"Journal and Logbook of an Anonymous Scotch Sailor, 1726–1729," HC 363/129

*Nationaal Archief, The Hague*

Records of the Dutch East India Company, VOC 1.04.02

*National Maritime Museum, Greenwich, London*

G251:18/11, 1824, Map of Boteler's River on the West Coast of Madagascar
RUSI 180/2, Log from India to Europe

## ONLINE DATABASES

The Dutch East India Company's Shipping between the Netherlands and Asia 1595–1795, Historici.nl, http://resources.huygens.knaw.nl/das/voyages?clear=1
Trans-Atlantic Slave Trade Database, http://www.slavevoyages.org
National Archives, British Library, Asian and African Studies, India Office Records, Maritime Department Records, Ships' Journals: IOR/L/MAR/A-B, http://discovery.nationalarchives.gov.uk/browse/r/937f93cc-ccf5-4c31-951c-af92be35ea66

## PUBLISHED PRIMARY SOURCES

Ahmed, Said Bakari bin Sultani. *The Swahili Chronicle of Ngazija*. Edited by Lyndon Harries. Bloomington: African Studies Program, Indiana University, 1977.

Beaulieu, Augustin de. *Mémoires d'un voyage aux Indes Orientales, 1619–1622: Un marchand normand à Sumatra*. Edited by Denys Lombard. Paris: École française d'Extrême-Orient; Maisonneuve & Larose, 1996.

Beehler, William Henry. *The Cruise of the Brooklyn: A Journal of the Principal Events of a Three Years' Cruise in the U.S. Flag-Ship Brooklyn, in the South Atlantic Station*. Philadelphia: J. B. Lippincott, 1885.

Behrendt, Stephen D., A. J. H. Latham, and David Northrup, eds. *The Diary of Antera Duke, an Eighteenth-Century African Slave Trader*. Oxford: Oxford University Press, 2010.

Bennett, Norman R., and George E. Brooks, eds. *New England Merchants in Africa: A History through Documents, 1802–1865*. Boston: Boston University Press, 1965.

Benyowsky, Maurice-Auguste. *Voyages et mémoires de Maurice-Auguste, Comte de Benyowsky*. 2 vols. Paris: F. Buisson, 1791.

Birdwood, George, and William Foster, eds. *The Register of Letters etc. of the Governour and Company of Merchants of London Trading into the East Indies, 1600–1619*. London: Quartich, 1893.

Birkeli, Emil. *Folklore Sakalava, recueilli dans la région de Morondava*. Antananarivo: Imp. G. Pitot de la Beaujardière, 1924; originally published in *Bulletin de l'Académie Malgache*, n.s., 6 (1922–23): 185–417.

Bontekoe, Willem Ysbrantsz. *Journael ofte gedenckwaerdige beschrijvinghe vande Oost-Indische reyse*. Hoorn: Printed by I. Willemsz, 1646.

———. *Memorable Description of the East Indian Voyage, 1618–25*. Translated by C. B. Bodde-Hodgkinson and Pieter Geyl. London: RoutledgeCurzon, 2005. Originally published in Dutch in 1646. First published in English in 1929.

Boothby, Richard. *A Briefe Discovery or Description of the Most Famous Island of Madagascar or St. Laurence in Asia Neare unto East-India*. London: Printed by E. G. for John Hardesty, 1646.

Boteler, Thomas. *Narrative of a Voyage of Discovery to Africa and Arabia . . . from 1821 to 1826, under the Command of Capt. F. W. Owen*. 2 vols. London: Richard Bentley, 1835.

Browne, John Ross. *Etchings of a Whaling Cruise, with Notes of a Sojourn on the Island of Zanzibar*. New York: Harper & Brothers, 1846.

Buckeridge, Nicholas. *Journal and Letter Book of Nicholas Buckeridge, 1651–1654*. Edited by John R. Jenson. Minneapolis: University of Minnesota Press, 1973.

Callet, François, ed. *Histoire des rois, traduction du "Tantaran'ny Andriana."* 5 vols. Antananarivo: Académie Malgache, 1953–78.

[Carmichael, Dugald]. *Account of the Conquest of Mauritius: With Some Notices on the History, Soil, Products, Defences, and the Political Importance, of This Island: To Which Is Added, a Sketch, Explanatory of the Military Operations.* London: Printed for T. Egerton, 1811.

Colomb, Philip H. *Slave-Catching in the Indian Ocean: A Record of Naval Experiences.* London: Longmans, Green, 1873. Facsimile reprint, London: Dawsons of Pall Mall, 1968.

Copland, Samuel. *A History of the Island of Madagascar.* London: R. Clay for Burton and Smith, 1822.

Coppalle, André. *Voyage dans l'intérieur de Madagascar et à la capitale du roi Radama Ier: Un peintre découvre la Grande Île, 1825–1826.* Besançon: La lanterne magique, 2006.

Corfield, Justin, and Ian Morson, eds. *British Sea-Captain Alexander Hamilton's "A New Account of the East Indies" (17th–18th Century).* Lewiston, NY: Edwin Mellen, 2001.

Dale, John. *Narrative of the Loss of the Winterton East Indiaman.* London: Tegg & Castleman, 1802.

Dandouau, André. *Contes populaires des Sakalava et des Tsimihety de la région d'Analalava.* Algiers: Jules Carbonel, 1922.

Danvers, Frederick Charles, ed. *Letters Received by the East India Company from Its Servants in the East.* Vol. 1. London: Sampson Low, Marston, 1896.

Darell, John. *Strange News from th' Indies; or, East India Passages Further Discovered: . . . Partly Discovering the Manner, and Tenour of East-India-Trade Hitherto, Together, with Part of the Wofull, and Sad Sufferings of William Courten.* London: Printed for Stephen Bowtel, 1652.

Davenant, William. *Madagascar, with Other Poems.* London: Printed by John Haviland for Thomas Walkly, 1638.

Decary, Raymond, ed. *Les voyages du chirurgien Avine à l'Île de France et dans la mer des Indes au début du XIXe siècle.* Paris: G. Durassié, 1961.

Dellon, Gabriel. *A Voyage to the East-Indies.* Translated by Jodocus Crull. London: Printed for D. Browne, 1698. Originally published in French in 1685.

*Documents on the Portuguese in Mozambique and Central Africa, 1497–1840.* 9 vols. Lisbon: National Archives of Rhodesia and Nyasaland, Centro de Estudos Históricos Ultramarinos, 1962–89.

Downing, Clement. *A Compendious History of the Indian Wars.* London: Printed for T. Cooper, 1737.

Drury, Robert. *The Adventures of Robert Drury.* London: Printed by W. Meadows, 1729. Reprint, Hull: Stodart and Craggs, 1807. Page references are to the 1807 edition.

Ellis, Stephen. "Un texte du XVIIe siècle sur Madagascar." *Omaly sy anio* (Université d'Antananarivo) 9 (1979): 151–66.

Everard, Robert. "A Relation of Three Years Sufferings of Robert Everard, upon the Coast of Assada near Madagascar, in a Voyage to India, in the Year 1686: And of His Wonderful Preservation and Deliverance, and Arrival at London, Anno 1693." In *A Collection of Voyages and Travels*, vol. 6, edited by Awnsham Churchill and John Churchill, 259–82. London: Churchill, 1732.

Findlay, Alexander George. *A Directory for the Navigation of the Indian Ocean: With Descriptions of Its Coasts, Islands, Etc., from the Cape of Good Hope to the Strait of Sunda and Western Australia, Including Also the Red Sea and the Persian Gulf; the Winds, Monsoons, and Currents, and the Passages from Europe to Its Various Ports.* 3rd ed. London: Richard Holmes Laurie, 1876.

Flacourt, Étienne de. *Histoire de la Grande Isle Madagascar.* 1658. Edited by Claude Allibert. Paris: Karthala, 1995.

Foster, William, ed. *Letters Received by the East India Company from Its Servants in the East.* Vol. 2. London: Sampson Low, Marston, 1897.

———. *Letters Received by the East India Company from Its Servants in the East.* Vol. 3. London: Sampson Low, Marston, 1899.

Frappé, Hendrik, and Willem van der Lint. *Slawehandel met Madagaskar: Die joernale van die Kaapse slaweskip Leijdsman, 1715.* Edited by Piet E. Westra and James C. Armstrong. Cape Town: Africana Uitgewers, 2006.

Freeman-Grenville, G. S. P., ed. *The French at Kilwa Island: An Episode in Eighteenth-Century East African History.* Oxford: Clarendon, 1965.

———. *The Mombasa Rising against the Portuguese, 1631: From Sworn Evidence.* London: Oxford University Press for the British Academy, 1980.

Fryer, John. *A New Account of East-India and Persia, in Eight Letters.* London: R. Chiswell, 1698.

Galaisière, Guillaume Joseph. *Voyage dans les mers de l'Inde, fait par ordre du Roi, à l'occasion du passage de Vénus, sur le disque du soleil, le 6 juin 1761, & le 3 du même mois 1769.* Vol. 2. Paris: Imprimerie Royale, 1781.

Gautier, Emile-Félix and Henri Froidevaux. *Un manuscrit arabico-malgache sur les campagnes de La Case dans l'Imoro de 1659 à 1663.* Paris: Imprimerie nationale, 1907.

Gourlet, Jean-François, ed. *Chroniques Mahoraises.* Paris: L'Harmattan, 2001.

Grandidier, Alfred, Jules Charles-Roux, Clément Delhorbe, Henri Froidevaux, and Guillaume Grandidier, eds. *Collection des ouvrages anciens concernant Madagascar.* 9 vols. Paris: Comité de Madagascar, 1903–20.

Grant, Charles, ed. *The History of Mauritius, or the Isle of France, and the Neighbouring Islands; from Their First Discovery to the Present Time:*

*Composed Principally from the Papers and Memoirs of Baron Grant, Who Resided Twenty Years in the Island*. London: W. Bulmer, 1801.

Grose, John-Henry. *A Voyage to the East-Indies, with Observations on Various Parts There*. London: S. Hooper and A. Morley, 1757.

Guillain, Charles. *Documents sur l'histoire, la géographie et le commerce de la partie occidentale de Madagascar*. Paris: Imprimerie Royale, 1845.

Hamond, Walter. *Madagascar, the Richest and Most Fruitful Island in the World*. London: Nicholas Bourne, 1643.

———. *A Paradox: Prooving, That the Inhabitants of the Isle Called Madagascar, or St. Laurence, (in Temporall Things) Are the Happiest People in the World*. London: Nathaniell Butter, 1640.

Hébert, Jean-Claude. "Documents sur les razzias Malgaches aux îles Comores et sur la côte orientale africaine." *Études océan Indien*, no. 3 (1983): 5–60.

Hill, Pascoe Grenfell. *Fifty Days on Board a Slave-Vessel in the Mozambique Channel, in April and May, 1843*. London: John Murray, 1844.

Hunt, Robert. *The Island of Assada, Neere Madagascar Impartially Defined: Being a Succint, Yet Plenary Discription of the Situation, Fertility and People Therein Inhabiting*. London: Printed for Nicholas Bourne, 1650.

"Isula S. Laurentii, vulgo Madagascar." Map. Amsterdam, 1665. Northwestern University Library, Map Collection, http://hdl.library.northwestern.edu/2166.DL/inu-afrmap-4264860-recto-ah.

James, Silas. *A Narrative of a Voyage to Arabia, India, &c*. London: W. Glindon, 1797.

Kermel, René-Marie. "Journal historique de la campagne de l'Inde (1803–1806)." Edited by Dast de Boisville. *Bulletin de géographie historique et descriptive*, vol. 13, *Année 1898* (1900): 170–98.

Kerr, Robert, ed. *A General History and Collection of Voyages and Travels, Arranged in Systematic Order: Forming a Complete History of the Origin and Progress of Navigation, Discovery, and Commerce, by Sea and Land, from the Earliest Ages to the Present Time*. 18 vols. Edinburgh: W. Blackwood, 1824.

Kestell-Cornish, Robert. *Journal of a Tour of Exploration in the North of Madagascar*. London: Society for the Propagation of the Gospel in Foreign Parts, 1877.

Lacombe, B.-F. Leguével de. *Voyage à Madagascar et aux îles Comores (1823 à 1830)*. Vol. 2. Paris: Louis Desessart, 1840.

Leibbrandt, H. C. V., ed. *Precis of the Archives of the Cape of Good Hope: December 1651–December 1653: Riebeeck's Journal, &c*. Pt. 1. Cape Town: W. A. Richards & Sons, 1897.

———. *Precis of the Archives of the Cape of Good Hope: January 1656–December 1658: Riebeeck's Journal, &c.* Pt. 2. Cape Town: W. A. Richards & Sons, 1897.
———. *Precis of the Archives of the Cape of Good Hope: Journal, 1662–1670*. Cape Town: W. A. Richards & Sons, 1901.
———. *Precis of the Archives of the Cape of Good Hope: Journal, 1671–1674, & 1676*. Cape Town: W. A. Richards & Sons, 1902.
———. *Precis of the Archives of the Cape of Good Hope: Letters Despatched from the Cape, 1652–1662*. Vol. 3. Cape Town: W. A. Richards & Sons, 1900.
———. *Precis of the Archives of the Cape of Good Hope: Letters Despatched, 1696–1708*. Cape Town: W. A. Richards & Sons, 1896.
———. *Precis of the Archives of the Cape of Good Hope: Letters Received, 1695–1708*. Cape Town: W. A. Richards & Sons, 1896.
Lougnon, Albert, ed. *Correspondance du conseil supérieur de Bourbon et de la Compagnie des Indes*. 2 vols. Paris: Ernest Leroux, 1933–34.
MacCarthy, Oscar. "Les Îles Arabes." In *Îles de l'Afrique*, edited by Marie Armand Pascal d'Avezac, 115–144. Part 3. Paris: Firmin Didot Frères, 1848.
MacIntosh, William. *Travels in Europe, Asia, and Africa*. 2 vols. London: J. Murray, 1782.
Majid al-Najdi, Ahmad ibn. *Arab Navigation in the Indian Ocean before the Coming of the Portuguese: Being a translation of* "Kitāb al-Fawā'id fī uṣūl al-baḥr wa'l-qawā'id *of Ahmad b. Mājid al-Najdī.*" Edited by G. R. Tibbetts. London: Royal Asiatic Society of Great Britain and Ireland, 1972.
McLeod, Lyons. *Madagascar and Its People*. New York: Negro Universities Press, 1969. Originally published 1865.
Molet-Sauvaget, Anne, ed. *Documents anciens sur les îles Comores: 1591–1800, Supplément / II*. Paris: Institut national des langues et civilisations orientales, 1996.
———, ed. *Documents anciens sur les îles Comores: 1591–1810*. Paris: Institut national des langues et civilisations orientales, 1994.
———. "La *Relation de Robert Everard*, ébauche probable du *Journal de Robert Drury* de Daniel Defoe." *Studies on Voltaire and the Eighteenth Century* 241 (1986): 1–28.
Mullens, Joseph. *Twelve Months in Madagascar*. New York: Robert Carter & Brothers, 1875.
Noël, Vincent. *Île de Madagascar: Recherches sur les Sakkalava*. Extrait du *Bulletin de la Société de Géographie*, 1843. Paris: Bourgogne et Martinet, 1844.
Nordhoff, Charles. *Whaling and Fishing*. New York: Dodd, Mead, 1855.

Osgood, Joseph Barlow Felt. *Notes of Travel; or, Recollections of Majunga, Zanzibar, Muscat, Aden, Mocha, and Other Eastern Ports.* Salem, MA: George Creamer, 1854.

Ovington, John. *A Voyage to Suratt, in the Year, 1689.* London: Jacob Tonson, 1696.

Péron, Françoise. *Mémoires du Capitaine Péron, sur ses voyages aux côtes d'Afrique, en Arabie, à l'île d'Amsterdam.* Vol. I. Paris: Brissot-Thivars, 1824.

Prior, James. *Voyage along the Eastern Coast of Africa, to Mosambique, Johanna, and Quiloa; to St. Helena; to Rio de Janeiro, Bahia, and Pernambuco in Brazil, in the Nisus Frigate.* London: Sir Richard Phillips, 1819.

"Proclamation of Radama, King of Madagascar, for the Abolition of the Slave Trade, 23rd October, 1817." Translated. In *British and Foreign State Papers, 1824–1825*, compiled by the Librarian and Keeper of the Papers, Foreign Office, 461–62. London: James Ridgway and Sons, 1846.

Rochon, Alexis-Marie de. *Voyage à Madagascar et aux Indes orientales.* Paris: Prault, 1791. Translated by Joseph Trapp as *A Voyage to Madagascar and the East Indies* (London: G. G. J. and J. Robinson, 1792).

Rooke, Henry. *Travels to the Coast of Arabia Felix.* 2nd. ed. London: R. Blamire, 1784.

Roque, Jean de la. *A Voyage to Arabia Felix.* Translated by Dominique de Moulins. New York: Oleander, 2004.

Ross, Robert, ed. "The Dutch on the Swahili Coast, 1776–1778: Two Slaving Journals." Pts. 1 and 2. *International Journal of African Historical Studies* 19, no. 2 (1986): 305–60; 19, no. 3 (1986): 479–506.

Saussay, Carpeau du. *Voyage de Madagascar.* Paris: Jean-Luc Nyon, 1722.

Sewell, Joseph S. *The Sakalava: Being Notes of a Journey Made from Antananarivo to Some Towns on the Border of the Sakalava Territory, in June and July, 1875.* Antananarivo: Abraham Kingdon, 1875.

Smith, George Herbert. *Among the Menabe; or, Thirteen months on the West Coast of Madagascar.* London: Society for Promoting Christian Knowledge, 1896.

Smyth, William Henry. *The Life and Services of Captain Philip Beaver, Late of His Majesty's Ship Nisus.* London: John Murray, 1829.

Sonnerat, Pierre. *A Voyage to the East-Indies and China; Performed by Order of Lewis XV between the Years 1774 and 1781.* Translated by Francis Magnus. Vol. 3. Calcutta: Joseph Cooper, 1789.

Theal, George McCall, ed. *Records of South-Eastern Africa Collected in Various Libraries and Archive Departments in Europe.* 9 vols. Cape Town: Printed for the Government of the Cape Colony, 1898–1903.

"Treaty between Great Britain and Madagascar, signed at Tamatave, 23 October, 1817." In *Hertslet's Commercial Treaties: A Complete Collection of the Treaties and Conventions, and Reciprocal Regulations, at Present Subsisting between Great Britain and Foreign Powers*, compiled by Lewis Hertslet, 1:354–56. London: Richard Clay & Sons, 1840.

Unienville, Antoine Marrier. *Statistique de l'Île Maurice et ses dépendances, suivie d'une notice historique sur cette colonie et d'un essai sur l'île de Madagascar.* Paris: Gustave Barba, 1838.

Valette, Jean. "Quelques textes relatifs aux expéditions Malgaches aux Comores." *Bulletin de Madagascar*, no. 304 (1971): 761–64.

van Linschoten, Jan Huygen. *The Voyage of John Huyghen van Linschoten to the East Indies: From the Old English Translation of 1598*. Edited by P. A. Tiele. Vol. 2. London: Printed for the Hakluyt Society, 1885.

van Riebeeck, Jan. *Journal of Jan van Riebeeck*. Edited by Hendrik Bernardus Thom, translated by W. P. L. van Zyl, C. K. Johnman, A. Ravenscroft, J. Smuts, C. van Oordt. 3 vols. Cape Town: Van Riebeeck Society, 1952–58.

Waldegrave, Powle. *An Answer to Mr Boothbies Book, of the Description of the Island of Madagascar.* London: Printed by T. N., 1649.

Walen, A. "Two Years among the Sakalava (Part I)." *Antananarivo Annual and Madagascar Magazine*, no. 5 (1881): 1–12.

Whitecar, William B, Jr.. *Four Years Aboard the Whaleship: Embracing Cruises in the Pacific, Atlantic, Indian, and Antarctic Oceans, in the Years 1855, '6, '7, '8, '9*. Philadelphia: J. B. Lippincott, 1864.

## PUBLISHED SECONDARY SOURCES

Ahuja, Ravi. "State Formation and 'Famine Policy' in Early Colonial South India." In Subramanyam, *Land, Politics, and Trade in South Asia*, 147–85.

Alexander, Andrew. "Negotiation, Trade and the Rituals of Encounter: An Examination of the Slave-Trading Voyage of *De Zon*, 1775–1776." *Itinerario* 31, no. 3 (2007): 39–58.

———. "Shipboard Slave Uprisings on the Malagasy Coast: The '*Meermin*' (1766) and '*De Zon*' (1775)." *Kronos*, no. 33 (2007): 84–111.

Allen, Richard B. "The Constant Demand of the French: The Mascarene Slave Trade and the Worlds of the Indian Ocean and Atlantic during the Eighteenth and Nineteenth Centuries." *Journal of African History* 49, no. 1 (2008): 43–72.

———. *European Slave Trading in the Indian Ocean, 1500–1850*. Athens: Ohio University Press, 2015.

———. *Slaves, Freedmen, and Indentured Laborers in Colonial Mauritius.* Cambridge: Cambridge University Press, 1999.

Allibert, Claude. "Les Hollandais et Madagascar." In Evers and Spindler, *Cultures of Madagascar*, 87–100.

———. *Mayotte: Plaque tournante et microcosme de l'océan Indien occidental: Son histoire avant 1841*. Paris: Anthropos, 1984.

Alpers, Edward A. *East Africa and the Indian Ocean*. Princeton, NJ: Markus Wiener, 2009.

———. "The French Slave Trade in East Africa (1721–1810)." *Cahiers d'études africaines* 10, no. 37 (1970): 80–124.

———. "Gujarat and the Trade of East Africa, c. 1500–1800." In Alpers, *East Africa and the Indian Ocean*, 3–22.

———. *The Indian Ocean in World History*. Oxford: Oxford University Press, 2014.

———. *Ivory and Slaves: Changing Pattern of International Trade in East Central Africa to the Later Nineteenth Century*. Berkeley: University of California Press, 1975.

———. "Littoral Society in the Mozambique Channel." In Alpers, *East Africa and the Indian Ocean*, 167–80.

———. "Madagascar and Mozambique in the Nineteenth Century: The Era of the Sakalava Raids (1800–1820)." *Omaly sy anio* (Université d'Antananarivo) 5–6 (1977): 37–53.

———. "The Somali Community at Aden in the Nineteenth Century." *Northeast African Studies* 8, nos. 2–3 (1986): 143–68.

———. "The Western Indian Ocean as a Regional Food Network in the Nineteenth Century." In Alpers, *East Africa and the Indian Ocean*, 23–38.

Alpers, Edward A., and Matthew S. Hopper. "Parler en son nom? Comprendre les témoignages d'esclaves africains originaires de l'océan Indien (1850–1930)." *Annales: Histoire, sciences sociales* 63, no. 4 (2008): 799–828.

Ames, Glenn J. "An African Eldorado? The Portuguese Quest for Wealth and Power in Mozambique and the Rios de Cuama, C. 1661–1683." *International Journal of African Historical Studies* 31, no. 1 (1998): 91–110.

———. *Colbert, Mercantilism, and the French Quest for Asian Trade*. DeKalb: Northern Illinois University Press, 1996.

Amrith, Sunil S. *Crossing the Bay of Bengal: The Furies of Nature and the Fortunes of Migrants*. Cambridge, MA: Harvard University Press, 2013.

Anderson, J. L. "Piracy and World History: An Economic Perspective on Maritime Predation." *Journal of World History* 6, no. 2 (1995): 175–99.

Andrade, Tonio. "Beyond Guns, Germs, and Steel: European Expansion and Maritime Asia, 1400–1750." *Journal of Early Modern History* 14, no. 1 (2010): 165–86.

———. "The Company's Chinese Pirates: How the Dutch East India Company Tried to Lead a Coalition of Pirates to War against China, 1621–1662." *Journal of World History* 15, no. 4 (2004): 415–44.

———. *How Taiwan Became Chinese: Dutch, Spanish, and Han Colonization in the Seventeenth Century.* New York: Columbia University Press, 2007.

Andrianaivoarivony, Rafolo. "Regards furtifs sur les poteries importées à Madagascar avant l'arrivée des Portugais (VIIIe–début XVIe siècle après J.-C.)." In *Civilisations des mondes insulaires*, edited by Chantal Radimilahy and Narivelo Rajaonarimanana, 337–55. Paris: Karthala, 2011.

Arasaratnam, Sinnappah. "The Rice Trade in Eastern India, 1650–1740." *Modern Asian Studies* 22, no. 3 (1988): 531–49.

Armitage, David, and Sanjay Subrahmanyam. "Introduction: The Age of Revolutions, c. 1760–1840." In *The Age of Revolutions in Global Context, c. 1760–1840*, edited by David Armitage and Sanjay Subrahmanyam, xii–xxxii. London: Palgrave Macmillan, 2010.

Armstrong, James C. "Madagascar and the Slave Trade in the Seventeenth Century." *Omaly sy anio* (Université d'Antananarivo) 17–20 (1983): 211–33.

Armstrong, James C., and Nigel A. Worden. "The Slaves, 1652–1834." In *The Shaping of South African Society, 1652–1840*, edited by Richard Elphick and Hermann Giliomee, 109–83. Middletown, CT: Wesleyan University Press, 1988.

Aslanian, Sebouh. *From the Indian Ocean to the Mediterranean: The Global Trade Networks of Armenian Merchants from New Julfa.* Berkeley: University of California Press, 2011.

Astuti, Rita. *People of the Sea: Identity and Descent among the Vezo of Madagascar.* Cambridge: Cambridge University Press, 1995.

Athale, Anil. *Struggle for Empire: Anglo-Maratha Wars, 1679–1818.* New Delhi: Reliance, 2001.

Atwell, William S. "Another Look at Silver Imports into China, ca. 1635–1644." *Journal of World History* 16, no. 4 (2005): 467–89.

Baldry, John. *Textiles in Yemen: Historical References to Trade and Commerce in Textiles in Yemen from Antiquity to Modern Times.* London: British Museum, 1982.

Ballarin, Marie-Pierre. *Les reliques royales à Madagascar: Source de légitimation et enjeu de pouvoir, XVIIIe–XXe siècles.* Paris: Karthala, 2000.

Banallec, Yves, and Jean-Yves Le Lan. "La Compagnie des Indes et la traite des noirs." In Dodille, *Idées et représentations coloniales*, 33–55.

Bang, Anne K. *Sufis and Scholars of the Sea: Family Networks in East Africa, 1860–1925.* London: RoutledgeCurzon, 2003.

Baré, Jean François. *Sable rouge: Une monarchie du nord-ouest malgache dans l'histoire*. Paris: L'Harmattan, 1980.

Barendse, R. J. *Arabian Seas, 1700–1763*. 4 vols. Leiden: Brill, 2009.

———. *The Arabian Seas: The Indian Ocean World of the Seventeenth Century*. Armonk, NY: M. E. Sharpe, 2002.

———. "Slaving on the Malagasy Coast, 1640–1700." In Evers and Spindler, *Cultures of Madagascar*, 137–56.

Barrett, Christopher B. "Understanding Uneven Agricultural Liberalisation in Madagascar." *Journal of Modern African Studies* 32, no. 3 (1994): 449–76.

Battistini, René, and Pierre Vérin. "Irodo et la tradition Vohémarienne: Les découverts d'Irodo et les civilisations du nord-est." *Revue de Madagascar* 36 (1966). Reprinted in Rakotoarisoa, *Arabes et Islamisés à Madagascar*, 22–46.

Bauer, Arnold J. *Goods, Power, History: Latin America's Material Culture*. Cambridge: Cambridge University Press, 2001.

Bayly, C. A. *The Birth of the Modern World, 1780–1914: Global Connections and Comparisons*. Malden, MA: Blackwell, 2004.

Beaujard, Philippe. "East Africa, the Comoros Islands and Madagascar before the Sixteenth Century: On a Neglected Part of the World System." *Azania* 42, no. 1 (2007): 15–35.

———. *Les mondes de l'océan Indien*. 2 vols. Paris: Armand Colin, 2012.

Behrendt, Stephen D. "Crew Mortality in the Transatlantic Slave Trade in the Eighteenth Century." In *Routes to Slavery: Direction, Ethnicity and Mortality in the Atlantic Slave Trade*, edited by David Eltis and David Richardson, 49–71. London: Frank Cass, 1997.

———. "Seasonality in the Trans-Atlantic Slave Trade." *Voyages: The Trans-Atlantic Slave Trade Database*. 2008. http://www.slavevoyages.org/assessment/essays#.

Bentley, Jerry H. "Sea and Ocean Basins as Frameworks of Historical Analysis." *Geographical Review* 89, no. 2 (1999): 215–24.

Berg, Gerald M. "Riziculture and the Founding of Monarchy in Imerina." *Journal of African History* 22, no. 3 (1981): 289–308.

———. "The Sacred Musket: Tactics, Technology, and Power in Eighteenth-Century Madagascar." *Comparative Studies in Society and History* 27, no. 2 (1985): 261–79.

Berthelot, Lilian. *La petite Mascareigne: Aspects de l'histoire de Rodrigues*. Port-Louis, Mauritius: Centre Culturel Africain, 2002.

Bethencourt, Francisco. "Political Configurations and Local Powers." In Bethencourt and Curto, *Portuguese Oceanic Expansion*, 197–254.

Bethencourt, Francisco, and Diogo Ramada Curto. Introduction to Bethencourt and Curto, *Portuguese Oceanic Expansion*, 1–18. Translated by Neil Safier.

———, eds. *Portuguese Oceanic Expansion, 1400–1800*. Cambridge: Cambridge University Press, 2007.

Bialuschewski, Arne. "Daniel Defoe, Nathaniel Mist, and the 'General History of the Pyrates.'" *Papers of the Bibliographical Society of America* 98, no. 1 (2004): 21–38.

———. "Pirates, Slavers, and the Indigenous Population in Madagascar, c. 1690–1715." *International Journal of African Historical Studies* 38 (2005): 401–25.

———. "Thomas Bowrey's Madagascar Manuscript of 1708." *History in Africa* 34 (2007): 31–42.

———. "*A True Account of the Design, and Advantages of the South-Sea Trade*: Profits, Propaganda, and the Peace Preliminaries of 1711." *Huntington Library Quarterly* 73, no. 2 (2010): 273–85.

Bissoondoyal, U., and S. B. C. Servansing, eds. *Slavery in South West Indian Ocean*. Moka, Mauritius: Mahatma Gandhi Institute, 1989.

Blanchy, Sophie. *Karana et Banians: Les communautés commerçantes d'origine indienne à Madagascar*. Paris: L'Harmattan, 1995.

Bloch, Maurice. "The Ethnohistory of Madagascar." *Ethnohistory* 48, nos. 1–2 (2001): 293–99.

Boivin, Nicole, Alison Crowther, Richard Helm, and Dorian Q. Fuller. "East Africa and Madagascar in the Indian Ocean World." *Journal of World Prehistory* 26, no. 3 (2013): 213–81.

Bose, Sugata. *A Hundred Horizons: The Indian Ocean in the Age of Global Empire*. Cambridge, MA: Harvard University Press, 2006.

———. "Space and Time on the Indian Ocean Rim: Theory and History." In Fawaz and Bayly, *Modernity and Culture*, 365–88.

Bouchon, Genevieve, and Denys Lombard. "The Indian Ocean in the Fifteenth Century." In *India and the Indian Ocean, 1500–1800*, edited by Ashin Das Gupta and Michael N. Pearson, 46–70. Calcutta: Oxford University Press, 1987.

Bowen, H. V. *The Business of Empire: The East India Company and Imperial Britain, 1756–1833*. Cambridge: Cambridge University Press, 2005.

Boxberger, Linda. *On the Edge of Empire: Hadhramawt, Emigration, and the Indian Ocean, 1880s–1930s*. Albany: State University of New York Press, 2002.

Boxer, C. R. *Portuguese Conquest and Commerce in Southern Asia, 1500–1750*. London: Variorum Reprints, 1985.

———. *The Portuguese Seaborne Empire, 1415–1825*. London: Hutchinson, 1969.

Boyajian, James C. *Portuguese Trade in Asia under the Habsburgs, 1580–1640*. Baltimore: Johns Hopkins University Press, 1993.

Brockey, Liam Matthew. "Introduction: Nodes of Empire." In Brockey, *Portuguese Colonial Cities*, 1–16.

———, ed. *Portuguese Colonial Cities in the Early Modern World*. Burlington, VT: Ashgate, 2008.

Brouwer, C. G. *Al-Mukha: Profile of a Yemeni Seaport as Sketched by Servants of the Dutch East India Company (VOC), 1614–1640*. Amsterdam: D'Fluyte Rarob, 1997.

———. "Non-Western Shipping Movements in the Red Sea and Gulf of Aden during the 2nd and 3rd Decades of the 17th Century, according to the Records of the Dutch East India Company." Pts. 1 and 2. *Die Welt des Islams* 31, no. 2 (1991): 105–67; 32, no. 1 (1992): 6–40.

Brown, Lester R. "The New Geopolitics of Food." *Foreign Policy*, no. 186 (2011): 54–63.

Bruijn, Jaap R. "Between Batavia and the Cape: Shipping Patterns of the Dutch East India Company." *Journal of Southeast Asian Studies* 11, no. 2 (1980): 251–65.

———. *Commanders of Dutch East India Ships in the Eighteenth Century*. Woodbridge, Suffolk: Boydell, 2011.

Bruijn, Jaap R., and Femme S. Gaastra, eds. *Ships, Sailors and Spices: East India Companies and Their Shipping in the 16th, 17th and 18th Centuries*. Amsterdam: NEHA, 1993.

Bruijn, Jaap R., Femme S. Gaastra, and Ivo Schöffer. *Dutch-Asiatic Shipping in the 17th and 18th Centuries*. 3 vols. The Hague: Martinus Nijhoff, 1979–87.

Burke, Edmund, III. "The Big Story: Human History, Energy Regimes, and the Environment." In *The Environment and World History*, edited by Edmund Burke III and Kenneth Pomeranz, 33–53. Berkeley: University of California Press, 2009.

Burney, David A., Lida Pigott Burney, Laurie R. Godfrey, William L. Jungers, Steven M. Goodman, Henry T. Wright, and A. J. Timothy Jull. "A Chronology for Late Prehistoric Madagascar." *Journal of Human Evolution* 47, nos. 1–2 (2004): 25–63.

Campbell, Gwyn. "Africa, the Indian Ocean World, and the 'Early Modern': Historiographical Conventions and Problems." In *Africa, Empire, and Globalization: Essays in Honor of A. G. Hopkins*, edited by Toyin Falola and Emily Brownell, 81–92. Durham, NC: Carolina Academic Press, 2011.

———. *David Griffiths and the Missionary "History of Madagascar."* Leiden: Brill, 2012.

———. "Disease, Cattle, and Slaves: The Development of Trade between Natal and Madagascar, 1875–1904." *African Economic History* 19 (1990): 105–33.

———. *An Economic History of Imperial Madagascar, 1750–1895: The Rise and Fall of an Island Empire*. Cambridge: Cambridge University Press, 2005.
———. "Forest Depletion in Imperial Madagascar, c. 1790–1861." In Evers et al., *Contest for Land in Madagascar*, 63–95. Leiden: Brill, 2013.
———. "Introduction: Slavery and Other Forms of Unfree Labour in the Indian Ocean World." In *The Structure of Slavery in Indian Ocean Africa and Asia*, edited by Gwyn Campbell, vii–xxxi. London: Frank Cass, 2004.
———. "Madagascar and Mozambique in the Slave Trade of the Western Indian Ocean, 1800–1861." In *The Economics of the Indian Ocean Slave Trade in the Nineteenth Century*, edited by William Gervase Clarence-Smith, 166–93. London: Frank Cass, 1989.
———. "Madagascar and the Slave Trade, 1810–1895." *Journal of African History* 22, no. 2 (1981): 203–27.
———. "Piracy in the Indian Ocean World." *Interventions* 16, no. 6 (2014): 775–94.
———. "The Role of Africa in the Emergence of the 'Indian Ocean World' Global Economy." In Gupta et al., *Eyes across the Water*, 170–96.
———. "Servitude and the Changing Face of the Demand for Labor in the Indian Ocean World, c. 1800–1900." In Harms et al., *Indian Ocean Slavery in the Age of Abolition*, 23–44.
———. "Slave Trades and the Indian Ocean World." In *India in Africa, Africa in India: Indian Ocean Cosmopolitanisms*, edited by John C. Hawley, 17–51. Bloomington: Indiana University Press, 2008.
———. "The Structure of Trade in Madagascar, 1750–1810." *International Journal of African Historical Studies* 26, no. 1 (1993): 111–48.
Carney, Judith A. *Black Rice: The African Origins of Rice Cultivation in the Americas*. Cambridge, MA: Harvard University Press, 2001.
Carney, Judith A., and Richard Nicholas Rosomoff. *In the Shadow of Slavery: Africa's Botanical Legacy in the Atlantic World*. Berkeley: University of California Press, 2009.
Casale, Giancarlo. *The Ottoman Age of Exploration*. Oxford: Oxford University Press, 2010.
Chan Low, Jocelyn. *"La VOC, t'Eylandt Mauritius et Rodrigues": Avec le voyage de Wolfert Harmensz vers les Îles Rodrigues et Maurice, 1601*. Port-Louis, Mauritius: National Library, 2001.
Chanudet, Claude, and Jean-Aimé Rakotoarisoa. *Mohéli: Une île des Comores à la recherche de son identité*. Paris: L'Harmattan, 2000.
Chapus, G. S., and André Dandouau. *Manuel d'histoire de Madagascar*. Paris: Larose, 1961.
Chastanet, Monique, Gérard Chouin, Dora de Lima, and Thomas Guindeuil, eds. "Eating and Drinking in Africa before the 20th Century: Cuisines,

Exchanges, Social Constructions." Special issue, *Afriques: Débats, methods et terrains d'histoire* 5 (2014). https://afriques.revues.org/1346.

Chaudhuri, K. N. *Asia before Europe: Economy and Civilisation of the Indian Ocean from the Rise of Islam to 1750*. Cambridge: Cambridge University Press, 1990.

———. "The English East India Company's Shipping (c. 1660–1760)." In Bruijn and Gaastra, *Ships, Sailors, and Spices*, 49–80.

———. *Trade and Civilisation in the Indian Ocean: An Economic History from the Rise of Islam to 1750*. Cambridge: Cambridge University Press, 1985.

Chazan-Gillic, Suzanne. "Le fitampoha de 1968 ou l'efficacité symbolique du mythe de la royauté Sakalava dans l'actualité politique et économique malgache." In Raison-Jourde, *Les souverains*, 451–76.

Cheke, Anthony, and Julian Hume. *Lost Land of the Dodo: The Ecological History of Mauritius, Réunion, and Rodrigues*. New Haven, CT: Yale University Press, 2010.

Chouzour, Sultan. *Le pouvoir de l'honneur: Tradition et contestation en Grande Comore*. Paris: L'Harmattan, 1994.

Christopher, Emma. *Slave Ship Sailors and Their Captive Cargoes, 1730–1807*. New York: Cambridge University Press, 2006.

Clulow, Adam. *The Company and the Shogun: The Dutch Encounter with Tokugawa Japan*. New York: Columbia University Press, 2014.

———. "The Pirate and the Warlord." *Journal of Early Modern History* 16, no. 6 (2012): 523–42.

Cook, Edward R., Kevin J. Anchukaitis, Brendan M. Buckley, Rosanne D. D'Arrigo, Gordon C. Jacoby, and William E. Wright. "Asian Monsoon Failure and Megadrought during the Last Millennium." *Science*, n.s., 328, no. 5977 (23 April 2010): 486–89.

Crossland, Zoë. *Ancestral Encounters in Highland Madagascar: Material Signs and Traces of the Dead*. Cambridge: Cambridge University Press, 2014.

Curry-Machado, Jonathan. "Global Histories, Imperial Commodities, Local Interactions: An Introduction." In *Global Histories, Imperial Commodities, Local Interactions*, edited by Jonathan Curry-Machado, 1–14. New York: Palgrave Macmillan, 2013.

Curtin, Philip D. *Cross-Cultural Trade in World History*. Cambridge: Cambridge University Press, 1984.

———. *Economic Change in Precolonial Africa: Senegambia in the Era of the Slave Trade*. Madison: University of Wisconsin Press, 1975.

Davis, Mike. *Late Victorian Holocausts: El Niño Famines and the Making of the Third World*. London: Verso, 2001.

Degryse, K., and J. Parmentier. "Maritime Aspects of the Ostend Trade to Mocha, India and China (1715–1732)." In Bruijn and Gaastra, *Ships, Sailors and Spices*, 139–75.

Deng, Kent G. "Miracle or Mirage? Foreign Silver, China's Economy and Globalization from the Sixteenth to the Nineteenth Centuries." *Pacific Economic Review* 13, no. 3 (2008): 320–57.

Deschamps, Hubert Jules. *Les pirates à Madagascar aux XVIIe et XVIIIe siècles*. Paris: Berger-Levrault, 1949.

Dewar, Robert E. "Early Human Settlers and Their Impact on Madagascar's Landscapes," in Scales, *Conservation and Environmental Management*, 44–64.

———. "Of Nets and Trees: Untangling the Reticulate and Dendritic in Madagascar's Prehistory." *World Archaeology* 26, no. 3 (1995): 301–18.

———. "Processual Assessment of Population Changes in Western Avaradrano." In *Early State Formation in Central Madagascar: An Archaeological Survey of Western Avaradrano*, edited by Henry Tutwiler Wright, 101–3. Ann Arbor: Museum of Anthropology, University of Michigan, 2007.

Dewar, Robert E., and Henry T. Wright. "The Culture History of Madagascar." *Journal of World Prehistory* 7, no. 4 (1993): 417–66.

Dez, Jacques. "De l'influence arabe à Madagascar à l'aide de faits de linguistique." In Rakotoarisoa, *Arabes et Islamisés à Madagascar*, 1–20.

Dietler, Michael. "Theorizing the Feast: Rituals of Consumption, Commensal Politics, and Power in African Contexts." In *Feasts: Archaeological and Ethnographic Perspectives on Food, Politics, and Power*, edited by Michael Dietler and Brian Hayden, 65–114. Tuscaloosa: University of Alabama Press, 2010.

Disney, A. R. *A History of Portugal and the Portuguese Empire*. 2 vols. Cambridge: Cambridge University Press, 2009.

Dodille, Norbert, ed. *Idées et représentations coloniales dans l'océan Indien*. Paris: Presses de l'Université Paris-Sorbonne, 2009.

Douteau, Robert. "La croisière extraordinaire de la galiote 'St Pierre et St Paul' dans la mer de Béring et sur les côtes du Japon (1771)." *Monumenta Nipponica* 1, no. 2 (1938): 439–50.

Driessen, Henk. "Mediterranean Port Cities: Cosmopolitanism Reconsidered." *History and Anthropology* 16, no. 1 (2005): 129–41.

Dubins, Barbara Dorothy. "A Political History of the Comoro Islands, 1795–1886." PhD Diss., Boston University, 1972.

Dubois, Colette. "The Red Sea Ports during the Revolution in Transportation, 1800–1914." In Fawaz and Bayly, *Modernity and Culture*, 58–74.

Duindam, Jeroen. "Early Modern Europe: Beyond the Strictures of Modernization and National Historiography." *European History Quarterly* 40, no. 4 (2010): 606–23.

Dull, Jonathan R. *The French Navy and the Seven Years' War*. Lincoln: University of Nebraska Press, 2005.

Duncan, T. Bentley. *Atlantic Islands: Madeira, the Azores, and the Cape Verdes in Seventeenth-Century Commerce and Navigation*. Chicago: University of Chicago Press, 1972.

Dvoichenko-Markov, Eufrosina. "Benjamin Franklin and Count M. A. Benyowski." *Proceedings of the American Philosophical Society* 99, no. 6 (1955): 405–17.

Ellis, Stephen. "The History of Sovereigns in Madagascar: New Light from Old Sources." In *Madagascar revisitée: En voyage avec Françoise Raison-Jourde*, edited by Didier Nativel and Faranirina V. Rajaonah, 405–31. Paris: Karthala, 2009.

———. "Tom and Toakafo: The Betsimisaraka Kingdom and State Formation in Madagascar, 1715–1750." *Journal of African History* 48, no. 3. (2007): 439–55.

Ellis, Stephen, and Solofo Randrianja. "Les archives de la compagnie néerlandaise des Indes orientales et l'histoire de Madagascar: L'expédition du navire de la V.O.C. le *Schuylenburg*, septembre 1752." In Rakoto, *La route des esclaves*, 47–73.

El-Sharkawy, Mabrouk A. "Drought-Tolerant Cassava for Africa, Asia, and Latin America." *BioScience* 43, no. 7 (1993): 441–51.

Eltis, David. "The Slave Trade and Commercial Agriculture in an African Context." In *Commercial Agriculture, the Slave Trade and Slavery in Atlantic Africa*, edited by Robin Law, Suzanne Schwarz, and Silke Strickrodt, 28–53. Woodbridge, Suffolk: James Currey, 2013.

Erikson, Emily. *Between Monopoly and Free Trade: The English East India Company, 1600–1757*. Princeton, NJ: Princeton University Press, 2014.

Evers, Sandra J. T. M. *Constructing History, Culture, and Inequality: The Betsileo in the Extreme Southern Highlands of Madagascar.* Leiden: Brill, 2002.

Evers, Sandra J. T. M., Gwyn Campbell, and Michael Lambek, eds. *Contest for Land in Madagascar: Environment, Ancestors and Development*. Leiden: Brill, 2013.

———. "Land Competition and Human-Environment Relations in Madagascar." In Evers et al., *Contest for Land in Madagascar*, 1–19.

Evers, Sandra, and Marc Spindler, eds. *Cultures of Madagascar: Ebb and Flow of Influences*. Leiden: International Institute for Asian Studies, 1995.

Ewald, Janet J. "African Bondsmen, Freedmen, and the Maritime Proletariats of the Northwestern Indian Ocean World, c. 1500–1900." In Harms et al., *Indian Ocean Slavery in the Age of Abolition*, 200–22.

———. "Crossers of the Sea: Slaves, Freedmen, and Other Migrants in the Northwestern Indian Ocean, c. 1750–1914." *American Historical Review* 105, no. 1 (2000): 69–91.

Fagan, Brian. *Fish on Friday: Feasting, Fasting, and the Discovery of the New World*. New York: Basic Books, 2006.

Fawaz, Leila Tarazi, and C. A. Bayly, eds. *Modernity and Culture: From the Mediterranean to the Indian Ocean*. New York: Columbia University Press, 2002.

Feeley-Harnik, Gillian. *A Green Estate: Restoring Independence in Madagascar.* Washington, DC: Smithsonian Institution Press, 1991.

———. "The King's Men in Madagascar Slavery, Citizenship and Sakalava Monarchy." *Africa: Journal of the International African Institute* 52, no. 2 (1982): 31–50.

———. "Sakalava Royal Work: A Study of Aesthetics in Labor and Government." PhD diss., New York University, 1976.

Ferrand, Gabriel. *Les musulmans à Madagascar et aux îles Comores*. 3 vols. Paris: Ernest Leroux, 1891–1902.

Fields-Black, Edda L. *Deep Roots: Rice Farmers in West Africa and the African Diaspora*. Bloomington: Indiana University Press, 2008.

Filliot, Jean-Michel. *La traite des esclaves vers les Mascareignes au XVIIIe siècle*. Paris: ORSTOM, 1974.

———. "La traite vers l'Île de France." In Bissoondoyal and Servansing, *Slavery in South West Indian Ocean*, 84–95.

Fisher, Michael H. "Working across the Seas: Indian Maritime Labourers in India, Britain, and in Between, 1600–1857." In "Coolies, Capital, and Colonialism," supplement, *International Review of Social History* 51, no. S14 (2006): 21–45.

Fleisher, Jeffrey. "Rituals of Consumption and the Politics of Feasting on the Eastern African Coast, AD 700–1500." *Journal of World Prehistory* 23, no. 4 (2010): 195–217.

Flynn, Dennis O., and Arturo Giráldez. "Cycles of Silver: Global Economic Unity through the Mid-Eighteenth Century." *Journal of World History* 13, no. 2 (2002): 391–427.

———. "Globalization Began in 1571." In *Globalization and Global History*, edited by Barry K. Gills and William R. Thompson, 232–47. New York: Routledge, 2012.

Foster, William. "An English Settlement in Madagascar in 1645–6." *English Historical Review* 27, no. 106 (1912): 239–50.

Freitag, Ulrike. *Indian Ocean Migrants and State Formation in Hadhramaut: Reforming the Homeland*. Leiden: Brill, 2003.

Frykman, Niklas, Clare Anderson, Lex Heerma van Voss, and Marcus Rediker. "Mutiny and Maritime Radicalism in the Age of Revolution: An Introduction." In "Mutiny and Maritime Radicalism in the Age of Revolution: A Global Survey," supplement, *International Review of Social History* 58, no. S21 (2013): 1–14.

Furber, Holden. *Rival Empires of Trade in the Orient, 1600–1800*. Minneapolis: University of Minnesota Press, 1976.

Gaastra, Femme S. "Soldiers and Merchants: Aspects of Migration from Europe to Asia in the Dutch East India Company in the Eighteenth Century." In *Migration, Trade, and Slavery in an Expanding World: Essays in Honor of Pieter Emmer*, edited by Wim Klooster, 99–116. Leiden: Brill, 2009.

Games, Alison. *The Web of Empire: English Cosmopolitans in an Age of Expansion, 1560–1660*. Oxford: Oxford University Press, 2008.

Garenne, Michel. "An Atypical Urban Famine: Antananarivo, Madagascar, 1985–1986." In *The New Famines: Why Famines Persist in an Era of Globalization*, edited by Stephen Devereux, 178–96. New York: Routledge, 2006.

Gaspar, David Barry. Review of *The Diligent: A Voyage through the Worlds of the Slave Trade*, by Robert Harms. *American Historical Review* 109, no. 1 (2004): 144–45.

Gevrey, Alfred. *Essai sur les Comores*. Pondichery: A. Saligny, 1870.

Godinho, V. Magelhães. "The Portuguese and the 'Carreira da India,' 1497–1810." In Bruijn and Gaastra, *Ships, Sailors and Spices*, 1–47.

Ghosh, Devleena, and Stephen Muecke, eds. *Cultures of Trade: Indian Ocean Exchanges*. Newcastle: Cambridge Scholars Publishing, 2007.

Gilbert, Erik. "Coastal East Africa and the Western Indian Ocean: Long-Distance Trade, Empire, Migration, and Regional Unity, 1750–1970." *History Teacher* 36, no. 1 (2002): 7–34.

Gøbel, E. "Danish Companies' Shipping to Asia, 1616–1807." In Bruijn and Gaastra, *Ships, Sailors and Spices*, 99–120.

Goedefroit, Sophie. *À l'ouest de Madagascar: Les Sakalava du Menabe*. Paris: Karthala, 1998.

Goedefroit, Sophie, and Jacques Lombard, *Andolo: L'art funéraire Sakalava à Madagascar*. Paris: Biro, 2007.

Goldstone, Jack A. "The Problem of the 'Early Modern' World." *Journal of the Economic and Social History of the Orient* 41, no. 3 (1998): 249–84.

Goodman, Steven M., and Jonathan P. Benstead, eds. *The Natural History of Madagascar*. Chicago: University of Chicago Press, 2006.

Gordon, Stewart. *The Marathas: 1600–1818*. Cambridge: Cambridge University Press, 1993.

Grandidier, Alfred, and Guillaume Grandidier. *Les Anglais à Madagascar au XVIIe siècle*. Paris: G. de Malherbe, 1903.

Green, Toby, ed. *Brokers of Change: Atlantic Commerce and Cultures in Precolonial Western Africa*. Oxford: Oxford University Press, 2012.

———. *The Rise of the Trans-Atlantic Slave Trade in Western Africa, 1300–1589*. Cambridge: Cambridge University Press, 2012.

Grove, Richard. "Conserving Eden: The (European) East India Companies and Their Environmental Policies on St. Helena, Mauritius and in Western India, 1660 to 1854." *Comparative Studies in Society and History* 35, no. 2 (1993): 318–51.

———. *Ecology, Climate and Empire: Colonialism and Global Environmental History, 1400–1940*. Cambridge: White Horse, UK, 1997.

———. "The Great El Niño of 1789–93 and Its Global Consequences: Reconstructing an Extreme Climate Event in World Environmental History." *Medieval History Journal* 10, nos. 1–2 (2007): 75–98.

Guelke, Leonard. "Frontier Settlement in Early Dutch South Africa." *Annals of the Association of American Geographers* 66, no. 1 (1976): 25–42.

Gupta, Pamila, Isabel Hofmeyr, and Michael N. Pearson, eds. *Eyes across the Water: Navigating the Indian Ocean*. Pretoria: Unisa Press, 2010.

Hafkin, Nancy Jane. "Trade, Society, and Politics in Northern Mozambique, c. 1753–1913." PhD diss., Boston University, 1973.

Haider, Najaf. "The Network of Monetary Exchange in the Indian Ocean Trade, 1200–1700." In *Cross Currents and Community Networks: The History of the Indian Ocean World*, edited by Himanshu Prabha Ray and Edward A. Alpers, 181–205. New York: Oxford University Press, 2007.

Håkansson, N. Thomas. "The Human Ecology of World Systems in East Africa: The Impact of the Ivory Trade." *Human Ecology* 32, no. 5 (2004): 561–91.

Hall, Kenneth R. *A History of Early Southeast Asia: Maritime Trade and Societal Development, 100–1500*. Lanham, MD: Rowman & Littlefield, 2011.

———. "Local and International Trade and Traders in the Straits of the Melaka Region: 600–1500." *Journal of the Economic and Social History of the Orient* 47, no. 2 (2004): 213–60.

Harms, Robert. *The Diligent: A Voyage through the Worlds of the Slave Trade*. New York: Basic Books, 2002.

———. "Introduction: Indian Ocean Slavery in the Age of Abolition," in Harms et al., *Indian Ocean Slavery*, 1–19.

Harms, Robert, Bernard K. Freamon, and David W. Blight, eds. *Indian Ocean Slavery in the Age of Abolition*. New Haven: Yale University Press, 2013.

Haudrère, Philippe. "The 'Compagnie des Indes' and Maritime Matters (c. 1725–1770)." In Bruijn and Gaastra, *Ships, Sailors and Spices*, 81–97.

———. *La compagnie française des Indes au XVIIIe siècle*. 2 vols. 2nd ed. Paris: Les Indes savantes, 2005.

Havik, Philip J., and Toby Green. "Introduction: Brokerage and the Role of Western Africa in the Atlantic World." In Green, *Brokers of Change*, 1–24.

Hawthorne, Walter. *From Africa to Brazil: Culture, Identity, and an Atlantic Slave Trade, 1600–1830*. Cambridge: Cambridge University Press, 2010.

———. *Planting Rice and Harvesting Slaves: Transformations along the Guinea-Bissau Coast, 1400–1900*. Portsmouth, NH: Heinemann, 2003.

Hébert, Jean-Claude. "Sur des ports esclavagistes de la côte nord-ouest de Madagascar dont le nom est devenu obsolète: Maringado ou Moringambo et Lulangani/Langany/Morumgany." In *Navires, ports, itinéraires*, edited by Claude Allibert, 11–60. Paris: Institut national des langues et civilisations orientales, 1999.

Heeringa, K. "De Nederlanders op Mauritius en Madagascar." In *De Indische gids*, edited by C. E. van Kesteren, R. A. van Sandick, and J. E. de Meyier, 864–92. Amsterdam: J. H. de Bussy, 1895.

Heuzé, V., G. Tran, and M. Boval. "Black Gram (Vigna Mungo)." In *Feedipedia, a Programme by INRA, CIRAD, AFZ and FAO*. Last modified 30 March 2016. http://www.feedipedia.org/node/236.

Ho, Engseng. *The Graves of Tarim: Genealogy and Mobility across the Indian Ocean*. Berkeley: University of California Press, 2006.

Hooper, Jane. "An Empire in the Indian Ocean: The Sakalava Empire of Madagascar." PhD diss., Emory University, 2010.

———. "*Flux du sang et sauterelles:* How the People and Environment of Madagascar Thwarted French Commercial Expansion." *Proceedings of the Western Society for French History* 37 (2009): 49–60.

———. "Pirates and Kings: Power on the Shores of Early Modern Madagascar and the Indian Ocean." *Journal of World History* 22, no. 2 (2011): 215–42.

Hooper, Jane, and David Eltis. "The Indian Ocean in Transatlantic Slavery." *Slavery & Abolition* 34, no. 3 (2013): 353–75.

Horton, Mark. *Shanga: The Archaeology of a Muslim Trading Community on the Coast of East Africa*. London: British Institute in Eastern Africa, 1996.

Horton, Mark, and John Middleton. *The Swahili: The Social Landscape of a Mercantile Society*. Oxford: Blackwell, 2000.

Hume, Douglas W. "Swidden Agriculture and Conservation in Eastern Madagascar: Stakeholder Perspectives and Cultural Belief Systems." *Conservation and Society* 4, no. 2 (2006): 287–303.

Inikori, J. E. *Africans and the Industrial Revolution in England: A Study in International Trade and Economic Development*. New York: Cambridge University Press, 2002.

———. "The Import of Firearms into West Africa 1750–1807: A Quantitative Analysis." *Journal of African History* 18, no. 3 (1977): 339–68.

"International Human Development Indicators." 2014, United Nations Development Programme, Human Development Reports. Accessed 5 January 2017. http://hdr.undp.org/sites/default/files/ranking.pdf.

Ipsen, Pernille. *Daughters of the Trade: Atlantic Slavers and Interracial Marriage on the Gold Coast*. Philadelphia: University of Pennsylvania Press, 2015.

Irigoin, Alejandra. "The End of a Silver Era: The Consequences of the Breakdown of the Spanish Peso Standard in China and the United States, 1780s–1850s." *Journal of World History* 20, no. 2 (2009): 207–44.

Jaovelo-Dzao, Robert. *Mythes, rites et transes à Madagascar.* Paris: Karthala, 1996.

Jones, William O. *Manioc in Africa*. Stanford, CA: Stanford University Press, 1959.

Judd, Jacob. "Frederick Philipse and the Madagascar Trade." *New York Historical Society Quarterly* 55, no. 4 (1971): 354–74.

Jury, M. R. "The Climate of Madagascar." In Goodman and Benstead, *Natural History of Madagascar*, 75–87.

Karasch, Mary. "Manioc." In Kiple and Ornelas, *The Cambridge World History of Food*, 1:181–87.

Kaufmann, Jeffrey C. "Doubting Modernity for Madagascar's Cactus Pastoralists." *History in Africa* 38 (2011): 123–51.

———. "Forget the Numbers: The Case of a Madagascar Famine." *History in Africa* 27 (2000): 143–57.

———. "Prickly Pear Cactus and Pastoralism in Southwest Madagascar." *Ethnology* 43, no. 4 (2004): 345–61.

———. "*La Question des Raketa*: Colonial Struggles with Prickly Pear Cactus in Southern Madagascar, 1900–1923." *Ethnohistory* 48, nos. 1–2 (2001): 87–121.

Kearney, Milo. *The Indian Ocean in World History.* London: Routledge, 2004.

Kennedy, Paul. *The Rise and Fall of the Great Powers: Economic Change and Military Conflict from 1500 to 2000*. New York: Random House, 1987.

Kent, Raymond K. *Early Kingdoms in Madagascar, 1500–1700*. New York: Holt, Rinehart and Winston, 1970.

———. "Madagascar and Africa: II. The Sakalava, Maroserana, Dady and Tromba before 1700." *Journal of African History* 9, no. 4 (1968): 517–46.

———. "Note sur l'introduction et la propagation du manioc à Madagascar." *Terre Malgache*, 5 (1969): 177–83.

Kiple, Kenneth F. *A Movable Feast: Ten Millennia of Food Globalization*. Cambridge: Cambridge University Press, 2007.

Kiple, Kenneth F., and Kriemhild Coneè Ornelas, eds. *The Cambridge World History of Food*. 2 vols. Cambridge: Cambridge University Press, 2000.

Klein, Herbert S. *The Atlantic Slave Trade*. 2nd ed. Cambridge: Cambridge University Press, 2010.

Klein, Martin A. "The Slave Trade and Decentralized Societies." *Journal of African History* 42, no. 1 (2001): 49–65.

Koninckx, C. "The Swedish East India Company (1731–1807)." In Bruijn and Gaastra, *Ships, Sailors and Spices*, 121–38.

Kottak, Conrad P. "The Process of State Formation in Madagascar." *American Ethnologist* 4, no. 1 (1977): 136–55.

Kurlansky, Mark. *Cod: A Biography of the Fish That Changed the World*. New York: Penguin Books, 1998.

Kusimba, Chapurukha Makokha. *The Rise and Fall of Swahili States*. Walnut Creek, CA: Alta Mira, 1999.

La Fleur, James D. *Fusion Foodways of Africa's Gold Coast in the Atlantic Era*. Leiden: Brill, 2012.

Lambek, Michael. "Reflections on the 'Ethno-' in Malagasy Ethnohistory." *Ethnohistory* 48, nos. 1–2 (2001): 301–8.

———. "The Sakalava Poiesis of History: Realizing the Past through Spirit Possession in Madagascar." *American Ethnologist* 25, no. 2 (1998): 106–27.

———. "The Value of Coins in a Sakalava Polity: Money, Death, and Historicity in Mahajanga, Madagascar." *Comparative Studies in Society and History* 43, no. 4 (2001): 735–62.

Lamphear, John. Introduction to *African Military History*, edited by John Lamphear, xi–xli. Burlington, VT: Ashgate, 2007.

Larson, Pier M. "A Census of Slaves Exported from Central Madagascar to the Mascarenes between 1769 and 1820." In *L'esclavage à Madagascar: Aspects historiques et résurgences contemporaines: Actes du colloque international sur l'esclavage, Antananarivo (24–28 septembre 1996)*, edited by Ignace Rakoto, 131–45. Antananarivo: Institut de civilisations, Musée d'art et d'archéologie, 1997.

———. "Colonies Lost: God, Hunger, and Conflict in Anosy (Madagascar) to 1674." *Comparative Studies of South Asia, Africa and the Middle East* 27, no. 2 (2007): 345–66.

———. "A Cultural Politics of Bedchamber Construction and Progressive Dining in Antananarivo: Ritual Inversions during the *Fandroana* of 1817." In *Ancestors, Power and History in Madagascar*, edited by Karen Middleton, 37–70. Leiden: Brill, 1999.

———. "Enslaved Malagasy and 'Le Travail de La Parole' in the Pre-Revolutionary Mascarenes." *Journal of African History* 48, no. 3 (2007): 457–79.

———. "Fragments of an Indian Ocean Life: Aristide Corroller between Islands and Empires." *Journal of Social History* 45, no. 2 (2011): 366–89.

———. *History and Memory in the Age of Enslavement: Becoming Merina in Highland Madagascar, 1770–1822*. Portsmouth, NH: Heinemann, 2000.

———. "Multiple Narratives, Gendered Voices: Remembering the Past in Highland Central Madagascar." *International Journal of African Historical Studies* 28, no. 2 (1995): 295–325.

———. *Ocean of Letters: Language and Creolization in an Indian Ocean Diaspora*. Cambridge: Cambridge University Press, 2009.

———. "Reconsidering Trauma, Identity, and the African Diaspora: Enslavement and Historical Memory in Nineteenth-Century Highland Madagascar." *William and Mary Quarterly* 56, no. 2 (1999): 335–62.

———. "The Route of the Slave from Highland Madagascar to the Mascarenes: Commercial Organization, 1770–1820." In Rakoto, *La route des esclaves*, 119–80.

Law, Robin. *The Slave Coast of West Africa, 1550–1750: The Impact of the Atlantic Slave Trade on an African Society*. Oxford: Oxford University Press, 1991.

Lawson, Philip. *The East India Company: A History*. New York: Routledge, 2014.

Leib, Arthur. "The Mystical Significance of Colours in the Life of the Natives of Madagascar." *Folklore* 57, no. 3 (1946): 128–33.

Lieberman, Victor B. *Strange Parallels: Southeast Asia in Global Context, c. 800–1830*. Vol. 1, *Integration on the Mainland*. New York: Cambridge University Press, 2003.

———. *Strange Parallels: Southeast Asia in Global Context, c. 800–1830*. Vol. 2, *Mainland Mirrors: Europe, Japan, China, South Asia, and the Islands*. Cambridge: Cambridge University Press, 2009.

Lincoln, Margarette. *British Pirates and Society, 1680–1730*. London: Ashgate, 2014.

Lindsay, Lisa A. "Extraversion, Creolization, and Dependency in the Atlantic Slave Trade." *Journal of African History* 55, no. 2 (2014): 135–45.

Linebaugh, Peter, and Marcus Rediker. *The Many-Headed Hydra: Sailors, Slaves, Commoners, and the Hidden History of the Revolutionary Atlantic*. Boston: Beacon Press, 2000.

Liszkowski, Henri Daniel. *Mayotte et les Comores: Escales sur la route des Indes aux XVe et XVIIe siècles*. Mamoudzou, Mayotte: Baobab, 2000.

Lombard, Jacques. *Le royaume Sakalava du Menabe, 17è–20è: Essai d'analyse d'un système politique à Madagascar*. Paris: Editions de l'ORSTOM, 1988.

Lovejoy, Paul E. “The Impact of the Atlantic Slave Trade on Africa: A Review of the Literature.” *Journal of African History* 30, no. 3 (1989): 365–94.

———. *Transformations in Slaves: A History of Slavery in Africa*. 3rd ed. Cambridge: Cambridge University Press, 2011.

Lovejoy, Paul E., and David Richardson. “Trust, Pawnship, and Atlantic History: The Institutional Foundations of the Old Calabar Slave Trade.” *American Historical Review* 104, no. 2 (1999): 333–55.

Lutjeharms, J. R. E. *The Agulhas Current*. New York: Springer, 2006.

Ly-Tio-Fane, Madeleine. “Problèmes d’approvisionnement de l’Île de France au temps de l’Intendant Poivre.” *Proceedings of the Royal Society of Arts and Sciences of Mauritius* 3, pt. 1 (1968): 101–15.

Ly-Tio-Fane Pineo, Huguette. “Food Production and Plantation Economy of Mauritius.” In Bissoondoyal and Servansing, *Slavery in South West Indian Ocean*, 210–22.

Lynn, Martin. “From Sail to Steam: The Impact of the Steamship Services on the British Palm Oil Trade with West Africa, 1850–1890.” *Journal of African History* 30, no. 2 (1989): 227–45.

———. “Technology, Trade and ‘A Race of Native Capitalists’: The Krio Diaspora of West Africa and the Steamship, 1852–95.” *Journal of African History* 33, no. 3 (1992): 421–40.

Machado, Pedro. “A Forgotten Corner of the Indian Ocean: Gujarati Merchants, Portuguese India and the Mozambique Slave-Trade, c. 1730–1830.” *Slavery & Abolition* 24, no. 2 (2004): 17–32.

———. *Ocean of Trade: South Asian Merchants, Africa and the Indian Ocean, c. 1750–1850*. Cambridge: Cambridge University Press, 2014.

“Madagascar: Current Issues and What the World Food Programme is Doing.” World Food Programme. Accessed 5 January 2017. https://www.wfp.org/countries/madagascar.

“Madagascar: Overview.” World Food Programme. Accessed 5 January 2017. https://www.wfp.org/countries/madagascar/overview.

Mahan, Alfred Thayer. *The Influence of Sea Power upon History, 1660–1783*. Boston: Little, Brown, 1890.

Mann, Kristin. *Slavery and the Birth of an African City: Lagos, 1760–1900*. Bloomington: Indiana University Press, 2007.

Manning, Patrick. “African and World Historiography.” *Journal of African History* 54, no. 3 (2013): 319–30.

———. *Slavery and African Life: Occidental, Oriental, and African Slave Trades*. Cambridge: Cambridge University Press, 1990.

Margariti, Roxani Eleni. “Mercantile Networks, Port Cities, and ‘Pirate’ States: Conflict and Competition in the Indian Ocean World of Trade before the Sixteenth Century.” *Journal of the Economic and Social History of the Orient* 51, no. 4 (2008): 543–77.

Martin, Jean. *Comores: Quatre îles entre pirates et planteurs.* 2 vols. Paris: L'Harmattan, 1983.

McCann, James C. *Maize and Grace: Africa's Encounter with a New World Crop, 1500–2000*. Cambridge, MA: Harvard University Press, 2005.

McCants, Anne E. C. "Exotic Goods, Popular Consumption, and the Standard of Living: Thinking about Globalization in the Early Modern World." *Journal of World History* 18, no. 4 (2007): 433–62.

McConnell, William J., and Christian A. Kull. "Deforestation in Madagascar: Debates over the Island's Forest Cover and Challenges of Measuring Forest Change." In Scales, *Conservation and Environmental Management*, 67–104.

McDonald, Kevin P. *Pirates, Merchants, Settlers, and Slaves: Colonial America and the Indo-Atlantic World*. Berkeley: University of California Press, 2015.

McPherson, Kenneth. "Port Cities as Nodal Points of Change: The Indian Ocean, 1890s–1920s." In Fawaz and Bayly, *Modernity and Culture*, 75–95.

Médard, Henri. "La traite et l'esclavage en Afrique orientale et dans l'océan Indien: Une historiographie éclatée." In Médard et al., *Traites et esclavages*, 31–63.

Médard, Henri, Marie-Laure Derat, Thomas Vernet, and Marie Pierre Ballarin, eds. *Traites et esclavages en Afrique orientale et dans l'océan Indien*. Paris: Karthala, 2013.

Metcalf, Thomas R. *Imperial Connections: India in the Indian Ocean Arena, 1860–1920*. Berkeley: University of California Press, 2007.

Middleton, Karen. "Power and Meaning on the Periphery of a Malagasy Kingdom." *Ethnohistory* 48, nos. 1–2 (2001): 171–204.

———. "Who Killed 'Malagasy Cactus'? Science, Environment and Colonialism in Southern Madagascar (1924–1930)." *Journal of Southern African Studies* 25, no. 2 (1999): 215–48.

Miller, Joseph C. "A Theme in Variations: A Historical Schema of Slavery in the Atlantic and Indian Ocean Regions." *Slavery & Abolition* 24, no. 2 (2003): 169–94.

———. *Way of Death: Merchant Capitalism and the Angolan Slave Trade, 1730–1830*. Madison: University of Wisconsin Press, 1988.

Milton, Giles. *Nathaniel's Nutmeg*. London: Hodder & Stoughton, 2012.

Miran, Jonathan. *Red Sea Citizens: Cosmopolitan Society and Cultural Change in Massawa*. Bloomington: Indiana University Press, 2009.

Misevich, Philip. "The Sierra Leone Hinterland and the Provisioning of Early Freetown, 1792–1803." *Journal of Colonialism and Colonial History* 9, no. 3 (2008). doi:10.1353/cch.0.0032.

Molet-Sauvaget, Anne. "La *Relation de Robert Everard*, ébauche probable du *Journal de Robert Drury* de Daniel Defoe." *Studies on Voltaire and the Eighteenth Century*, no. 241 (1986): 1–28.

Molnár, Miklós. "Héros ou imposteur? Un aventurier au XVIIIe siècle." *Revue européenne des sciences sociales* 27, no. 85 (1989): 75–91.

Monnier, Jehanne-Emmanuelle. *Esclaves de la canne à sucre: Engagés et planteurs à Nossi-Bé, Madagascar 1850–1880*. Paris: L'Harmattan, 2006.

Monroe, J. Cameron. *The Precolonial State in West Africa: Building Power in Dahomey.* Cambridge: Cambridge University Press, 2014.

Monroe, J. Cameron, and Anneke Janzen. "Le festin dahoméen: Femmes du palais, politiques internes et pratiques culinaires en Afrique de l'Ouest au XVIIIe–XIXe siècle." *Afriques: Débats, méthodes et terrains d'histoire*, no. 5 (2014). https://afriques.revues.org/1632.

Moree, P. J. *A Concise History of Dutch Mauritius, 1598–1710: A Fruitful and Healthy Land*. London: Kegan Paul International, 1998.

Mosca, Liliana. "La traite à Madagascar dans la seconde moitié du XVIIe siècle à la lumière de quelques documents anglo-américains." In Rakoto, *La route des esclaves*, 75–90.

Mouser, Bruce L., ed. *A Slaving Voyage to Africa and Jamaica: The Log of the Sandown, 1793–1794*. Bloomington: Indiana University Press, 2002.

Mukherjee, Rila, ed. *Networks in the First Global Age, 1400–1800*. Delhi: Primus Books, 2011.

Muntaner, Antoni Picazo. "Ports and Commercial Networks in the Indian and Pacific Oceans: Models and Flows of Capitalism." In Mukherjee, *Networks in the First Global Age*, 35–52.

Nadri, Ghulam A. *Eighteenth-Century Gujarat: The Dynamics of Its Political Economy, 1750–1800*. Leiden: Brill, 2009.

Nash, David J., Kathleen Pribyl, Jørgen Klein, Georgina H. Endfield, Dominic R. Kniveton, and George C. D. Adamson. "Tropical Cyclone Activity over Madagascar during the Late Nineteenth Century." *International Journal of Climatology* 35, no. 11 (2015): 3249–61, published online 13 November 2014.

Newitt, Malyn. "The Comoro Islands in Indian Ocean Trade before the 19th Century." *Cahiers d'études africaines* 23, nos. 89–90 (1983): 139–65.

———. *A History of Mozambique*. Bloomington: Indiana University Press, 1995.

———. *A History of Portuguese Overseas Expansion, 1400–1668*. London: Routledge, 2005.

———. "Mozambique Island: The Rise and Decline of a Colonial Port City." In Brockey, *Portuguese Colonial Cities*, 105–27.

———. "The Southern Swahili Coast in the First Century of European Expansion." *Azania* 13, no. 1 (1978): 111–26.

Newman, James L. "Africa South from the Sahara." In Kiple and Ornelas, *The Cambridge World History of Food*, 2:1330–39.

Newson, Linda A., and Susie Minchin. "Diets, Food Supplies, and the African Slave Trade in Early Seventeenth-Century Spanish America." *Americas* 63, no. 4 (2007): 517–50.

Nierstrasz, Chris. *In the Shadow of the Company: The Dutch East India Company and Its Servants in the Period of Its Decline (1740–1796)*. Leiden: Brill, 2012.

Northrup, David. *Africa's Discovery of Europe, 1450–1850*. 2nd ed. New York: Oxford University Press, 2009.

———. "The Growth of Trade among the Igbo before 1800." *Journal of African History* 13, no. 2 (1972): 217–36.

Nutting, P. Bradley. "The Madagascar Connection: Parliament and Piracy, 1690–1701." *American Journal of Legal History* 22, no. 3 (1978): 202–15.

Olson, Sherry. "Red Destinies: The Landscape of Environmental Risk in Madagascar." *Human Ecology* 15, no. 1 (1987): 67–89.

Paine, Lincoln. *The Sea and Civilization: A Maritime History of the World*. New York: Knopf, 2013.

Parker Pearson, Mike. "Close Encounters of the Worst Kind: Malagasy Resistance and Colonial Disasters in Southern Madagascar." *World Archaeology* 28, no. 3 (1997): 393–417.

———. *Pastoralists, Warriors and Colonists: The Archaeology of Southern Madagascar*. Oxford: Archaeopress, 2010.

———. "Reassessing 'Robert Drury's Journal' as a Historical Source for Southern Madagascar." *History in Africa* 23 (1996): 233–56.

Parker Pearson, Mike, and Karen Godden. *In Search of the Red Slave: Shipwreck and Captivity in Madagascar*. Stroud, UK: Sutton, 2002.

Parthesius, Robert. *Dutch Ships in Tropical Waters: The Development of the Dutch East India Company (VOC) Shipping Network in Asia 1595–1660*. Amsterdam: Amsterdam University Press, 2010.

Payet, Jean Valentin. *Histoire de l'esclavage à l'Île Bourbon (Réunion)*. Paris: L'Harmattan, 1990.

Pearson, Michael N. "Connecting the Littorals: Cultural Brokers in the Early Modern Indian Ocean." In Gupta et al., *Eyes across the Water*, 32–47.

———. "The Idea of the Ocean." In Gupta et al., *Eyes across the Water*, 7–14.

———. *The Indian Ocean*. London: Routledge, 2003.

———. "Littoral Society: The Case for the Coast." *Great Circle* 7, no. 1 (1985): 1–8.

———. "Littoral Society: The Concept and the Problems." *Journal of World History* 17, no. 4 (2006): 353–73.

———. "Markets and Merchant Communities in the Indian Ocean: Locating the Portuguese." In Bethencourt and Curto, *Portuguese Oceanic Expansion*, 88–108.

———. *Merchants and Rulers in Gujarat: The Response to the Portuguese in the Sixteenth Century*. Berkeley: University of California Press, 1976.

———. *Port Cities and Intruders: The Swahili Coast, India, and Portugal in the Early Modern Era*. Baltimore: Johns Hopkins University Press, 1998.

Peerthum, Sateeanund. "Resistance against Slavery." In Bissoondoyal and Servansing, *Slavery in South West Indian Ocean*, 124–30.

Pérotin-Dumon, Anne. "The Pirate and the Emperor: Power and the Law on the Seas, 1450–1850." In *The Political Economy of Merchant Empires: State Power and World Trade, 1350–1750*, edited by James D. Tracy, 196–227. Cambridge: Cambridge University Press, 1991.

Picard, David. "Cultivating Human Gardens: Tropical Island Tourism in the South-Western Indian Ocean." In Gupta et al., *Eyes across the Water*, 326–43.

Pilcher, Jeffrey M. *¡Que Vivan Los Tamales!: Food and the Making of Mexican Identity*. Albuquerque: University of New Mexico Press, 1998.

Prakash, Om. "Cooperation and Conflict among European Traders in the Indian Ocean in the Late Eighteenth Century." In Subrahmanyam, *Land, Politics, and Trade in South Asia*, 20–43.

———. *Precious Metals and Commerce: The Dutch East India Company in the Indian Ocean Trade*. Aldershot, UK: Variorum, 1994.

Prange, Sebastian R. "A Trade of No Dishonor: Piracy, Commerce, and Community in the Western Indian Ocean, Twelfth to Sixteenth Century." *American Historical Review* 116, no. 5 (2011): 1269–93.

Prestholdt, Jeremy. *Domesticating the World: African Consumerism and the Genealogies of Globalization*. Berkeley: University of California Press, 2008.

Prosper, Eve. *Les esclaves de Bourbon, la mer et la montagne*. Paris: Karthala, 2003.

Rabesahala-Randriamananoro, Charlotte Liliane. *Ambohimanga-Rova: Approche anthropologique de la civilisation merina (Madagascar)*. Paris: Publieur, 2005.

Racault, Jean-Michel. "Les premières tentatives coloniales à Madagascar (XVIIe–XVIIIe siècles): Échos dans la fiction." In Dodille, *Idées et représentations coloniales*, 285–98.

Radimilahy, Chantal. *Mahilaka: An Archaeological Investigation of an Early Town in Northwestern Madagascar*. Uppsala: Department of Archaeology and Ancient History, Uppsala University, 1998.

———. "Sacred Sites in Madagascar." In *Sacred Sites, Sacred Places*, edited by David L. Carmichael, Jane Hubert, Brian Reeves, and Audhild Schanche, 82–88. London: Routledge, 1994.

Radimilahy, Chantal, and Barthélémy Manjakahery. "Archaeology of St. Augustine's Bay, Lower and Middle Onilahy Valley, Southwestern Madagascar." In *The African Archaeology Network: Research in Progress*, Studies in the African Past 5, 60–94. Dar es Salaam: Dar es Salaam University Press, 2006.

Rakoto, Ignace, ed. *La route des esclaves: Système servile et traite dans l'est Malgache*. Paris: L'Harmattan, 2000.

Rakotoarisoa, Jean-Aimé, ed. *Arabes et Islamisés à Madagascar et dans l'océan Indien*. Antananarivo: Revue de Madagascar, distributed by Hachette-Madagascar, 1967.

Raison, Jean-Pierre. "L'introduction du manioc à Madagascar: Un problème non résolu." *Terre Malgache* 13 (1972): 223–28.

Raison-Jourde, Françoise. Introduction to Raison-Jourde, *Les souverains de Madagascar*, 7–68.

———, ed. *Les souverains de Madagascar: L'histoire royale et ses résurgences contemporaines*. Paris: Karthala, 1983.

Raison-Jourde, Françoise, and Solofo Randrianja, eds. *La nation malgache au défi de l'ethnicité*. Paris: Karthala, 2002.

Ramilisonina. "Topographies religieuse d'un terroir et relations entre vivants et ancêtres à Madagascar: Les Bezanozano Zanadroandrena et Tsimifahy (Mandialaza-Moramanga)." In *Ancestralité et Identité à Madagascar*, Études océan Indien 30, 99–129. Paris: Institut national des langues et civilisations orientales, 2001.

Ranaivoson, Dominique. *Madagascar: Dictionnaire des personnalités historiques*. Saint-Maur-des-Fossés, France: Sépia, 2005.

Randrianja, Solofo, and Stephen Ellis. *Madagascar: A Short History*. Chicago: University of Chicago Press, 2009.

Ranjeva-Rabetafika, Yvette, René Baesjou, and Natalie Everts. "Of Paper and Men: A Note on the Archives of the VOC as a Source for the History of Madagascar." *Itinerario* 24, no. 1 (2000): 45–67.

Rantoandro, G. A. "Hommes et réseaux Malata de la côte orientale de Madagascar à l'époque de Jean René (1773–1826)." *Annuaire des pays de l'Océan Indien* 17 (2001–2): 103–21.

Ratsivalaka, Gilbert. "Éléments de Biographie de Nicolas Mayeur (1747–1809)." *Omaly sy Anio* (Université d'Antananarivo) 5–6 (1977): 77–89.

Ratsivalaka, Ranaivo G. *Les Malgaches et l'abolition de la traite européenne des esclaves (1810–1817): Histoire de la formation du Royaume de Madagascar*. Antananarivo: Hery Arivo, 1999.

Ray, Aniruddha. "French Colonial Policy in Seventeenth Century Madagascar: François Martin's Account." *Archipel* 17 (1979): 81–97.

———. *Trade, Politics, and Plunder: The Marathas at Cambay, c. AD 1725–1825*. New Delhi: Munshiram Manoharlal, 2006.

Ray, Indrani. *The French East India Company and the Trade of the Indian Ocean: A Collection of Essays by Indrani Ray*. Edited by Lakshmi Subramanian. New Delhi: Munshiram Manoharlal, 1999.

Rediker, Marcus. *Between the Devil and the Deep Blue Sea: Merchant Seamen, Pirates and the Anglo-American Maritime World, 1700–1750*. Cambridge: Cambridge University Press, 1989.

———. *The Slave Ship: A Human History*. New York: Viking Penguin, 2007.

———. *Villains of All Nations: Atlantic Pirates in the Golden Age*. Boston: Beacon Press, 2004.

Reid, Anthony. "The Structure of Cities in Southeast Asia, Fifteenth to Seventeenth Centuries." *Journal of Southeast Asian Studies* 11, no. 2 (1980): 235–50.

Richards, John F. *The Unending Frontier: An Environmental History of the Early Modern World*. Berkeley: University of California Press, 2003.

Richards, W. A. "The Import of Firearms into West Africa in the Eighteenth Century." *Journal of African History* 21, no. 1 (1980): 43–59.

Risso, Patricia. "Cross-Cultural Perceptions of Piracy: Maritime Violence in the Western Indian Ocean and Persian Gulf during a Long Eighteenth Century." *Journal of World History* 12, no. 2 (2001): 293–319.

Ritchie, Robert C. *Captain Kidd and the War against the Pirates*. Boston: Harvard University Press, 1989.

Robineau, Claude. "L'Islam aux Comores: Une étude d'histoire culturelle de l'île d'Anjouan." Revue de Madagascar, 35 (1966). Reprinted in Rakotoarisoa, *Arabes et Islamisés à Madagascar*, 39–56.

Rodrigues, Eugénia. "Eating and Drinking at the Royal Hospital of Mozambique Island: Medicine and Diet Change between the End of the 18th and the Early 19th Century." *Afriques: Débats, méthodes et terrains d'histoire*, no. 5 (2014). http://afriques.revues.org/1553.

Rönnbäck, Klas. "The Speed of Ships and Shipping Productivity in the Age of Sail." *European Review of Economic History* 16, no. 4 (2012): 469–89.

Sacleux, Charles. *Dictionnaire Swahili-Français, Tome 1*. Paris: Institut d'Ethnologie, 1939.

Sanchez, Samuel F. "Plans de colonisation, idées chimériques? Nosy Be et Mayotte dans les projets francais d'expansion dans l'océan Indien occidental et vers Madagascar (1839–1857)." In Dodille, *Idées et représentations coloniales*, 167–98.

Scales, Ivan R. "A Brief History of the State and the Politics of Natural Resource Use in Madagascar." In Scales, *Conservation and Environmental Management*, 129–45.

———, ed. *Conservation and Environmental Management in Madagascar.* New York: Routledge, 2014.

———. "The Drivers of Deforestation and the Complexity of Land Use in Madagascar." In Scales, *Conservation and Environmental Management*, 105–25.

———. "Introduction: Conservation at the Crossroads: Biological Diversity, Environmental Change and Natural Resource Use in Madagascar." In Scales, *Conservation and Environmental Management*, 1–13.

Schlemmer, Bernard. "La domination royal au Menabe: Détournement colonial, survivance et décomposition." In Raison-Jourde, *Les souverains*, 391–408.

Schmitt-Pantel, Pauline. "Greek Meals: A Civic Ritual." In *Food: A Culinary History from Antiquity to the Present*, edited by Jean-Louis Flandrin and Massimo Montanari, 90–95. New York: Columbia University Press, 1999.

Schreurs, Guido, Sandra J. T. M. Evers, Chantal Radimilahy, and Jean-Aimé Rakotoarisoa. "The Rasikajy Civilization in Northeast Madagascar: A Pre-European Chinese Community?" *Études océan Indien*, nos. 46–47 (2011): 107–32.

Schwartz, Stuart B. "The Economy of the Portuguese Empire." In Bethencourt and Curto, *Portuguese Oceanic Expansion*, 19–48.

Searing, James F. *West African Slavery and Atlantic Commerce: The Senegal River Valley, 1700–1860.* Cambridge: Cambridge University Press, 1993.

Sen, S. P. *The French in India: 1763–1816.* 2nd ed. New Delhi: Munshiram Manoharlal, 1971.

Serjeant, R. B. *The Portuguese off the South Arabian Coast: Hadrami Chronicles, with Yemeni and European Accounts of Dutch Pirates off Mocha in the Seventeenth Century.* Oxford: Clarendon, 1963.

Shepherd, Gill. "The Comorians and the East African Slave Trade." In *Asian and African Systems of Slavery*, edited by James L. Watson, 73–99. Berkeley: University of California Press, 1980.

Sheriff, Abdul. *Dhow Cultures of the Indian Ocean: Cosmopolitanism, Commerce and Islam.* New York: Columbia University Press, 2010.

Shumway, Rebecca. "Castle Slaves of the Eighteenth-Century Gold Coast (Ghana)." *Slavery & Abolition* 35, no. 1 (2014): 84–98.

———. *The Fante and the Transatlantic Slave Trade.* Rochester, NY: University of Rochester Press, 2011.

Sleigh, Daniel. "The Economy of Mauritius during the Second Dutch Occupation (1664–1710)." In *Globalisation and the South-West Indian Ocean*, edited by Sandra Evers and V. Y. Hookoomsingh, 51–56. Réduit: University of Mauritius and International Institute for Asian Studies, 2000.

Sleigh, Daniel, and Piet Westra. *The Taking of the Slaver Meermin, 1766*. Cape Town: Africana, 2013.

Smallwood, Stephanie E. *Saltwater Slavery: A Middle Passage from Africa to American Diaspora*. Cambridge, MA: Harvard University Press, 2007.

Stanziani, Alessandro. *Sailors, Slaves, and Immigrants: Bondage in the Indian Ocean World, 1750–1914*. New York: Palgrave Macmillan, 2014.

Starn, Randolph. "The Early Modern Muddle." *Journal of Early Modern History* 6, no. 3 (2002): 296–307.

Stern, Philip J. "Soldier and Citizen in the Seventeenth-Century English East India Company." *Journal of Early Modern History* 15, no. 1 (2011): 83–104.

Subrahmanyam, Sanjay. "Connected Histories: Notes towards a Reconfiguration of Early Modern Eurasia." *Modern Asian Studies* 31, no. 3 (1997): 735–62.

———. "Introduction: The Indian Ocean between Empire and Nation." In *Maritime India*, edited by Sanjay Subrahmanyam, xi–xvii. New Delhi: Oxford University Press, 2004.

———, ed. *Land, Politics, and Trade in South Asia*. New Delhi: Oxford University Press, 2004.

———. "Of Imarat and Tijarat: Asian Merchants and State Power in the Western Indian Ocean, 1400 to 1750." *Comparative Studies in Society and History* 37, no. 4 (1995): 750–80.

———. *The Portuguese Empire in Asia, 1500–1700: A Political and Economic History*. 2nd ed. West Sussex, UK: Wiley-Blackwell, 2012.

Subramanian, Lakshmi. "Of Pirates and Potentates: Maritime Jurisdiction and the Construction of Piracy in the Indian Ocean." In Ghosh and Muecke, *Cultures of Trade*, 19–30.

Sutton, Jean. *The East India Company's Maritime Service, 1746–1834: Masters of the Eastern Seas*. Rochester, NY: Boydell, 2010.

Svalesen, Leif. *The Slave Ship Fredensborg*. Translated by Pat Shaw and Selena Winsnes. Bloomington: Indiana University Press, 2000.

Sylla, Yvette. "Les Malata: Cohésion et disparité d'un 'groupe.'" *Omaly sy anio* (Université d'Antananarivo) 21–22 (1985): 19–32.

Teelock, Vijaya. *Bitter Sugar: Sugar and Slavery in 19th Century Mauritius*. Moka, Mauritius: Mahatma Gandhi Institute, 1998.

Thornton, John Kelly. *Africa and Africans in the Making of the Atlantic World, 1400–1800*. 2nd ed. Cambridge: Cambridge University Press, 1998.

Toussaint, Auguste. *History of the Indian Ocean*. Translated by June Guicharnaud. Chicago: University of Chicago Press, 1966.

Tuchscherer, Michel. "Trade and Port Cities in the Red Sea–Gulf of Aden Region in the Sixteenth and Seventeenth Century." In Fawaz and Bayly, *Modernity and Culture*, 28–45.

Tuck, Michael W. "Everyday Commodities, the Rivers of Guinea, and the Atlantic World: The Beeswax Export Trade, c. 1450–c. 1800." In Green, *Brokers of Change*, 285–303.

Turner, Jack. *Spice: The History of a Temptation*. New York: Alfred A. Knopf, 2004.

United Nations Children's Fund and World Food Programme. "Rural Madagascar Comprehensive Food and Nutrition Security and Vulnerability Analysis." Data collected August–September 2010, drafted by WFP Madagascar and UNICEF Madagascar, published November 2011. documents.wfp.org/stellent/groups/public/documents/ena/wfp246796.pdf.

Valette, Jean. "Le Commerce de Madagascar vers les Mascareignes au XVIIIe siècle." *La revue de Madagascar* 33 (1966): 36–52.

———. *Études sur le règne de Radama Ier.* Antananarivo, Madagascar: Imprimerie nationale, 1962.

van Duivenvoorde, Wendy. *Dutch East India Company Shipbuilding: The Archaeological Study of Batavia and Other Seventeenth-Century VOC Ships*. College Station: Texas A&M University Press, 2015.

Vaughan, Megan. *Creating the Creole Island: Slavery in Eighteenth-Century Mauritius*. Durham, NC: Duke University Press, 2005.

Vérin, Pierre. *The History of Civilisation in North Madagascar.* Translated by David Smith. Rotterdam: A. A. Balkema, 1986.

Vérin, Pierre, and Narivelo Rajaonarimanana. "Divination in Madagascar: The Antemoro Case and the Diffusion of Divination." In *African Divination Systems: Ways of Knowing*, edited by Philip M. Peek, 53–68. Bloomington: Indiana University Press, 1991.

Vernet, Thomas. "Avant le giroflier: Esclavage et agriculture sur la côte swahili, 1590–1812." In Médard et al., *Traites et esclavages*, 245–306.

———. "Le commerce des esclaves sur la côte Swahili, 1500–1750." *Azania* 38 (2003): 69–97.

———. "La première traite française à Zanzibar: Le journal de bord du vaisseau *l'Espérance*, 1774–1775." In *Civilisations des mondes insulaires*, edited by Chantal Radimilahy and Narivelo Rajaonarimanana, 477–521. Paris: Karthala, 2011.

———. "Slave Trade and Slavery on the Swahili Coast, 1500–1750." In *Slavery, Islam and Diaspora*, edited by Paul Lovejoy, Behnaz A. Mirzai, and Ismael M. Montana, 37–76. Trenton, NJ: Africa World Press, 2009.

Vink, Markus P. M. "Indian Ocean Studies and the 'New Thalassology.'" *Journal of Global History* 2, no. 1 (2007): 41–62.

———. "A Match Made in Heaven? World-Systems Analysis and Dutch Indian Ocean Studies." In *Rivalry and Conflict: European Traders and Asian Trading Networks in the 16th and 17th Century*, edited by Leonard Blusse and Ernst van Veen, 267–314. Leiden: CNWS, 2005.

———. "'The World's Oldest Trade': Dutch Slavery and Slave Trade in the Indian Ocean in the Seventeenth Century." *Journal of World History* 14, no. 2 (2003): 131–77.

Walshaw, Sarah C. "Converting to Rice: Urbanization, Islamization and Crops on Pemba Island, Tanzania, AD 700–1500." *World Archaeology* 42, no. 1 (2010): 137–54.

Ward, Kerry. *Networks of Empire: Forced Migration in the Dutch East India Company*. Cambridge: Cambridge University Press, 2009.

Wellington, Donald C. *French East India Companies: A Historical Account and Record of Trade*. Lanham, MD: Hamilton Books, 2006.

Whatley, Warren. "The Gun-Slave Cycle in the 18th Century British Slave Trade in Africa." *Munich Personal RePEc Archive (MPRA)*, December 2012. http://mpra.ub.uni-muenchen.de/44492/1/MPRA_paper_44492.pdf.

Whatley, Warren, and Rob Gillezeau, "The Fundamental Impact of the Slave Trade on African Economies." In *Economic Evolution and Revolution in Historical Time*, edited by Paul W. Rhode, Joshua L. Rosenbloom, and David F. Weiman, 86–110. Stanford, CA: Stanford University Press, 2011.

Wilkinson, J. C. "Oman and East Africa: New Light on Early Kilwan History from the Omani Sources." *International Journal of African Historical Studies* 14, no. 2 (1981): 272–305.

Wills, John E., Jr. "Maritime Asia, 1500–1800: The Interactive Emergence of European Dominance." *American Historical Review* 98, no. 1 (1993): 83–105.

Wilson, David. "Piracy, Patronage & Political Economy: Captain Kidd and the East India Trade." *International Journal of Maritime History* 27, no. 1 (2015): 26–40.

Wilson-Fall, Wendy. "Women Merchants and Slave Depots: Saint-Louis, Senegal, and St. Mary's, Madagascar." In *Paths of the Atlantic Slave Trade: Interactions, Identities, and Images*, edited by Ana Lucia Araujo, 273–303. Amherst, NY: Cambria Press, 2011.

Winius, George D., and Marcus P. M. Vink. *The Merchant-Warrior Pacified: The VOC (the Dutch East India Company) and Its Changing Political Economy in India*. Delhi: Oxford University Press, 1991.

Wright, Henry T. "Early State Dynamics as Political Experiment." *Journal of Anthropological Research* 62, no. 3 (2006): 305–19.

Wright, Henry T., and Jean-Aimé Rakotoarisoa, "The Rise of Malagasy Societies: New Developments in the Archaeology of Madagascar." In Goodman and Benstead, *Natural History of Madagascar*, 112–19.

Wright, Henry T., Pierre Vérin, Ramilisonina, David Burney, Lida Piggott Burney, and Katsumi Matsumoto. "The Evolution of Settlement Systems in the Bay of Boeny and the Mahavavy River Valley, North-Western Madagascar." *Azania* 31, no. 1 (1996): 37–73.

# Index